Hand Book of Perfumes and Flavours

Directory Of Plant and Equipments, Raw Materials and Manufacturer/ Exporters/Suppliers of Perfumes

OTHER RELATED BOOKS

- Fruits & Vegetables Processing Hand Book
- Fruit Beverages & Processing With Mango Products
- Food Processing & Agro Based Industries
- Manufacturing Technology of Snacks Food, Namkeen, Pappad & Potato Products
- Preservation & Canning of Fruits and Vegetables
- Hand Book of Food Dehydration & Drying
- Meat Processing & Meat Products Hand Book
- Technology of Food Preservation & Processing
- Hand Book of Food Packaging Technology
- Agro Based & Processed Food Products
- Potato & Potato Processing Technology
- Technology of Maize & Allied Com. Products
- Technology of Food Processing Industries
- Technology of Sweets (Mithai) with Formulae
- Hand Book of Organic Farming And Organic Foods With Vermi-Composting and Neem Products
- Hand Book of Fish Farming And Fishery Products
- Hand Book of Mushroom Cultivation, Processing And Packaging
- Hand Book of Spices & Packaging With Formulaes
- Start Your Own Cold Storage Unit
- Hand Book of Bakery Industries
- Hand Book of Confectionery With Formulations
- Breakfast, Dietary Food, Pasta & Cereal Products Technology
- Hand Book of Modern Bakery Products
- Modern Bakery Technology & Fermented Cereal Products With Formulae
- Technology of Confectionery, Chocolates, Toffee, Candy, Chewing & Bubble Gums, Lollipop and Jelly Products with Formulations
- Hand Book of Poultry Farming & Feed Formulations
- Hand Book of Pig Farming
- Agro Based Hand Book of Plantation, Cultivation & Farming
- Agro Based Plantation Cultivation & Farming
- Agro Chemical Industries (Insecticide & Pesticides)
- Modern Bee Keeping & Honey Processing
- Technology of Modern Rice Milling And Basmati Rice
- Hand Book of Goat Farming
- Floriculture Hand Book (Flowers Growing Technology)
- Aloe Vera Cultivation, Processings, Formulations And Manufacturing Technology
- Hand Book of Dairy Formulations, Processes & Milk Processing Industries
- Milk Processing And Dairy Products Industries
- Hand Book of Dairy Farming to Produce Milk with Packaging
- Hand Book of Ice Cream Technology And Formulae
- Hand Book of Milk Processing Dairy Products And Packaging Technology
- Dairy Farming for Milk Production Technology
- Ayurvedic & Herbal Medicines With Formulaes
- Hand Book of Ayurvedic Medicines With Formulations (A Complete Hand Book of Ayurvedic & Herbal Medicines)

Hand Book of Perfumes and Flavours

Directory Of Plant and Equipments, Raw Materials and Manufacturer/ Exporters/Suppliers of Perfumes

Written By

EIRI Board of Consultants & Engineers

ENGINEERS INDIA RESEARCH INSTITUTE

4449, Nai Sarak, Main Road, Delhi - 110006 (India)
Ph: +91-11-23918117, 23916431, 45120361, 23947058, 64727385
* E-Mail: eiritechnology@gmail.com & eiriprojects@gmail.com
*Website: www.eiriindia.org & www.industrialprojects.in

PRINTED & PUBLISHED BY

ENGINEERS INDIA RESEARCH INSTITUTE

4449, Nai Sarak, Main Road, Delhi - 110006 (India)

Ph: +91-11-23918117, 23916431, 45120361, 23947058, 64727385

* E-Mail: eiritechnology@gmail.com & eiriprojects@gmail.com

*Website: www.eiriindia.org & www.industrialprojects.in

Distributors:

EIRI PROJECT CONSULTANTS AND PUBLISHERS
4/54 Roop Nagar, Delhi-110007
and
INDUSTRIAL TECHNOLOGIES, INDIA
Nai Sarak, Delhi-110006

ISBN: 9788186732304

Printed in New Delhi (INDIA)

₹ 975/- or US $ 100

Printed & Published by Sudhir Gupta for "Engineers India Research Institute", 4449 Nai Sarak, Main Road, New Delhi -110006

Preface

The basic object of this book is to furnish a comprehensive treatment on the latest methods & formulaes of perfumes & flavours. The book also covers new addresses of plant & equipments suppliers. The book has been written for the benefit and to prove an asset and a handy reference guide in the hands of new entrepreneurs & well established industrialists.The perfume & flavour industry has become a major business. Mans search for substances which can produce new flavours & perfumes, substitute for expensive & or scarce ones, or augment & enhance existing desirable ones continuous a pace. The manufacture of perfume oils & flavouring compounds is an art & it means metering of the individual components in accordance with the formula, followed by blending for homogenization.

But in all perfume & flavour house the oil formulas are among the best kept secrets & represent the knowhow. They play a major role in the success of the companies. Odors are also commonly called scents, which can refer to both pleasant and unpleasant odors. The terms fragrance and aroma are used primarily by the food and cosmetic industry to describe a pleasant odor, and are sometimes used to refer to perfumes. The odours are classified in various kinds such as floral, woody, rustic, balsamic, fruity, animal etc. There are numerous types of applications of perfumes in modern industrialized society such as perfumes used in soaps & detergents, paints, adhesives, air deodorants, cosmetics, toilet & beauty preparations, textiles, beverages, foods, medicines, and many more. The global flavour industry can be characterized as highly technical, specialized, and innovative. This industry is highly competitive and concentrated, compared to other product categories within the food and beverage market. The global flavours market is predicted to grow at a Compound Annual Growth Rate (CAGR) of 2% per annum. The present book deals with the new techniques & manufacturing processes with formulae of different useful and demandable perfumes and flavours

The book named ***HAND BOOK OF PERFUMES & FLAVOURS*** covers new formulaes of various kinds of perfumes & flavours. The major chapters of the book are Perfumes, Formulary of Perfumes, Formulary of Flavours, Chemicals Specifications for Perfume & Flavour Components, Plant & Equipment Suppliers, Suppliers of Raw Materials, Manufacturer/ Exporters/Suppliers of Perfumes. At the end of the book the last but not the least chapter project profiles has also included for the benefits of the new entrepreneurs.

EIRI Board of Consultants & Engineers

CONTENTS AND SUBJECT INDEX

CHAPTERS **PAGE NO.**

FORMULARY OF PERFUMES 29 - 73

Chapter-1

PERFUMES

Natural Odors Simulated with Aromatic Chemicals

BALSAMIC

DESCRIPTION: Chemicals with a penetrating, plesant odor similar to the fragrant resin or oleoresin flowering from various plants containing benzoic or cinnamic acid.

COMMON VARIETIES: Peru Balsam, from Central America; Tolu Balsam, from Colombia; Copaiba Balsam, from Brazil and Venezuela; Balm of Gilead, shrub, Middle East, Africa; Canada Balsam, North America fir tree; Benzoin, from Styrax tree in Southeast Asia and Sumatra.

CHEMICALS FOR SCENT MATCHING: (1) Benzyl benzoate; (2) Benzyl cinnamate; (3) Cinnamic alcohol; (4) Cinnamyl acetate; (5) Cinnamyl anthranilate; (6) Cinnamyl butyrate; (7) Cinnamyl isobutyrate; (8) Isobutyl cinnamate; (9) Phenyl ethyl salicylate; (10) Phenyl propyl cinnamate

CITRUS

DESCRIPTION: Chemicals with odor similar to the citrus trees and shrubs flowers *(Aurantiaceae)*. Citrus is a generic name referring to a group of trees and shrubs of the Rutaceae whose fruits are edible, with juice, rinds, oils, and acids, all useful.

Citrus trees are thorny, evergreen, with long shiny, pointed leaves. The leaves and the flowers are fragrant. Citrus plants grow in warm climates where there is no frost or wind. They contain large amounts of vitamins and minerals and are high in Vitamin C. Ripe citrus fruits are yellow to orange red in colour.

Bergamot is only used in perfumery and as a histological clearing agent.

COMMON VARIETIES: *Citrus aurantium*, sweet orange; *Citrus aurantium*, var. *Bigaradia*, bitter orange; *Citrus medica*, citron; *Citrus medica*, var. Limonum, lemon; *Citrus medica*, var. Acida, lime; *Citrus decumana*, grapefruit (shaddock); *Citrus bergamia*, bergamot

CHEMICAL FOR SCENT MATCHING: (1) Acetate C-12; (2) Alcohol C-7; (3) Alcohol C-8; (4) Alcohol C-9; (5) Alcohol C-11, undecylenic; (6) Alcohol C-11, undecylic; (7) Aldehyde C-8; (8) Citral; (9) Linalyl butyrate; (10) Methyl heptenone, pure; (11) Methyl nonyl ketone; (12) Neryl acetate

FATTY

DESCRITION: Chemicals with a fatty odour
CHEMICALS FOR SCENT MATCHING: (1) Benzyl laurate; (2) Nonoic acid

FLOWERY

DESCRIPTION: Chemicals with a floral odour

CHEMICALS FOR SCENT MATCHING: (1) Acetanisole; (2) Acetate C-9; (3) Acetate C-11; (4) Amyl cinnamic alcohol; (5) Anisyl alcohol; (6) Benzyl isovalerate; (7) Benzyl propionate; (8) Cinnamic alcohol; (9) Cinnamyl acetate; (10); Cinnamyl propionate; (11) Ethyl laurate; (12) Hydroxycitronellal dimethyl acetal; (13) Linalool; (14) p Methyl acetophenone; (15) Methyl phenyl carbinol; (16) Methyl phenyl propionate; (17) Phenyl acetaldehyde ; (18) Phenyl acetic acid; (19) Phenyl propyl acetate; (20) Phenyl propyl cinnamate; (21) Phenyl propyl formate

GRASSY

DESCRIPTION: Chemicals with a grassy odour

CHEMICALS FOR SCENT MATCHING: (1) Isocyclocitral

GREEN- FLORAL

DESCRIPTION: Chemicals with green top note and floral background odour

CHEMICALS FOR SCENT MATCHING: (1) Methyl heptyne carbonate; (2) Methyl octine carbonate; (3) Methyl phenyl carbinol; (4) Phenyl acetaldehyde

HARSH PUNGENT

DESCRIPTION: Chemicals with an harsh pungent penetrating odour

CHEMICALS FOR SCENT MATCHING: (1) Aldehyde C-7; (2) Methyl quinoline

HERB- LIKE

DESCRIPTION: Chemicals with an herb like odour

CHEMICALS FOR SCENT MATCHING: (1) α–Phellandrene

LEAF- GREEN

DESCRIPTION: Chemicals with an odor similar to green leaves

CHMICALS FOR SCENT MATCHING: (1) Acetal R; (2) p Methyl hydratropic aldehyde; (3) Phenyl acetaldehyde dimethyl acetal; (4) Phenyl acetaldehyde ethylene acetal; (5) Phenyl ethyl acetal; (6) n Propyl acetal

MUSKY

DESCRIPTION: Chemicals with a persistent odour similar to musk

CHEMICALS FOR SCENT MATCHING: (1) Civettal; (2) Skatole

ODORLESS- FAINT

DESCRIPTION: Chemicals with an almost imperceptible odor

CHEMICALS FOR SCENT MATCHING: (1) Benzyl alcohol; (2) Cetyl alcohol

WAXY

DESCRIPTION: Chemicals with a waxy odour

CHEMICALS FOR SCENT MATCHING: (1) Myristic alcohol

WOODY

DESCRIPTION: Chemicals with an odour similar to wood

CHEMICALS FOR SCENT MATCHING: (1) Dimethyl benzyl carbinal ; (2) Isobutyl quinoline (3) Isopropyl quinolone (4) Vetaccetyl

Simulated Flower Scents

ACACIA

BOTANICAL: *Family: Leguminosae; Genus; Acacia; Species; Greggii*

OCCURRENCE: About 450 kinds of acacia grow in tropical regions and lands close to the tropics. Twelve varieties grow in the U.S mostly in Texas and California.

DESCRIPTION: The flowers are bright yellow with a sweet odour. In some plants they cluster together forming balls. Others have white flowers.

CHEMICALS FOR SCENT MATCHING: (1) Anisic aldehyde; (2) Isobutylbenzoate; (3) Methyl anthranilate; (4) Phenyl acetic aldehyde; (5) Yara yara *Basis*:* (1) Alcohol C-9; (2) Alcohol C-10; (3) Aldehyde C-9; (4) Aldehyde C-10

BERGAMOT

BOTANICAL: *Family; Rutaceae; Genus; Citrus; Species; Bergamia; Subspecies; Risso, Poiteau*

CHEMICALS FOR SCENT MATCHING: (1) Citronellyl acetate; (2) Limonene; (3) Linalool; (4) Linaly acetate; (5) Linalyl formate; (6) Linalyl propionate; (7) Menthanyl acetate; (8) Terpinyl acetate

CARNATION

BOTANICAL: Family: Caryophyllaceae; Genus; Dianthus; Species; Caryophyllus (common garden)

DESCRIPTION : There are pink, purple, red, white, and yellow carnation flowers

CHEMICAL FOR SCENT MATCHING: (1) Acetyl isoeugenol; (2) Benzyl isoeugenol; (3) Coumarin; (4) Eugenol; (5) Methyl eugenol; (6) Methyl isoeugenol; (7) Nerol; (8) Terpineol; (9) Vanillin

Basis; (1) Alcohol C-9; (2) Aldehyde C-8; (3) Aldehyde C-9

CASSIA

BOTANICAL: *Family: Leguminosae; Genus; Cassia; Species; Acutifolia, Angustifolia* (Indian), *Matilandia* (wild Surna), *Fassciculate* (partirdge peas); There are more than 400 species of cassia

CHEMICALS FOR SCENT MATCHING: (1) Anisic aldehyde; (2) Anisyl acetate; (3) Ionone; (4) Methyl acetophenone
Basis: (1) Aldehyde C-8; (2) Anisyl acetate; (3) Ionone; (4) Methyl acetophenone

Basis: (1) Aldehyde C-8; (2) Aldehyde C-9; (3) Aldehyde C-10; (4) Aldehyde C-12

CHRYSANTHEMUM

BOTANICAL: *Family: Compositae; Ganus; Chrysanthemum*

DESCRIPTION: A strong scented shrubby herb growing in

temperate regions worldwide. The name is from the Greek word meaning "golden flower". Because of its beautiful and abundant blooms, it is extensively cultivated. The flowers are white, yellow, pink, or red.

CHEMICALS FOR SCENT MATCHING: (1) Phenylethyl formate

CLOVE

SYNONYMS: *Eugenia caryophyllata*

BOTANICAL: *Family; Myrtaceae; Genus; Caryophyllus; Species; Aromaticus*

OCCURRENCE: The tree grows wild in the Moluccas (also called Spice Islands), in Sumatra, Jamaica, West Indies, and Brazil

DESCRIPTION: The name clove refers to the dried flowers (buds) of a tropical tree. The buds are picked before they open to become a flower. They are used as a spice and are called cloves.

An oil distilled from the dried buds and stems is widely used in the flavor and perfumery industry.

CHEMICALS FOR SCENT MATCHING: (1) Caryophyllene; (2) Eugenol; (3) Eugenol acetate; (4) Isoeugenol phenyl acetate

CLOVER

SYNONYMS: New mown hay; Foin coupe

BOTANICAL: *Family: Leguminosae; Genus and Species;*

COMMON VARIETIES: *Trifolium pratense* (red clover); *Trifoliumrepens, hybridum, crimson, incarnatum, alsike* (white clover); *Melilotus alba* (white sweet clover); *Melilotus officinalis* (yellow sweet clover); *Melilotus indica* (sour clover)

DESCRIPTION: About 300 different kinds of clover plants exist, growing wild in fields, lawns, and along roadsides. Some species are cultivated for livestock food.

Red clover provides pasture for farm animals and enriches

the soil because of its high nitrogen content. It is also the main source of hay. *White clover,* in addition to being a valuable pasture corp, provides its blossom nectar to bees for the making of superior honey. *Alsike clover,* also called Swedish clover, is white or pink in color. *Crimson clover* has a variety of colors: red, white, yellow, scarlet. It is also called "Italian type clover. *Sweet clover* is called "Melilot" from the Latin word "miele" (honey). *Sour clover* is primarily used for improving the soil.

Clover generally has three leaves. According to superstition,four leaved clover brings luck while five or six leaved clovers bring misfortune.

CHEMICALS FOR SCENT MATCHING: (1) Benzylidene acetone; (2) Benzyl salicylate; (3) Coumarin; (4) Linalyl acetate; (5) Methyl salicylate

CYCLAMEN

BOTANICAL: Family: Primulaceae (primrose); Genus; Cyclamen

CHEMICALS FOR SCENT MATCHING: (1) Cyclamen aldehyde; (2) Hydroxycitronellal; (3) Ionone; (4) Rhodinol

Basis: (1) Alcohol C-9; (2) Aldehyde C-9; (3) Aldehyde C-10 (4) Aldehyde C-12

FERN

SYNONYMS: Fougere

BOTANICAL: The ferns are classified into 12 families.

The most common and widely distributed family is: *Family: Polypodiaceae* which includes several genera: *Genus: Pteridium* (the bracken), *Adiantum* (maidenhair), *Dryopteris* (woodfern), *Asplenium* (spleenworts), *Polypodium* (polypody), *Comptosorus* (walking leaf), *Onoclea* (sensitive fern), *Polystichum* (holly ferns).

Other families include: *Family: Trichomanes* (filmy fern), *Lygodium* (climbing fern), *Ophioglossum* (adder's tongue), *Botrychium* (rattlesnake fern)

OCCURRENCE: Ferns grow worldwide but more commonly in the tropics. About 300 varieties grow in the U.S

DESCRIPTION: There are about 10,000 kinds of ferns in different sizes and shapes, from moss-like to 40 foot tall trees. The fern is a flowerless plant.

The basic "fougere" perfume is made by simple blending of oakmoss, coumarin, and amyl salicylate, or just oakmoss and amyl salicylate.

CHEMICALS FOR SCENT MATCHING: (1) Ethyl phenyl acetate; (2) Isobutyl salicylate; (3) Linalyl acetate

Basis: (1) Alcohol C-8; (2) Alcohol C-9; (3) Aldehyde C-8; (4) Aldehyde C-9; (5) Aldehyde C-10; (6) Aldehyde C-11; (7) ıdehyde C-12 MNA

FRANGIPANI

BOTANICAL: *Family: Apocynaceae; Genus; Plumeria; Species; Acutifolia* (yellowish), *Alba* (white), *Rubra* (pink)

OCCURRENCE: The plant grows extensively in all tropical areas, particularly in the eastern part of central Africa.

DESCRIPTION: Frangipani is one of the most beautiful and pleasantly scented flowers. Like other tropical fragrant flowers, trangipani is more frangrant at night than during the day. It is a decorative plant, especially in India. Since no synthetic imitation can really match the exceptionally pleasant fragrance of the frangipani, it is obtained using an odourless solvent such as hexane, or by enfleurage.

CHEMICALS FOR SCENT MATCHING: (1) Cinnamic aldehyde;(2) Citral; (3) Coumarin; (4) Eugenol; (5) Ionone; (6) Linalyl acetate; (7) Rhodinyl butyrate; (8) Terpineol; (9) Vetiverol

GARDENIA

BOTANICAL: *Family: Rubiaceae: Ganus: Jasminoides*

DESCRIPTION: The name gardenia was given to this plant in honor of Alexander Garden, a Scottish naturalist, who collected plants in South Carolina before the Revolutionary War.

Gardenia is an ornamental plant in subtropical warm temperate areas. The flower has a very outstanding fragrance.

It's essential oil occurs in a very minimal amount (1x5000). Therefore, it's fragrance is synthetically imitated.

CHEMICALS FOR SCENT MATCHING: (1) Ethyl acetate; (2) Methyl phenyl carbinyl acetate

Basis: (1) Aldehyde C-8; (2) Aldehyde C-10; (3) Aldehyde C-12; (4) Aldehyde C-14

GERANIUM

BOTANICAL: *Family: Geraniaceae; Genus; Pelargonium; Species; Graveolens* (rose geranium), *Domesticus* (Lady Washington), *Robertianum* (herb Robert, red robin), *Erodium cicutarium* (Alfilaria, red stem filareae), *Peltatum* (ivy geranium)

DESCRIPTION: It grows widely in home and gardens. Leaves of the rose geranium are used to flavor jellies and for the extraction of geranium rose essential oil, particularly that of African origin. Alfilaria or red stem filareae is grown for forage in wastern and southwestern U.S. Herb Robert or red robin has been used in medicine.

CHEMICALS FOR SCENT MATCHING: (1) Benzophenone; (2) Diphenyl methane; (3) Diphenyl oxide; (4) Isobutyl benzoate; (5) Isopulegol extra

HAWTHORN

BOTANICAL: *Family; Roseceae; Genus; Crataegus; Species; Oxyacantha* (English), *Mollis* (downy hawthorn), *Crus galli* (cockspur thorn)

DESCRIPTION: Its fruit called "haw" looks like a small apple. The flowers are white and bloom in May with a fragrant rose like odor. In Autumn, the small leaves have a brilliant colour.

CHEMICALS FOR SCENT MATCHING: (1) Acetophenone; (2) Anisic aldehyde; (3) Anisyl acetate; (4) Citral

Basis: (1) Alcohol C-9; (2) Aldehyde C-9; (3) Aldehyde C-10

HELIOTROPE

BOTANICAL: *Family: Boraginaceae; Genus; Heliotropium; Species; Arborescence* (Peruvian type)

DESCRIPTION: The plant has beautiful flowers with a vanilla honey fragrance and a delicate bitter almond scent. It is also known as a "cherry pie blossom"

CHEMICALS FOR SCENT MATCHING: (1) Coumarin; (2) Helioptropin; (3) Hydroxycitronellal; (4) Vanillin

HONAYSUCKLE

SYNONYMS: Chevrefeuille

BOTENICAL: *Family: Caprifoliaceae; Genus; Lonicera; Species; Caprifolium, Sempervirens* (coral type or trumpet), *Peryclymenum* (woodbine), *Tatarica* (landscaping type), *Fragrantissima* (landscaping type), *Nitida* (box evergreen), *Pileata* (privet)

DESCRIPTION: Honeysuckle is also called "woodbine". The bush honeysuckle attracts bees. It has yellow blossoms. The coral or trumpet honeysuckle has a blossom which is red outside and orange yellow inside. Honeysuckle produces trumpet shaped flowers. Some people believe that it was the "trusted eglantin" referred to in the poems of Milton.

CHEMICALS FOR SCENT MATCHING: (1) Benzyl acetate; (2) Cresyl acetate; (3) Rhodinol; (4) Vanillin

Basis: (1) Alcohol C-9; (2) Aldehyde C-9 MNA (methyl nonyl acetaldehyde)

HYSCINTH

SYNONYMS: Jacynth

BOTANICAL: *Family: Liliaceae: Genus; Hyacinthus; Species; Orientalis*

DESCRIPTION: Hyacinth flowers have a variety of colors from white, pink, blue, yellow to purple, with a characteristic delicate fragrance

CHEMICALS FOR SCENT MATCHING: (1) Cinnamic alcohol; (2) Bromystyrot; (3) Hydratropic aldehyde; (4) Phenyl acetaldehyde; (5) Phenyl ethyl formate; (6) Phenyl ethyl phenyl acetate; (7) Phenyl propyl alcohol; (8) Phenyl propyl aldehyde

Basis: (1) Alcohol C-8; (2) Aldehyde C-8; (3) Aldehyde C-10

IRIS

BOTANICAL: *Family: Iridiceae: Genus; Iris* (yellow flag iris); *Species; P seudacorus* (blue flag), *Versicolor* (blue flag), *Kaempferi* (Japanese iris), *Sibirica* (Siberian iris), *Spuria* (butterfly iris), *Pumila* (dwarf bearded iris); *Genus; Freesia; Species; Refracta*

DESCRIPTION: Iris has a faint violet like odour. The name iris comes from the Greek word "rainbow". The roots of iris (orris roots) are dried and employed in perfumes, cosmetics, and medicine. The French name "fleur de lis" (flower of the lily) is also applied in the manufacture of specific perfumes with a characteristic iris odor.

CHEMICALS FOR SCENT MATCHING: (1) Anisic aldehyde;(2) Cuminic aldehyde;(3) Methyl ionone; (4) Irone

Basis: (1) Alcohol C-9; (2) Alcohol C-10; (3) Aldehyde C-9; (4) Aldehyde C-10; (5) Aldehyde C-12

JASMINE

BOTANICAL: *Family: Oleaceae; Genus; Jasminum; Species; Officialis or officinale, Grandiflorum* (Spanish)

CHEMICALS FOR SCENT MATCHING: (1) Acetate C-8; (2) Amyl cinnamic aldehyde; (3) α–Amyl cinnamic aldehyde; (4) α–Amyl cinnamic aldehyde dimethyl acetal; (5) Benzyl acetate; (6) Benzyl butyrate; (7) Benzyl isobutyrate; (8) Hexyl cinnamic aldehyde; (9) Indole; (10) Ionone; (11) Isojasmone; (12) Linalool; (13) Methyl anthranilate

Basis: (1) Alcohol C-10; (2) Aldehyde C-8; (3) Aldehyde C-10

JONQUIL

SYNONYMS: Narcissus jounquil

BOTANICAL: *Family: Amaryllidaceae;Genus; Narcissus odorous*

DESCRIPTION: It is the name of several yellow narcissus. The jonquil fragrance, sweet scented is, that of the common jonquil classified as Narcissus odorous. The name jonquil is from the Latin word "juncus" meaning "rush".

CHEMICALS FOR SCENT MATCHING: (1) Benzyl acetate; (2) Cinnamic alcohol; (3) Hydratropic aldehyde; (4) Hydroxycitronellal; (5) Indole; (6) Isoeugenol; (7) Linalool; (8) Musk ambrette; (9) Phenyl acetate; (10) Terpineol

Basic : (1) Alcohol C-9; (2) Aldehyde C-9

LAVENDER

BOTANICAL: *Family: Labiatae; Genus; Lavandula; Species; Vera; Officinalis*

DESCRIPTION: The name "lavender" comes from the Latin word 'lavo' meaning 'to wash' as the Romans used the leaves and flowers of this plant when they were bathing. Traditionally 'lavender' represents 'purity'. The expression 'lavender' is also used with reference to some one with gentle manners. The fragrance of the lavender lasts even after the plant is totally dry.

CHEMICALS FOR SCENT MATCHING: (1) Citronellyl butyrate; (2) Geranyl acetate; (3) Linalyl acetate; (4) Linalyl butyrate; (5) Menthanyl acetate; (6) Perpinyl acetate (7) Terpinyl propionate

Basis: (1) Alcohol C-9; (2) Aldehyde C-10

LILAC

BOTANICAL: *Family: Oleaceae; Genus; Syringa; Species; Vulgaris*

DESCRIPTION: Lilac has white or purple flowers with a peculiar fresh green fragrance. It is one of the odors imitated and synthesized for multiple purposes in perfuming.

CHEMICALS FOR SCENT MATCHING: (1) Anisyl acetate; (2) Anisic alcohol; (3) Cinnamic alcohol; (4) Dimethyl acetophenone; (5) Heliotropin; (6) Hydroxycitronellal; (7) Indole; (8) Isoeugenol; (9) Phenyl ethyl alcohol; (10) Terpineol

Basis: (1) Alcohol C-9; (2) Aldehyde C-9; (3) Aldehyde C 10; (4) Aldehyde C-12 MNA

LILY OF THE VALLEY

SYNONYMS: Muguet

BOTANICAL: *Family: Lilaceae; Genus; Convallaria; Species; Majallis, Montana*

DESCRIPTION: In Germany it is also called "mayflower" because it is one of the special flowers of the month of May. It has one of the most delightful fragrances. A toilet water imitating its odor, a fresh rosy lemon note of distinct greenness, is called "eau d oro" (golden water) by the French.

CHEMICALS FOR SCENT MATCHING: (1) Amyl cinnamic aldehyde; (2) Cinnamyl acetate; (3) Cyclamen aldehyde; (4) Ethyl phenyl acetate; (5) Hydroxycitronellal; (6) Ionone; (7) Linalool; (8) Linalyl propionate; (9) Phenyl ethyl propionate; (10) Tetrahydro linalool

Basis: (1) Alcohol C-9; (2) Alcohol C-10; (3) Alcohol C-11; (4) Aldehyde C-9; (5) Aldehyde C-10; (6) Aldehyde C-12; (7) Aldehyde C-16

LINDEN

SYNONYMS: Basswood

BONTANICAL : *Family: Tiliaceae; Genus; Tilia; Species; Americana, Platy phyllos, Lacimata* (European cut linden), *Cordate* (little leaf linden)

DESCRIPTION: It is a graceful cone shaped tree, growing in many areas of the world. It is also called lime tree or basswood. The flowers are small, white or yellowish with fragrant lime odor. The European "cut leaf" linden and the "little leaf" linden are extensively planted as oranamentals. The nectar of its fragrant flowers is a source of honey.

CHEMICALS FOR SCENT MATCHING: (1) Benzyl benzoate; (2) Farnesol; (3) Hydroxycitronellal; (4) Methyl anthranilate; (5) Verdantol

MAGNOLIA

BOTANICAL: *Family: Magnoliaceae; Genus; Magnolia; Species; Grandiflora* (southern type), *Virginiana* (sweet bay, swamp magnolia), *Tripetala* (umbrella tree), *Macrophylla* (big leaf magnolia), *Acuminata* (cucumber tree)

DESCRIPTION: There are 35 kinds of magnolia trees. Eight varieties grow widely in the eastern part of the U.S. The southern magnolia (grandiflora) is popular because of the beauty and fragrance of its large whitish flowers. Its flowers have an extremely delicate, sweet fragrance of rose, violet, and orange flowers.

CHEMICALS FOR SCENT MATCHING: (1) Amyl cinnamic aldehyde; (2) Anisic aldehyde; (3) Benzyl acetate; (4) Citral; (5) Heliotropin; (6) Hydroxycitronellal; (7) Linalool; (8) Linalyl acetate; (9) Methyl ionone; (10) Musk ketone

Basis: Aldehyde C-10

MIGNONETTE

SYNONYMS: Reseda
BOTANICAL: *Family: Resedaceae; Genus; Reseda; Species; Odorata*

DESCRIPTION: The name comes from the French word "mignonette" which means "little darling". Mignonette has a very pleasant fragrance, particularly from small flowers.

CHEMICALS FOR SCENT MATCHING: (1) Benzyl acetate; (2) Cinnamic alcohol; (3) Ethyl laurinate; (4) Geraniol; (5) Guaiacol acetate; (6) Linalool; (7) Ionone; (8) Methyl heptyne carbonate; (9) Methyl ionone; (10) Methyl nonyl ketone; (11) Phenyl ethyl acetate; (12) Phenyl propyl acetate; (13) Santolol or cedrol; (14) Terpineol; (15) Vetiverol

Basis: (1) Alcohol C-9; (2) Aldehyde C-10; (3) Aldehyde C-12

MIMOSA

BOTANICAL: *Family: Leguminosae; Genus; Mimosa*

OCCURRENCE: Mimosa is a plant growing mostly in tropical lands and in warm, areas worldwide.

DESCRIPTION: It is similar to acacia. Its flowers are small and yellow, pink, lavender, or purple. The fragrance of mimosa is very strong.

CHEMICALS FOR SCENT MATCHING: (1) Acetophenone; (2) Dimethyl acetophenone; (3) Hydroxycitronellal; (4) Terpineol
Basis: (1) Alcohol C-10; (2) Alcohol C-11; (3) Aldehyde C-10; (4) Aldehyde C-11

MOON FLOWER

BOTANICAL: *Family: Convolvulaceae; Genus; Calonyction; Species; Aculeatum*

DESCRIPTION: The scent is very delicate. It is also of the

morning glory flower family.

CHEMICALS FOR SCENT MATCHING: (1) Benzo dihydropyrone; (2) Coumarin; (3) Dimethyl hydroquinone; (4) Methyl anisate

MORNING GLORY

BOTANICAL: *Family; Convolvulaceae; Genus; Ipomoeae; Species; Purpurea*

DESCRIPTION: It is a climbing plant with a funnel like flower with a mixture of purple, blue, red, pink, and white colors. The fragrant flower opens in the morning and closes later in the evening.

CHEMICALS FOR SCENT MATCHING: (1) Benzo dihydropyrone; (2) Coumarin; (3) Dimethyl hydroquinone; (4) Methyl anisate

MOSS

BOTANICAL: *Family: Lichens; Genus; Evernia; Species; Prunastri* (oak moss), *Furfuraceae* (tree moss); *Genus; Urnea; Species; Barbata* (tree moss)

DESCRIPTION: E. *prunastri* grows mostly on oak trees and is celled oak moss. the *furfuraceae* and the barbata species grow on spruce and fir trees and are called "tree moss".

CHEMICALS FOR SCENT MATCHING: (1) Cinnamic alcohol; (2) Coumarin; (3) Benzyl benzoate; (4) Benzyl cinnamate; (5) Heliotropin; (6) Ionone; (7) Linalool; (8) Linalyl acetate; (9) Musk; (10) Vetiverol

MUSK

DESCRIPTION: It is an oily substance with a strong, persistent odor. It is from a gland of the male musk deer. The finest quality is from China and is called tog king. Artifical musk, however, is used more often in the manufacture of perfumes to give a more permanent odor than the natural musk.

The musk deer is a small animal about 2 feet tall. It lives in the Himalaya mountains and in the high regions of the northern hemisphere at an altitude of 8000-12000 feet. It lives alone contrary to habits of deer in herds. It feeds on lichens, grass, roots, and twigs of shrubs and comes out only at night.

The musk product derives from a globe shaped gland in the skin of the male deer abodomen.

CHEMICALS FOR SCENT MATCHING: (1) Musk ambrette; (2) Musk ketone; (3) Musk tibetene; (4) Musk xylol

NARCISSUS

SYNONYMS: Daffodil

BOTANICAL: *Family: Amaryllidaceae; Genus; Narcissus; Species; Pseudo-narcissus* (daffodil), *Poeticus, Tazetta, Poet's Poeticus* (hybrid of tazetta), *Polyanthus*

DESCRIPTION: Narcissus flowers are white or yellow and have a very delicate, fragrant odor similar to that of hyacinth

CHEMICALS FOR SCENT MATCHING: (1) Cinnamic alcohol; (2) p-Cresyl acetate; (3) p Cresyl phenyl acetate; (4) Phenyl ethyl alcohol

Basis: (1) Alcohol C-9; (2) Aldehyde C-9

ORANGE BLOSSOM

SYNONYMS: Neroli

BOTANICAL: *Family: Rutaceae; Genus; Citrus; Species; Sinensis, Aurantium* (bitter orange); *Subspecies; Amara*

DESCRIPTION: Neroli is extracted from fresh picked flowers of the bitter orange (Citrus aurantium amara) whose leaves and twigs are also the source of petitgrain.

CHEMICALS FOR SCENT MATCHING: (1) Dimethyl anthranilate; (2) Ethyl anthranilate; (3) Methyl anthranilate; (4) Methyl B-naphthyl Ketone; (5) Nerolin; (6) Neryl acetate; (7) Yara yara

Basis: (1) Alcohol C-9; (2) Alcohol C-10; (3) Alcohol C-12; (4) Aldehyde C-9; (5) Aldehyde C-12

ORCHID

BOTANICAL: Family: Orchidaceae; Genus; Cypripedium (peristeria dove), *Arethusa, Calypso, Calopogen, Habernaria, Elata* (dove plant).

DESCRIPTION: There are more than 6000 species of orchids, one of which furnishes vanilla.

CHEMICALS FOR SCENT MATCHING: (1) Amyl salicylate; (2) Isobutyl salicylate; (3) Isoeugenol; (4) Linalool; (5) Nerolin; (6) Terpineol

PATCHOULI

BOTANICAL: *Family: Labiatae; Genus; Pogostemon; Species; Hyeneanus*

OCCURRENCE: India; also widely cultivated in the Phillppines and Malaya.

DESCRIPTION: The patchouli plant is 2 or 3 feet high with a purple flower or small white spikes. The oil from the leaves has a musty odor. It is used in tropical Asia.

CHEMICALS FOR SCENT MATCHING: (1) Benzyl salicylate (2) Cinnamic alcohol; (3) Cinnamic aldehyde; (4) Coumarin; (5) Geraniol; (6) Heliotropin; (7) Methyl salicylate; (8) Musk xylene; (9) Phenyl ethyl alcohol; (10) Rhodinol; (11) Vanillin

PINE (NEEDLES)

BOTANICAL: *Family: Pinaceae; Genus; Pinus; Species; Strobus* (white pine), *Lambertiana* (sugar pine), *Banksiana* (jack pine), *Palustris* (longleaf pine), *Ponderosa* (Ponderosa)

DESCRIPTION: The common name 'pine' refers to the largest and most important group of conifers, cone bearing trees. Among these are larch, spruce, hemlock, and fir. These differ from the tree of the pine genus which comprises about 80 different kinds of pine, growing mostly in the northern hemisphere. Of these, 35 species grow in the U.S.

Pinus are evergreen trees. They are mostly used for timber and for the extraction of the resin which provides turpentine and sub derivatives through distillation. A pure essential oil employed in perfumery and flavors in small amounts is also extracted from the pine needles. Turpentine, obtained chiefly by steam distillation of pine palustris resin, is extensively used in blending with rosemary oil, camphene, isobornyl acetate, coumarin, oakmoss, etc. and for the fractional distillation of its many components: terpineol, estragole, fenchone, fenchyl alcohol, borneol. Turpentine is an excellent solvent, particularly in the paint industry.

CHEMICALS FOR SCENT MATCHING: (1) Bornyl acetate; (2) Isobornyl acetate

ROSE

BOTANICAL: *Family: Rosaceae; Genus; Ros; Spaecies; Centifolia; Variety; Muscosa, Setigera* (climbing type), *Damascena* (rose, otto)

DESCRIPTION: Attar, oil from rose petals, is used to make toilet water perfumes. In the rose family there are about 2000 species of trees, shrubs, and herbs. These include apple, apricot, berries, cherries, peach, pear, plum, quince, and strawberry.

CHEMICALS FOR SCENT MATCHING: (1) Acetate C-10; (2) Acetate C-12; (3) Anisic aldehyde; (4) Benzophenone; (5); Benzyl butyrate; (6) Benzyl isoeugenol; (7) Butyl phenyl acetate; (8) Cinnamic isovalerate; (9) Citronellal; (10) Citronellol; (11) Citronellyl acetate; (12) Citronellyl butyrate; (13) Citronellyl formate; (14); Citronellyl isobutyrate; (15) Citronellyl propionate; (16) Citronellyl oxycetaldehyde; (17) Dimethyl octanol; (18) Ethyl pelargonate; (19) Ethyl phenyl acetate; (20) Geraniol; (21) Geranyl acetate; (22) Geranyl butyrate; (23) Geranyl formate; (24) Geranyl phenyl acetate; (25) Geranyl propionate; (26) Guaiacwood acetate; (27) Hydroxycitronellal; (28) Isobutyl benzoate; (29) Isbutyl phenyl acetate; (30) Isopulegol extra; (31) Linalyl formate; (32) Methyl acetate, racemic; (33) Methyl diphenyl ether; (34) Nerol; (35) Nerolidol; (36) Phenoxy isobutyrate; (37) Phenyl ethyl acetate; (38) Phenyl ethyl alcohol; (39) Phenyl ethyl benzoate; (40) Phenyl ethyl butyrate; (41) Phenyl ethyl cinnamate; (42) Phenyl ethyl isobutyrate; (43) Phenyl ethyl phenyl acetate; (44) Phenyl ethyl propionate; (45) Phenyl ethyl salicylate; (46) Rhodinol extra, (47) Rhodinyl acetate; (48) Rhodinyl butyrate; (49) Rhodinyl formate; (50) Rhodinyl phenyl acetate; (51) Rosacetol; (52) Tetrahydrolinalool

Basis: Rosa centifolia; (1) Alcohol C-9; (2) Aldehyde C-9 (3) Aldehyde C-11 (4) Aldehyde C-16; Rose blanche (white) (1) Alcohol C-8; (2) Aldehyde C-8; Rose rouge (red); (1) Alcoho C-9; (2) Alcohol C-11; Rose d oriente: (1) Alcohol C-9; (2 Aldehyde C-11

SWEET PEA

BOTANICAL: *Family: Leguminosae; Genus; Lathyrus; Species Odoratus; Latifolius*

DESCRIPTION: More than 1000 species of sweet peas exist i two types: (1) dwarf, only a few inches high; (2) climbing growing along strings or trellises. The fragrance of sweet pe is vary pleasant.

CHEMICALS FOR SCENT MATCHING: (1) Amyl cinnami aldehyde; (2) Benzyl acetate; (3) Benzylidene acctone; (4 Cinnamic alcohol; (5) Dimethyl benzyl carbinol acetate; (6 Heliotropin; (7) Hydroxycitronellal; (8) Ionone ; (9) Isobut phenyl acetate; (10) Linalool; (11) Methyl anthranlate; (12 Methyl naphthyl ketone; (13) Methyl nonyl acetic acid; (14 Musk ambrette; (15) Phenyl acetic aldehyde; (16) Phenyl eth acetate; (17) Phenyl ethyol alcohol; (18) Rhodinol; (19 Terpineol; (20) Vanillin

Basis: (1) Alcohol C-10; (2) Aldehyde C-9; (3) Aldehyde C1 (4) Aldehyde C-12

SYRINGA

SYNONYMS: Mock orange

BOTANICAL: *Family: Saxifragraceae; Genus; Philadelphus; Species; Virginalis, Coronarius*

DESCRIPTION: The syringa is a flower with white ivory color and a strong lilacorange blossom type fragrance. It is used mostly as a border around lawns and gardens. The Philadelphus virginalis type is among the best and most fragrant of the mock orange.

CHEMICALS FOR SCENT MATCHING: (1) Anisyl formate; (2) Hydroxycitronellal; (3) Isobutyl anthranilate; (4) Isobutyl benzoate

TOBACCO

BOTANICAL: *Family: Solanaceae; Genus; Nicotiana; Species; Tabacum, Petunoids, Affinis*

DESCRIPTION: The fragrance of the tobacco flowers is extremely delicate, sweet, spice like, and reminiscent of fresh carnation. Phenyl acetic acid is its major constituent.

CHEMICALS FOR SCENT MATCHING: (1) Heliotropin; (2) Methyl ionone; (3) Methyl phenyl acetate; (4) Musk ketone; (5) Phenyl acetic acid; (6) y-Valerolactone; (7) Vanillin; (8) Vetiverol

TREFLE

SYNONYMS: Trefoil

BOTANICAL: *Family: Leguminosae; Genus; Lotus* (bird's foot as it bears clusters of pods resembling a croce's foot); *Species; Corniculatus, Uliginous, Bertholeti* (coralgem deervetch)

DESCRIPTION: Trefle or trefoil means “three lead”. It is applied to plants having compound leaves with three leaflets, e.g. clover. Any of several trifoliate leguminous herbs.

CHEMICALS FOR SCENT MATCHING: (1) Amyl cinnamic aldehyde; (2) Ethyl salicylate; (3) Heliotropin; (4) Isobutyl phenyl acetate; (5) Isoeugenol; (6) Musk ketone; (7) Rhodinol; (8) Vanillin

Basis: (1) Aldehyde C-9; (2) Aldehyde C-11; (3) Aldehyde C-12; (4) Aldehyde C-12 MNA

TUBEROSE

BOTANICAL: *Family: Amaryllidaceae; Genus; Polianthes; Species; Tuberosa*

DESCRIPTION: Tuberose has been described as a "lump of cloying sweetness" It has a heavy fragrance. Mare than 100, 000 pounds of tuberose flowers are employed each year for essential oil production.

CHEMICALS: FOR SCENT MATCHING: (1) Benzyl acetate; (2) Butyl benzyl oxide; (3) Butyl phenyl acetate; (4) Hydroxycitronellal; (5) Methyl benzoate; (6) Methyl nonyl acetaldehyde; (7) Methyl salicylate; (8) Propyl phenyl alcohol

Basis: (1) Alcohol C-10; (2) Alcohol C-12; (3) Aldehyde C-10; (4) Aldehyde C-12

VERBENA

SYNONYMS: Eau de verveine

BOTANICAL: *Family; Verbenaceae; Genus; Verbena; Species; Hybrida, Erinoides* (moss verbene), *Lippia citriodora*

DESCRIPTION: The verbena flowers are pink, purple, red, white, and other colors except yellow. Their fragrance is citrus lilac like.

CHEMICALS FOR SCENT MATCHING: (1) Benzyl isoeugenol; (2) Citral ; (3) Cyclamen aldehyde; (4) Hydroxycitronellal; (5) Isobutyl benzoate; (6) Linalool; (7) Linalyl acetate; (8) Neroli

Basis: (1) Aldehyde C-8; (2) Aldehyde C-10

VIOLET

BOTANICAL: *Family: Violaceae; Genus; Viola; Species; Pepilionaceae* (the bird's foot violet), *Tricolor* (pansy violet), *Canina* (dog violet), *Odorata* (Victoria variety)

DESCRIPTION: More than 300 species of violets are grown worldwide with about 100 in the U.S. Some have white and yellow flowers. The blue and purple types are more abundant. The dog violet has no fragrance. The pansy is a cultivated species.

CHEMICALS FOR SCENT MATCHING: (1) Benzyl acetate; (2) Ethyl myristate; (3) Heliotropin; (4) Ionone; (5) α–Ionone; (6) ß-Ionone; (7) α–Irone; (8) α–Isoamyl ionone; (9) α–Isomethyl ionone; (10) Methyl heptyne carbonate; (11) y Methyl ionone; (12) Methyl 2 nonanoate; (13) Methyl octine carbonate

Basis: (1) Alcohol C-9; (2) Alcohol C-10; (3) Alcohol C-12; (4) Aldehyde C-9; (5) Aldehyde C-10; (6) Aldehyde C-11, undecylenic; (7) Aldehyde C-12, lauric; (8) Aldehyde C-14, myristic

WALLFLOWER

SYNONYMS: Goldenlack, Germany

BOTANICAL: *Family: Cruciferae; Genus; Cheiranthus; Species; Cheiri*

DESCRIPTION: The name comes from the fact that it grows on walls over strong cliffs and supporting places. It is a plant related to the mustard. It has a purple flower with a lilac violet jasmine orange flower-ylang ylang-narcissus-carnation-like fragrance with green top note.

CHEMICALS FOR SCEBN MATCHING: (1) Anisic aldehyde; (2) Heliotropin; (3) Hydroxycitronellal; (4) Ionone; (5) Isoeugenol; (Methyl p cresol; (7) Methyl ß-naphthyl ketone

Basis: (1) Alcohol C-9; (2) Aldehyde C-9

WISTERIA

BOTANICAL: *Family: Leguminosae; Genus; Wisteria; Species; Sinensis*

OCCURRENCE: It is a native of China. It is often seen around homes in the U.S.

DESCRIPTION: Wisteria is a climbing plant with beautiful clusters of bluish lavender blossom flowers similar to pea blossom. This plant grows fast and covers large areas with its branches. It is one of the most attractive vining plants.

CHEMICALS FOR SCENT MATCHING: Basis: (1) Alcohol C-8; (2) Aldehyde C-8; (3) Aldehyde C-12

WINTERGREEN

BOTANICAL: *Family: Ericaceae; Genus; Gaultheria; Species; Procumbens*

DESCRIPTION: The name of this plant refers to its leaves which remain green all winter. Its berries heve a pleasant smell and their oil is used in chewing gum, tooth paste and powder, and medicine because of the agreeable flavour.

It is a low growing shrub with creeping or subterranean stems. The berries are bright red. The flowers which are like urns, are covered by the leaves.

CHEMICALS FOR SCENT MATCHING: (1) Ethyl benzoate; (2) Ethyl salicylate; (3) Methyl salicylate

YLANG YLANG

SYNONYMS: Cananga odoroata

BOTANICAL: *Family: Anonaceae; Genus; Anona odoratissima; Species; Uvaria odorate, Cananga odorata*

DESCRIPTION: Ylang ylang is employed as a base in muguet type perfumes: gardenia, honeysuckle, hyacinth, lilac, lily, narcissus, peonia freesia, sweet pea, and many other delicate floral compositions of oriental type such as sandalwood, opopanax, and spice. It is also used in flavors such as peach, apricot, and sweet type.

CHEMICALS FOR SCENT MATCHING: (1) m Cresyl phenyl acetate; (2) Ethyl acetate; (3) Geranyl benzoate; (4) Methyl benzoate; (5) Methyl p cresol

Basis: (1) Alcohol C-9; (2) Aldehyde C-9

Simulated Marine Scents (Algae)

SEAWEED (ALGAE)

BOTANICAL: Phyla; Algae; Family; Thallophyta
Genus: Macrocystis; Species; Pyrifera
Genus: Phylum; Species; Phacophyta (brown algae)
Genus: Sargassum (gulfweed); Species; Bacciferum
Genus: Phylum; Species; Rodophyta (red algae)
Genus: Chondrus; Species; Crispus (Irish moss)
Genus: Phylum; Species; Cyanophyta (blue green)
Genus: Phylum; Species; Chlorophyta (green)

DESCRIPTION: The seaweeds of cold water are mostly brown algae. Those of the tropics are mainly red algae. Seaweeds contain large amounts of iodine as well as algin which is used in cream for its nonfoaming capacity to hold different liquids together in milk. Agar and carrageen, from seaweeds, are also employed in foods and drugs.

Seaweeds reach more than 200 feet, Particularly in the South Pacific, and occur in large masses in the Sargasso Sea, floating in the Atlantic Ocean east of Florida. Agar agar is a gelatinous substance from seaweeds particularly from the algae classified as Galidium. It occurs in tropical Asia and along the Pacific coast of America.

CHEMICALS FOR SCENT MATCHING: (1) Acetaldehyde; (2) Alcohol C-7; (3) Butyraldehyde; (4) Butyric acid; (5) Propionic acid; (6) Valeraldehyde

Suggested New Perfumes

The creation of the following perfumes is suggested:

1. Adonis, a mythological subject
2. Forsythia, the golden spring bell of the U.S.
3. Fringe, the botanical splendor of the southern U.S.

ADONIS

BOTANICAL: *Family: Ranunculaceae; Genus; Adonis; Anemone* (wind flower); *Species; Quinquifolia*

DESCRIPTION: A group of plants native to Europe and Asia, they also grow in North America. The flowers may be yellow or red with 5-16 petals.

Even though this plant has no fragrance it stimulates the fantasy in compounding a fine perfume.

COMPONENTS: *Basis:* (1) Benzyl acetate; (2) Hydroxycitronellal; (3) Isobutyl phenyl acetate

FORSYTHIA

SYNONYMS: Golden bell

BOTANICAL: *Family: Oleaceae; Genus; Forsythia; Species; Suspensa; Spectabilis; Viridissima, Intermedia*

DESCRIPTION: Forsythia is a shrub about nine feet high, Because the flowers have a beautiful golden color, they are called golden bells and spring garden flower."

In early spring forsythia blossoms are the earliest sign of flowers. The leaves grow to about 3 inches long and are egg shaped.

The name is from the English botanist William Forsyth (1737-1804).

Forsythia flowers have no fragrance, but as it is the first beautiful flower in the begining of spring, it invokes agreeable feelings. Therefore, the creation of a special perfume with the forsythia name would certainly be appreciated.

FRINGE TREE

BOTANICAL: *Family: Oleaceae; Genus; Chionanthus; Spe Virginicus*

DESCRIPTION: It is a fragrant, small tree, sometimes reaching 30 feet high, with delicate white flowers with four slim petals blooming in early spring. It is native to the middle and southern U.S. from southern Pennsylvania to Florida, and also in the West Brazos River in Taxas.

A perfume similar to the "fringe" would be valued.

Fixatives for Perfumes

The formulation of well compounded perfume is usually based on three basic odors: the one first perceived with its peculiar tonality; the second floral portion well in harmony with the tonality; and the third longer lasting fixative. Consequently, the fixative is the most difficult part of preparing a perfume in the search to harmonize all elements for a very pleasant and lasting scent.

There are perfumes which contain 50-100 different compounds each compound itself containing other compounds. In fact, as many as 300 ingredients may be employed in a perfume. There are about 500 natural and 3000 synthetic oils available for the production of perfumes.

Two of the preferred fixatives are ambergris and musk, both of natural origin.

AMBERGRIS

DESCRIPTION: Ambergris is a wax like substance occurring in the sperm whale's intestine. It is found floating on the oceans or seashores as waste. It has a disagreeable odor when inside the whale's intestines but on exposure to air, it acquires a sweet earthy smell and combines very well in the manufacture of perfumes.

COMPONENTS: *Basis:* (1) Aldehyde C-8; (2) Aldehyde C9; (3) Aldehyde C-10

Chapter 2

FORMULARY OF PERFUMES

NOTE :

A. All formulaes are specified by the name of each perfume. If the formula is prevalently made with natural products, such as essential oils, it is called "imitation". If the formula is prevalently made with chemical products, it is called "synthetic".

B. The amount of each ingredient in all formaulaes is by weight (g).

C. All formulaes are alphabetically listed including their ingredients. The solvents (ethyl alcohol - 95% and distilled water) are included at the end of each formula.

D. Ingredients denoted by an asterisk (*) are formulaes which may by found in this book.

E. The polysolvent for the perfumes is :

1.	Propylene Glycol	500
2.	Triton	250
3.	Tween	250
		1000

ACACIA

1.	Acetophenone	50
2.	Alcohol C-9	12
3.	Alcohol C-10	5
4.	Alcohol C-11	5
5.	Aldehyde C-9	13
6.	Aldehyde C-10	5
7.	Aldehyde C-14	5
8.	Aldehyde C-18	5
9.	Anethole	125
10.	Anisaldehyde	125
11.	Bergamot Oil	50
12.	Bromostyrol	10
13.	Geranium Oil	100
14.	Hydroxycinnamic Aldehyde	10
15.	Ionone	5
16.	Isobutyl Benzoate	200
17.	Jasmine Oil	25
18.	Linalool	25
19.	Methyl Anthranilate	25
20.	Musk Ketone	30
21.	Musk Xylene	30
22.	Naphthol Methyl Ether	10
23.	Nerolin	15
24.	Phenyl Acetic Aldehyde	15
25.	Styrax	15
26.	Terpineol	5
27.	Vanillin	50
28.	Vetiverol Oil	10
		1000

ACETIC ACID TINCTURE

1.	Glacial Acetic Acid	10
2.	Ethyl Alcohol 95%	990
		1000

ALPESTRINE, PERFUME

1.	Lavender, Oil	30
2.	Lavandin, Oil	50
3.	Rosemary, Oil	40
4.	Sage, Oil	30
5.	Spike, Oil	50
6.	Ethyl Alcohol 95%	400
7.	Distilled Water	400
		1000

AMBER, BASE

1.	Aldehyde C-8	60
2.	Aldehyde C-9	200
3.	Aldehyde C-10	150
4.	Aldehyde C-12	90
5.	Ethyl Alcohol 95%	500
		1000

AMBER, CONCRETE (FIXATIVE)

1.	Balsam Tolu	100
2.	Benzyl Benzoate	500
3.	Jasmine, Oil	10
4.	Labdanum, Resinoid	250
5.	Musk Ambrette	40
6.	Oakmoss, Oil	50
7.	Vanillin	50
		1000

AMBER, LIQUID (CHYPRE BASIS)

1.	Benzyl Benzoate	500
2.	Clary Sage	175
3.	Musk Ambrette	125
4.	Musk Xylol	50
5.	Oakmoss, Oil	150
		1000

AMBERGRIS TINCTURE IMITATION NO. 1

1.	Amber, Base*	70
2.	Ambergris Tincture*	500
3.	Musk Ambrette	100
4.	Rose, Oil	20
5.	Vanilla, Oil	10
6.	Ethyl Alcohol 95%	300
		1000

AMBERGRIS PERFUME IMITATION NO. 2

1.	Benzoin	125
2.	Castor, Oil	125
3.	Civet	125
4.	Jasmine, Oil	10
5.	Labdanum, Oil	50
6.	Musk	125
7.	Oakmoss, Oil	50
8.	Peru Balsam	125
9.	Rose, Oil	10
10.	Storax	125
11.	Tolu Balsam	125
12.	Vanillin	5
		1000

AMBERGRIS, TINCTURE

1.	Ambergris	100
2.	Ethyl Alcohol 95%	900
		1000

Macerate for a three month period. Filter.

BERGAMMONIA DISINFECTANT

1.	Ammonia	100
2.	Bergamot	500
3.	Limonene	100
4.	Terpineyl Acetate	100
5.	Ethyl Alcohol 95%	200
		1000

BERGAMOT, ESSENCE (NATURAL) NO. 1

1.	Bergamot, Oil	300
2.	Limonene	300
3.	Linalool	60
4.	Linalyl Acetate	300
5.	Terpinyl Acetate	40
		1000

BERGAMOT ESSENCE (NATURAL) NO. 2

1.	Bergamot, Oil	430
2.	Bois de Rose, Oil	80
3.	Geranyl Acetate	30
4.	Linalyl Acetate	150
5.	Nerolin	10
6.	Petitgrain, Paraguay	20
7.	Terpineol	190
8.	Tripinyl Acetate	90
		1000

BOUQUET, NO. 1 (FOR SOAP)

1.	Bergamot, Oil	325
2.	Clove, Oil	25
3.	Geranium, Oil	200
4.	Gingergrass, Oil	150
5.	Lemongrass, Oil	75
6.	Methyl Anthranilate	60
7.	Musk Xylene	40
8.	Patchouli, Oil	75

9.	Styrax	50
		1000

BOUQUET NO.2 (FOR SOAP)

1.	Aldehyde C-10 (10% solution)	25
2.	Linalool	300
3.	Linalyl Acetate	100
4.	Methyl Anthranilate	100
5.	Orange (Sweet) Oil	125
6.	Phenyl Ethyl Alcohol	350
		1000

BOUVARDIA

1.	Acetyl Isoeugenol	5
2.	Alcohol C-9	2
3.	Aldehyde C-9	5
4.	Aldehyde C-10	6
5.	Aldehyde C-12	3
6.	Hydroxycitronellal	20
7.	Jasmine Oil	6
8.	Linalool	50
9.	Methyl Heptyne Carbonate	4
10.	Methyl Ionone	5
11.	Ethyl Alcohol 95%	894
		1000

CALAMUS IMITATION NO. 1

1.	Benzyl Alcohol (10% solution)	300
2.	Eucalyptol	100
3.	Limonene (10% soln.)	300
4.	Phellandrene	50
5.	Alpha Pinene	50
6.	Terpinyl Acetate	200
		1000

CALAMUS, IMITATION NO. 2

1.	Calamus	800
2.	Calamus, Oil	200
		1000

CAMPHOR, TINCTURE

1.	Camphor	10
2.	Ethyl Alcohol 95%	990
		1000

CANANGA (FOR SOAP)

1.	Bromostyrene	25
2.	Cedarwood, Oil	75
3.	p-Cresyl Methyl Ether	25
4.	Geranium Palmarosa, Oil	37
5.	Methyl Anthranilate	50
6.	Musk Xylene	50
7.	Sassafras, Oil	25
8.	Terpineol	375
		1000

CAPSICUM

1.	Capsicum, Oleoresin (10% soln.)	750
2.	Cotton Seeds, Oil	200
3.	Paprika, Oleoresin	50
		1000

CARNATION, IMITATION NO.1

1.	Cinnamon Oil	55
2.	Clary Sage	30
3.	Eugenol	100
4.	Heliotropin	50
5.	Hydroycitronellal	30
6.	α–Ionone	20

7. Isoeugenol (10% solution) 400
8. Methyl Isoeugenol 100
9. Musk 50
10. Neroli, Oil 50
11. Pimento Oil 50
12. Rose Oil 30
13. Vanillin 5
14. Ylang Ylang Oil 30

1000

CARNATION, IMITATION NO- 2.

1. Cinnamon Oil 10
2. Clary Sage Oil 40
3. Eugenol 150
4. Heliotropin 100
5. Hydroxycitronellal 40
6. Ionone 10
7. Isoeugenol 150
8. Methyl Isoeugenol 150
9. Neroli Oil 100
10. Pimento Oil 150
11. Rose Oil (10% solution). 60
12. Ylang Ylang Oil 40

1000

CARNATION (FOR SOAP)

1. Benzyl Acetate 75
2. Benzyl Benzoate 30
3. Cananga Oil 250
4. Cinnamon Oil 10
5. Eugenol 500
6. Heliotropin 20
7. Nutmag Concrete 20
8. Nutmeg Oil 20
9. Orris Absolute 50
10. Rose Oil 5
11. Ylang Ylang Oil 20

1000

CARNATION, PINK (PERFUME)

1. Alcohol c-7 2
2. Alcohol c-9 2
3. Aldehyde c-8 1
4. Aldehyde c-9 1
5. Amyl Salicylate 1
6. Bay oil 5
7. Benzyl Isoeugenol 5
8. Cinnamon Oil 1
9. Clary Sage Oil 2
10. Coumarin 5
11. Heliotropin 5
12. Hydroxycitronellal 2
13. α–Ionone 1
14. Isobutyl Phenyl Acetate 1
15. Isoeugenol 45
16. Musk Ambrette 4
17. Neroli Oil 5
18. Rose Oil 3
19. Terpineol 45
20. Vanillin 2
21. Ylang ylang 2
22. Ethyl Alcohol 95% 860

1000

CASTOR, TINCTURE NO. 1

1. Castor, Brown (finely cut)80
2. Ethyl Alcohol 95 % 920

1000

CASTOR, TINCTURE NO.2

1. Castor, Brown (finely cut) 486
2. Ethyl Alcohol 95% 514

1000

CEDRELA, "WOOD TYPE"

1.	Cedarwood, Oil	5
2.	Geranium, Oil	2
3.	Patchouli, Oil	1
4.	Sandalwood, Oil	2
5.	Ethyl Alcohol 95%	990
		1000

CITRONELLA (FOR SOAP)

1.	Benzaldehyde	25
2.	Bergamot, Oil	200
3.	Caraway, Oil	225
4.	Citronella, Oil	275
5.	Geranium Palmarosa, Oil	225
6.	Musk Xylene	25
7.	Terpineol	25
		1000

COCONUT, EXTRACT (NATURAL)

1. Coconut, Rasped (pulp fresh, not rancid) 10 kg
2. Ethyl Alcohol 95 % 30 l

Macerate for 10 days, stirring each day for 1 h. Collect, without pressure, 20 l of extract. To the residue add:

3. Distilled Water 20 l

Let stand for another 3 days, and add:

4. Aldehyde C-18 1 ml
5. Amyl Formate 45 ml
6. Ethyl Oenanthate 24 ml
7. Vanilla Beans, Tincture 100 ml

Distill altogether.

Yield: 40 liters

COCONUT, PASTE

1. Coconut (desiccated) fine powder 4 kg
2. Corn Syrup 3 kg
3. Creme, Fondant (80% sugar + 20% distilled water) 2 kg
4. Milk, Condensed Sweet 2 kg
5. Sugar 10 kg

Mix milk and syrup (#2 and 3) hot. Stir with desiccated powdered coconut. Cool.

COLOGNE

1.	Bergamot, Oil	200
2.	Lemon, Oil	100
3.	Musk Ambrette	1
4.	Neroli, Oil	20
5.	Orange, Oil	50
6.	Rosemary, Oil	1
7.	Ethyl Alcohol 95%	314
8.	Distilled Water	314
		1000

COLOUR BASE STANDARD FORMULA NO. 1

1. Distilled Water 847 ml
2. Dyestuff 50 g
3. Glycerin (28 Be) 100 ml
4. Sodium Benzoate 3 g

Heat to 100 C. Dissolve well. Cool. Filter.

COLOUR BASE STANDARD FORMULA NO. 2

1. Colour 10 g
2. Ethyl Alcohol 95% 190 ml
3. Distilled Water 800 ml

COLOUR MIXTURE

		dye**	g
1.	Cherry	Blue	2.5
		Red	97.5
2.	Green	Blue	10.0
		Yellow	90.0
3.	Orange	Red	10.0
		Yellow	90.0

** The dye, as per the specified amount, must be dissolved as in Colour Base Standard Formula No. 2.

4.	Peach	Orange	75.0
		Yellow	25.0
5.	Pineapple	Brown	50.0
	(Ananas)	Peach	50.0
6.	Pomegranate	Red	97.0
		Yellow	2.5
7.	Raspberry	Red	90.0
		Yellow	10.0

COLOURS (NATURAL DYES)

1.	Blue	Indigo
2.	Brown	Burnt sugar
3.	Green	Chlorophyll
4.	Red	Malva arborea; berries; cochineal
5.	Yellow	Bixa orellana
6.	Violet	Indigo; cochineal

COVER ODOUR, PERFUME NO. 1

1.	Almond, Oil	100
2.	Apricot, Oil	100
3.	Formaldehyde	100
4.	Peach, Oil	100
5.	Propylene Glycol	600
		1000

COVER ODOUR, PERFUME No.2

1.	Ambergris	20
2.	Castor, Oil	40
3.	Hyacinth Oil	100
4.	Jasmine, Absolute	100
5.	Lilac, Oil	100
6.	Neroli, Oil	100
7.	Rose, Bulgarian Absolute	100
8.	Tuberose, Oil	100
9.	Violet, Oil	100
10.	Zibet, Oil	40
11.	Ethyl Alcohol 95%	100
12.	Distilled Water	100
		1000

COVER ODOUR, PERFUME NO. 3

1.	Anisic Alcohol	15
2.	Benzyl Acetate	15
3.	Benzyl Formate	30
4.	Cinnamic Alcohol	15
5.	Coumarin	84
6.	Ethyl Vanillin	110
7.	Heliotropin	105
8.	Hydroxycitronellal	42
9.	Ionone	6
10.	Linalool	90
11.	Methyl Anthranilate	30
12.	Phenyl Acetic Aldehyde	18
13.	Phenyl Ethyl Alcohol	60
14.	Rhodinol	10
15.	Terpineol	240
16.	Ethyl Alcohol 95%	130
		1000

CYCLAMEN, BASE (SYNTHETIC)

1.	Alcohol C-9	1
2.	Aldehyde C-9	1

3. Aldehyde C-10 1
4. Aldehyde C-11 1
5. Aldehyde C-12 1
6. Hydroxycitronellal 20
7. Ionone 25
8. α–Methyl Benzyl Acetate (garden) 25
9. Ethyl Alcohol 95% 463
10. Distilled Water 462

1000

CYCLAMEN (FOR SOAP)

1. Amyl Cinnamic Aldehyde 65
2. Anisaldehyde 85
3. Cananga, Oil 85
4. Cyclamen Aldehyde 100
5. Geraniol 150
6. Hydroxycitronellal 100
7. Inonoe 85
8. Musk Xylene 25
9. Phenyl Acetic Acid 25
10. Rosewood, Oil 65
11. Styrax Resinoid 65
12. Terpineol 150

1000

DEODORANT FOR CREAM

1. Clove, Oil 6
2. Ethyl Acetate 6
3. Rose, Oil 28
4. Ethyl Alcohol 95% 500
5. Distilled Water 460

1000

DEODORANT FOR VESSELS

1. Potatoes, Raw Smashed (amount depends on the size of the vessel) 1/3
2. Hot Water (to fill the vessel) 2/3

Let stand for 1 h. Repeat if necessary.

DEODORANT FOR WATER

1. Magnesia Oixde 30
2. Rose, Tincture 120
3. Distilled water, warm 4000

Filler.

DEODORANTS (MASKING AGENT)

1. Eucalyptus, Citriodora Oil 60
2. Formaldehyde 40% 120
3. Lemon, Oil 60
4. Ethyl Alcohol 95% 760

1000

DEODORANTS (MASKING AGENT / FOR HEAVY ODORS

1. Pine, Oil 30
2. Potassium Permanganate 16
3. Spoke Lavender 30
4. Thymol 160
5. Isopropyl Alcohol 95% 700
6. Distilled Water 64

1000

DEODORANTS (MASKING AGENT) GRASSY ODOURS

1. Ammonia 1
2. Bergamot, Oil 40
3. Cineol 20
4. Citronellol 40

5.	Lemon, Oil	40
6.	Lemongrass, Oil	10
7.	Menthol	20
8.	Thymol	10
9.	Ethyl Alcohol 95%	819
		1000

DIACETYL, TINCTURE

1.	Diacetyl	10
2.	Ethyl Alcohol 95%	990
		1000

EAU DE COLOGNE

1.	Bergamot, Oil	500
2.	Lavender, Oil	40
3.	Lemon, Oil	250
4.	Melissa, Oil	40
5.	Neroli, Oil	40
6.	Ethyl Alcohol 95%	130
		1000

EAU DE COLOGNE (FOR SOAP)

1.	Cadarwood, Oil	100
2.	Cinnamyl Butyrate,	30
3.	Citronella, Oil	100
4.	Clove, Oil	50
5.	Diphenyl Oxide	100
6.	Lavender, Oil	100
7.	Linalyl Acetate	50
8.	Musk Xylene	30
9.	Rosewood, Oil	200
10.	Styrax, Resinoid	20
11.	Terpineol	200
12.	Thyme, Oil	20
		1000

EGLANTINE (WILD ROSE)

1.	Anisaldehyde	30
2.	Geraniol	40
3.	Isobutyl Phenyl Acetate	30
4.	Ethyl Alcohol 95%	450
5.	Distilled Water	450
		1000

ESTERS, GENERAL BASE

1.	Amyl Acetate	225
2.	Amyl Butyrate	75
3.	Ethyl Acetate	385
4.	Ethyl Formate	225
5.	Ethyl Alcohol 95%	90
		1000

FENUGREEK, TINCTURE

1.	Fenugreek, Powdered after Roasting	100
2.	Propylene Glycol	225
3.	Ethyl Alcohol 95%	450
4.	Distilled Water	225
		1000

Filter.

FERN (FOR SOAP)

1.	Benzoin, Resinoid	65
2.	Bergamot, Oil	125
3.	Bornyl Acetate	25
4.	Coumarin	125
5.	Geranyl Acetate	85
6.	Lavender	150
7.	Linalool	125
8.	Musk Ketone	125
9.	Oakmoss, Resinoid	65
10.	Patchouli, Oil	25
11.	Terpenyl Isobutyrate	85

FLORAL FRAGRANCE (FOR SOAP)

1. Carnation (for Soap) 100
2. Jasmine, Oil 100
3. Lilac Imitation No. 1 366
4. Muguet (Lily of the valley) Imitation No. 2* 234
5. Rose, Imitation No. 6* 200

1000

FLORAL, IMITATION NO.1

1. Jasmine, Absolute 100
2. Muguet, Absolute 200
3. Rose, Absolute (10% solution) 450
4. Violet, Leaf, Absolute 150
5. Orange Flower, Absolute 100

1000

FLORAL, IMITATION NO. 2

1. Jonquil, absolute (10% sol' n.) 500
2. Muguet, Absolute 200
3. Rose, Petals 100
4. Violet, Leaf Absolute 200

1000

Note : For Floral Imitation No. 1 amd No. 2 add to each double the amount of ethyl alcohol 95% (1000) and distilled water (1000) Macerate for 5 days and distill over 1800 cc.

FOUGERE

1. Aldehyde C-14 Myristic 30
2. Bergamot, Oil 75
3. Labdanum, Resinoid 70
4. Lavender, Oil 70
5. Lavender Spike, Oil 240
6. Oakmoss, Resin 50
7. Vanillin 30
8. Ethyl Alcohol 95% 225
9. Distitted Water 210

1000

FOUGERE, BASE (FERN)

1. Alcohol C-8 10
2. Alcohol C-9 30
3. Aldehyde C-8 5
4. Aldehyde C-9 5
5. Aldehyde C-10 5
6. Aldehyde C-11 50
7. Aldehyde C-12 25
8. Ethyl Phenyl Acetate 25
9. Isobutyl Acetate 15
10. Lavender 50
11. Musk Xylene 10
12. Ethyl Alcohol 95% 770

1000

FRANGIPANNI, IMITATION NO. 1 (ACUTIFOLIA, ALBA, RUBRA)

1. Balsam Peru 25
2. Bergamot, Oil 125
3. Carnation 125
4. Cinnamic Alcohol 25
5. Coumarin 25
6. Lemon, Oil 125
7. Lily of the Valley 125
8. Orange Flower, Oil 125
9. Terpineol 175
10. Tuberose 125

1000

FRANGIPANNI, IMITATION NO. 2

1.	Gardenia	100
2.	Honeysuckle	50
3.	Jasmine	300
4.	Lilac	100
5.	Mimosa	100
6.	Muguet	100
7.	Orange Flowers, Oil	50
8.	Tuberose	100
9.	Ylang Ylang	100
		1000

FRANGIPANNI, IMITATION NO. 3

1.	Ambergris	8
2.	Jasmine, Oil (10% solution)	100
3.	Musk Ambrette	15
4.	Neroli, Oil	1
5.	Orris, Powder	750
6.	Rose, Oil	1
7.	Sandalwood, Oil	1
8.	Sandalwood, Powder	62
9.	Vetiver, Powder	62
		1000

FRANGIPANNI, IMITATION NO. 4

1.	Bergamot, Oil	30
2.	Cassia, Oil	174
3.	Civet	45
4.	Geranium, Palmarosa	40
5.	Musk Ambrette	70
6.	Neroli, Oil	36
7.	Orange, Oil	140
8.	Rose Otto, Tincture (10% solution)	320
9.	Sandalwood, Oil	5
10.	Tonquin, Musk	70
11.	Vanillin	70
		1000

FRESHENER, PERFUME

1.	Eucalyptol, Oil	200
2.	Eugenol, Oil	10
3.	Formaldehyde	70
4.	Methyl Eugenol	20
5.	Ethyl Alcohol 95%	350
6.	Distilled Water	350
		1000

GARDENIA, BASE

1.	Acetate C-9	1
2.	Alcohol C-9	2
3.	Aldehyde C-8	1
4.	Aldehyde C-10	1
5.	Aldehyde C-12	1
6.	Aldehyde C-14 (pure)	2
7.	Aldehyde C-18	2
8.	Amyl Cinnamic Aldehyde	30
9.	Anisyl Acetate	30
10.	Benzyl Acetate	50
11.	Isoamyl Benzyl Ether	10
12.	Linalyl Benzoate	50
13.	Methyl Anthranilate	45
14.	Methyl Heptyna Carbonate	5
15.	Methyl Phenyl Carbinyl Acetate	50
16.	Phenyl Ethyl Acetate	50
17.	Ethyl Alcohol 95%	670
		1000

GERANIUM

1.	Bois De Rose, Oil	250
2.	Geranium Bourbon, Oil	250
3.	Ethyl Alcohol 95%	250
4.	Distilled Water	250
		1000

GERANIUM, IMITATION (FOR SOAP)

1.	Cedarwood, Oil	150
2.	Citronella, Oil	150
3.	Clove, Oil	25
4.	Diphenyl Oxide	75
5.	Linalyl Acetate	75
6.	Musk Xylene	25
7.	Rosewood, Oil	150
8.	Spike Lavender, Oil	150
9.	Styrax, Resinoid	25
10.	Terpineol	150
11.	Thyme	25
		1000

GERANIUM, SYNTHETIC

1.	Citronellol	250
2.	Diphenyl Oxide	100
3.	Geraniol	300
4.	Phenyl Ethyl Alcohol	175
5.	Rosewood, Oil (Bois de Rose)	175
		1000

GINGERGRASS (FOR SOAP)

1.	Cassia, Oil	75
2.	Cedarwood, Oil	150
3.	Clove, Oil	75
4.	Geranium Palmarose, Oil	225
5.	Gingergrass, Oil	275
6.	Musk Xylene	25
7.	Spike Lavender, Oil	150
8.	Styrax, Resinoid	25
		1000

GIROFLE, IMITATION NO. 1

1.	Amyl Salicylate (10% sol' n.)	250
2.	Isobutyl Salicylate (10% sol' n.)	250
3.	Methyl Salicylate (10% sol' n.)	250
4.	Vanillin (10% sol' n.)	250
		1000

GIROFLE, IMITATION NO. 2

1.	Amyl Salicylate (10% sol' n.)	150
2.	Benzyl Isoeugenol	50
3.	Benzylidene Acetone	50
4.	Clary Sage	50
5.	Isobutyl Salicylate (10% sol' n.)	150
6.	Linalyl Acetate	50
7.	Methyl Salicylate (10% sol' n.)	150
8.	Musk Ambrette	50
9.	Oak Moss, Resin	50
10.	Venillin (10% sol' n.)	100
11.	Ylang Ylang, Oil	150
		1000

HALO, SEA SALT ODOUR

1.	Aldehyde C-20	20
2.	Coumarin	10
3.	Geranyl Acetate	100
4.	Geranyl Formate	10
5.	Lavender, Oil	450
6.	Linalool, Ex Bois de Rose	120
7.	Musk Xylene	10
8.	Sage, Oil	50
9.	Linalyl Acetate	230
		1000

HAWTHORN

1.	Acetophenone	68
2.	Alcohol C-9	20
3.	Aldehyde C-9	4

4. Aldehyde C-10 1
5. Anisaldehyde 200
6. Benzaldehyde (pure) 2
7. Benzal Benzoate 165
8. Citral 5
9. Geraniol 400
10. Methyl Ionone 50
11. Methyl p Tolyl Ketone 80
12. Rose, Oil 5

1000

HAWTHORN (FOR SOAP)

1. Acetophenone 25
2. Anisaldehyde 300
3. Benzaldehyde 1
4. Benzoin, Resinoid 123
5. Methyl Ionone 100
6. Mimosa, Absolute 30
7. Musk Ambratte 25
8. Petitgrain 71
9. Rhodinol 300
10. Rose, Oil 25

1000

HELIOTROPE (FOR SOAP)

1. Aldehyde C-18 5
2. Anisaldehyde 5
3. Anisic Alcohol 45
4. Benzyl Acetate 45
5. Cinnamic Alcohol 50
6. Coumarin 40
7. Heliotropin 175
8. Hydroxycitronellal 5
9. α–Ionone 80
10. Methoxy Acetophenone 5
11. Musk Ketone 30
12. Phenyl Ethyl Alcohol 150
13. Rhodinol 150
14. Vanillin 175

15. Ylang Ylang, Oil 40

1000

HERBAL BASE, " GOLD WATER"

1. Angelic Root, Oil 16
2. Basil, Oil 34
3. Caraway, Oil 34
4. Cherry, Essence (Natural)* 115
5. Cinnamon, Oil 34
6. Clove Flowers, Oil 34
7. Coriander, Oil 34
8. Fennel Seeds, Oil 34
9. Lemon, Oil 16
10. Mandarin, Oil 34
11. Marjoram, Oil 50
12. Orange (Bitter), Oil 50
13. Peppermint, Oil 16
14. Rose, Oil 16
15. Star Anise, Oil 150
16. Sugar 100
17. Ethyl Alcohol 95% 233

1000

HIP, EXTRACT (NATURAL)

1. Hips, Crushed 10 kg
2. Ethyl Alcohol 95% 10 1
3. Distilled Water 10 1

Macerate for 3 days. Express and to the residue add:

4. Distilled Water 20 1

Let stand for another 3 days Add:

5. Amyl Valerianate 5 ml
6. Ethyl Acetate 45 ml

Distill altogether.
Yield: 40 liters

HIP, IMITATION NO. 1

1.	Amyl Acetate	240
2.	Amyl Butyrate	250
3.	Anisaldehyde	5
4.	Butyric Acid	6
5.	Clove, Oil	3
6.	Ethyl Acetate	240
7.	Ethyl Valerianate	250
8.	Heliotropin	5
9.	Rose, Oil	1
		1000

HONEY, SYNTHETIC (FOR PERFUME)

1.	Acetophenone	10
2.	Diisobutyl Pyrocatehol Ketal (10 sol' n.)	750
3.	Methy Ionone	60
4.	Phenyl Acetic Acid (10 sol' n.)	30
5.	Rose Oil (1% sol' n.)	150
		1000

HONEYSUCKLE

1.	Alcohol C-9	5
2.	Aldehyde C-9	10
3.	Aldehyde C12 MNA	20
4.	Amyl Cinnamic Aldehyde	10
5.	Benzyl Acetate	100
6.	Citronellyl Propionate	15
7.	Dimethyl Benzyl Carbinyl Acetate	15
8.	Geraniol	200
9.	Heliotropin	10
10.	Hydroxycitronellal	100
11.	Jasmine (10% solution)	50
12.	Linalool	100
13.	Linaly Acetate	50
14.	Methyl Anthranilate	100
15.	Methyl Heptyne Carbonate	1
16.	Narcissus Absolute	50
17.	Phenyl Ethyl Alcohol	34
18.	Phenyl Ethyl Isobutyrate	15
19.	Rhodinol	100
20.	Rose Oil (10% solution)	10
21.	Vanillin	5
		1000

HYACINTH

1.	Alcohol C-8	10
2.	Aldehyde C-8	5
3.	Aldehyde C-10	5
4.	Benzyl Alcohol	100
5.	Bromostyrol	25
6.	Cinnamic Alcohol	25
7.	Phenyl Acetic Aldehyde	150
8.	Phenyl Ethyl Formate	25
9.	Phenyl Propyl Alcohol	50
10.	Terpineol	25
11.	Ethyl Alcohol 95%	290
12.	Distilled Water	290
		1000

IONONE

1.	Acetone	500
2.	Citral or Lemongrass	250
3.	Sodium Hydroxide	250
		1000

Stir for 72 h. Let stand. Separate the liquids layers. Distill the reddish brown layer.

IRIS

1.	Orris, Concrete	50
2.	Orris, Oil	100
3.	Methylionone (10% sol' n.)	840

4. Santalyl Acetate 10

1000

IRIS, SYNTHETIC

1.	Alcohol C-9	10
2.	Alcohol C-10	10
3.	Aldehyde C-9	10
4.	Aldehyde C-10	5
5.	Aldehyde C-12	5
6.	Anisaldehyde	25
7.	Cuminic Aldehyde	25
8.	α–Irone	60
9.	Methyl Ionone	100
10.	Ethyl Alcohol 95%	375
11.	Distilled Water	375
		1000

JASMINE (FOR BRILLIANTINE)

1.	L-Amylcinnamic Aldehyde (10% solution)	380
2.	Benzyl Acetate (10% solution)	250
3.	Benzyl Propionate	20
4.	Cinnamic Alcohol	100
5.	Cyclamen, Oil	20
6.	Jasmine, Concrete	20
7.	Linalool	50
8.	Musk Ambrette	30
9.	Neroli, Oil	50
10.	Orange Flower, Oil	30
11.	Terpineol	50
		1000

JASMINE "GRANDIFLORA"

1.	Acetate C-8	5
2.	Acetate C-10	5
3.	Alcohol C-7	5
4.	Alcohol C-8	5
5.	Alcohol C-9	5
6.	Aldehyde C-8	5
7.	Aldehyde C-10	5
8.	Aldehyde C-11	5
9.	Amyl Cinnamic Aldehyde	5
10.	Amyl Alcohol	50
11.	Benzyl Acetate	160
12.	Benzyl Alcohol	100
13.	Benzyl Butyrate	160
14.	Benzyl Formate	50
15.	Benzyl losbutyrate	50
16.	Benzyl Propionate	50
17.	Citral	21
18.	Dimethyl Benzyl Carbinol	50
19.	Dimethyl Benzyl Carbinyl Acetate	50
20.	Ethyl Anthranilate	27
21.	Hexyl Cinnamic Aldehyde	5
22.	Hydroxcitronellal	5
23.	Indole	5
24.	Isojasmone	12
25.	Linalool	12
26.	Linalyl Acetate	12
27.	Methyl Anthranilate	15
28.	Methyl Benzoate	12
29.	Methyl p Cresol	12
30.	Phenoxy Ethyl Isobutyrate	12
31.	Phenyl Ethyl Alcohol	25
32.	Phenyl Ethyl Isobutyrate	12
33.	Phenyl Ethyl Phenyl Acetate	12
34.	Phenyl Propyl Acetate	12
35.	Phenyl Propyl Alcohol	12
36.	Phenyl Propyl Aldehyde	12
		1000

JASMINE, IMITATION NO. 1

1.	α–Amylcinnamic Aldehyde	200
2.	Benzyl Acetate	300
3.	Benzyl Alcohol	100
4.	Benzyl Chloroacetate	100
5.	Benzyl Formate	30

6.	Benzyl Propionate	20
7.	Methyl Anthranilate	50
8.	Phenyl Allylic Alcohol	100
9.	Phenyl Ethyl Acetate	100
		1000

JASMINE, IMITATION NO. 2

1.	Jasmine, Absolute (10% solution)	500
2.	Jasmine, Imitation No. 1*	500
		1000

JASMINE, IMITATION NO.3 (FOR SOAP)

1.	Amyl Cinnamic Aldehyde	75
2.	Benzyl Acetate	250
3.	Benzyl Phenyl Acetate	75
4.	Hydroxycitronellal	250
5.	Indole	15
6.	Jasmine, Absolute	50
7.	Methyl Ionone	75
8.	Orris, Concrete	10
9.	Phenyl Ethyl Alcohol	125
10.	Ylang Ylang, Oil	75
		1000

JASMINE, INFUSION

1.	Jasmine, Fresh Flowers	1 kg
2.	Ethyl Alcohol 95%	500 ml
3.	Distilled Water	500 ml
4.	Indole (10% solution)	10 ml

Let stand until the odour is well developed.Express and filter.

Yield: 1 liter.

JASMINE, SYNTHETIC NO. 1

1.	Alcohol C-8	30
2.	Alcohol C-10	25
3.	Aldehyde C-10	40
4.	Benzyl Acetate	25
5.	Benzyl Butyrate	25
6.	Linalool	25
7.	Indole	10
8.	Ionone	5
9.	Methyl Anthranilate	25
10.	Ethyl Alcohol 95%	395
11.	Distilled Water	395
		1000

JASMINE, SYNTHETIC NO. 2

1.	Alcohol C-10	10
2.	Aldehyde C-10	12
3.	Amyl Cinnamic Aldehyde	40
4.	Benzyl Acetate	25
5.	Benzyl Propionate	2
6.	Cinnamic Alcohol	10
7.	Cyclamen Aldehyde	10
8.	Linalool	5
9.	Musk Ambrette	3
10.	Neroli Oil	3
11.	Terpineol	5
12.	Ethyl Alcohol 95%	438
13.	Distilled Water	437
		1000

JASMINE, SYNTHETIC NO. 3

1.	Benzyl Acetate	650
2.	Benzyl Alcohol	60
3.	Indole	30
4.	Linalool	150
5.	Linalyl Acetate	70
6.	Methyl Anthranilate	10

7. Phenyl Ethyl Alcohol 30

1000

JASMINE, SYNTHETIC NO. 4

1.	Benzyl Acetate	300
2.	Benzyl Alcohol	300
3.	Benzyl Formate	150
4.	Benzyl Propionate	150
5.	Geraniol	25
6.	Linalool	35
7.	Menthyl Anthranilate	20
8.	Musk Ketone	10
9.	Paracresol	10
		1000

JASMINE, SYNTHETIC NO. 5

1.	ß-Acetophenone	50
2.	α–Amyl Cinnamic Aldehyde Dimethyl Acetal	200
3.	Benzyl Acetate	300
4.	Benzyl Salicylate	20
5.	Cinnamic Alcohol	30
6.	Hydroxycitronellal	60
7.	Indole (10% solution)	50
8.	Linalool	100
9.	Linalyl Acetate	30
10.	Methyl Amyl Pyrocatechol Ketal	60
11.	Phenyl Ethyl Alcohol	100
		1000

JASMINE, SYNTHETIC NO.6

1.	α–Amyl Cinnamic Aldehyde	100
2.	Benzyl Acetate	150
3.	Benzyl Alcohol	100
4.	Benzyl Formate	20
5.	Benzyl Propionate	20
6.	α–Ionone	20
7.	Methyl Anthranilate	30
8.	Phenyl Ethyl Acetate	30
9.	Phenyl Ethyl Alcohol	30
10.	Rhodinol	10
11.	Ethyl Alcohol 95%	245
12.	Distilled Water	245
		1000

JONQUIL (DAFFODIL), IMITATION

1.	Alcohol C-9	8
2.	Aldehyde C-8	3
3.	Aldehyde C-9	7
4.	Benzyl Salicylate	75
5.	Cinnamic Alcohol	25
6.	Coumarin	25
7.	Hydroxycitronellal	32
8.	Jasmine, Oil	125
9.	Lilac, Imitation	25
10.	Linalool	25
11.	Methyl Ionone	12
12.	Methyl Isoeugenol	8
13.	Musk Ketone	33
14.	Nerol	25
15.	Neroli, Oil	25
16.	Patchouli, Oil	12
17.	Phenyl Acetaldehyde Dimethyl Acetal	15
18.	Phenyl Ethyl Acetate	125
19.	Phenyl Ethyl Alcohol	75
20.	Sandalwood, Oil	30
21.	Ylang Ylang, Oil	35
22.	Styrax, Resinoid	13
23.	Ethyl Alcohol 95%	242
		1000

JONQUIL (DAFFODIL), SYNTHETIC

1.	Benyl Benzoate	150
2.	Cinnamic Acid	150
3.	Indole (10% solution)	100
4.	Linalool	100
5.	Methyl Anthranilate	100
6.	Methyl Benzoate	150
7.	Methyl Cinnamate	150
8.	Phenyl Acetaldehyde Dimethyl Acetal	50
9.	Phenyl Ethyl Phenyl Acetal	50
		1000

LAVENDER, ESSENCE (NATURAL)

1.	Bergamot, Oil	150
2.	Clove, Oil	10
3.	Lavender, Oil	800
4.	Linalyl Acetate	10
5.	Neroli, Oil	10
6.	Patchouli Oil	10
7.	Rose, Oil	10
		1000

LAVENDER, IMITATION NO. 1

1.	Citronellol	190
2.	Geraniol	150
3.	Geranyl Acetate	70
4.	Heptyl Alcohol (Alcohol C-7)	10
5.	Lavendin (40% solution)	500
6.	Linalyl Acetate (75% solution)	80
		1000

LAVENDER, IMITATION NO. 2

1.	Bergamot, Oil	150
2.	Clary Sage, Oil	5
3.	Clove, Oil	7
4.	Geranyl Benzoate	5
5.	Lavender Oil (10% solution)	800
6.	Linalool	5
7.	Linalyl Acetate	5
8.	Linalyl Butyrate	5
9.	Methtyl Amyl Ketone	5
10.	Neroli, Oil	3
11.	Patchouli, Oil	3
12.	Rose, Oil	7
		1000

LAVENDER, IMITATION NO. 3

1.	Cedarwood, Oil (10% solution)	460
2.	Lavender, Oil (10% solution)	500
3.	Musk Ambrette	20
4.	Musk Xylol	10
5.	Oak Moss Resin Extract	10
		1000

LAVENDER, IMITATION NO. 4

1.	Citronellyl Acetate	30
2.	Lavendin (10% solution)	270
3.	Lavender 40/42 (10% solution)	440
4.	Linalyl Acetate (10% solution)	230
5.	Octyl Acetate	30
		1000

LAVENDER, IMITATION NO. 5

1.	Citronellyl Acetate	180
2.	Geraniol	70
3.	Lavandin (10% solution)	750
		1000

LAVENDER, IMITATION NO.6

1.	Aspic (Lavandula spica)	60
2.	Lavandin (10% solution)	250
3.	Marjoram	30
4.	Musk xylene	10
5.	Petitgrain	10
6.	Sage	30
7.	Terpinolene (10% solution)	300
8.	Venillin (10% solution)	10
9.	Ethyl Alcohol 95%	300
		1000

LAVENDER, IMITATION NO. 7

1.	Citronellyl Acetate	60
2.	Lavender 40/42 (10% solution)	520
3.	Linalyl Acetate	130
4.	Spike, Oil	160
5.	Terpinyl Acetate	130
		1000

LAVENDER, IMITATION NO. 8

1.	Geranyl Acetate	200
2.	Heliotropine	70
3.	Isobornyl Acetate	20
4.	Lavender (10% solution)	300
5.	Linalyl Acetate	150
6.	Linalyl Formate	30
7.	Musk Ambrette	40
8.	Terpineol	100
9.	Terpinyl Acetate	80
10.	Vanillin (10% solution)	10

LAVENDER, IMITATION NO. 9

1.	Geranyl Acetate (10% solution)	250
2.	Geranyl Formate	15
3.	Linalyl (10% solution)	220
4.	Linalyl Acetate (10% solution)	500
5.	Nonyl Acetate	5
6.	Vanillin (10% solution)	10
		1000

LAVENDER, IMITATION NO. 10

1.	Lavender, Imitation No. 8	475
2.	Lavender, Imitation No. 9	375
3.	Musk Xylol (10% solution)	150
		1000

LAVENDER, IMITATION NO . 11

1.	Alcohol C-9	25
2.	Aldehyde C-10	25
3.	Clary Sage, Oil	200
4.	Coumarin	50
5.	Geranyl Acetate	100
6.	Geranyl Benzoate	100
7.	Linalool	100
8.	Linalyl Acetate	100
9.	Linalyl Butyrate	100
10.	Terpinyl Acetate	100
11.	Terpinyl Propionate	100
		1000

LAVENDER, IMITATION NO. 12 (FOR SOAP)

1.	Benzyl Acetate	40
2.	Bergamot, Oil	125
3.	Borneol	30
4.	Coumarin	30
5.	Geranium, Oil	200
6.	Lavender, Oil	200
7.	Patchouli, Oil	40
8.	Musk Xylene	25
9.	Rosemary, Oil	60
10.	Spike, Oil	200
11.	Thyme Oil	50
		1000

LAVENDER, SWEET

1.	Bergamot Oil	110
2.	Citral	10
3.	Coumarin	10
4.	Geranyl Acetate	20
5.	α–Ionone	20
6.	Isobornyl Acetate	50
7.	Lavender Oil	110
8.	Linalyl Acetate	50
9.	Musk Ketone	10
10.	Pine White Oil	10
11.	Terpinyl Acetate	10
12.	Ethyl Alcohol 95%	295
13.	Distilled Water	295
		1000

LEATHER

1.	Amyl Salicylate	50
2.	Balsam Peru	100
3.	Birch Tar Rectified	100
4.	Coumarin	30
5.	Methyl Salicylate	50
6.	Ethyl Alcohol 95%	335
7.	Distilled Water	335
		1000

LILAC, IMITATION NO. 1

1.	Anisic Aldehyde	10
2.	Benzyl Acetate	30
3.	Benzyl Alcohol	40
4.	Benzyl Formate	10
5.	Benzyl Salicylate	10
6.	Cananga, Oil	40
7.	Cinnamic Alcohol	100
8.	p-Cresyl Acetate	10
9.	Cuminic Aldehyde	10
10.	Decyl Alcohol	10
11.	Farnesol	10
12.	Heliotropin	60
13.	Hydroxycitronellal	150
14.	Isoeugenol	10
15.	Methyl Anthranilate	10
16.	Linalool	40
17.	Phenylacetaldehyde	10
18.	Phenyl Ethyl Acetate	50
19.	Phenyl Ethyl Alcohol	150
20.	Phenylpropyl Acetate	40
21.	Rose Oil	10
22.	Terpineol	150
23.	p-Tolyl Aldehyde	10
24.	Tuberose Oil	20
25.	Vanillin (10% solution)	10
		1000

LILAC, IMITATION NO. 2

1.	Anisic Aldehyde	140
2.	Benzyl Alcohol	110
3.	Citronellol	150
4.	α–Ionone	10
5.	Musk Ketone	10
6.	Phenylacetaldehyde	10

7. Phenyl Ethyl Alcohol (10% solution) 200
8. Terpineol 350
9. Tuberose, Oil 10
10. Vanillin (10% solution) 10

1000

LILAC, IMITATION NO. 3

1. Anisic Alcohol 40
2. Benzaldehyde (pure, 10% solution) 10
3. Cananga, Oil 20
4. Cinnamic Alcohol 150
5. Heliotropin 50
6. Hydroxycitronellal (10% solution) 230
7. Neroli 100
8. Phenyl Ethyl Alcohol (10% solution) 250
9. Terpineol 150

1000

LILAC, IMITATION NO. 4

1. Benzyl Benzoate (10% solution) 275
2. Benzyl Formate (10% solution) 275
3. Cananga, Oil 30
4. Cinnamic Alcohol 30
5. Hydroxycitronellal 100
6. Linalool 120
7. Phenyl Ethyl Alcohol 100
8. Terpineol 70

1000

LILAC, IMITATION No. 5

1. Benzoin 100
2. Cananga, Oil 80
3. Hydroxycitronellal 150
4. Musk Ketone 20
5. Terpineol (10% solution) 600
6. Vanillin (10% solution) 50

1000

LILAC, IMITATION NO. 6

1. Benzyl Benzoate 150
2. Lilac, Imitation No. 1 140
3. Lilac, Imitation No. 2 140
4. Lilac, Imitation No. 3 140
5. Lilac, Imitation No. 4 140
6. Lilac, Imitation No. 5 140
7. Terpineol 150

1000

LILAC, IMITATION NO. 7

1. Dimethyl Benzyl Carbinol 50
2. Heliotropin 10
3. Hydroxycitronellal 100
4. Phenyl Ethyl Alcohol 350
5. Terpineol 200
6. Vanillin 5
7. Ylang Ylang Oil 285

1000

LILAC, IMITATION NO . 8

1. Benzoin 50
2. Heliotropin 10
3. Jasmine, Absolute 55
4. Musk Ketone 30
5. Phenyl Ethyl Alcohol 350
6. Rosewood, Oil 300
7. Terpineol 200
8. Vanillin 5

1000

LILAC, IMITATION NO.9 (FOR SOAP)

1.	Amyl Cinnamic Aldehyde	30
2.	Anisic Aldehyde	75
3.	Benzyl Acetate	40
4.	Cyclamen Aldehyde	30
5.	Hydroxycitronellal	75
6.	Methyl Anthranilate	75
7.	Musk Xylene	40
8.	Petitgrain, Oil	40
9.	Terpineol	275
10.	Phenyl Ethyl Alcohol	275
11.	Tolu Balsam	45
		1000

LILAC, SYNTHETIC NO. 1 (FOR SOAP)

1.	Heliotropin	100
2.	Hydroxycitronellal	150
3.	Methyl Anthranilate	50
4.	Musk Ketone	50
5.	Phenyl Ethyl Acohol	350
6.	Terpineol	300
		1000

LILAC, SYNTHETIC NO. 2 (FOR SOAP)

1.	Alcohol C-9	5
2.	Aldehyde C-9	5
3.	Aldehyde C-10	5
4.	Aldehyde C-12, MNA	10
5.	Aldehyde C-14 (pure)	15
6.	Anisic Alcohol	50
7.	Cinnamic Alcohol	70
8.	Heliotropin	150
9.	Indole	10
10.	Hydroxycitronellal	200
11.	Isoeugenol	30
12.	Phenyl Ethyl Alcohol	250
13.	Terpineol	200
		1000

LILY, BASE

1.	Hydroxycitronellal	400
2.	Linalool	300
3.	Terpineol	300
		1000

MAGNOLIA

1.	Cinnamic Alcohol	75
2.	Hydroxycitronellal	225
3.	Isoeugenol	5
4.	Jasmine, Oil	150
5.	Lemon Oil	75
6.	Musk Ketone	30
7.	Nerol	225
8.	Vanilla, Oil	15
9.	Ylang Ylang, Oil	200
		1000

MIGNONETTE (RESEDA)

1.	Alcohol C-9	10
2.	Aldehyde C-12 (lauric)	10
3.	Cassia Absolute	20
4.	Clary Sage, Oil	20
5.	Jasmine Absolute	20
4.	Methyl Inonoe	10
7.	Tolu Balsam	10
8.	Ethyl Alcohol 95%	450
9.	Distilled Water	450
		1000

MIMOSA, IMITATION

1.	Hydroxycitronellal	150

2.	Jasmine Concrete	60
3.	Methyl Acetophenone	30
4.	Methyl Heptyne Carbonate	10
5.	Peru Balsam	50
6.	Styrax Resinoid	50
7.	Terpineol	150
8.	Ethyl Alcohol 95%	250
9.	Distilled Water	250
		1000

MIMOSA, SYNTHETIC

1.	Alcohol C-10	20
2.	Alcohol C-12	10
3.	Aldehyde C-10	50
4.	Aldehyde C-11	20
5.	Hydroxycitronellal	150
6.	Methyl Acetophenone	150
7.	Terpineol	100
8.	Ethyl Alcohol 95%	250
9.	Distilled Water	250
		1000

MOSS

1.	Ambergris Tincture	50
2.	Benzyl Acetate	100
3.	Cinnamic Alcohol	100
4.	Coumarin	25
5.	Heliotropin	100
6.	Ionone	50
7.	Linalool	100
8.	Linalyl Acetate	100
9.	Musk Ambrette	25
10.	Patchouli, Oil	100
11.	Peru Balsam	25
12.	Vetiverol	25
13.	Ethyl Alcohol 95%	100
14.	Distilled Water	100
		1000

MUGUET (LILY OF THE VALLEY), IMITATION NO. 1

1.	Civet	10
2.	Jasmine, Oil	75
3.	Lime, Oil	25
4.	Linalool	150
5.	Musk Ambertte	15
6.	Rose, Oil	10
7.	Terpineol	150
8.	Ylang Ylang, Oil	25
9.	Ethyl Alcohol 95%	270
10.	Distilled Water	270
		1000

MUGUET (LILY OF THE VALLEY), IMITATION NO. 2

1.	Aldehyde C-11 (undecylenic)	5
2.	Aldehyde C-12 (lauric)	5
3.	Aldehyde C-14 (myristic)	5
4.	Almond (Bitter) Oil (pure)	10
5.	Cassie, Oil	20
6.	Jasmine, Oil	40
7.	Orange Flowers, Oil	45
8.	Rose, Oil	10
9.	Tuberose Oil	45
10.	Vanillia Beans Oil	15
11.	Ethyl Alcohol 95%	400
12.	Distilled Water	400
		1000

MUGUET (LILY OF THE VALLEY), IMITATION NO. 3 (FOR SOAP)

1.	Benzyl Acetate	50
2.	Civet Absolute	5
3.	Geranium Palmarosa, Oil	325
4.	Hydroxycitronellal	325
5.	Jasmine Absolute	20

6. Linalool 75
7. Terpineol 75
8. Ylang Ylang, Oil 125

1000

MUGUET (LILY OF THE VALLEY), SYNTHETIC NO. 1

1. Benzyl Acetate 200
2. Cinnamic Alcohol 200
3. Hydroxycitronellal (10% solution) 300
4. Musk Ambrette 50
5. Phenyl Ethyl Alcohol 100
6. Terpineol 100
7. Ylang Ylang, Oil 50

1000

MUGUET (LILY OF THE VALLEY), SYNTHETIC NO. 2

1. Alcohol C-9 6
2. Alcohol C-10 1
3. Alcohol C-11 (undecylenic) 5
4. Aldehyde C-9 4
5. Aldehyde C-10 3
6. Aldehyde C-12 4
7. Aldehyde C-16 2
8. Cinnamic Acetate 150
9. Ethyl Phenyl Acetate 150
10. Hydroxycitronellal 150
11. Ionone 25
12. Linalool 150
13. Ethyl Alcohol 95% 175
14. Distilled Water 175

1000

MUSK

1. Ambergris 50
2. Bergamot, Oil 250
3. Benzyl Salicylate (10% solution) 50
4. Heliotropine 150
5. Linalool 150
6. Orris, Oil 50
7. Vanillin (10% solution) 150
8. Vetiverol 150

1000

MUSK, IMITATION NO. 1 (FOR POWDER)

1. Amyl Benzoate 250
2. Cassia, Oil 55
3. Clary Sage, Oil 5
4. Ionone 50
5. Musk Ambrette 300
6. Rhodinol 300
7. Sandalwood, Oil 25
8. Vetiver, Oil 15

1000

MUSK, IMITATION NO. 2 (FOR SOAP)

1. Benzyl Acetate 50
2. Cassia, Oil 50
3. Castor Tincture 150
4. Cedarwood, Oil 100
5. Civet 5
6. Clove, Oil 75
7. Geranium Palmarosa, Oil 300
8. Musk Xylene 100
9. Lemon, Oil 75
10. Musk Ambrette 55
11. Sandalwood, Oil 25
12. Vetiver, Oil 15

1000

NARCISSUS, IMITATION NO. 1 (FOR POWDER)

1.	Hydroxycitronellal	150
2.	Jasmine, Oil	70
3.	Linalool	50
4.	Methyl Anthranilate	150
5.	Methyl Ionone	25
6.	Musk Ketone	5
7.	Neroli, Oil	10
8.	Phenyl Ethyl Acetate	2
9.	Styrax Resinoid	150
10.	Ylang Ylang, Oil	25
11.	Ethyl Alcohol 95%	363
		1000

NARCISSUS, IMITATION NO. 2 (FOR COLOGNE)

1.	Aldehyde C-10	4
2.	Aldehyde C-11	6
3.	Civet Tincture	10
4.	Coumarin	3
5.	Jasmine, Oil	20
6.	Methyl Naphthyl Ketone	3
7.	Musk Ketone	5
8.	Orange (Sweet), Oil	10
9.	Orange Flowers, Oil	50
10.	Rose Otto, Oil	4
11.	Sandalwood, Oil	2
12.	Vanillin	3
13.	Ethyl Alcohol 95%	440
14.	Distilled Water	440
		1000

NARCISSUS, IMITATION NO.3 (FOR COLOGNE)

1.	Aldehyde C-16	9
2.	Amyl Salicylate	10
3.	Geraniol	40
4.	Geranyl Formate	1
5.	Hydroxycitronellal	40
6.	Linalool	15
7.	Musk Ketone	15
8.	Neroli, Oil	86
9.	Phenyl Ethyl Alcohol	70
10.	Rhodinol	100
11.	Styrax Resinoid	5
12.	Ylang Ylang, Oil	75
13.	Ethyl Alcohol 95%	260
14.	Distilled Water	260
		1000

NARCISSUS, IMITATION NO.4 "POETICUS" (FOR COLOGNE)

1.	Alcohol C-9	10
2.	Aldehyde C-8	10
3.	Aldehyde C-10	10
4.	Ambergris	10
5.	Benzoin	10
6.	Chamomile, Oil	10
7.	Cinnamic Alcohol	50
8.	Clary Sage	10
9.	Honey Synthetic No. 1*	110
10.	Hydratropic Aldehyde	50
11.	Jasmine, Oil	50
12.	Orange Flower Imitation No.1*	50
13.	Phenyl Acetaldehyde Dimethyl Acetal	50
14.	Phenyl Acetaldehyde	50
15.	Phenyl Ethyl Acetate	50
16.	Phenyl Ethyl Alcohol	30
17.	Rose, Oil	50
18.	Terpineol	250
19.	Vanillin	10
20.	Ethyl Alcohol 95%	110
21.	Tolu Balsam	20
		1000

NARCISSUS, IMITATION NO. 5 (FOR SOAP)

1.	Anisaldehyde	110
2.	Isoeugenol	110
3.	Linalool	250
4.	Methyl-p-Cresol	15
5.	Petigrain, Oil	115
6.	Phenyl Acetaldehyde	100
7.	Rose, Absolute	25
8.	Terpineol	250
9.	Tuberose Absolute	25
		1000

NARCISSUS, SYNTHETIC NO. 1

1.	Alcohol C-9	20
2.	Aldehyde C-9	15
3.	Benzyl Benzoate	150
4.	Benzyl Cinnamate	50
5.	Cinnamic Alcohol	60
6.	Phenyl Acetaldehyde	25
7.	Phenyl Ethyl Alcohol	30
8.	Terpineol	150
9.	Ethyl Alcohol 95%	250
10.	Distilled Water	250
		1000

NARCISSUS, SYNTHETIC NO. 2

1.	Benzaldehyde (pure)	25
2.	Benzoic Acid	50
3.	Benzyl Alcohol	300
4.	Cinnamic Alcohol	200
5.	Eugenol	50
6.	Ethyl Alcohol 95%	375
		1000

NARCISSUS, SYNTHETIC NO. 3

1.	Aldehyde C-14 (10% solution)	50
2.	Benzyl Acetate	200
3.	Indole (10% solution)	50
4.	Linalool	200
5.	Phenyl Propyl Acetate	250
6.	Phenyl Propyl Alcohol	250
		1000

NARCISSUS SYNTHETIC NO. 4

1.	Alcohol C-10	1
2.	Benzyl Acetate	12
3.	Benzyl Alcohol	12
4.	§-3- Carene	2
5.	Cinnamyl Alcohol	6
6.	Cineol	30
7.	p-Cymol	15
8.	Geraniol	2
9.	Indole (10% solution)	16
10.	Limonene	15
11.	Linalool	16
12.	Methyl Anthranilate	17
13.	Methyl Benzoate	3
14.	Methyl Cinnamate	9
15.	Methyl Phenyl Acetate	2
16.	Nerol	1
17.	α–Pinene	8
18.	ß-Pinene	2
19.	Sabinene	20
20.	ß-Sitosterol	1
21.	α–Terpineol	95
22.	Terpinolene	13
23.	Ethyl Alcohol 95%	702
		1000

NEROLI, IMITATION NO. 1

1.	Bergamot, Oil	80
2.	Citronellol	80
3.	Geraniol	80
4.	Geranyl Acetate	80
5.	Hydroxycitronellal	40
6.	α–Ionone	100
7.	Lemon, Oil (terpeneless)	10
8.	Linalool	200
9.	Linalyl Acetate	80
10.	Methyl Anthranilate	60
11.	Methyl Naphthyl Ketone	60
12.	Nerol	30
13.	Orange, Oil (terpeneless)	10
14.	Petitgrain, Oil (terpeneless)	80
15.	Vanillin (10% solution)	10
		1000

NEROLI, IMITATION NO. 2

1.	Acetate C-8	30
2.	Alcohol C-9	30
3.	Alcohol C-12	30
4.	Aldehyde C-9	15
5.	Aldehyde C-12	15
6.	Bergamot, Oil	10
7.	Citronellol	10
8.	Geraniol	10
9.	Hydroxycitronellal	4
10.	Ionone	1
11.	Lemon, Oil	1
12.	Linalool	20
13.	Linalyl Acetate	10
14.	Methyl Anthranilate	6
15.	Methyl Naphthyl Ketone	6
16.	Nerol	15
17.	Petitgrain, Oil	10
18.	Orange, Oil	1
19.	Vanillin	1
20.	Ethyl Alcohol 95%	388
21.	Distilled Water	387
		1000

NEROLI IMITATION NO. 3 (FOR SOAP)

1.	Alcohol C-12 (lauric)	30
2.	Amyl Cinnamic Aldehyde	25
3.	Indole (10% solution)	10
4.	Linalool	225
5.	Linalyl Acetate	60
6.	Methyl Anthranilate	30
7.	Nerol	120
8.	Nonyl Acetate	100
9.	Petitgrain, Oil	325
10.	Phenyl Acetic Acid	25
11.	Terpineol	50
		1000

NEROLIN

(ß-naphthyl mehtyl ether or ß-naphthyl ethyl ether)

(a) Yara Yara

1.	Methyl Alcohol	60
2.	ß-Naphthol	36
3.	Zine Chloride	4

(b) Bromelia

1.	Ethyl Alcohol	60
2.	ß-Naphthol	36
3.	Sulfuric Acid	4

Heat in autoclave at 150^0 C.
Uses: (a) Perfumes, soaps

NEUTROLEUM, DEODORIZING PERFUME

1.	Ambergris	10
2.	Benzylidene Acetone	100
3.	Butyric Acid	10
4.	Caryophylene	

5. Cedar Leaf, Oil 50
6. Cinnamic Aldehyde 10
7. Cinnamon Leaf, Oil 50
8. Clove Leaf, Oil 50
9. Clove Terpenes, Oil 50
10. Isovaleric Acid 10
11. Mercaptan 10
12. Orange, Oil 50
13. Pimento Leaf, Oil 50
14. Propylene Glycol 100
15. Rosemary, Oil 200
16. Sage, Oil 200

1000

NEWMOWN HAY (FOIN COUPE), IMITATION NO. 1

1. Acetophenone 55
2. Benzophenone 15
3. Benzyl Acetate 55
4. Bergamot, Oil 55
5. Clary Sage, Oil 55
6. Coumarin 100
7. Geranium, Oil 100
8. Lavender, Oil 225
9. Linalool 225
10. Musk Xylene 40
11. Oakmoss Resinoid 15
12. Patchouli, Oil 40
13. Sandalwood, Oil 20

1000

NEW MOWN HAY (FOIN COUPE), IMITATION NO. 2

1. Anisic Aldehyde 23
2. Anisyl Alcohol 22
3. Benzyl Benzoate 100
4. Bergamot, Oil 150
5. Cananga, Oil 25
6. Cassia Absolute 25
7. Citral 5
8. Coumarin 20
9. Geranium, Oil 30
10. Hydroxycitronellal 100
11. α–Ionone 5
12. Isobutyl Salicylate 5
13. Jasmine, Oil 25
14. Lavender, Oil 150
15. Lemon, Oil 20
16. Linalool 150
17. Methyl Acetophenone 15
18. Orange, Oil 25
19. Orange Flower, Oil 25
20. Rhodinol 30
21. Rose, Oil 25
22. Vanillin 15
23. Vetiver, Oil 10

1000

OPOPONAX, IMITATION NO. 1

1. Bergamot (terpeneless) 300
2. Heliotropin 70
3. Ionone 50
4. Linalyl Acetate 50
5. Musk Ambrette 60
6. Opoponax Resinoid 150
7. Peru, Resinoid 80
8. Santalol 80
9. Vanilla Resinoid 100
10. Vetiverol 60

1000

OPOPONAX, IMITATION NO. 2

1. Bergamot, Oil 360
2. Castoreum, Oil 50
3. Musk Ambrette 150
4. Neroli, Oil 40
5. Patchouli, Oil 100

6.	Santalol	100
7.	Vetiverol	100
8.	Vanillin (10% solution)	100
		1000

OPOPONAX, IMITATION NO. 3

1.	Bergamot, Oil	300
2.	Citral	5
3.	Geraniol	150
4.	Jasmine, Oil	35
5.	Musk Ambrette	75
6.	Opoponax Resinoid	50
7.	Rhodinol	150
8.	Rose, Oil	15
9.	Vanillin	5
10.	Violet, Oil	15
11.	Ethyl Alcohol 95%	100
12.	Distilled Water	100
		1000

OPOPONAX, IMITATION NO. 4 (FOR SOAP)

1.	Amber, Resinoid	50
2.	Benzoin, Resinoid	50
3.	Benzoyl Acetone	60
4.	Bergamot, Oil	200
5.	Labdanum Resinoid	55
6.	Musk Ambrette	85
7.	Opoponax Resinoid	60
8.	Rhodinyl Acetate	55
9.	Sandalwood, Oil	150
10.	Sweet Orange, Oil	150
11.	Vanillin	85
		1000

ORANGE BLOSSOM, BOUQUET (FOR SOAP)

1.	Benzyl Acetate	100
2.	Bois De Rose, Oil	175
3.	Bromostyrol	25
4.	Clove, Oil	40
5.	Geranium Palmarosa, Oil	150
6.	Hydroxycinnamic Aldehyde	25
7.	Linalyl Acetate	75
8.	Mehtyl Anthranilate	50
9.	Methyl Naphthyl Ketone	50
10.	Musk Ambrette	40
11.	Petitgrain, Oil	150
12.	Phenyl Ethyl Alcohol	50
13.	Terpineol	70
		1000

ORANGE FLOWER, IMITATION NO. 1

1.	Aldehyde C-12 (lauric)	30
2.	Cinnamic Alcohol	30
3.	Geraniol	15
4.	Indole (10% solution)	20
5.	Isoeugenol	10
6.	Jasmine, Oil	50
7.	Linalool	100
8.	Linalyl Acetate	30
9.	Methyl Anthranilate	40
10.	Methyl Benzoate	10
11.	Methyl Cinnamate	5
12.	Methyl Naphthyl Ketone	20
13.	Musk Ketone	50
14.	Nerol	50
15.	Orange Sweet, Oil	40
16.	Petitgrain, Oil	280
17.	Phenyl Acetaldehyde Dimethyl Acetal	10
18.	Phenyl Ethyl Alcohol	200
19.	Sandalwood, Oil	10
		1000

ORANGE FLOWER, IMITATION NO. 2

1.	Acetophenone	5
2.	Bergamot, Oil	10
3.	Geraniol	20
4.	Hydroycitronellal	50
5.	Linalool	160
6.	Linalyl Acetate	160
7.	Methyl Anthranilate	50
8.	Methyl Ionone	5
9.	Nutmeg	8
10.	Orange, Sweet, Oil	10
11.	Petitgrain	160
12.	Phenyl Acetaldehyde Dimethyl Acetal	2
13.	Phenyl Ethyl Alcohol	350
14.	Sandalwood, Oil	5
15.	Terpineol	5
		1000

ORANGE FLOWER, IMITATION NO. 3

1.	Aldehyde C-8	6
2.	Aldehyde C-10	8
3.	Benzyl Acetate	70
4.	Geranyl Formate	6
5.	Hydroxycitronellal	40
6.	Linalool	200
7.	Methyl Anthranilate	130
8.	Nerol	120
9.	Orange Flowers, Absolute	20
10.	Petitgrain	180
11.	Phenyl Ethyl Alcohol	220
		1000

ORANGE FLOWER, SYNTHETIC NO. 4

1.	Alcohol C-8	20
2.	Alcohol C-9	20
3.	Alcohol C-10	20
4.	Alcohol C-12	18
5.	Aldehyde C-8	18
6.	Aldehyde C-10	20
7.	Aldehyde C-12 (lauric)	20
8.	Aldehyde C-16	10
9.	Cimene	6
10.	Citronellol	20
11.	Citronellyl Acetate	10
12.	Eugenol	3
13.	Farnesol	1
14.	Geraniol	40
15.	Geraniol Acetate	16
16.	Jasmone	1
17.	Limonene	14
18.	Linalool	150
19.	Linalyl Acetate	50
20.	Methyl Anthranilate	150
21.	Nerol	40
22.	Nerolidol	40
23.	Neryl Acetate	40
24.	Phenyl Acetate Acid	1
25.	Phenyl Ethyl Alcohol	250
26.	α–Pinene	1
27.	ß-Pinene	1
28.	α–Terpineol	20
		1000

ORCHID, IMITATION

1.	Aldehyde C-9	10
2.	Aldehyde C-11 (undecylenic)	10
3.	Aldehyde C-12 MNA	10
4.	Amyl Benzoate	53
5.	Amyl Salicylate (10% solution)	250
6.	Anisic Aldehyde	54
7.	Ethyl Benzoate	53
8.	Geranium, Oil	50
9.	Isoeugenol	20
10.	Jasmine Absolute	10

1.	Lavender, Oil	10
2.	Linalool	200
3.	Nerolin	20
4.	Terpineol	200
5.	Ylang Ylang, Oil	50
		1000

ORRIS ROOT, EXTRACT (NATURAL)

1.	Orris Root, Florentine	10 kg
2.	Ethyl Alcohol 95%	10 l

Let stand for 3 days. Express and to the residue add:

3.	Ethyl Alcohol 95%	20 l
4.	Distilled Water	20 l

Let stand for one week, stirring for l h every day. Add:

5.	Distilled Water	20 l
6.	Amyl Acetate	25 ml
7.	Ethyl Acetate	120 ml
8.	Ethyl Oenanthate	45 ml

Distill altogether.
Yield 60 liters

ORRIS ROOT, FLORENTINE

1.	Citral	25
2.	Cedrol	50
3.	Heliotropin	15
4.	α–Ionone	100
5.	Methylionone (10% solution)	250
6.	Myristic Acid	200
7.	Methyl Myristate	25
8.	Orris, Concrete	25
9.	Orris, Resinoid	100
10.	Terpineol	75
11.	Stearic Acid	100
12.	Vetiverol	25
13.	Vanillin (10% solution)	10
		1000

ORRIS ROOT, SYNTHETIC

1.	Benzyl Alcohol	50
2.	Cineol	10
3.	Ethyl Acetate	250
4.	Ethyl Oenanthate	190
5.	Ethyl Pelargonate	62
6.	Ionone	10
7.	Isoamyl Acetate	420
8.	Linalool	8
		1000

PATCHOULI, IMITATION NO. 1 (FOR SOAP)

1.	Benzyl Acetate	75
2.	Civet Tincture	75
3.	Clove, Oil	50
4.	Coumarin	75
5.	Geranium, Oil	300
6.	Musk Ambrette	75
7.	Patchouli, Oil	150
8.	Sandalwood, Oil	100
9.	Vetiver, Oil	100
		1000

PATCHOULI, IMITATION NO. 2 (FOR TOILET POWDER)

1.	Aldehyde C-14 (pure)	10
2.	Amber, Tincture	20
3.	Anisaldehyde	50
4.	Benzoin, Resinoid	225
5.	Coumarin	20

6.	Ethyl Cinnamate	55
7.	Heliotropin	75
8.	Jasmine, Oil	75
9.	Linalyl Acetate	135
10.	Orris Root, Extract (Natural)*	225
11.	Patchouli, Oil	55
12.	Rose, Oil	55
		1000

PINE, IMITATION NO. 1

1.	α–Phellandrene	200
2.	Pine, Oil	200
3.	Terpineol	200
4.	Terpinolene	200
5.	Ethyl Alcohol 95%	200
		1000

PINE, IMITATION NO.2

1.	Pine, Oil	200
2.	Sassafras, Oil	40
3.	Terpineol	600
4.	Turpentine	160
		1000

PINE NEEDLE

1.	Pine Needles, Oil	300
2.	Ethyl Alcohol 95%	700
		1000

PINE NEEDLE, SIBERRIAN, IMITATION NO. 1

1.	Citral	50
2.	α–Ionone, White	10
3.	Isobornyl Acetate	800
4.	Limonene	100
5.	α–Pinene	10
6.	Rosemary, Oil	20
7.	Spruce, Oil	10
		1000

PINE NEEDLE, SIBERIAN, IMITATION NO. 2

1.	Aldehyde C-12	10
2.	Bois De Rose	10
3.	Diethylene Glycol Monoethyl Ether	80
4.	Geraniol	10
5.	Isobornyl Acetate	80
6.	Musk Ambrette	20
7.	Pine Needles, Siberian, Oil	100
8.	Spruce, Oil	160
9.	Tolu Balsam, Oil (10% solution)	20
10.	Vanillin (10% solution)	10
11.	Ethyl Alcohol 95%	500
		1000

PINE NEEDLE, SIBERIAN, IMITATION NO. 3

1.	Citral (10% solution)	250
2.	L-Ionone	50
3.	Isobornyl Acetate	200
4.	Limonene	100
5.	Pinene	100
6.	Rosemary, Oil	200
7.	Spruce, Oil	100
		1000

ROSE, BULGARIAN TYPE

1.	Alcohol C-8	5
2.	Alcohol C-10	5

3. Citronellol 23
4. Citronellyl Acetate 5
5. Citronellyl Formate 5
6. Decyl Aldehyde 5
7. Geraniol 25
8. Geranium Bourbon 2
9. Hydroxycitronellal 1
10. α–Ionone 5
11. Lemon, Oil (terpeneless) 5
12. Musk Ambrette 5
13. Nerol 1
14. Nonyl Aldehyde 5
15. Patchouli, Oil 5
16. Phenyl Ethyl Alcohol 13
17. Phenyl Ethyl Butyrate 1
18. Rhodinol 8
19. Rhodinyl Butyrate 1
20. Ylang Ylang, Oil 1
21. Ethyl Alcohol 95% 437
22. Distilled Water 437

1000

ROSE, FOR CREAM

1. Citronellal 180
2. Geraniol (10% solution) 500
3. Geranyl Acetate 20
4. Linalool 60
5. Phenyl Ethyl Alcohol (10%solution) 170
6. Rose, Oil (10% solution) 70

1000

ROSE, FOR FACE POWDER NO. 1

1. Ambrettolide 50
2. Benzyl Isoeugenol 20
3. Citronellol 100
4. Ethyl Cinnamate 5
5. Eugenol 10
6. Geraniol (10% solution) 330
7. Geranyl Acetate 30
8. Linalool 80
9. Linaly! Acetate 20
10. α–Ionone 43
11. Jasmine, Oil 40
12. Methyl Ionone 30
13. Methyl Nonyl Acetaldehyde 50
14. Musk Ketone 5
15. Pacthouli, Oil 20
16. Phenyl Ethyl Alcohol (10% solution) 120
17. Sandalwood, Oil 30
18. Vanillin (10% solution) 7
19. Vetivert, Oil 10

1000

ROSE, FOR FACE POWDER NO. 2

1. Anisic Aldehyde 50
2. Civet 2
3. Ionone 18
4. Jasmine, Oil (10% solution) 540
5. Isoeugenol 60
6. Neroli, Oil 50
7. Orris, Oil 10
8. Phenyl Acetaldehyde 10
9. Rose Otto, Oil (10% solution) 60
10. Sandalwood, Oil 60
11. Ylang Ylang, Oil 140

1000

ROSE, IMITATION NO .2

1. Aldehyde C-8 10
2. Citral 10
3. Citronellol 100
4. Geraniol 800
5. Linalool 20

6.	Phenyl Ethyl Alcohol	10
7.	Rose, Oil	50
		1000

ROSE, IMITATION NO. 3

1.	Alcohol C-8	5
2.	Alcohol C-10	5
3.	Aldehyde C-9	5
4.	Aldehyde C-10	5
5.	Citronellol	50
6.	Citronellyl Acetate	5
7.	Citronellyl Formate	5
8.	Geraniol	50
9.	Hydroxycitronellal	20
10.	Ionone	5
11.	Lemon, Oil	5
12.	Nerol	10
13.	Patchouli, Oil	5
14.	Phenyl Ethyl Alcohol	25
15.	Phenyl Ethyl Butyrate	10
16.	Rhodinol	15
17.	Rhodinol Butyrate	10
18.	Rosacetol	5
19.	Ylang Ylang, Oil	10
20.	Ethyl Alcohol 95%	750
		1000

ROSE, IMITATION NO. 4

1.	Aldehyde C-9	20
2.	Citronellol	250
3.	Geraniol	250
4.	Guaiacwood, Oil	5
5.	Methyl Ionone	40
6.	Nerol	50
7.	Phenyl Acetaldehyde (10% solution)	20
8.	Phenyl Acetic Acid (10% solution)	40
9.	Phenyl Ethyl Alcohol	325
		1000

ROSE, IMITATION NO. 5 (FOR COSMETIC CREAM)

1.	Dimethyl Octanol	75
2.	Geranium Palmarosa, Oil	275
3.	Geranyl Acetate	150
4.	Guaiacwood, Oil	75
5.	α–Ionone	30
6.	Musk Xylene	35
7.	Patchouli, Oil	35
8.	Phenyl Ethyl Alcohol	275
9.	Rose, Oil	50
		1000

ROSE, IMITATION NO. 6 (FOR SOAP)

1.	Bois De Rose	250
2.	Civet Absolute (10% solution)	25
3.	Geraniol	150
4.	Geranium Palmarosa, Oil	150
5.	Musk Xylene	25
6.	Patchouli, Oil	25
7.	Phenyl Ethyl Alcohol	350
8.	Styrax, Resinoid	25
		1000

ROSE, IMITATION NO.7

1.	Cinnamic Alcohol	200
2.	Ionone	225
3.	Jasmine, Oil	75
4.	Phenyl Ethyl Alcohol	175
5.	Rhodinol	175
6.	Rhodinyl Acetate	150
		1000

ROSE, IMITATION NO. 8

.	Aldehyde C-11	25
.	Cinnamic Alcohol	20
.	Citronellol	150
.	Eugenol	3
.	Geranium Palmarosa, Oil	300
.	Guaiacwood, Oil	75
.	L-Ionone	100
.	Phenyl Acetic Acid	25
.	Phenyl Acetic Aldehyde	2
0.	Phenyl Ethyl Alcohol	150
1.	Rhodinol	150
13.	Phenyl Ethyl Alcohol (10% solution)	250
14.	Phenyl Ethyl Butyrate	14
15.	Rhodinol	150
16.	Ylang Ylang, Oil	10
17.	Ethyl Alcohol 95%	404
		1000

ROSE, IMITATION NO.9 (FOR PERFUME)

1.	Geranium Palmarosa, Oil	50
2.	Jasmine, Oil	200
3.	Rose, Oil	300
4.	Ylang Ylang, Oil	50
5.	Ethyl Alcohol 95%	200
6.	Distilled Water	200
		1000

ROSE, IMITATION NO. 10

1.	Alcohol C-8	5
2.	Alcohol C-10	5
3.	Citronellol	50
4.	Citronellyl Acetate	5
5.	Citronellyl Formate	5
6.	Decyl Aldehyde	5
7.	Geraniol	50
8.	Hydroxycitronellal	20
9.	Lemon, Oil (terpeneless)	2
10.	Nerol, Oil	10
11.	Nonyl Aldehyde	5
12.	Patchouli, Oil	10

ROSE, IMITATION NO.11

1.	Geraniol Extra	40
2.	Geranium Rose, Oil	5
3.	Orange Bitter, Oil	25
4.	Orange Sweet, Oil	25
5.	Phenyl Ethyl Alcohol	180
6.	Rhodinol	30
7.	Rose Bulgarian, Oil (10% solution)	5
8.	Ethyl Alcohol 95%	690
		1000

ROSE, IMITATION NO. 12

1.	Citral	1
2.	Geraniol	100
3.	Geranium Rose, Oil	3
4.	Orange Sweet, Oil	25
5.	Rhodinol	25
6.	Rose, Turkish, Oil (10% solution)	5
7.	Ethyl Alcohol 95%	841
		1000

ROSE, IMITATION NO. 13

1.	Geranium Bourbon	100
2.	Rose, Imitation No. 1*	250
3.	Rose, Imitation No. 2*	250
4.	Rose, Imitation No. 3*	250
5.	Undecylenic Acid	150
		1000

ROSE, IMITATION NO. 14

1.	Geranium Bourbon	100
2.	Undecenal (10% solution)	450
3.	Undecylenic Acid (10% solution)	450
		1000

ROSE, IMITATION NO. 15

1.	Geranium Bourbon	50
2.	Geranium Palmarosa	50
3.	Undecanal (10% solution)	450
4.	Undecylenic Acid (10% solution)	450
		1000

ROSE, IMITATION NO. 16

1.	Rose Macedone, Oil (10% solution)	500
2.	Rose, Imitation No. 6*	500
		1000

ROSE, IMITATION NO.17

1.	Rose Macedone, Oil (10% solution)	500
2.	Rose, Imitation No. 7*	500
		1000

ROSE, IMITATION NO. 18

1.	Alcohol C-12	10
2.	Citronellol	60
3.	Cedar	30
4.	Geraniol	50
5.	Geranium Palmarosa	100
6.	Guaiacwood	50
7.	Phenyl Ethyl Alcohol (10% solution)	350
8.	Rose Bulgarian Oil (10% solution)	350
		1000

ROSE, IMITATION NO. 19

1.	Alcohol C-12	10
2.	Citronellol	60
3.	Cedarwood, Oil	30
4.	Geraniol	50
5.	Geranium Palmarosa	100
6.	Guaiacwood	50
7.	Phenyl Ethyl Alcohol (10% solution)	350
8.	Rose Turkish, Oil (10% solution)	350
		1000

ROSE, IMITATION NO. 20

1.	Alcohol C-12	10
2.	Citronellol	60
3.	Cedarwood, Oil	30
4.	Geraniol	50
5.	Geranium Palmarosa	100
6.	Guaiacwood	50
7.	Phenyl Ethyl Alcohol (10% solution)	350
8.	Rose May, Oil (10% solution)	350
		1000

ROSE MACEDONE

1.	Rose Macedone, Oil (10% solution)	500
2.	Undecylenic Acid (10% solution)	500
		1000

ROSE, MOSS

1.	Benzoin, Tincture (10% solution)	200
2.	Cinnamic Alcohol	150
3.	Geranium, Oil	100
4.	Musk Ketone	50
5.	Patchouli, Oil	100
6.	Phenyl Ethyl Alcohol (10% solution)	200
7.	Rhodinol, Oil	200
		1000

ROSE, OIL SYNTHETIC

1.	Citronellol (10% solution)	250
2.	Geraniol (10% solution)	500
3.	Geranium, Oil	30
4.	Geranyl Butyrate	20
5.	Phenyl Ethyl Alcohol	100
6.	Terpineol	100
		1000

ROSE, ORIENTAL

1.	Heliotropin	100
2.	Isoeugenol (10% solution)	250
3.	Labdanum, Resinoid	50
4.	Musk Ambrette	200
5.	Styrax, Tincture	200
6.	Vanillin (10% solution)	100
7.	Vetivert	100
		1000

ROSE OTTO

1.	Geranium Bourbon	50
2.	Geranium Palmarosa	50
3.	Undecylenic Acid (10% solution)	900
		1000

ROSE, SYNTHETIC NO.1 (GENERAL BASE FOR ROSE ODOR)

1.	Acetate C-8	10
2.	Acetate C-12	10
3.	Alcohol C-8	10
4.	Alcohol C-9	10
5.	Alcohol C-10	10
6.	Alcohol C-12	10
7.	Aldehyde C-9	10
8.	Aldehyde C-10	10
9.	Aldehyde C-11	10
10.	Aldehyde C-16	10
11.	Benzyl Acetate	100
12.	Benzyl Formate	100
13.	Benzyl Propionate	100
14.	Citronellol	100
15.	Geraniol	200
16.	Phenyl Ethyl Alcohol	100
17.	Rhodinol	100
18.	Rosacetol	100
		1000

ROSE, SYNTHETIC NO. 2

1.	Aldehyde C-9	100
2.	Aldehyde C-10	100
3.	Aldehyde C-11	100
4.	Aldehyde C-12	100
5.	Jasmine, Oil	10
6.	Violet, Oil	10
7.	Ethyl Alcohol 95%	300
8.	Distilled Water	280
		1000

ROSE, SYNTHETIC NO. 3

1.	Glycerin	390
2.	Rose, Oil	10
3.	Stearin	300
4.	Ethyl Alcohol 95%	150
5.	Distilled Water	150
		1000

ROSE, SYNTHETIC NO. 4 (MILK LIKE COMPOUND)

1.	Corn, Oil	165
2.	Rose, Imitation No. 1*	165
3.	Soap	165
4.	Spermaceti	165
5.	Wax	165
6.	Ethyl Alcohol 95%	175
		1000

ROSE, WHITE

1.	Aldehyde C-9 (10% solution)	100
2.	Aldehyde C-10 (10% solution)	100
3.	Aldehyde C-11 (10% solution)	100
4.	Aldehyde C-12 (10% solution)	100
5.	Benzyl Isoeugenol	50
6.	Phenyl Ethyl Alcohol (10% solution)	450
7.	Phenyl Ethyl Propionate	100
		1000

SANDALWOOD "SANTAL (FOR SOAP),"

1.	Benzyl Acetate	70
2.	Cedarwood, Oil	225
3.	Coumarin	55
4.	Geranium, Oil	75
5.	Ionone	70
6.	Mace (or Nutmeg), Oil	25
7.	Musk Xylene	55
8.	Orris, Oleoresin	75
9.	Patcholi, Oil	50
10.	Petitgrain, Oil	25
11.	Sandalwood, Oil	225
12.	Vetiver, Oil	50
		1000

SASSAFRAS, FOR SOAP NO. 1

1.	Camphene	50
2.	Phellandrene	150
3.	Pine, Oil	50
4.	Sassafras, Oil	750
		1000

SASSAFRAS, FOR SOAP NO. 2

1.	Camphene	100
2.	Ocotea Cymbarum	200
3.	Phellandrene	150
4.	Pine, Oil	50
5.	Sassafras, Oil	500
		1000

SEBACIC ACID, STABILIZER FOR PERFUME

1.	Propylene Glycol	750

2.	Sebacic Acid	250
		1000

SOAP, PERFUME NO. 1

1.	Amyl Acetate	10
2.	Citral	50
3.	Benzyl Benzoate	50
4.	Butyl Acetate	10
5.	Ethyl Acetate	10
6.	Ethyl Formate	10
7.	Jasmine, Oil	30
8.	Orris, Oil	10
9.	Rose, Concrete	10
10.	Triacetin	800
11.	Vanillin	10
		1000

SOAP, PERFUME NO. 2

1.	Amyl Acetate	20
2.	Butyl Acetate	20
3.	Citral	80
4.	Ethyl Acetate	20
5.	Ethyl Formate	20
6.	L-Ionone	20
7.	Jasmine, Oil	30
8.	Orris, Oil	30
9.	Rose, Concrete	10
10.	Triacetin	700
11.	Ylang Ylang, Oil	50
		1000

SOAP, PERFUME NO. 3

1.	Aldehyde C-20	250
2.	Soap Perfume No. 1*	500
3.	Soap Perfume No. 2*	250
		1000

SOAP, FERFUME NO. 4

1.	Amyl Acetate	25
2.	Butyl Acetate	25
3.	Citral	25
4.	Ethyl Acetate	25
5.	Ethyl Formate	25
6.	Ylang Ylang, Oil	875
		1000

SOAP, PERFUME NO. 5

1.	Apricot Kernel, Oil	250
2.	Pine, Oil	250
3.	Propylene Glycol	500
		1000

SWEET PEA, BLOSSOM

1.	Benzylidene Acetone	1
2.	Hyacinth, Oil	100
3.	Methyl Acetophenone	1
4.	Neroli, Oil	200
5.	Ethyl Alcohol 95%	349
6.	Distilled Water	349
		1000

SYRINGA, IMITATION NO. 1

1.	Lemon, Oil	250
2.	Lime, Oil	250
3.	Terpineol, Extra	500
		1000

SYRINGA IMITATION NO. 2

1.	Acetophenone	150
2.	Amyl Cinnamic Aldehyde	200
3.	Anisyl Formate	150

4.	Hydroxycitronellal	150
5.	Isobutyl Anthranilate	50
6.	Isobutyl Benzoate	50
7.	Linalool	200
8.	Methyl Ionone	50
		1000

TOBACCO FOR SNUFF

1.	Bergamot, Oil	100
2.	Cascarilla, Oil	400
3.	Cinnamon Leaf, Oil	100
4.	Geranium, Oil	100
5.	Lavender, Oil	100
6.	Nutmeg, Oil	100
7.	Vanilla Beans, Tincture	100
		1000

TOBACCO PERFUMES, GENERAL BASIC METERIAL NO. 1

1.	Cassia, Absolute	20
2.	Heliotropin	70
3.	Jasmine, Oil	50
4.	Labdanum Absolute	20
5.	Methyl Ionone	60
6.	Musk Ketone	40
7.	Neroli, Oil	30
8.	Rose, Oil	40
9.	Tuberose, Absolute	10
10.	Vanillin	10
11.	Vetiverol, Oil	60
12.	Ethyl Alcohol 95%	590
		1000

TOBACCO PERFUMES, GENERAL BASIC MATERIAL NO. 2

1.	Bergamot, Oil	110
2.	Birch Tar, Oil	5
3.	Castoreum, Resinoid	2
4.	Clary Sage, Oil	80
5.	Dimethyl Hydroquinone	80
6.	Isopropyl Quinoline	70
7.	Jasmine, Oil	14
8.	Methyl Nonyl	40
9.	Methyl Nonyl Acetaldehyde	2
10.	Methyl Phenyl Acetate	15
11.	Musk Ambrette	30
12.	Musk Ketone	80
13.	Neroli, Oil	14
14.	Orris, Oil	10
15.	Phenyl Acetic Acid	15
16.	Rose, Oil	35
17.	Sandalwood, Oil	42
18.	Tetrahydrofurfuryl Acetate	1
19.	Tobacco, Absolute	30
20.	Vanillin	25
21.	Ethyl Alcohol 95%	300
		1000

TOBACCO, STRONG ODOUR

1.	Birch Tar, Oil	100
2.	Hydroquinone Dimethyl Ether	100
3.	Immortelle	200
4.	Labdanum, Oil	200
5.	Olibanum, Oil	200
6.	Phenyl Propyl Alcohol	200
		1000

TREFLE (CLOVER, TREFOIL) (FOR SOAP)

1.	Amyl Salicylate	400
2.	Anisaldehyde	50
3.	Benzylidene Acetone	25
4.	Benzyl Salicylate	25
5.	Bergamot, Oil	50
6.	Cananga, Oil	225
7.	Clary Sage, Oil	5
8.	Coumarin	45
9.	α–Ionone	25
10.	Lavender, Oil	25
11.	Linalyl Acetate	50
12.	Oakmoss Resinoid	25
13.	Rose, Oil	35
14.	Vanillin	15
		1000

TUBEROSE, IMITATION (FOR SOAP)

1.	Aldehyde C-18	25
2.	Benzyl Acetate	70
3.	Benzyl Salicylate	70
4.	Hydroxycitronellal	150
5.	Linalool	100
6.	Linalyl Benzoate	175
7.	Methyl Anthranilate	150
8.	Methyl Benzoate	70
9.	Methyl Heptyne Carbonate	15
10.	Methyl Salicylate	70
11.	Tolu Balsam	25
12.	Tuberose	25
13.	Vanillin	5
14.	Ylang Ylang, Oil	50
		1000

TUBEROSE, SYNTHETIC

1.	Alcohol C-10	8
2.	Alcohol C-12	12
3.	Aldehyde C-9	3
4.	AldehydeC-10	8
5.	Aldehyde C-11	3
6.	Aldehyde C-12	12
7.	Aldehyde C-18	4
8.	Amyl Cinnamic Aldehyde	10
9.	Anisyl Formate	10
10.	Benzyl Alcohol	150
11.	Benzyl Benzoate	150
12.	Benzyl Propionate	150
13.	Butyl Phenyl Acetate	150
14.	Hydroxycitronellal	150
15.	Methyl Anthranilate	10
16.	Methyl Heptyne Carbonate	10
17.	Methyl Nonyl Acetaldehyde	5
18.	Methyl Salicylate	5
19.	Phenyl Propyl Alcohol	150
		1000

UNY COLOGNE, PERFUME BASE

1.	Bergamot, Oil	200
2.	Citral	100
3.	Citronella Formosa	150
4.	Lavender, Oil	100
5.	Musk Xylol	20
6.	Nerolin	60
7.	Petitgrain, Oil	100
8.	Rosemary, Oil	150
9.	Spike, Oil	120
		1000

VAPOROUS PERFUME, IMITATION NO. 1

1.	Cedarleaf, Oil	10

2.	Eucalyptol, Oil	350
3.	Isobornyl Acetate, Crystals	20
4.	Menthol	500
5.	Menthone, Oil	120
		1000

VAPOROUS PERFUME, IMITATION NO.2

1.	Eucalyptol, Oil	170
2.	Isoborneol, Crystals	50
3.	Menthol	500
4.	Menthone, Oil	250
5.	Peppermint, Oil	30
		1000

VAPOROUS PERFUME, IMITATION NO. 3

1.	Camphor, Oil	250
2.	Menthone, Oil	250
3.	Vaporous Perfume, Imitation No.1*	250
4.	Vaporous Perfume, Imitation No. 2*	250
		1000

VIOLET, FOR FACE POWDER

1.	Bergamot	100
2.	α–Ionone (10% solution)	350
3.	Jasmine, Oil	100
4.	Methyl Ionone	50
5.	Musk Ketone	50
6.	Orange, Flower	50
7.	Orris Concrete (10%solution)	200
8.	Vetiver	50
9.	Ylang Ylang	50
		1000

VIOLET, IMITATION NO. 1

1.	Aldehyde C-11	2
2.	Aldehyde C-12	5
3.	Aldehyde C-14	2
4.	Aldehyde C-18	2
5.	Citral	10
6.	Ethyl Myristate	5
7.	Ionone	10
8.	Orris Roots, Oil	15
9.	Ylang Ylang, Oil	10
10.	Ethyl Alcohol 95%	465
11.	Methyl Heptyne Carbonate	10
12.	Distilled Water	464
		1000

VIOLET, IMITATION NO. 2

1.	Aldehyde C-18	20
2.	Bergamot, Oil	20
3.	α–Ionone	2
4.	Methyl Heptyne Carbonate	2
5.	Neroli, Oil	2
6.	Orris, Roots	130
7.	Rhodinol	10
8.	Vanilla Beans, Oil	10
9.	Ethyl Alcohol 95%	402
10.	Distilled Water	402
		1000

VIOLET, IMITATION NO. 3

1.	Aldehyde C-12 (lauric)	20
2.	Bergamot, Oil	50
3.	Eugenol	25
4.	Helitropin	25
5.	Hydroxycitronellal	25
6.	α–Ionone	85
7.	ß-Ionone	75
8.	Methyl Heptyne Carbonate	15
9.	Methyl Ionone	75

10.	Musk Ambrette	5
11.	Rose, Oil	25
12.	Sandalwood, Oil	10
13.	Vanillin	10
14.	Ylang Ylang	25
15.	Ethyl Alcohol 95%	265
16.	Distilled Water	265
		1000

VIOLET, IMITATION NO. 4 (FOR SOAP)

1.	Cassia, Oil	75
2.	Ethyl Myristate	75
3.	Guaiacwood, Oil	75
4.	α–Ionone	250
5.	Methyl Heptyne Carbonate	50
6.	Orris Root Concrete	350
7.	Sandalwood, Oil	50
8.	Violet Leaves Concrete	75
		1000

VIOLET, IMITATION NO. 5 (FOR SOAP)

1.	Anisaldehyde	10
2.	Bergamot, Oil	50
3.	Cassia Absolute	15
4.	Heliotropin	60
5.	Ionone	250
6.	Methyl Heptyne Carbonate	15
7.	Methyl Ionone	250
8.	Orris Root, Oil	250
9.	Violet Leaf, Absolute	100
		1000

VIOLET, IMITATION NO. 6

1.	Bergamot, Oil	50
2.	Eugenol	20
3.	Heliotropin	40
4.	Hydroxycitronellal	30
5.	α–Ionone (10% solution)	335
6.	ß-Ionone (10% solution)	335
7.	Lauric Aldehyde	20
8.	Methyl Ionone	100
9.	Rose Oil (10% solution)	30
10.	Ylang Ylang, Oil	40
		1000

VIOLET LEAF

1.	Alcohol C-12 (10% solution)	100
2.	Aldehyde C-10 (10% solution)	100
3.	Aldehydde C-12 (10% solution)	100
4.	α–Ionone	100
5.	Methyl Heptyne Carbonate	10
6.	Orris Concrete (10% solution)	100
7.	Phenyl Ethly Alcohol	100
8.	Ethyl Alcohol 95%	390
		1000

VIOLET, SYNTHETIC

1.	Alcohol C-10	10
2.	Alcohol C-12	50
3.	Aldehyde C-10	5
4.	Aldehyde C-12	15
5.	Cassia, Oil	25
6.	Jasmine, Oil	25
7.	Methyl Heptyne Carbonate	20
8.	Ionone	100
9.	Irone	100
10.	Orris Root, Absolute	50
11.	Ethyl Alcohol 95%	300
12.	Distilled Water	300
		1000

WALLFLOWER

1.	Alcohol C-9	75
2.	Aldehyde C-9	25
3.	Anisaldehyde	25
4.	Heliotropin	25
5.	Hydroxycitronellal	100
6.	Isoeugenol	15
7.	Methyl-ß- Naphthyl Ketone	10
8.	Ethyl Alcohol 95%	250
9.	Mehtyl Ionone	25
10.	Methyl-p-Cresol	200
11.	Distilled Water	250
		1000

WINTERGREEN, IMITATION (FOR SOAP)

1.	Cinnamon Bark, Oil	50
2.	Clove, Oil	100
3.	Methyl Salicylate	200
4.	Peppermint, Oil	350
5.	Rhodinol	150
6.	Spearmint, Oil	150
		1000

STIR-FILTER

YLANG YLANG, IMITATION NO. 1

1.	Benzyl Alcohol	250
2.	Benzyl Benzoate	250
3.	Heliotropine	100
4.	α–Ionone White	20
5.	Vanillin	100
6.	Ylang Ylang, Oil	30
7.	Ethyl Alcohol 95%	125
8.	Distilled Water	125
		1000

YLANG YLANG, IMITATION NO.2

1.	Benzyl Alcohol	180
2.	Cassia, Oil	30
3.	Citral	50
4.	Ethyl Enanthate	50
5.	Heliotropin	20
6.	Orris, Oil	70
7.	Ylang Ylang, Oil (10% solution)	600
		1000

YLANG YLANG, IMITATION NO. 3

1.	Cananga, Oil (10% solution)	250
2.	α–Ionone	100
3.	Orris Concrete	150
4.	Ylang Ylang, A	500
		1000

YLANG YLANG, IMITATION NO. 4

1.	Benzyl Alcohol (10% solution)	250
2.	Benzyl Benzoate (10% solution)	250
3.	Heliotropin (10% solution)	100
4.	α–Ionone	20
5.	Phenyl Ethyl Alcohol (10% solution)	250
6.	Vanillin (10% solution)	100
7.	Ylang Ylang, Oil	30
		1000

YLANG YLANG, IMITATION NO. 5

1.	Anisic Aldehyde	100
2.	Benzyl Acetate	20
3.	Benzyl Benzoate	100
4.	Cananga, Oil	10
5.	Cinnamic Acid	10
6.	Citral	10
7.	p-Cresol Methyl Ether	10
8.	p-Cresyl Acetate	10
9.	p-Cresyl Phenyl Acetate	20
10.	Ethyl Benzoate	100
11.	Eugenol	10
12.	Geraniol	100
13.	Geranyl Phenyl Acetate	10
14.	Iraldeine, Balsam	10
15.	Methyl Benzoate	100
16.	Methyl Eugenol	10
17.	Methyl Phenyl Acetate	10
18.	Opoponax, Oil	10
19.	Phenyl Ethyl Alcohol	100
20.	Phenyl Acetic Acid	20
21.	Phenyl Ethyl Cinnamate	20
22.	Terpineol	100
23.	Terpinyl Acetate	100
24.	Vetivert	10
		1000

YLANG YLANG, SYNTHETIC NO. 1

1.	Alcohol C-9	25
2.	Aldehyde C-9	20
3.	Benzyl Acetate	50
4.	Benzyl Alcohol	50
5.	Benzyl Benzoate	50
6.	Cadinene, Oil	50
7.	Eugenol	10
8.	Geraniol	250
9.	Geranyl Benzoate	250
10.	Isoeugenol	20
11.	Linalool	50
12.	Methyl Anthranilate	20
13.	Methyl Benzoate	150
14.	Methyl Salicylate	5
		1000

YLANG YLANG, SYNTHETIC NO. 2

1.	Aldehyde C-18	25
2.	Benzyl Acetate	25
3.	Geraniol	250
4.	Geranyl Benzoate	250
5.	Linalool	100
6.	Linalyl Acetate	50
7.	Methyl Benzoate	250
8.	Methyl Eugenol	25
9.	Terpineol	25
		1000

Chapter-3

FORMULARY OF FLAVOURS

NOTES:

A. The esters of amyl, benzyl, butyl, methyl, and propyl alcohols with acetic, anthranilate, butyric, capric, formic,propionic, and valeric acids are employed to simulate the fruit flavours. For example, a peach flavour is enhanced by Aldehyde C-14, a strawberry flavor by Aldehyde C-16, and a pineapple flavor by ethyl butyrate. All the formulas of these flavours are made with these esters.

B. The proportion used for making essences is 2 or 3 volumes (2 or 3 cc per liter of solvent) for each completed formula.

C. All formulas are alphabetically listed, including their ingredients. The ethyl alcohol 95% and distilled water are always listed last in each formula.

D. Ingredients denoted by an asterisk (*) are formulas which may be found in this book.

GENERAL METHOD FOR THE EXTRACTION OF NATURAL FLAVOURS FROM FRESH OR DRY FRUITS

1.	Fruits (fresh, ripe or dry, not rancid) well crushed, rasped, or ground)	10 kg
2.	Ethyl Alcohol 95%	10 l
3.	Distilled Water	10 l

Let stand for several days (either 10, 8, or 3, depending on the maximum flavour and odour development which can also be obtained by fermentation with the addition of sugar in double amount before the addition of alcohol and distilled water). Stir for 1 h daily.Separate the juice. To the residue add:

4.	Ethyl Alcohol 95%	10 l
5.	Distilled Water	10 l

Let stand for another 3 days. Add:

6.	Amyl Valerianate	5 ml

for fresh fruits or

Ethyl Oenenthate	25 ml
Amyl Formate	45 ml

for dry fruits.

Distill altogether. Filter.

Yield : Proportionate to the amount of fruits and doubled ethyl alcohol 95% and distilled water.

"NEUTRAL" ESTERS MIXTURE BASE

1.	Ethyl Acetate	420
2.	Ethyl Formate	250
3.	Isoamyl Acetate	250
4.	Isoamyl Butyrate	80

Note: This is a general base. It can be used with the simple addition of one or more components for a specific flavour. For example by increasing the isoamyl acetate in this base the characteristic banana flavour is obtained.

ABBEY, BENEDICTINE TYPE

1.	Angelica, Oil (terpeneless)	2
2.	Camomile, German, Oil (terpeneless)	8
3.	Celery, Oil (terpeneless)	4
4.	Cinnamon, Ceylon, Oil (terpeneless)	8
5.	Mace, Oil (terpeneless)	4
6.	Cognac, Oil	200
7.	Maraschino	350
8.	Orange Bitter, Oil (terpeneless)	6
9.	Orange Sweet, Oil (terpeneless)	4
10.	Peppermint, Oil (terpeneless)	14
11.	Ethyl Alcohol 95%	400
		1000

Note : Abbey is the name of a monastery or convent.

ABSINTHE

1.	Absinthe, Oil (10% solution)	50
2.	Anise, Oil	5
3.	Fennel, Oil	2
4.	Lemon, Oil	5
6.	Sugar	238
7.	Ethyl Alcohol 95%	325
8.	Distilled Water	325
		1000

Dissolve sugar in the water stir together; filter.

Note: Absinthe is not allowed as an alcoholic beverage in the U.S. A.

ADVOCAAT (ADVOKAAT)

1.	Clove, Oil	1
2.	Cloves	2
3.	Cognac	65
4.	Coriander, Oil	1
5.	Mace, Oil	5
6.	Maraschino, Essence	35
7.	Neroli, Oil	1
8.	Nutmag, Oil	5
9.	Rum, Jamaica	25
10.	Saffron	10
11.	Sassafras, Wood	25
12.	Vanilla, Oil	25
13.	Vanillin (100 %)	10
14.	Ethyl Alcohol 95%	395
15.	Distilled Water	395
		1000

Macerate for 10 days, warm. Press the liquid off. Filter through paper. Add:

1.	Yellow Colour Sol'n.	2
2.	Ethyl Alcohol 95%	100

Note: Advocaat is a sweet thick yellow Dutch liqueur. This essence is a Dutch specialty. It has a peculiar taste, similar to egg yolk. It is also suitable for soft chocolate cream at 1 - 2 cc/ 1000 cc.

ALLSPICE, OIL

1.	Caraway, Seeds Oil	100
2.	Celery, Seeds Oil	100
3.	Cinnamon Seeds Oil	300
4.	Cloves, Seeds Oil	100
5.	Coriander, Seeds Oil	100
6.	Nutmeg, Seeds Oil	100
		1000

ALMOND, BITTER

A variety of the common almond (Prunus amygdalus amara) having bitter kernels that yield a highly poisonous oil. It is used for flavouring only when the prussic acid in it has been totally removed.

ALMOND BITTER, ESSENCE (NATURAL)

1.	Almond Bitter, Oil (pure)	160
2.	Benzaldehyde (pure)	5
3.	Benzyl Alcohol	15
4.	Ethyl Alcohol 95%	410
5.	Distilled Water	410
		1000

ALMOND, BITTER (FOR SOAP)

1.	Benzaldehyde	300
2.	Caraway, Oil	25
3.	Cedarwood, Oil	25
4.	Citronella, Oil	50
5.	Geranium Palmarosa, Oil	150
6.	Phenyl Ethyl Alcohol	150
7.	Terpineol	300
		1000

ALMOND, BITTER IMITATION

1.	Benzaldehyde (pure)	10
2.	Geraniol	70

3.	Petitgrain, Paraguay	50
4.	Phenyl Ethyl Alcohol	80
5.	Ethyl Alcohol 95%	790
		1000

ALMOND, BITTER NO. 1

1.	Benzaldehyde (pure 10% solution)	450
2.	Benzyl Alcohol (10% solution)	544
3.	Bromelia	1
4.	Vanillin	5
		1000

ALMOND, BITTER NO. 2

1.	Benzaldehyde (pure 10% solution)	100
2.	Ethyl Acetate (10% solution)	450
3.	Ethyl Benzoate	50
4.	Ethyl Formate (10% solution)	250
5.	Isoamyl Acetate	150
		1000

ALMOND, BITTER NO.3

1.	Almond Bitter Oil (cyanide free)	200
2.	Benzaldehyde (pure 10% solution)	50
3.	Benzyl Alcohol	100
4.	Ethyl Alcohol 95%	325
5.	Distilled Water	325
		1000

ALMOND, BITTER NO. 4

1.	Almond Bitter, Oil (cyanide free)	500
2.	Benzaldehyde (pure 10% solution)	150
3.	Benzyl Alcohol (10% solution)	343
4.	Neroli, Oil	2
5.	Vanillin	5
		1000

ALMOND, BITTER NO. 5

1.	Benzaldehyde (pure, 10% solution)	150
2.	Benzyl Alcohol (10% solution)	844
3.	Bromelia	1
4.	Vanillin	5
		1000

ALMOND, BITTER NO. 6

1.	Benzaldehyde (pure, 10% solution)	100
2.	Ethyl Acetate (10% solution)	450
3.	Ethyl Benzoate	50
4.	Ethyl Formate (10% solution)	250
5.	Isoamyl Acetate	150
		1000

ALMOND, BITTER NO. 7

1.	Almond Bitter No. 1*	750
2.	Almond Bitter No. 2*	250
		1000

ALMOND, BITTER, SYNTHETIC NO. 1

1.	Benzaldehyde (pure)	10
2.	Ethyl Alcohol 95%	350
3.	Distilled Water	640
		1000

ALMOND, BITTER, SYNTHETIC NO. 2

1.	Benzaldehyde (pure)	5
2.	Benzyl Alcohol	60
3.	Ethyl Benzoate	5
4.	Ethyl Formate	5
5.	Vanillin	5
6.	Ethyl Alcohol 95%	460
7.	Distilled Water	460
		1000

ALMOND, BITTER, SYNTHETIC NO. 3

1.	Benzaldehyde (pure)	12
2.	Benzyl Alcohol	42
3.	Ethyl Acetate	22
4.	Ethyl Benzoate	2
5.	Ethyl Formate	12
6.	Hydrocinnamic Aldehyde	1
7.	Isoamyl Acetate	7
8.	ß-Naphthyl Ethyl Ether	2
9.	Rhodinyl Propionate	2
10.	Vanillin	5
11.	Ethyl Alcohol 95%	447
12.	Distilled Water	446

ALMOND, BITTER SYNTHETIC NO. 4

1.	Anisette, Essence	100
2.	Cognac (liquor at 60%)	50
3.	Curacao, Essence	150
4.	Maraschino Essence	50
5.	Orange Flowers (collected early morning)	195
6.	Vanillin	5
7.	Ethyl Alcohol 95%	150
8.	Distilled Water	300

Macerate for 8 days. Agitate with stirrer 1 h daily. Filter.

ALMOND, IMITATION

1.	Benzaldehyde (pure 10% solution)	9
2.	Isoamyl Isovalerate	10
3.	Malic Acid	1
4.	Ethyl Alcohol 95%	980
		1000

ALMOND, MILK (ORZATA)

1.	Almond, Bitter Essence (Natural)* (pure)	40
2.	Benzoin	10
3.	Sugar	200
4.	Distilled Water	750
		1000

Note: Barley, basis, Barley is a widely cultivated cereal grass (Hordeum, Family Graminaceae). The grain of this plant is used as food and in making beer ale and whiskey.

ALMOND, PEACH

1.	Maraschino, Essence	25
2.	Orange Flowers	

	Imitation No.1*	25
3.	Peach Extract (Natural)*	38
4.	Rose Imitation No. 1*	25
5.	Undelactone (Aldehyde C-14)	2
6.	Vanillin	3
7.	Ethyl Alcohol 95%	460
8.	Distilled Water	422
		1000

Note: Essence of kernel of maraschino "wild cherry" free of cyanuric acid.

ANGELIC, TINCTURE

1.	Angelic Root (pulverized)	400
2.	Ethyl Alcohol 95%	500
3.	Distilled Water	100
		1000

ANGOSTURA, BITTER

1.	Angostura, Bark (pulverized)	110
2.	Cardamom, Seeds (pulverized)	3
3.	Cinnamon, Bark (pulverized)	40
4.	Clove, Flowers (dry and pulverized)	30
5.	Galangal, Root (pulverized)	7
6.	Gentian, Root (pulverized)	7
7.	Ginger, Root (pulverized)	2
8.	Lemon, Peels (pulverized)	20
9.	Orange (bitter), Peels (pulverized)	40
10.	St. John's Bread (pulverized)	2
11.	Sugar (pulverized)	345
12.	Sweet Flag, Root (pulverized)	7
13.	Tonka Beans, Seeds (pulverized)	40
14.	Ethyl Alcohol 95%	174
15.	Distilled Water	173
		1000

Pulverize # 1-13. Macerate with sugar and alcohol (# 11, 14) for 10 days stirring every day for 1 h. Filter. To the residue add double amount of ethyl alcohol 95% and distilled water. Let stand for another 3 days stirring every day for 1 h. Filter. To the residue add double amount of ethyl alcohol 95% and distilled water. Let stand for another 3 days stirring every day for 1 h. Put altogether and distill.

Yield: 2 liters

ANISE BASE

1.	Anise Seeds, Oil	820
2.	Cardamom, Oil	20
3.	Cinnamon, Oil	20
4.	Clove, Oil	40
5.	Coriander, Oil	80
6.	Lemon, Oil	20
		1000

ANISEED

1.	Almond, Bitter, Oil (cyanide free)	2
2.	Angelica, Oil (terpeneless)	2
3.	Anise, Oil (terpenelass)	25
4.	Badiane (Star Anise), Oil	10
5.	Coriander, Oil	6
6.	Fennel, Oil	15
7.	Rose Bulgarian Oil (10% solution)	6
8.	Ethyl Alcohol 95%	934
		1000

ANISETTE, OIL NO. 1

1.	Anise, Oil	770
2.	Cardamom, Oil	5
3.	Coriander, Oil	20
4.	Fennel (Sweet), Oil	200
5.	Lemon, Oil	5
		1000

Note: Mix well and let stand for 24 h or more. Use 15 cl of this oil to make 1 part of anisette extract.

ANISETTE, OIL NO. 2

1.	Amber, Oil	2
2.	Anise Seeds, Oil	55
3.	Coriander, Oil	3
4.	Fennel (sweet), Oil	6
5.	Orris Roots, Oil	9
6.	Sugar	450
7.	Ethyl Alcohol 95%	240
8.	Distilled Water	235
		1000

APPLE, BASE

1.	Apples (freshly sliced)	450
2.	Ethyl Alcohol 95%	550
		1000

Let macerate for 6 days. Then add:

3.	Distilled Water	1250

Distilled 1125 cc. Use the distillate to macerate:

4.	Apple (sliced)	450

After 3 days add:

5.	Amyl Valerate	20
6.	Ethyl Butyrate	5
7.	Ethyl Valerate	5
8.	Isobutyl Valerate	100
9.	Distilled Water	200

Distil to obtain a final yield of 1000 cc.

APPLE, ESSENCE (NATURAL) NO. 1

1.	Apples (freshly sliced and chopped)	1000
2.	Salt	150

Macerate for 10 days.

3.	Ethyl Alcohol 95%	250
4.	Wine White	1000

Macerate for another 8 days Distill over 1000 cml.

Note: Employ 5-10 cml per liter.

APPLE, ESSENCE (NATURAL) NO. 2

1.	Apple Essence No.1 (Natural)*	500
2.	Ethyl Acetate	3
3.	Ethyl Malonate	3
4.	Isobutyl Valerianate	1
5.	Ethyl Alcohol 95%	247
6.	Distilled Water	246
		1000

Distill

Note: Employ 1/2 cml per liter.

APPLE, ESSENCE (NATURAL) NO. 3

1.	Apple, Concentrated Juice	240
2.	Apple, Essence No. 1 (Natural)*	80
3.	Apple, Essence No. 2 (Natural)*	350
4.	Ethyl Alcohol 95%	165
5.	Propylene Glycol	165
		1000

Distill

APPLE, ESSENCE (NATURAL) NO. 4

1.	Apples or Apple Peels (dried)	10
2.	Ethyl Alcohol 95%	30

Macerate for 3 days

3.	Distilled Water	30

Distill.

4. Amyl Valerianate in small amount to achieve the best odour and flavour.

APPLE, IMITATION NO. 1

1.	Amyl Acetate	34
2.	Amyl Valerate	30
3.	Apples Base*	200
4.	Benzaldehyde (pure)	1
5.	Clove, Oil	4
6.	Cognac, Oil	1
7.	Ethyl Acetate	65
8.	Ethyl Butyrate	20
9.	Ethyl Valerate	45
10.	Ethyl Pelargonate	15
11.	Isobutyl Valerate	60
12.	Lemon Oil (terpenaless)	1
13.	Orange Bitter, Oil (terpeneless)	1
14.	Orange Sweet, Oil (terpeneless)	3
15.	Ethyl Alcohol 95%	520
		1000

APPLE, IMITATION NO. 2

1.	Amyl Valerianate	125
2.	Ethyl Acetate	85
3.	Ethyl Butyrate	45
4.	Ethyl Malonate	20
5.	Ethyl Nitrate	85
6.	Isobutyl Valerianate	100
7.	Ethyl Alcohol 95%	540
		1000

APPLE, IMITATION NO. 3

1.	Acetaldeyde	20
2.	n-Caprylate	10
3.	Geraniol	10
4.	Geranyl Acetate	10
5.	Geranyl Formate	10
6.	Isoamyl Acetate	100
7.	Isoamyl-n-Caproate	50
8.	Isoamyl Formate	100
9.	Ethyl Alcohol 95%	345
10.	Distilled Water	345
		1000

APPLE, IMITATION NO.4

1.	Amyl Acetate	75
2.	Amyl Valerianate	60
3.	Benzaldehyde (pure)	1
4.	Citronellyl Valerate	5
5.	Clove, Oil	10
6.	Ethyl Acetate	140
7.	Ethyl Butyrate	50
8.	Ethyl Malonate	35
9.	Ethyl Valerianate	75
10.	Geranyl Butyrate	5
11.	Isoamyl Valerate	35
12.	Ethyl Alcohol 95%	255
13.	Distilled Water	254
		1000

APPLE, SYNTHETIC NO. 1

1.	Amyl Acetate	13
2.	Amyl Valerianate	26
3.	Benzaldehyde (pure)	2
4.	Ethyl Acetate	13
5.	Ethyl butyrate	13
6.	Ethyl Valerianate	13
7.	Ethyl Alcohol 95%	460
8.	Propylene Glycol	460
		1000

APPLE, SYNTHETIC NO. 2

1.	Aldehyde C-14	2
2.	Amyl Valerianate	10
3.	Chloroform	1
4.	Ethyl Acetate	1
5.	Ethyl Nitrate	1
6.	Glycerin (neutral)	40
7.	Tartaric Acid	1
8.	Ethyl Alcohol 95%	472
9.	Distilled Water	472
		1000

APPLE, SYNTHETIC NO. 3

1.	Acetaldehyde	1
2.	Amyl Valerianate	10
3.	Chloroform	1
4.	Ethyl Acetate	10
5.	Ethyl Benzoate	10
6.	Ethyl Butyrate	10
7.	Ethyl Nitrate	10
8.	Ethyl Oenanthate	1
9.	Glycerin (neutral)	472
10.	Tartaric Acid	1
11.	Vanillin	2
12.	Ethyl Alcohol 95%	236
13.	Distilled Water	236
		1000

APPLE, SYNTHETIC NO. 4

1.	Amyl Acetate	4
2.	Amyl Valerianate	5
3.	Benzaldehyde (pure)	1
4.	Clove, Oil	1
5.	Ethyl Acetate	3
6.	Ethyl Oenanthate	1
7.	Ethyl Valerianate	5
8.	Ethyl Alcohol 95%	490
9.	Distilled Water	490
		1000

APPLE, SYNTHETIC NO. 5

1.	Apple, Synthetic No. 1*	30
2.	Ethyl Butyrate	5
3.	Isobutyl Valerianate	5
4.	Methyl Ethyl Phenyl Glycidate	5
5.	Ethyl Alcohol 95%	475
6.	Distilled Water	480
		1000

APPLE, SYNTHETIC NO. 6

1.	Acetaldehyde	1
2.	Amyl Valerianate	6
3.	Ethyl Acetate	4
4.	Ethyl Alcohol 95%	492
5.	Ethyl Nitrate	4
6.	Distilled Water	493
		1000

APPLE, SYNTHETIC NO. 7

1.	Acetaldehyde	2
2.	Benzaldehyde	1
3.	n-Caprylate	1
4.	Citronellyl Valerianate	22
5.	Ethyl Acetate	3
6.	Ethyl Butyrate	11
7.	Ethyl Isovalerianate	30
8.	Ethyl Malonate	10
9.	Ethyl Oenanthate	16
10.	Eugenol	4
11.	Geranyl Acetate	28
12.	Geranyl Butyrate	26
13.	Isoamyl Acetate	9
14.	Isoamyl Caproate	6
15.	Isoamyl Oenanthate	1
16.	Isoamyl Valerianate	50
17.	Isobutyl Valerianate	10
18.	Malonic Acid	10
19.	Ethyl Alcohol 95%	380
20.	Distilled Water	380
		1000

APPLE, SYNTHETIC NO. 8

1.	Aldehyde C-14	2
2.	Amyl Butyrate	10
3.	Chloroform	1
4.	Ethyl Acetate	1
5.	Ethyl Nitrate	1
6.	Glycerin (neutral)	328
7.	Tartaric Acid	1
8.	Ethyl Alcohol 95%	328
9.	Distilled Water	328
		1000

APPLE, SYNTHETIC NO. 9

1.	Amyl Butyrate	4
2.	Chloroform	3
3.	Ethyl Butyrate	30
4.	Ethyl Salicylate	3
5.	Ethyl Valerianate	15
6.	Glycerin (neutral)	315
7.	Ethyl Alcohol 95%	315
8.	Distilled Water	315
		1000

APPLE, SYNTHETIC NO. 10

1.	Acetaldehyde	2
2.	Amhyl Acetate	10
3.	Amyl Valerianate	10
4.	Chloroform	10
5.	Ethyl Acetate	10
6.	Ethyl Nitrate	10
7.	Ethyl Alcohol 95%	474
8.	Distilled Water	474
		1000

APPLE, SYNTHETIC NO. 11

1.	Aldehyde C-14 (pure)	1
2.	Amyl Valerianate	8
3.	Chloroform	2
4.	Ethyl Acetate	2
5.	Ethyl Nitrate	1
6.	Glycerin (neutral)	328
7.	Ethyl Alcohol 95%	330
8.	Distilled Water	328
		1000

APPLE, SYNTHETIC NO. 12

1.	Acetaldehyde	12
2.	Amyl Valerianare	12
3.	Chloroform	12
4.	Ethyl Nitrate	12
5.	Ethyl Acetate	12
6.	Ethyl Alcohol 95%	470
7.	Distilled Water	470
		1000

APPLE, SYNTHETIC NO. 13

1.	Amyl Valerianate	12
2.	Ethyl Acetate	8
3.	Ethyl Butyrate	4
4.	Ethyl Malonate	2
5.	Ethyl Nitrate	8
6.	Isobutyl Valerianate	10
7.	Ethyl Alcohol 95%	478
8.	Distilled Water	478
		1000
9.	Magnesium Oxide	2

Distill over 1250 cl
Add:

10.	Apple Essence (Natural) No.1*	500
11.	Apple Essence (Natural) No.2*	500

Filter
Note: Employ 3 cl per liter.

APPLE, SYNTHETIC NO. 14

1.	Acetaldehyde	1
2.	Isoamyl Acetate	13
3.	Isoamyl-n-Caproate	5
4.	Isoamyl-n-Caprylate	2
5.	Isoamyl Valerianate	21
6.	Ethyl Alcohol 95%	479
7.	Distilled Water	479
		1000

APRICOT, ESSENCE (NATURAL) NO. 1

1.	Apricots (chopped, without seeds)	10 kg
2.	Ethyl Alcohol 95%	20 l

Macerate for 3 days

3.	Distilled Water	10 l

Macerate for another 3 days

4.	Distilled Water	10 cl
5.	Ethyl Valerianate	5 cml

Distill

APRICOT, ESSENCE (NATURAL) NO. 2

1.	Apricot, Essence (Natural) No. 1*	500

2.	Benzyl Cinnamate	1
3.	Ethyl Cinnamate	1
4.	Lactone Undecyyenic Acid (persicol)	5
5.	Nonyl Aldehyde (Apricolin)	5
6.	Tannic Acid	1
7.	Vanilla, Oil	2
8.	Vanillin	1
9.	Ethyl Alcohol 95%	242
10.	Distilled Water	242
		1000

APRICOT, IMITATION NO. 1

1.	Almond, Bitter, Oil (cyanide free)	8
2.	Amyl Butyrate	150
3.	Amyl Propionate	10
4.	Benzaldehyde (pure 10% solution)	4
5.	Ethyl Butyrate	100
6.	Ethyl Valerate	50
7.	Methyl Salicylate	25
8.	Phenyl Methyl Acetate	25
9.	Phenyl Methyl Formate	25
10.	Y-Undelactone	3
11.	Ethyl Alcohol 95%	600
		1000

APRICOT, IMITATION NO. 2

1.	Almond, Bitter, Oil (cyanide free)	6
2.	Amyl Butyrate	75
3.	Amyl Propionate	5
4	Apricot, Base	25
5.	Methyl Heptyne Carbonate	25
6.	Methyl Phenyl Acetate	25
7.	Methyl Phenyl Formate	35
8.	Peach Base	25
9.	y-Undelactone	5
10.	Ethyl Alcohol 95%	774
		1000

APRICOT, IMITATION NO. 3

1.	Almond, Bitter, Oil (cyanide free)	5
2.	Amyl Butyrate	150
3.	Amyl Valerate	25
4.	Benzaldehyde (pure 10% solution)	5
5.	Ethyl Butyrate	125
6.	Ethyl Valerate	50
7.	Methyl Salicylate	25
8.	Phenyl Methyl Acetate	50
9.	Phenyl Methyl Formate	35
10.	y-Undelactone	4
11.	Ethyl Alcohol 95%	526
		1000

APRICOT, IMITATION NO. 4

1.	Anethole	5
2.	Amyl Acetate	50
3.	Amyl Alcohol	5
4.	Amyl Butyrate	75
5.	Butyl Butyrate	100
6.	Ethyl Acetate	50
7.	Ethyl Butyrate	75
8.	Ethyl Valerate	55
9.	Eugenol	3
10.	Jasmine, Oil (10% solution)	10
11.	Petitgrain, Oil	10
12.	Phenyl Methyl Carbinyl Acetate	50
13.	Vanillin	12
14.	Ethyl Alcohol 95%	250

15.	Distilled Water	250
		1000

APRICOT, IMITATION NO. 5

1.	Amyl Alcohol	15
2.	Benzaldehyde (pure 10% solution)	70
3.	Benzyl Acetate	70
4.	Cinnamon, Ceylon, Oil	12
5.	Clove, Oil	6
6.	Cognac, Oil	15
7.	Coriander, Oil	2
8.	Ethyl Acetate	110
9.	Ethyl Butyrate	200
10.	Ethyl Formate	5
11.	Ethyl Pelargonate	25
12.	Ethyl Valerate	40
13.	Geraniol	12
14.	Orange Sweet, Oil	30
15.	Rose, Oil	3
16.	Vanillin (10% solution)	35
17.	Ethyl Alcohol 95%	350
		1000

APRICOT, SYNTHETIC NO. 1

1.	Amyl Butyrate	1
2.	Chloroform	1
3.	Ethyl Butyrate	10
4.	Ethyl Oenanthate	1
5.	Ethyl Salicylate	2
6.	Ethyl Valerianate	5
7.	Glycerin (neutral)	4
8.	Tartaric Acid	1
9.	Ethyl Alcohol 95%	488
10.	Distilled Water	487
		1000

APRICOT, SYNTHETIC NO.2

1.	Amyl Acetate	1
2.	Amyl Alcohol	5
3.	Amyl Butyrate	2
4.	Benzyl Acetate	1
5.	Benzyl Propionate	1
6.	Butyl Butyrate	1
7.	Chloroform	2
8.	Ethyl Acetate	5
9.	Ethyl Butyrate	4
10.	Ethyl Oenanthate	2
11.	Ethyl Salicylate	2
12.	Ethyl Valerianate	10
13.	Eugenol	1
14.	Glycerin (neutral)	36
15.	Tartaric Acid	1
16.	Vanillin	1
17.	Ethyl Alcohol 95%	463
18.	Distilled Water	462
		1000

APRICOT, SYNTHETIC NO. 3

1.	Aldehyde C-16	5
2.	Amyl Butyrate	2
3.	Chloroform	1
4.	Ethyl Oenanthate	1
5.	Ethyl Salicylate	2
6.	Ethyl Valerianate	4
7.	Glycerin (neutral)	327
8.	Phenyl Ethyl Acetate	4
9.	Ethyl Alcohol 95%	327
10.	Distilled Water	327
		1000

APRICOT, SYNTHETIC NO. 4

1.	Aldehyde C-16	1
2.	Anethole	1
3.	Apricot Essence	

	(Natural) No. 1*	20
.	Benzaldehyde (pure)	3
.	Benzyl Acetate	2
.	Butyl Butyrate	2
.	Ethyl Acetate	5
.	Ethyl Butyrate	15
.	Ethyl Formate	4
0.	Ethyl Isovalerianate	8
1.	Ethyl Oenanthate	1
2.	Ethyl Salicylate	1
3.	Eugenol	1
4.	Glycerin (neutral)	300
5.	Isoamyl Acetate	6
6.	Isoamyl Alcohol	2
7.	Isoamyl Butyrate	22
8.	Isoamyl Isovalerianate	2
9.	Isoamyl Propionate	1
0.	Linalool	1
1.	Methyl Heptyne Carbonate	1
2.	Vanillin	1
3.	Ethyl Alcohol 95%	300
4.	Distilled Water	300
		1000

PRICOT, SYNTHETIC NO. 5

	Aldehyde C-14	25
	Amyl Acetate	16
	Amyl Butyrate	16
	Amyl Valerianate	16
	Benzaldehyde	4
	Cinnamic Aldehyde	1
	Ethyl Caprylate	18
	Ethyl Valerianate	18
	Geraniol	1
.	Neroli, Oil	4
.	Vanillin	16
.	Ethyl Alcohol 95%	433
.	Distilled Water	432
		1000

AUBEPINE (HAWTHORN)

1.	Alcohol C-9	2
2.	Aldehyde C-9	1
3.	Aldehyde C-10	2
4.	Anisic Aldehyde	75
5.	Citral	20
6.	Ethyl Alcohol 95%	450
7.	Distilled Water	450
		1000

AVOCADO

1.	Cloves	3
2.	Cognac	125
3.	Coriander	1
4.	Maraschino	75
5.	Neroli, Oil	1
6.	Nutmeg	15
7.	Rum, Jamaica	50
8.	Saffron	25
9.	Vanilla Beans	20
10.	Ethyl Alcohol 95%	343
11.	Distilled Water	342
		1000

Macerate for 10 days Press Filter Add certified yellow color (2 g) triacetin 100 cc.

BANANA, ESSENCE (NATURAL) NO. 1

1.	Bananas, Peeled (not overripened, only the pulp is used)	20 kg
2.	Ethyl Alcohol 95%	20 l

Macerate for 3 days Express at least 20l. To the residue add:

3. Distilled Water 2 cl
4. Amyl Butyrate 6 ml
5. Coriander, Oil 12 ml

Macerate for another 3 days Distill altogether.

Yield : 15ltr

BANANA, ESSENCE (NATURAL) NO. 2

1. Bananas, Peeled 10 kg
2. Ethyl Alcohol 95% 10 l

Press after I week. Add:

3. Wine, Brand 2 l
4. Vanilin 15 g
5. Ethyl Butyrate 3 ml

BANANA, IMITATION NO. 1

1.	Amyl Acetate	20
2.	Amyl Butyrate	30
3.	Benzyl Benzoate	20
4.	Chamomile, Oil	3
5.	Cinnamon, Oil	2
6.	Eugenol	3
7.	Ethyl Butyrate	3
8.	Lemon, Oil	30
9.	Mandarin, Oil	10
10.	Orange, Sweet, Oil	20
11.	Petitgrain, Oil	7
12.	Vanillin	10
13.	Ethyl Alcohol 95%	421
14.	Distilled Water	421
		1000

BANANA, IMITATION NO. 2

1.	Banana, Essence (Natural) No. 1*	1
2.	Banana, Essence (Natural) No. 2*	3
3.	Amyl Acetate	
4.	α–Ionone	
5.	Vanillin	
6.	Ethyl Alcohol 95%	2
7.	Distilled Water	2
		10

BANANA, IMITATION NO.

1.	Amyl Acetate	
2.	Benzyl Propionate	
3.	Butyl Butyrate	
4.	Ethyl Butyrate	
5.	Lemon, Oil	
6.	Orange, Sweet, Oil	
7.	Propyl Acetate	
8.	Vanillin	
9.	Ethyl Alcohol 95%	
10.	Distilled Water	
		1

BANANA, IMITATION NO.

1.	Acetaldehyde	
2.	Amyl Alcohol	
3.	Benzyl Propionate	
4.	Chloroform	
5.	Clove, Oil	
6.	Glycerin (neutral)	
7.	Petitgrain, Oil	
8.	Vanillin	
9.	Ethyl Alcohol 95%	
10.	Distilled Water	
		1

BANANA, IMITATION NO. 5

Ingredient	Parts
Capraldehyde	1
Benzyl Benzoate	12
Cinnamic Aldehyde	1
Ethyl Acetate	12
Ethyl Butyrate	20
Ethyl Sebacate	10
Eugenol	1
Glycerin (neutral)	289
Isoamyl Acetate	37
Isoamyl Butyrate	20
Lemon, Oil	1
§-Limonene	8
Linalool	6
Methyl Anthranilate	1
Vanillin	3
Ethyl Alcohol 95%	289
Distilled Water	289
	1000

BANANA, SYNTHETIC NO 1

Ingredient	Parts
Amyl Acetate	30
Ethyl Butyrate	30
Ethyl Alcohol 95%	470
Distilled Water	470
	1000

BANANA, SYNTHETIC NO. 2

Ingredient	Parts
Amyl Acetate	40
Amyl Butyrate	8
Benzyl Acetate	40
Ethyl Butyrate	8
Vanillin	4
Ethyl Alcohol 95%	450
Distilled Water	450
	1000

BANANA, SYNTHETIC NO. 3

No.	Ingredient	Parts
1.	Amyl Acetate	90
2.	Amyl Butyrate	12
3.	Benzyl Acetate	20
4.	Ethyl Butyrate	7
5.	Ethyl Alcohol 95%	436
6.	Distilled Water	435
		1000

BANANA, SYNTHETIC NO. 4

No.	Ingredient	Parts
1.	Amyl Acetate	10
2.	Amyl Butyrate	20
3.	Benzyl Acetate	20
4.	Benzyl Propionate	20
5.	Ethyl Butyrate	18
6.	Vanillin	2
7.	Glycerin (neutral)	20
8.	Ethyl Alcohol 95%	445
9.	Distilled Water	445
		1000

BANANA, SYNTHETIC NO. 5

No.	Ingredient	Parts
1.	Amyl Acetate	20
2.	Amyl Butyrate	10
3.	Benzyl Acetate	20
4.	Benzyl Phenyl Acetate	2
5.	Ethyl Butyrate	5
6.	Glycerin (neutral)	10
7.	Vanillin, Tincture 1/10%	50
8.	Ethyl Alcohol 95%	442
9.	Distilled Water	441
		1000

BARBECUE

No.	Ingredient	Parts
1.	Bay, Leaves	25
2.	Capsicum, Oleoresin	150

3.	Cloves	175
4.	Coriander	50
5.	Garlic Extract	50
6.	Ginger, Oleoresin	100
7.	Marjoram, Sweet	125
8.	Onion, Extract	50
9.	Pepper, Black	100
10.	Pimenta, Leaves	150
11.	Thyme White	25
		1000

BARBECUE SAUCE, "HUNT" TYPE

1.	Carrots, Dehydrated	20
2.	Celery, Dehydrated	15
3.	Corn Syrup	60
4.	Flavours, Natural: Basil, Laurel Leaves, Oregano, Parsley, Rosemary, Sage (Oils), I ml each	6
5.	Onions, Dehydrated	25
6.	Pectin	5
7.	Pepper, Green Bell,Dehydrated	15
8.	Salt	1
9.	Spices: Cinnamon, Clove, Nutmeg, Paprika, Pepper(Oils) 1 ml each	5
10.	Sugar	20
11.	Tomatoes, Dehydrated	300
12.	Tomatoes, Sauce	350
13.	Vinegar, Distilled	3
14.	Distilled Water	175
		1000

Note: The amount of each ingredient can be increased or decreased in accordance with individual taste.

BARBERRY, ESSENCE (NATURAL)

1. Barberries, Juice (express from fully ripe berries) 7 l

Macerate the residue for 3 days with:

2. Ethyl Alcohol 95% 3 l

Mix the residue of the maceration with the juice. Add:

3. Ethyl Butyrate 12 ml

Distilled altogether. Redistill for retification.
Yield 5 liters.

BENEDICTINE NO. 1

Liquor made originally by Benedictine monks.

1.	Absinthe, Oil	250
2.	Angelica, Oil	80
3.	Cardamom, Oil	40
4.	Cinnamon, Oil	20
5.	Coriander, Oil	40
6.	Lemon, Oil	270
7.	Nutmug, Oil	20
8.	Orange, Oil	90
9.	Peppermint, Oil	170
10.	Thyme, Oil	20
		1000

BENEDICTINE NO. 2

1.	Angelica, Oil	80
2.	Cardamom, Oil	40

3. Cinnamon, Oil 20
4. Coriander, Oil 40
5. Lemon, Oil 270
6. Nutmeg, Oil 20
7. Orange, Oil 90
8. Peppermint, Oil 170
9. Thyme, Oil 20
10. Ethyl Alcohol 95% 250

1000

BERGAMOT, FLAVOUR

1. Bergamot, Oil 100
2. Lemon, Oil 150
3. Orange, Oil 50
4. Ethyl Alcohol 95% 350
5. Distilled Water 350

1000

BILBERRY, ESSENCE (NATURAL) NO.1

1. Bilberries, Black (crushed) 20 kg
2. Sugar 20 kg

Let ferment for serveral days untill the flavor is developed. Express the juice. Macerate the residue for 3 days with.

3. Amyl Butyrate 4 ml
4. Coriander, Oil 2 ml
5. Ethyl Acetate 12 ml
6. Fennel, Sweet, Oil 2 ml
7. Ethyl Alcohol 95% 15 l
8. Distilled Water 15 l

Distill altogether, Redistill for rectification.
Yield 20 liters.

BILBERRY, ESSENCE (NATURAL) NO. 2, RED

1. Bilberries, Black (crushed) 20 kg
2. Sugar 20 kg

Let ferment for several days until the flavor is developed Express the juice Macerate the residue for 3 days with

3. Ethyl Alcohol 95% 15 l
4. Distilled Water 15 l
5. Rose, Oil 1 ml
6. Ethyl Benzoate 30 ml
7. Methyl Salicylate 4 ml

Distill altogether Redistill for rectification.
Yield 20 liters.

BILBERRY, ESSENCE (NATURAL) NO. 3 SCANDINAVIAN TYPE

1. Bilberries, Juice 485
2. Amyl Butyrate 5
3. Benzoic Acid 2
4. Coriander, Oil 2
5. Ethyl Acetate 5
6. Fennel, Sweet, Oil 1
7. Ethyl Alcohol 95% 500

1000

Macerate for 2 days. Distill
Note. Employ 3 ml per liter

BILBERRY, IMITATION NO. 1

1. Bilberries (crushed) 250
2. Bilberries, Juice (distilled) 250
3. Amyl Butyrate 20
4. Benzoic Acid 1

5.	Coriander	2
6.	Ethyl Acetate	20
7.	Fennel, Oil	2
8.	Ethyl Alcohol 95%	250
9.	Distilled Water	205
		1000

Macerate for 2 days Distill slowly over 800 cc.

BILBERRY, IMITATION NO. 2

1.	Amyl Acetate	22
2.	Amyl Butyrate	14
3.	Benzyl Acetate	4
4.	Bilberry, Imitation No. 1*	50
5.	Coriander, Oil	1
6.	Ethyl Acetate	38
7.	Ethyl Benzoate	30
8.	Ethyl Valerate	16
9.	Fennel, Oil	2
10.	Methyl Salicylate	1
11.	Petitgrain, Oil	1
12.	Vanillin	3
13.	Ethyl Alcohol 95%	409
14.	Distilled Water	409
		1000

BILBERRY, IMITATION NO. 3

1.	Bilberry Imitation No. 1*	600
2.	Bilberry Imitation No. 2*	200
3.	Ethyl Alcohol 95%	200
		1000

BITTER NO. 1, "UNICUM"

1.	Absinthe	1
2.	Angelica, Root	30
3.	Angostura, Bark	75
4.	Centaury, Root	75
5.	Calamius, Root	60
6.	Cinchona (Red), Bark	30
7.	Cinnamon, Bark	35
8.	Ginger, Root	60
9.	Gentian, Root	60
10.	Honey	64
11.	Lemon Balm, Balsam	35
12.	Lemon, Peels	26
13.	Orange, Peels	35
14.	Rhubarb, Roots and Stalks	30
15.	Spearmint, Leaves	30
16.	Sugar	80
17.	Ethyl Alcohol 95%	137
18.	Distilled Water	137
		1000

Macerate the whole pulverized material for 7 days. Express and filter.

BITTER NO. 2, " SPANISH"

1.	Angelica, Oil	3
2.	Angelica, Root	66
3.	Calamus, Oil	5
4.	Calamus, Root	100
5.	Cascarilla, Bark	33
6.	Chamomile, Flowers	33
7.	Chamomile, Oil	5
8.	Clove, Flowers	33
9.	Clove, Oil	3
10.	Coriander, Fruits	33
11.	Galangal, Root	66
12.	Gentian, Bark	66
13.	Juniper, Oil	5
14.	Marjoram	33
15.	Orange, Bitter, Peels	100
16.	Orange, Bitter, Oil	5
17.	Peppermint	33
18.	Pimento, Berry	33
19.	Wormwood, Leaves and Tops	33

20.	Ethyl Alcohol 95%	156
21.	Distilled Water	156
		1000

BITTER NO. 3, "STOMACH"

1.	Aloe, Roots	8
2.	Angelica, Root	8
3.	Calamus, Root	8
4.	Clove, Flowers	8
5.	Gentian, Root	15
6.	Lemon, Peels	15
7.	Licorice, Root	70
8.	Orange, Bitter, Peels	35
9.	Rhubarb, Root	35
10.	Star Anise, Root	49
11.	St. John's Bread (Carob)	70
12.	Wormwood, Leaves and Tops	15
13.	Ethyl Alcohol 95%	332
14.	Distilled Water	332
		1000

BLACKBERRY, ESSENCE (NATURAL)

1.	Blackberries (ripe, crushed)	20 kg
2.	Sugar	20 kg

Let ferment for several days until the flavour is strongly developed Express the juice Macerate the residue for 3 days with

3.	Ethyl Alcohol 95%	15 l
4.	Distilled Water	15 l
5.	Methyl Salicylate	6 ml

Distill Redistill.
Yield 20 liters.

BLACKBERRY, IMITATION NO. 1

1.	Apricot, Imitation No. 1*	260
2.	Cherry, Imitation No. 1*	180
3.	Cinnamon, Ceylon, Oil	8
4.	Peach, Imitation No. 1*	60
5.	Pineapple, Imitation No. 1*	40
6.	Raspberry, Imitation No. 1*	140
7.	Ethyl Alcohol 95%	312
		1000

BLACKBERRY, IMITATION NO. 2

1.	Ethyl Acetate	100
2.	Ethyl Butyrate	40
3.	Ethyl Formate	20
4.	Ethyl Pelargonate	30
5.	Isoamyl Butyrate	15
6.	y-Nonyl Lactone	1
7.	Ethyl Alcohol 95%	794
		1000

BLACKBERRY, IMIATION NO. 3

1.	Amyl Butyrate	6
2.	Benzaldehyde (pure, 10% solution)	4
3.	Benzyl Acetate	100
4.	Ethyl Formate	170
5.	Ethyl Oenanthate	60
6.	Isoamyl Acetate	125
7.	Isoamyl Butyrate	130
8.	Isoamyl Isovalerate	5
9.	Ethyl Alcohol 95%	400
		1000

BLACKBERRY, SYNTHETIC

1.	Amyl Methyl Ketone	1
2.	Benzaldehyde (pure)	4
3.	Benzyl Acetate	10
4.	Ethyl Formate	7
5.	Ethyl Oenanthate	6
6.	Isoamyl Acetate	22
7.	Isoamyl Butyrate	43
8.	Isoamyl Isovalerianate	5
9.	Methyl Salicylate	5
10.	Ethyl Alcohol 95%	449
11.	Distilled Water	448
		1000

BLACK CHERRY

1.	Benzoic Acid (1% solution)	80
2.	Ethyl Acetate (10% solution)	400
3.	Ethyl Benzoate	200
4.	Isoamyl Isovalerate	120
5.	Isoamyl Butyrate	200
		1000

BLACK CURRANT

1.	Acetaldehyde	40
2.	Amyl Acetate	60
3.	Amyl Butyrate	250
4.	Anisaldehyde	15
5.	Buchu, Oil	15
6.	Cinnamon, Oil	20
7.	Ethyl Acetate	160
8.	Ethyl Benzoate	30
9.	Ethyl Heptanoate	20
10.	Ethyl Pelargonate	50
11.	Geraniol	5
12.	Isobutyl Acetate (10% solution)	250
13.	Lemon, Oil (terpeneless)	30
14.	Nerol, Oil	5
15.	Orris, Oil	40
16.	Vanillin	10
		1000

BLACK CURRANT, SYNTHETIC

1.	Acetaldehyde	4
2.	Anisaldehyde	1
3.	Amyl Acetate	5
4.	Amyl Butyrate	25
5.	Cinnamon, Oil	1
6.	Ethyl Acetate	16
7.	Ethyl Benzoate	3
8.	Ethyl Oenanthate	2
9.	Ethyl Pelargonate	5
10.	Geraniol	1
11.	Isobutyl Acetate	25
12.	Neroli, Oil	1
13.	Lemon, Oil	3
14.	Orris, Oil	4
15.	Vanillin	3
16.	Ethyl Alcohol 95%	451
17.	Distilled Water	450
		1000

BLACK PEPPER, IMITATION NO. 1

1.	Borneol	60
2.	Guaiacwood	340
3.	Pepper, Black, Oil	340
4.	Phellandrene (10% sol'n.)	260
		1000

BLACK PEPPER, IMITATION NO. 2

1.	Black Pepper, Oil	350
2.	Borneol	100
3.	Guaiacwood	50
4.	Pepper, Black, Oil	350
5.	Phellandrene	200
		1000

BLUEBERRY ESSENCE, (NATURAL)

1.	Blueberries (ripe, crushed)	20 kg
2.	Sugar	20 kg

Let ferment for several days until the flavour is strongly developed. Express the juice Macerate the residue for 3 days with.

3.	Ethyl Alcohol 95%	15 l
4.	Distilled Water	15 l
5.	Isoamyl Hexanoate	1 l
6.	Methyl Ionone	1 l
7.	Rhodinyl Butyrate	1 l

Distill Redistill
Yield 20 liters..

BRANDY (COGNAC) NO. 1

1.	Acetic Acid	60 ml
2.	Acetate Ether	60 ml
3.	Kino Tincture	75 ml
4.	Raisins, Bruised	3 kg
5.	Syrup (simple)	1 kg

Add burnt sugar for colour Let stand 12 days. Filter.

Yield 20 gal pure 50% proof spirit

BRANDY (COGNAC) NO. 2

1.	Acetaldehyde	3
2.	Amyl Isobutyrate	3
3.	Benzaldehyde (pure)	1
4.	Cinnamon, Oil	1
5.	Cinnamyl Propionate	1
6.	Cinnamyl Butyrate	1
7.	Coganc, Oil	12
8.	Ethyl Acetate	55
9.	Ethyl Butyrate	2
10.	Fusel, Oil	5
11.	Heliotropine	1
12.	Methyl Eugenol	2
13.	Neroli, Oil	12
14.	Pelargonic Ether	3
15.	Vanillin	6
16.	Ethyl Alcohol 95%	892
		1000

BREAD FRESH, ROASTED FLAVOUR

1.	Bread Fresh Roasted (ground)	2
2.	Propylene Glycol	1
3.	Distilled Water	1

Filter.

BUTTER, FLAVOUR, IMITATION NO. 1

1.	Butyl Acetate	60
2.	Butyl Butyrate	20
3.	Diacetyl (10% solution)	350
4.	Ethyl Butyrate	40
5.	Ethyl Alcohol 95%	530
		1000

BUTTER, FLAVOUR, IMITATION NO. 2

1.	Butyl Acetate	55
2.	Butyl Butyrate	25
3.	Diacetyl (10% solution)	310
4.	Ethyl Butyrate	35
5.	Ethyl Pelargonate	25
6.	Ethyl Alcohol 95%	550
		1000

BUTTER, FLAVOUR, IMITATION NO. 3

1.	Butyl Acetate	15
2.	Butyl Butyrate	5
3.	Diacetyl	170
4.	Ethyl Butyrate	10
5.	Ethyl Alcohol 95%	800
		1000

BUTTER, FLAVOUR, IMITATION NO. 4

1.	Butyl Acetate	140
2.	Butyl Butyrate	70
3.	Diacetyl	155
4.	Ethyl Butyrate	70
5.	Ethyl Pelargonate	70
6.	Ethyl Alcohol 95%	495
		1000

BUTTER, FLAVOUR, IMITATION NO. 5

1.	Butyl Acetate (10% solutionn)	250
2.	Butyl Butyrate (10% solution)	250
3.	Diacetyl	200
4.	Ethyl Butyrate	200
5.	Ethyl Pelargonate	100
		1000

BUTTER, FLAVOUR, IMITATION NO. 6

1.	Amyl Butyrate	80
2.	Amyl Isobutyrate	130
3.	Butyl Butyrate	65
4.	Ethyl Isobutyrate	155
5.	Ethyl Myristate	55
6.	Ethyl Alcohol 95%	515
		1000

BUTTER, FLAVOUR, SYNTHETIC

1.	Amyl Butyrate	7
2.	Butyl Acetate	11
3.	Butyl Butyrate	1
4.	Butyric Acid	12
5.	Diacetyl	43
6.	Ethyl Butyrate	22
7.	Ethyl Myristate	4
8.	Ethyl Pelargonate	1
9.	Triacetin	8
10.	Vanillin	1
11.	Ethyl Alcohol 95%	445
12.	Distilled Water	445
		1000

BUTTER, RUM

1.	Butter, Flavor, Imitation No. 1*	50
2.	Butter, Flavor, Imitation No. 2*	50
3.	Honey	50
4.	Rum, Essence	845
5.	Vanillin	5
		1000

BUTTERSCOTCH, IMITATION NO. 1

1.	Butyl Acetate	120
2.	Butyl Butyrate (10% solution)	570
3.	Cognac, Oil	230
4.	Ethyl Pelargonate	80
		1000

BUTTERSCOTCH, IMITATION NO. 2

1.	Almond, Oil (pure)	75
2.	Amyl Butyrate	35
3.	Butyl Acetate	73
4.	Butyric Acid	100
5.	Butyl Butyric (10% solution)	250
6.	Butyl Ethyl Ether	35
7.	Ethyl Heptanoate	92
8.	Ethyl Pelargonate	180
9.	Geranium, Oil	40
10.	Lemon, Oil	40
11.	Methyl Salicylate	5
12.	Orange, Oil	20
13.	Pelargonic Aldehyde	20
14.	Vanillin (10% solution)	35
		1000

BUTTERSCOTCH, IMITATION NO. 3

1.	Butyl Acetate	2
2.	Butyl Butyrate	25
3.	Butyric Acid	17
4.	Capraldehyde	1
5.	Cinnamic Aldehyde	1
6.	Ethyl Butyrate	13
7.	Ethyl Oenanthate	9
8.	Ethyl Pelargonate	19
9.	Isoamyl Acetate	11
10.	Isobutyl α–Toluate	1
11.	Ethyl Alcohol 95%	451
12.	Distilled Water	450
		1000

BUTTERSCOTCH, IMITATION NO.4

1.	Almond, Oil	18
2.	Amyl Butyrate	5
3.	Butyl Butyrate	5
4.	Butyric Acid	15
5.	Ethyl Butyrate	6
6.	Ethyl Oenanthate	4
7.	Ethyl Pelargonate	4
8.	Geranium Oil	5
9.	Lamon, Oil	10
10.	Methyl Salicylate	1
11.	Orange, Oil	5
12.	Ethyl Alcohol 95%	457
13.	Vanillin	8
14.	Distilled Water	457
		1000

BUTTERSCOTCH, IMITATION NO. 5

1.	Amyl Acetate	12
2.	Cinnamon Oil	2

3. Butyl Butyrate 13
4. Butyric Acid 3
5. Ethyl Butyrate 15
6. Ethyl Cinnamate 7
7. Ethyl Oenanthate 15
8. Ethyl Pelargonate 10
9. Homoquinoline 2
10. Honey 6
11. Ethyl Alcohol 95% 458
12. Distilled Water 457

1000

BUTTERSCOTCH, IMITATION NO. 6

1. Butyl Acetate 80
2. Butyl Butyrate (10% solution) 420
3. Ethyl Oenanthate 170
4. Ethyl Pelargonate (10% solution) 330

1000

CACAO, EXTRACT (NATURAL) NO. 1, COLOURLESS

1. Cacao Beans Roasted and Ground 10 kg
2. Ethyl Alcohol 95% 20 l

Macerate for one week Add:

3. Distilled Water 3 cl
4. Cinnamon Oil 3 ml
5. Vanillin 20 g

Distill
Yield 20 liters.

CACAO, EXTRACT (NATURAL) NO. 2, BROWN

1. Cacao Beans, Roasted and Ground 10 kg
2. Ethyl Alcohol 95% 20 1

Macerate for one week. Add

3. Distilled Water 3 cl
4. Cinnamon, Oil 3 ml
5. Vanillin 20 g

Filter.
Yield 20 liters

CACAO, IMITATION

1. Benzyl Alcohol 70
2. Cinnamaldehyde 20
3. Ethyl Acetate (10% solution) 250
4. Ethyl Oenanthate 80
5. Eugenol 20
6. Isoamyl Acetate (10% solution) 250
7. Isoamyl Butyrate 175
8. Theobroma, Oil 100
9. Vanillin (10% solution) 35

1000

CACAO, SYNTHETIC

1. Amyl-α–Toluate 1
2. Benzyl Alcohol 7
3. Cinnamic Aldehyde 2
4. Etnyl Acetate 35
5. Ethyl Oenanthate 8
6. Eugenol 2
7. Eugenol Isoamyl Ether 1
8. Isoamyl Butyrate 25
9. Isoamyl Butyrate 16

10.	Ethyl Alcohol 95%	450
11.	Distilled Water	450
12.	Vanillin	3
		1000

CAPER, EXTRACT (NATURAL)

1. Capers 2 kg

Cut up small and remove the juice. Macerate with

2. Alcohol 95% 4 l

for 3 days Express. To the residue add:

3. Ethyl Alcohol 95% 4 l

Macerate for another 3 days Distill altogether

Yield 10 liters

CAPSICUM, EXTRACT (NATURAL)

1. Capsicum 2 kg

Cut up small and remove the juice (if fresh) or if dry macerate with

2. Ethyl Alcohol 95% 4 l
for 3 days. Express. To the residue add

3. Ethyl Alcohol 95% 4 l

Macerate for another 3 days Distill altogether.

Yield 10 liters.

CARAMEL, FLAVOUR NO. 2

1.	Almond, Oil (pure)	480
2.	Heliotropin	10
3.	Musk	10
4.	Vanillin (10% solution)	500
		1000

CARAWAY, IMITATION NO. 1

1.	Benzyl Benzoate	200
2.	Orange, Oil	600
3.	Terpineol	200
		1000

CARAWAY, IMITATION NO. 2

1.	Caraway, Imitation No.1*	320
2.	Caraway, Oil	320
3.	Dill Weed (Anethum graveolens)	320
4.	Guaiacwood, Oil	40
		1000

CARAWAY, IMITATION NO. 3

1.	Carvone	200
2.	Limonene (10% solution)	700
3.	Phellandrene	100
		1000

CARAWAY, IMITATION NO. 4

1.	Caraway, Imitation No.2*	800
2.	Caraway, Oil	200
		1000

CARAWAY, IMITATION NO. 5

1. Caraway

	Imitation No.3	800
2.	Dill Wood, Oil	200
		1000

CARDAMOM, IMITATION NO. 1

1.	Cineol	200
2.	Limonene	200
3.	Terpineol (10% solution)	300
4.	Terpinyl Acetate (10% solution)	300
		1000

CARDAMOM, IMITATION NO. 2

1.	Cardamom, Imitation No. 1*	800
2.	Cardamom, Oil	200
		1000

CARNATION, FLAVOUR

1.	Cinnamon, Oil	5
2.	Eugenol	50
3.	Heliotropin	50
4.	Hydroxycitronellal	20
5.	Ionone	10
6.	Isoeugenol (10% solution)	350
7.	Mehtyl Isoeugenol	50
8.	Musk	1
9.	Neroli, Oil	50
10.	Pimento, Oil	50
11.	Rose, Oil	30
12.	Sage, Clary, Oil	20
13.	Vanillin	4
14.	Ylang Ylang, Oil	20
15.	Ethyl Alcohol 95%	290
		1000

CARROT, EXTRACT (NATURAL)

1. Carrot 2 kg

Scrape and express to remove the juice Macerate with.

2. Alcohol 95% 4 1

for 3 days. Express. To the residue add;

3. Ethyl Alcohol 95% 4 1

Macerate for another 3 days. Distill altogether.
Yield 10 liters.

CASCARILLA, TINCTURE

1.	Cascarilla Bark (ground)	282
2.	Ethyl Alcohol 95%	178
3.	Distilled Water	540
		1000

CASHEW, EXTRACT (NATURAL)

1. Cashew, Rasped Kernels 10 kg
2. Ethyl Alcohol 95% 30 l

Macerate for 10 days, stirring often Collect all liquid. Add to the residue

3. Distilled Water 20 1
4. Amyl Formate 12 ml
5. Ethyl Oenanthate 12 ml

Distill altogether.

Yield 50 liters

CASSIA, IMITATION NO. 1

1.	Cinnamic Aldehyde (10% solution)	958
2.	Clove, Oil	30
3.	Heptaldehyde	2
4.	Menthone	1
5.	α–Methylcinnamic Aldehyde	6
6.	Salicylate Aldehyde	3
		1000

CASSIA, IMITATION NO. 2

1.	Cassia, Imitation No. 1*	200
2.	Cinnamic Aldehyde (10% solution)	800
		1000

CASSIA, IMITATION NO. 3

1.	Cassia, Imitation No. 2*	200
2.	Cedarwood, Oil	100
3.	Cinnamic Aldehyde (10% solution)	700
		1000

CASSIA, IMITATION NO. 4

1.	Cassia, Imitation No. 1*	333
2.	Cassia, Imitation No. 2*	333
3.	Cassia, Imitation No. 3*	334
		1000

CASSIA, IMITATION NO. 5

1.	Cassia, Imitation No. 4*	995
2.	α–Methylcinnamic Aldehyde	5
		1000

CASSIA, IMITATION NO. 6

1.	Cedarwood, Oil	50
2.	Cinnamic Aldehyde (10% solution)	540
3.	Clove, Oil (10% solution)	350
4.	Heptaldehyde	20
5.	Menthone	10
6.	Salicylate Aldehyde (10% solution)	30
		1000

CASSIA, IMITATION NO. 7

1.	Cassia, Imitation No.5*	790
2.	Cinnamic Aldehyde	30
3.	Propylene Glycol	180
		1000

CASSIA, IMITATION NO. 8

1.	Aldehyde C-10	2
2.	Benzyl Alcohol	40
3.	Cuminic Aldehyde	3
4.	Geraniol	2
5.	Linalool	8
6.	Ionone	2
7.	Irone	5
8.	Methyl Salicylate	35
9.	Terpineol	3
10.	Ethyl Alcohol 95%	450
11.	Distilled Water	450
		1000

CASSIA, IMITATION NO. 9

1.	Acetate C-8	1
2.	Alcohol C-8	2
3.	Alcohol C-11	2
4.	Aldehyde C-9	1
5.	Aldehyde C-10	1
6.	Anisic Aldehyde	5
7.	Benzaldehyde	4
8.	Benzyl Alcohol	45
9.	Isobutyl Salicylate	12
10.	Methyl Acetophenone	4
11.	Methyl Salicylate	23
12.	Ethyl Alcohol 95%	900
		1000

CHAMPAGNE, CEDAR, IMITATION

1.	Amyl Acetate	100
2.	Amyl Valerianate	25
3.	Ethyl Acetate	50
4.	Ethyl Butyrate	100
5.	Ethyl Nitrate	10
6.	Ethyl Valerianate	25
7.	Ginger, Oil	3
8.	Peach, Imitation No. 1*	100
9.	Vanillin	5
10.	Ethyl Alcohol 95%	582
		1000

CHAMPAGNE, FLAVOUR

1.	Amyl Acetate	20
2.	Amyl Isobutyrate	4
3.	Cognac, Oil	10
4.	Ethyl Acetate	8
5.	Ethyl Butyrate	40
6.	Lemon, Oil	6
7.	Neroli, Oil	10
8.	Vanillin	2
9.	Ethyl Alcohol 95%	900
		1000

CHARTREUSE

1.	Absinthe, Oil (10% solution)	10
2.	Angelica, Oil	200
3.	Cinnamon, Oil	100
4.	Coriander, Oil	100
5.	Lemon, Oil	60
6.	Neroli, Oil	15
7.	Nutmeg, Oil	100
8.	Orange, Oil	400
9.	Rose, Oil	15
		1000

CHARTREUSE LIQUEUR) NO.1

1.	Angelica, Oil	10
2.	Anise, Oil	150
3.	Clove, Oil	150
4.	Hyssop, Oil	150
5.	Lemon, Oil	150
6.	Nugmeg, Oil	150
7.	Peppermint,Oil	20
9.	Ethyl Alcohol 95%	220
		1000

Note: Yellow or green color sugar and distilled water may be added accroding to personal preference.

CHARTREUSE (LIQUEUR) NO.2

1.	Absinthe, Oil	7
2.	Angelica, Oil	20
3.	Cinnamon, Oil	10
4.	Coriander, Oil	10
5.	Lamon, Oil	4
6.	Nutmeg, Oil	6
7.	Neroli, Oil	2
8.	Orange (Sweet), Oil	40
9.	Rose, Oil	1
10.	Ethyl Alcohol 95%	450
11.	Distilled Water	450
		1000

CHEESE, BLUE, SYNTHETIC NO. 1

1.	Acetoin	1
2.	n-Butanol	1
3.	Butanone	1
4.	n-Butyric Acid	8
5.	Capric Acid	3
6.	Caproic Acid	21
7.	Caprylic Acid	21
8.	d-Decalactone	35
9.	Diacetyi	1
10.	d-Dodecalactone	6
11.	Ethyl Acetate	1
12.	Ethyl Butyrate	2
13.	Ethyl Lactate	1
14.	2-Heptanol	3
15.	2-Heptanone	5
16.	cis-3-Hexenol	1
17.	2-Nonanone	2
18.	8-Nonen-2-one	23
19.	2-Pentanol	3
20.	2-Pentanone	3
21.	Vegetable Oil	858
		1000

CHEESE, BLUE, SYNTHETIC NO.2

1.	Acetic Acid	9
2.	Butyric Acid	17
3.	Cinnamic Acid	1
4.	Decanoic Acid	134
5.	5-Decannolide	1
6.	5-Dodecanolide	1
7.	Glycoxylic Acid	71
8.	Heptanoic Acid	12
9.	2-Heptanone	64
10.	Hexanoic Acid	265
11.	Indole	1
12.	Isobuturic Acid	13
13.	Methional	1
14.	3-Methyl Butanoic Acid	3
15.	Nonanone Acid	5
16.	2-Nonanone	117
17.	Octanoic Acid	90
18.	1-Octen-3-ol	20
19.	2-Oxo-Butanedioic Acid	52
20.	2-Oxo-3-Methyl Pentanoic Acid	18
21.	2-Oxo-4-Methyl Pentanoic Acid	44
22.	2-Oxo-Pentanoic Acid	4
23.	Pentanoic Acid	13
24.	2-Pentanone	10
25.	Pyruvic Acid	21
26.	2-Tridecanone	3
27.	2-Undecanone	10
		1000

CHEESE "ROQUEFORT" TYPE

1.	Ammonium Isovalerianate	20
2.	Butyric Acid	100
3.	Caproic Acid	50

4. Ethyl Butyrate 200
5. Ispvaleric Acid (pure) 100
6. Methyl n Amyl Ketone (free of Fusel) 50
7. Ethyl Alcohol 95% 240
8. Distilled Water 240

1000

CHEESE, SYNTHETIC

1. Caproic Acid 50
2. Butyl Butyryl Lactate 100
3. Butyric Acid 100
4. Ethyl Butyrate 100
5. Isovaleric Acid (pure) 100
6. Methyl n Amyl Ketone (free of fusel) 50
7. Ethyl Alcohol 95% 250
8. Propylene Glycol 250

1000

CHERIMOYA, SYNTHETIC

1. Aldehyde C-10 5
2. Aldehyde C-14 5
3. Ally Caproate 10
4. Amyl Acetate 30
5. Amyl Butyrate 28
6. Benzyl Acetate 50
7. Ethyl Butyrate 30
8. Ethyl Heptylate 20
9. Ethyl Valerianate 20
10. Geraniol 100
11. Isobutyl Butyrate 50
12. Phenyl Ethyl Alcohol 150
13. Vanillin 2
14. Ethyl Alcohol 95% 500

1000

CHERRY "BLACK" "ESSENCE", (NATURAL)

1. Cherries, Bleck (crushed) 100 kg
2. Sugar 5 kg

Let ferment for several days Express the juice Macerate the residue for another 3 days with

3. Ethyl Alcohol 95% 20 1

Express, and add

4. Ethyl Benzoate 2 ml
5. Amyl Formate 3 ml

Distill
Yield 20 liters.

CHERRY BLOSSOM, N0. 1

1. Amyl Acetate 100
2. Amyl Butyrate 50
3. Benzaldehyde 5
4. Cherry Fruit Juice 160
5. Cinnamon Leaf 10
6. Clove, Leaf 10
7. Lemon, Oil 100
8. Neroli, Oil 10
9. Orange, Oil 100
10. Vanillin 5
11. Ethyl Alcohol 95% 225
12. Distilled Water 225

1000

CHERRY BLOSSOM NO. 2

1. Almond, Bitter (cyanide free) 10
2. Amyl Acetate 20
3. Amyl Butyrate 10
4. Benzaldehyde

	(pure, 10% solution)	10
5.	Benzyl Alcohol	40
6.	Cinnamon, Leaf	2
7.	Clove, Leaf	2
8.	Lemon, Oil	2
9.	Orange, Oil	2
10.	Vanillin (10% solution)	10
11.	Ethyl Alcohol 95%	446
12.	Distilled Water	446
		1000

Distilled over 900 cc.

CHERRY BRANDY, NO. 1

1.	Almond, Bitter Oil (cyanidefree)	10
2.	Cherry, Juice	500
3.	Cognac, Oil	50
4.	Ethyl Methylphenylgly cidate	32
5.	Neroli, Oil	6
6.	Pineapple, Juice	50
7.	Raspberry, Juice	250
8.	Rum, Essence	100
9.	Vanillin	2
		1000

Distill Over 900 cc.

CHERRY BRANDY, NO. 2

1.	Almond, Bitter, Oil (cyanidefree)	8
2.	Cherry, Juice	250
3.	Cognac, Oil	26
4.	Ethyl Methylphenylglycidate	26
5.	Neroli, Oil	2
6.	Pineapple, Juice	50
7.	Respberry, Juice	250
8.	Rum, Essence	100
9.	Vanillin	2
10.	Ethyl Alcohol 95%	286
		1000

CHERRY BRANDY, SYNTHETIC

1.	Amyl Methyl Ketone	1
2.	Benzyldehyde (pure)	4
3.	Benzyl Alcohol	50
4.	Benzoic Acid	1
5.	Benzyl Benzoate	8
6.	Cinnamic Aldehyde	1
7.	Ethyl Oenanthate	25
8.	Ethyl Pelargonate	5
9.	Eugenol	1
10.	Isoamyl Alcohol	1
11.	Isoamyl Caprate	1
12.	Linalool	1
13.	Nerolin	1
14.	Vanillin	1
15.	Ethyl Alcohol 95%	450
16.	Distilled Water	449
		1000

CHERRY, IMITATION NO. 1

1.	Almond, Bitter, Oil (cyanidefree)	20
2.	Amyl Formate	10
3.	Cherry, Juice	260
4.	Ethyl Benzoate	10
5.	Ethyl Alcohol 95%	350
6.	Distilled Water	350
		1000

Distill over 900 cc.

CHERRY, IMITATION NO. 2

1.	Almond, Bitter, Oil (cyanide free)	15
2.	Amyl Acetate	15
3.	Amyl Alcohol	10
4.	Amyl Formate	60

5. Benzyl Benzoate 7
6. Cherry, Juice 150
7. Cinnamon, Ceylon Oil 2
8. Clove, Oil 3
9. Cognac, Oil 3
10. Ethyl Acetate 150
11. Ethyl Pelargonate 15
12. Raspberry, Juice 150
13. Ethyl Alcohol 95% 210
14. Distilled Water 210

1000

Distill over 900 cc.

CHERRY, IMITATION NO. 3

1. Almond, Bitter, Oil (cyanide free) 15
2. Amyl Acetate 15
3. Amyl Alcohol 10
4. Amyl Formate 60
5. Benzyl Acetate 150
6. Benzyl Benzoate 7
7. Cherry, Juice 150
8. Cinnamon, Ceylon, Oil 2
9. Clove, Oil 3
10. Cognac, Oil 3
11. Ethyl Acetate 150
12. Raspberry, Juice 150
13. Vanillin 5
14. Ethyl Alcohol 95% 140
15. Distilled Water 140

1000

Distill over 900 cc.

CHERRY, IMITATION NO. 4

1. Almond, Bitter, Oil (cyanide free) 10
2. Amyl Acetate 2
3. Amyl Butyrate 8
4. Cinnamon, Ceylon, Oil 2
5. Clove, Oil 2
6. Lemon, Oil 2
7. Orange, Sweet, Oil 14
8. Ethyl Alcohol 95% 960

1000

CHERRY, IMITATION NO. 5

1. Benzaldehyde (pure, 10% solution) 60
2. Benzyl Benzoate 25
3. Cinnamaldehyde 5
4. Ethyl Acetate (10% solution) 380
5. Ethyl Oenanthate 100
6. Ethyl Pelargonate 15
7. Eugenol 20
8. Isoamyl Alcohol 70
9. Isoamyl Formate (10% solution) 300
10. Vanillin (10% solution) 25

1000

CHERRY, IMITATION NO. 6

1. Benzaldehyde (pure 10% solution) 45
2. Citral 5
3. Ethyl Acetate (10% solution) 600
4. Ethyl Oenanthate 50
5. Isoamyl Butyrate 100
6. Isoamyl Formate 200

1000

CHERRY, IMITATION NO. 7

1. Benzaldehyde (pure, 10% solution) 100
2. Benzyl Benzoate 50

3. Ethyl Acetate (10% solution) 500
4. Ethyl Benzoate (pure 10% solution) 250
5. Ethyl Pelargonate 25
6. Isoamyl Alcohol 50
7. Vanillin (10% solution) 25

1000

CHERRY, IMITATION NO. 8

1. Benzaldehyde (pure, 10% solution) 49
2. Benzyl Benzoate 90
3. Bromelia 1
4. Cinnamaldehyde 20
5. Ethyl Acetate (10% solution) 540
6. Ethyl Oenanthate 180
7. Ethyl Pelargonate 35
8. Eugerol 60
9. Isoamyl Alcohol 15
10. Vanillin 10

1000

CHERRY, IMITATION NO. 9

1. Benzaldehyde (pure, 10% solution) 100
2. Benzoic Acid (1% solution) 100
3. Ethyl Acetate (10% solution) 400
4. Iso.amyl Formate (10% solution) 400

1000

CHERRY, IMITATION NO. 10

1. Benzoic Acid (1% solution) 75
2. Ethyl Acetate (10% solution) 425
3. Ethyl Pelargonate 75
4. Isoamyl Formate (10% solution) 425

1000

CHERRY, IMITATION NO. 11

1. Capraldehyde 5
2. Cinnamaldehyde 55
3. Citral 10
4. Ethyl Acetate (10% solution) 450
5. Eugenol 60
6. Isoamyl Butyrate 100
7. Isoamyl Formate (10% solution) 320

1000

CHERRY, IMITATION NO. 12

1. Benzaldehyde (pure 10% solution) 40
2. Benzoic Acid (1% sil n) 80
3. Ethyl Acetate (10% solution) 400
4. Ethyl Oenanthate 80
5. Isomyl Formate (10% solution) 400

1000

CHERRY, IMITATION NO. 13

1. Benzaldehyde (pure 10% solution) 80
2. Benzyl Alcohol 55
3. Cinnamic Aldehyde 30
4. Ethyl Anthranilate 30
5. Ethyl Caproate 20

6.	Ethyl Caprate	40
7.	Ethyl Phenyl Acetate	190
8.	Geraniol	60
9.	Geranyl Butyrate	20
10.	Heliotropin	50
11.	Isoamyl Acetate	120
12.	Isoamyl Acetate	120
13.	Methyl Acetate	110
14.	Terpinyl Acetate	5
15.	Vanillin (10% solution)	70
		1000

CHERRY, IMITATION NO. 14

1.	Amyl Acetate (10% solution)	300
2.	Benzaldehyde (pure 10% solution)	30
3.	Benzyl Benzoate	100
4.	Cinnamaldehyde	20
5.	Ethyl Acetate	200
6.	Ethyl Oenanthate	200
7.	Ethyl Pelargonate	90
8.	Eugenol	15
9.	Isoamyl Alcohol	15
10.	Isoamyl Butyrate	15
11.	Vanillin (10% solution)	15
		1000

CHERRY, IMITATION NO. 15

1.	Almond Bitter Oil (cyanide free)	100
2.	Amyl Acetate	150
3.	Amyl Butyrate	80
4.	Cinnamon, Ceylon, Oil	20
5.	Clove, Oil	20
6.	Lemon, Oil	20
7.	Orange, Sweet, Oil	10
8.	Ethyl Alcohol 95%	600
		1000

CHERRY, IMITATION NO. 16

1.	Almond, Bitter, Oil (pure)	50
2.	Amyl Formate	5
3.	Cherry Black Essence (Natural)*	500
4.	Ethyl Benzoate	5
5.	Ethyl Alcohol 95%	440
		1000

CHERRY, IMITATION NO. 17

1.	Aldehyde C-20	2
2.	Almond, Bitter, Oil (pure)	15
3.	Amyl Acetate	15
4.	Amyl Alcohol	10
5.	Amyl Formate	6
6.	Cherry "Black" Essence (Natural)*	175
7.	Benzyl Benzoate	7
8.	Cherry "Red" Essence (Natural) "Agriot"*	175
9.	Cinnamon, Oil	2
10.	Clove, Oil	5
11.	Cognac, Oil	3
12.	Ethyl Acetate	15
13.	Ethyl Heptoate	15
14.	Lauri Cerasi, Oil (pure)	10
15.	Vanillin	3
16.	Ethyl Alcohol 95%	542
		1000

CHERRY "RED" ESSENCE (NATURAL) "AGRIOT"

1.	Cherries, Red "Agriot" (crushed)	5 kg
2.	Sugar	5 kg

Let ferment for several days Express the juice Mecerate The

residue for another 3 days with

3. Ethyl Alcohol 95% 20 l

Express and add

4. Amyl Formate 4 ml
5. Cognac, Oil 4 ml
6. Ethyl Benzoate 2 ml

Distill
Yield 20 liters

CHERRY, SYNTHETIC NO. 1

1. Ethyl Acetate 50
2. Ethyl Benzoate 50
3. Ethyl Oenanthate 10
4. Glycerin (neutral) 30
5. Succinic Acid 10
6. Tartaric Acid 1
7. Ethyl Alcohol 95% 849

1000

CHERRY, SYNTHETIC NO.2

1. Almond, Bitter, Oil (pure) 30
2. Amyl Acetate 15
3. Chloroform 75
4. Ethyl Acetate 225
5. Ethyl Benzoate 225
6. Ethyl Alcohol 95% 430

1000

CHERRY, STNTHETIC NO. 3

1. Aldehyde C-16 10
2. Benzoic Acid 10
3. Ethyl Acetate 50
4. Ethyl Benzoate 50
5. Ethyl Oenanthate 10
6. Glycerin (natural) 30
7. Ethyl Alcohol 95% 840

1000

CHERRY, SYNTHETIC NO. 4

1. Aldehyde C-16 15
2. Benzoic Acid 10
3. Ethyl Acetate 45
4. Ethyl Benzoate 50
5. Ethyl Oenanthate 10
6. Glycerin (natural) 30
7. Alcohol 95% 840

1000

CHERRY, SYNTHETIC NO. 5

1. Amyl Formate 10
2. Benzaldehyde (pure) 1
3. Benzoic Acid 1
4. Clove, Oil 1
5. Ethyl Acetate 30
6. Ethyl Benzoate 15
7. Ethyl Cinnamate 1
8. Ethyl Oenanthate 8
9. Ethyl Pelargonate 2
10. Glycerin (natural) 9
11. Ethyl Alcohol 95% 922

1000

CHERRY, SYNTHETIC NO.6

1. Aldehyde C-16 3
2. Almond, Bitter, Oil (pure) 2
3. Amyl Acetate 20
4. Amyl Benzoate 10
5. Amyl Formate 2
6. Benzaldehyde (pure) 15
7. Benzyl Formate 2
8. Benzyl Propionate 2
9. Cassia, Oil 2

10. Cinnamon, Oil 1
11. Clove, Oil 4
12. Ethyl Acetate 8
13. Ethyl Benzoate 1
14. Ethyl Oenanthate 5
15. Lemon,Oil 2
16. Orange, Sweet, Oil 1
17. Phenyl Ethyl Cinnamate 5
18. Phenyl Ethyl Phenyl Acetate 4
19. Vanilla, Oil 1
20. Vanillin 1
21. Ethyl Alcohol 95% 909

1000

CHERRY, SYNTHETIC NO. 7

1. Aldehyde C-16 2
2. Almond, Bitter, Oil (pure) 50
3. Amyl Formate 5
4. Anisaldehyde 1
5. Ethyl Acetate 25
6. Ethyl Benzoate 25
7. Vanillin 1
8. Ethyl Alcohol 95% 891

1000

CHERRY, SYNTHETIC NO. 8

1. Benzaldehyde (pure) 2
2. Benzoic Acid 1
3. Benzyl Benzoate 1
4. Capraldehyde 1
5. Cinnamic Aldehyde 1
6. Citral 1
7. Ethyl Acetate 4
8. Ethyl Benzoate 3
9. Ethyl Oenanthate 3
10. Ethyl Pelargonate 3
11. Eugenol 1
12. Isoamyl Alcohol 1
13. Isoamyl Butyrate 4
14. Isoamyl Formate 5
15. Vanillin 1
16. Ethyl Alcohol 95% 473
17. Distilled Water 473

1000

CHERRY, SYNTHETIC NO. 9

1. Amyl Methyl Ketone 1
2. Benzoic Acid 1
3. Ethyl Acetate 43
4. Ethyl Benzoate 22
5. Isoamyl Butyrate 17
6. Isoamyl Valerianate 6
7. Ethyl Alcohol 95% 455
8. Distilled Water 455

1000

CHERRY "WILD," AGRIOT SYNTHETIC

1. Benzaldehyde (pure) 20
2. Benzoic Acid 2
3. Ethyl Acetate 10
4. Ethyl Benzoate 5
5. Ethyl Oenanthate 5
6. Tartaric Acid 3
7. Ethyl Alcohol 95% 955

1000

CHERVIL, ESSENCE (NATURAL)

1. Chervil 2 kg

Cut up small and add:

2. Ethyl Alcohol 95% 4 l

Macerate for 3 days Express the juice. To the residue add:

3. Ethyl Alcohol 95% 4 l

Macerate for another 3 days Distill altogether

Yield 10 Liters

CHOCOLATE, ESSENCE (FOR PRALINE LIQUEUR)

1.	Cacao (Brown)	498
2.	Cardamom Tincture	125
3.	Clove, Tincture	125
4.	Cinnamon Tincture	250
5.	Vanillin	2
		1000

CHOCOLATE, FLAVOUR (NATURAL)

1.	Amyl Phenyl Acetate	117
2.	Benzyl Butyrate	12
3.	Cocoa	500
4.	Propylene Glycol	300
5.	Vanillin	60
6.	Veratraldehyde	11
		1000

CHOCOLATE, HARDENER

1.	Albumin (Eggs) (10% solution)	100
2.	Arabic Gum (10% solution)	100
3.	Flour (10% solution)	100
4.	Gelatin (10% solution)	100
5.	Gluten (10% solution)	100
6.	Pectin (Apple Lemon Orange) (10% solution)	300
7.	Malt Dry	100
8.	Starch, Gum (Dextrin)	100
		1000

CHYPRE, BASE FOR BOUQUET

(Aroma of wine and liquor)

1.	Alcohol C-8	2
2.	Alcohol C-9	1
3.	Alcohol C-10	2
4.	Aldehyde C-8	2
5.	Aldehyde C-9	1
6.	Aldehyde C-10	1
7.	Aldehyde C-12	1
8.	Aldehyde C-16	2
9.	Amber, Tincture	200
10.	Musk Ambrette, Tincture	200
11.	Rose, Oil	2
12.	Tonka Beans, Tincture	200
13.	Vanilla, Tincture	200
14.	Ethyl Alcohol 95%	186
		1000

CINNAMON, IMITATION

1.	Aldehyde C-9	2
2.	Benzaldehyde (pure)	1
3.	Caryophyllene	5
4.	Cinnamic Aldehyde	20
5.	Cuminic Aldehyde	2
6.	Eugenol	5
7.	Isoeugenol	5
8.	Linalool	20
9.	Methyl Amyl Ketone	1
10.	Methyl Isoeugenol	1
11.	Phellandrene	2

12.	Ethyl Alcohol 95%	468
13.	Phenyl Propyl Aldehyde	1
14.	Distilled Water	467
		1000

CITRUS FRUITS, EXTRACT FROM PEELS

1.	Citrus Fruit, Peels from fresh lemon, lime, orange or tangerine	10 kg
2.	Ethyl Alcohol 95%	20 l

Macerate for 3 days Express To the residus add:

3.	Distilled Water	20 l

Distill to separate the terpenes. Redistill altogether with the expressed juice.

Yield 30 liters.

CLOVE

1.	Clove, Oil	750
2.	Caryophyllene	32
3.	Eugenol	174
4.	Eugenyl Acetate	24
5.	Methyl Eugenol	20
		1000

COCA, FLAVOUR

1.	Coca, Tincture	300
2.	Lemon, Oil	40
3.	Orange (Bitter), Oil	15
4.	Tonka Beans, Tincture	50
5.	Vanilla, Tincture	100
6.	Ethyl Alcohol 95%	495
		1000

COCOA, ESSENCE (NATURAL)

1.	Cacoa Beans (roasted and powdered)	300 g
2.	Vanilla, Beans	4
3.	Ethyl Alcohol 95%	1500 ml

Macerate for 3 days

4.	Distilled Water	200 ml

Distill.

COFFEE, EXTRACT (NATURAL) NO. 1, BROWN

1.	Coffee (freshly roasted)	5 kg
2.	Arrack (pure)	3 l
3.	Distilled Water	9 l

Macerate for 1 day Percolate.

4.	Ethyl Alcohol 95%	2 l
5.	Distilled Water	2 l

Percolate.
Yield: 15 liters.

Note: The residue of the percolate can be added as a menstruum to further preparation.

COFFEE, EXTRACT (NATURAL) NO.2, COLOURLESS

1.	Coffee (freshly roasted)	10 kg
2.	Ethyl Alcohol 95%	4 l
3.	Distilled Water	10 l

Macerate for 1 day.

4. Vanillin 10 g

Distill slowly.
Yield 10 liters.

COFFEE, EXTRACT (NATURAL) NO.3, BROWN

1. Coffee, Brown (freshly roasted) 5 kg
2. Ethyl Alcohol 95% 5 l
3. Distilled Water 5 l

Let stand 1 day.Percolate 10 l. Add:

4. Arrack (pure) 1500 ml
5. Cinnamon, Tincture 150 ml
6. Mace, Tincture 150 ml
7. Wine, Brandy (pure) 1000 ml

COFFEE, EXTRACT (NATURAL) NO. 4, COLOURLESS

1. Coffee, Extract (Natural) No. 1 Brown* 5 l
2. Ethyl Alcohol 95% 3 l
3. Distilled Water 3 l

Distill
Yield 5 liters

COFFEE, IMITATION NO. 1

1. Benzyl Acetate 60
2. Bromelia 1
3. Citral 10
4. Ethyl Acetate (10% solution) 360
5. Ethyl Oenanthate 4
6. Ethyl Formate 180
7. Ethyl Pelargonate 85
8. Isoamyl Acetate (10% solution) 280
9. Vanillin (10% solution) 20

1000

COFFEE, IMITATION NO. 2

1. Benzyl Benzoate 130
2. Bromelia 1
3. Citral 10
4. Ethyl Acetate (10% solution) 340
5. Ethyl Oenanthate 9
6. Ethyl Formate (10% solution) 340
7. Ethyl Pelargonate 170

1000

COFFEE, IMITATION NO. 3

1. Benzyl Benzoate 60
2. Bromelia 1
3. Citral 5
4. Ethyl Acetate (10% solution) 320
5. Ethyl Oenanthate 9
6. Ethyl Formate 200
7. Ethyl Pelargonate 100
8. Isoamyl Acetate (10% solution) 300
9. Vanillin (10% solution) 5

1000

COFFEE, SYNTHETIC

1. Benzyl Acetate 13
2. Benzyl Benzoate 14
3. Citral 2
4. Diacetyl 1
5. Ethyl Acetate 4
6. Ethyl Formate 6
7. Ethyl Oenanthate 2

8.	Ethyl Pelargonate	11
9.	Isoamyl Acetate	9
10.	Nerolin	1
11.	Propyl Oenanthate	1
12.	Vanillin	2
13.	Ethyl Alcohol 95%	467
14.	Distilled Water	467
		1000

COGNAC, BASE, SYNTHETIC

1.	Cognac, Oil	10
2.	Ethyl Caprate	10
3.	Ethyl Caproate	10
4.	Ethyl Caprylate	10
5.	Ethyl Oenanthate	10
6.	Ethyl Alcohol 95%	475
7.	Distilled Water	475
		1000

COGNAC, IMITATION NO. 1

1.	Almond Shales (broken)	83
2.	Cognac, White, Oil	22
3.	Ethyl Oenanthate	2
4.	Licorice (sticky)	2
5.	Orris Root (granulated)	16
6.	Peach Kernels (broken)	37
7.	Plums (dried)	66
8.	Raisins Blue (dried)	66
9.	Ethyl Alcohol 95%	353
10.	Distilled Water	353
		1000

Macerate for 24 h. Filter.

COGNAC, IMITATION NO. 2

1.	Benzaldehyde (pure)	1
2.	Amyl Acetate	10
3.	Amyl Butyrate	20
4.	Cognac, White, Oil	7
5.	Ethyl Acetate	11
6.	Ethyl Oenanthate	4
7.	Ethyl Pelargonate	20
8.	Neroli, Oil	1
9.	Petitgrain	10
10.	Vanillin	1
11.	Ethyl Alcohol 95%	458
12.	Distilled Water	457
		1000

COGNAC, IMITATION NO. 3

1.	Aldehyde C-20	30
2.	Amyl Butyrate	120
3.	Cardamom Oil	60
4.	Ethyl Acetate	60
5.	Ethyl Oenanthate	40
6.	Ethyl Pelargonate	50
7.	Mace, Oil	120
8.	Methyl Alcohol 95%	250
9.	Ethyl Salicylate	20
10.	Distilled Water	250
		1000

COGNAC, IMITATION NO. 4

1.	Acetaldehyde	30
2.	Almond, Oil (pure)	5
3.	Amyl Isobutyrate	30
4.	Cinnamon, Oil	5
5.	Cinnamyl Butyrate	10
6.	Cinnamyl Propionate	10
7.	Cognac, Oil	125
8.	Ethyl Acetate (10% solution)	500
9.	Ethyl Butyrate	20
10.	Fusel, Oil	50
11.	Heliotropin	5
12.	Methyl Eugenol	20
13.	Neroli, Oil	100
14.	Pelargonic Aldehyde	30

15.	Vanillin (10% solution)	60
		1000

COGNAC, IMITATION NO. 5

1.	Aldehyde C-20 (10% solution)	60
2.	Amyl Butyrate	180
3.	Cardamom, Oil	80
4.	Ethyl Acetate	90
5.	Ethyl Oenanthate (10% solution)	500
6.	Ethyl Pelargonate	60
7.	Methyl Salicylate (10% solution)	30
		1000

COGNAC, IMITATION NO. 5

1.	Almond, Barks (broken)	250
2.	Cognac, Oil	15
3.	Orris, Root (granulated)	5
4.	Licorice, Stick	5
5.	Peach, Kernels (broken)	100
6.	Plums (dried)	200
7.	Raisin (dried)	200
8.	Sassafras, Wood	225
		1000

Macerate for 24 h. Pour off the juice and filter.

COGNAC, IMITATION NO. 6

1.	Almond, Barks (broken)	24
2.	Cognac, Oil	2
3.	Licorice, Stick	1
4.	Orris, Root (granulated)	1
5.	Peach, Kernels (broken)	10
6.	Plums (dried)	20
7.	Raisin (dried)	20
8.	Sassafras, Wood	2
9.	Ethyl Alcohol 95%	460
10.	Distilled Water	460
		1000

Macerate for 24 h. Pour off the juice and filter.

COGNAC, IMITATION NO. 7

1.	Ethyl Caprate	10
2.	Ethyl Caproate	10
3.	Ethyl Caprylate	10
4.	Ethyl Oenanthate	10
5.	Ethyl Alcohol 95%	960
		1000

COLA, IMITATION NO.1 (SYRUP)

1.	Bergamot, Oil	25
2.	Cola Nuts, Tincture	400
3.	Orange Bitter, Oil	275
4.	Orange Sweet, Oil	275
5.	Tonka Beans, Tincture	100
6.	Vanilla Beans, Tincture	100
		1000

COLA, IMITATION NO. 2 (SYRUP)

1.	Acetic Acid, Glacial 99%	14
2.	Caffeine (powder)	55
3.	Cinnamon, Oil	2
4.	Citric Acid	28
5.	Clove, Oil	1
6.	Cola Tincture	22
7.	Glycerin (neutral)	110
8.	Lemon, Oil	8

9.	Lime, Oil	7
10.	Neroli, Oil	1
11.	Nutmeg, Oil	2
12.	Orange, Oil	78
13.	Patchouli, Oil	22
14.	Vanillin	1
15.	Ethyl Alcohol 95%	360
16.	Distilled Water	360
		1000

* Formulas which appear in this book

Dissolve caffeine in 722 g boiling water. Add 28 g citric acid. Add phosphoric acid syrup. Add glacial acetic acid. Add cola tincture. Dissolve vanillin and all the essential oils. Blend all with stirring. Let stand for 48 h stirring four times every 12 h. Let stand for another 48 h without any agitation. Separate the resins at the bottom. Separate the terpenes at the surface. Separate the clear middle portion siphoning with a rubber tube. Filter all cloudy parts of the bottom with filter paper. Place the oily upper portion in a narrow small container and siphon off the clear portion. Add to the other clear portion and shake well.

Use 35 ml of this extract and 15 ml of liquid caramel to make a finished syrup. Prepare a simple syrup by mixing 3 kg of sugar 700 ml of distilled water and 50 ml of this syrup to make a gallon of imitation cola syrup. Concentration: 30 ml/gal.

COLA, TINCTURE

1.	Cola Nuts (roasted)	10 kg
2.	Ethyl Alcohol 95%	5 1
3.	Distilled Water	5 1

Macerate for 1 week. Filter.

Yield 10 liters.

CORIANDER, IMITATION NO. 1

1.	Camphene	140
2.	Guaiacwood, Oil	20
3.	Limonene	100
4.	Linalool	40
5.	Pinene	150
6.	Terpineol	140
		1000

CORIANDER, IMITATION NO.2

1.	Coriander, Imitation No. 1*	800
2.	Coriander, Oil	200
		1000

CRANBERRY

1.	Benzyl Acetate	30
2.	Ethyl Acetate (10% solution)	360
3.	Ethyl Benzoate	90
4.	Ethyl Isovalerate	185
5.	Isoamyl Acetate	130
6.	Isoamyl Butyrate	170
7.	Linalool	10
8.	Methyl Salicylate	5
9.	Vanillin (10% solution)	20
		1000

CRANBERRY, SYNTHETIC

1.	Benzyl Acetate	3
2.	Ethyl Acetate	36
3.	Ethyl Benzoate	6
4.	Ethyl Isovalerianate	18
5.	Isoamyl Acetate	13
6.	Isoamyl Butyrate	17
7.	Linalool	1
8.	Methyl Salicylate	1
9.	Vanillin	2
10.	Ethyl Alcohol 95%	450
11.	Distilled Water	450
		1000

CREAM PASTE

1.	Corn Syrup	4 l
2.	Gelatin	60 g
3.	Sugar (fine)	10 kg

CRYSTAL BEVERAGES

1.	Any Flavour from Ethyl Alcohol Extraction	50 ml
2.	Ascorbic Acid	20 g
3.	Citric Acid	70g
4.	Dextrose	200 g
5.	Sodium Citrate	10 g
6.	Sugar	650 g

Preservative:
Sodium benzoate or
Sodium benzoate 10%
(90% distilled water,
10% sodium benzoate) 0.1%

Uses: 100 g of crystals in One Litre distilled water.

CUCUMBER, EXTRACT (NATURAL)

1.	Acetate C-8	1
2.	Citral	1
3.	Cucumber, Juice	97
4.	Methyl Heptyne Carbonate	1
5.	Ethyl Alcohol 95%	450
6.	Distilled Water	450
		1000

Express Filter.

CUCUMBER "MILK" (FOR COSMETICS)

1.	Cucumber Juice	150
2.	Olive, Oil	150
3.	Soap (White)	150
4.	Spermaceti (sperm whale)	150
5.	Wax (Beeswax or Lanolin)	150
6.	Ethyl Alcohol 95%	250
		1000

CULINARY, EXTRACT (NATURAL)

1. Allspice
2. Anise
3. Asparagus
4. Calamus
5. Caper
6. Capsicum
7. Caraway
8. Cardamom
9. Carrot
10. Champignon
11. Chervil
12. Chives
13. Cinnamon
14. Clove

15. Coriander
16. Cumin
17. Curcuma
18. Dill
19. Fennel
20. Garlic
21. Ginger
22. Horseradish
23. Juniper Berries
24. Laurel Leaves
25. Leek
26. Mace
27. Marjoram
28. Morel
29. Mushroom
30. Mustard
31. Nutmeg
32. Onion
33. Parsley
34. Pepper
35. Pimenta
36. Saffron
37. Sage
38. Savory
39. Shallot
40. Tarragon
41. Thyme
42. Truffle

For each listed product separately dry and cut in very small pieces. Roast slowly and gently stir untill each reaches a brownish color. To the weight of each add 50% ethyl alcohol 95% and 50% distilled water. Let stand for 1 week stirring every day for 1 h. Filter. Reuse the residue the residus for another three times adding 50% ethyl alcohol 95% and 50% distilled water each time Combine the extract and filter.

CURACAO, IMITATION NO. 1 LIQUOR BASE

1.	Almond, Bitter, Oil (cyanide free	2
2	Anise, Oil	1
3.	Cardamon, Oil	1
4.	Cinnamon, Oil	1
5.	Curacao, Oil	830
6.	Lemon, Oil	5
7.	Mace, Oil	2
8.	Neroli, Oil	2
9	Orange, Bitter, Oil	156
		1000

25 cc of formula dissolved in ethyl alcohol 95% is sufficient for 100 1 of liquor.

* Formulas which appear in this book

CURACAO, IMITATION NO. 2, LIQUOR BASE

1.	Curacao, Imitation No. 1*	50
2.	Curacao, Oil	900
3.	Orange, Bitter, Oil	50
		1000

25 cc of formula dissolved in ethyl alcohol 95% is sufficient for 100 l of liquor.

CURACAO, IMITATION NO. 3, LIQUOR BASE

1.	Almond, Bitter, Oil (cyanide free)	4
2.	Badian, Oil (terpenaless)	2

3. Cinnamon, Oil (terpeneless) 2
4. Curacao, Oil (terpeneless) 500
5. Lemon, Oil (terpeneless) 15
6. Mace, Oil (terpeneless) 2
7. Neroli, Oil 5
8. Orange, Bitter, Oil (terpeneless) 150
9. Ethyl Alcohol 95% 320

1000

25 cc of formula dissolved in ethyl alcohol 95% is sufficient for 100 1 of liquor.

CURACAO, IMITATION NO. 4, LIQUOR BASE

1. Curacao, Imitaiton No. 1* 333
2. Curacao, Imitation No. 2* 333
3. Curacao, Imitation No. 3* 334

1000

25 cc of formula dissolved in ethyl alcohol 95% is sufficient for 100 1 of liquor .

CURACAO, IMITATION NO. 5, LIQUOR BASE

1. Cinnamon, Oil 350
2. Coriander, Oil 100
3. Ginger, Oil 150
4. Lemon, Oil (terpeneless) 148
5. Neroli, Oil 1
6. Orange, Oil (terpeneless) 250
7. Rose, Oil 1

1000

25 cc formula dissolved in ethyl alcohol 95% is sufficient for 100 1 of liquor.

CURACAO, IMITATION NO. 6

1. Cinnamon 320
2. Coriander, Oil 80
3. Ginger, Oil 120
4. Lemon, Oil 140
5. Neroli, Oil 1
6. Orange, Oil 338
7. Rose, Oil 1

1000

CURRANT, EXTRACT (NATURAL) NO. 1

1. Currant (Black) Berries 50 kg
2. Currand (Red), Berries 50 kg
3. Sugar 10 kg

Ferment for 1 week or more untill flavour is totally develoved Add:

4. Ethyl Alcohol 95% 50 l

Distill

Yield 60 liters

CURRANT, EXTRACT (NATURAL) NO. 2

1. Currant (Black), Berries 50 kg
2. Currant (Red), Berries 50 kg
3. Sugar 10 kg

Ferment for 1 week or more untill flavour is totally develoved Express. To the residue add:

4. Currant Extract (Natural) No. 1* 50 l

Let macerate for another week Add:

* Formulas which appear in this book

5. Anisaldehyde 12 ml
6. Ethyl Acetate 22 ml
7. Ethyl Benzoate 24 ml
8. Ethyl Pelargonate 12 ml

Distill altogether.

Yield 60 liters

CURRANT, IMITATION NO. 1

1. Black Currant, Fresh Leaves 75
2. Black Currant 500
3. Ethyl Alcohol 95% 425

Macerate, moderately warm, for 6 days Shake often. Distill Add:

4. Distilled Water 875

Distill over 1000 cc. Redistill for above 750 cc.

CURRANT, IMITATION NO. 2

1. Bilberry, Imitation No. 1* 175
2. Currant, Imitation No. 1* 300
3. Ethyl Methylphenylglycidate22
4. Pineapple, Imitation No. 1* 15
5. Raspberry, Imitation No. 1* 60
6. Raspberry, Imitation No. 2* 12
7. Ethyl Alcohol 95% 208
8. Distilled Water 208

1000

CURRANT, IMITATION NO. 3

1. Currant, Imitation No. 1* 500
2. Currant, Imitation No. 2* 500

1000

CURRANT, IMITATION NO. 4

1. Currant, Imitation No. 3* 250
2. Raspberry, Imitation No. 3*250
3. Ethyl Alcohol 95% 250
4. Distilled Water 250

1000

CURRANT, IMITATION NO. 5

1. Amyl Butyrate 9
2. Benzyl Acetate 1
3. Cinnmon, Ceylon, Oil 2
4. Ethyl Acetate 5
5. Isoamyl Acetate 7
6. Lemon, Oil 5
7. Orange, Sweet, Oil 5
8. Orris, Liquid 2
9. Petitgrain, Oil 2
10. Rose, Oil 1
11. Vanillin 1
12. Ethyl Alcohol 95% 480
13. Distilled Water 480

1000

CURRANT, IMITATION NO. 6

1. Aldehyde C-8 1

2. Aldehyde C-16 1
3. Benzyl Acetate 4
4. Benzyl Phenyl Acetate 1
5. Clove, Tincture 5
6. Currant, Extract (Natural) No. 2* 463
7. Ethyl Benzoate 10
8. Ethyl Butyrate 20
9. Ethyl Oenanthate 10
10. Orange, Oil 5
11. Orris Root, Tincture 2
12. Petitgrain, Oil 1
13. Vanillin Beans, Tincture 5
14. Ethyl Alcohol 95% 472

1000

CURRANT, SYNTHETIC NO. 1

1. Ethyl Acetate (10% solution) 275
2. Ethyl Benzoate 60
3. Ethyl Butyrate 60
4. Ethyl Formate 60
5. Ethyl Oenanthate 60
6. Ethyl Sebacate 60
7. Isoamyl Acetate 60
8. Isoamyl Butyrate 60
9. Methyl Salicylate (10% solution) 60
10. Tartaric Acid (10% solution) 245

1000

CURRANT, SYNTHETIC NO. 2

1. Ethyl Acetate (10% solution) 930
2. Ethyl Benzoate 25
3. Isoamyl Acetate 10
4. Propyl Acetate 10
5. Propyl Propionate 25

1000

CURRANT, SYNTHETIC NO. 3

1. Ethyl Isovalerate (10% solution) 500
2. Ethyl Myristate 5
3. Ethyl Phenyl Acetate 5
4. Linalool 60
5. Methyl Cinnamate (10% solution) 400
6. Methyl Heptenone 10
7. Vanillin (10% solution) 20

1000

CURRANT, SYNTHETIC NO. 4

1. Aldehyde C-16 1
2. Benzoic Acid 1
3. Cyclohexyl Butyrate 10
4. Cyclohexyl Isovalerianate 18
5. Ethyl Acetate 10
6. Ethyl Benzoate 30
7. Ethyl Butyrate 2
8. Ethyl Formate 2
9. Ethyl Myristate 1
10. Ethyl Oenanthate 4
11. Ethyl Sebacate 1
12. Ethyl Acetate 2
13. Isoamyl Butyrate 1
14. Linalool 2
15. Methyl Cinnamate 8
16. Methyl Heptenone 1
17. Methyl Salicylate 1
18. Propyl Acetate 1
19. Propyl Propionate 1
20. Succinic Acid 1
21. Tartaric Acid 1
22. Vanillin 1
23. Ethyl Alcohol 95% 450
24. Distilled Water 450

1000

CURRANT, SYNTHETIC NO. 6

1.	Ethyl Acetate (10% solution)	350
2.	Ethyl Benzoate	70
3.	Ethyl Butyrate	70
4.	Ethyl Formate	70
5.	Ethyl Oenanthate	70
6.	Isoamyl Acetate	70
7.	Tartaric Acid (10% solution)	300
		1000

DATE, EXTRACT (NATURAL)

1.	Dates (dried and chopped)	10 kg
2.	Alcohol 95%	20 l

Macerate for 3 days. Add:

3.	Distilled Water	20 l

Distill. To the residue add:

4.	Ethyl Alcohol 95%	20 l

Macerate for another 3 days. Add:

5.	Ethyl Acetate	60 ml

* Formulas which appear in this book

Distill altogether.
Yield 60 liters.

DATE, IMITATION NO.1

1.	Amyl Acetate	75
2.	Amyl Butyrate	2
3.	Amyl Valerianate	150
4.	Cinnamon Oil	3
5.	Ethyl Acetate	75
6.	Ethyl Benzoate	150
7.	Eugenol	2
8.	Honey, Imitation No. 1*	20
9.	Nerolin	5
10.	Peach, Imitation No. 1*	6
11.	Ethyl Alcohol 95%	256
12.	Distilled Water	256
		1000

DATE, IMITATION NO.2

1.	Bromelia	15
2.	Cinnamaldehyde	10
3.	Ethyl Acetate (10% solution)	350
4.	Ethyl Butyrate	150
5.	Eugenol	5
6.	Isoamyl Acetate (10% solution)	250
7.	Isoamyl Butyrate	50
8.	Isoamyl Isovalerate	150
9.	Isoamyl Acetate	5
10.	y-Undecalactone (10% solution)	15
		1000

DATE, SYNTHETIC

1.	Aldehyde C-14	2
2.	Cinnamaldehyde	2
3.	Ethyl Acetate	30
4.	Ethyl Benzoate	3
5.	Ethyl Butyrate	6
6.	Eugenol	1
7.	Isoamyl Acetate	25
8.	Isoamyl Butyrate	15
9.	Isoamyl Isovalerianate	15
10.	Nerolin	1
11.	Ethyl Alcohol 95%	450

12. Distilled Water 450

1000

FERNET "BRANCA" ESSENCE

1.	Angelic, Root	110
2.	Calamus, Root	135
3.	Calisaya, Bark	70
4.	Cardamom, Seeds	15
5.	Curacao, Peels	70
6.	Gentian, Root	210
7.	Iva, Herb	55
8.	Lemon, Peels	40
9.	Orange, Bitter, Peels	160
10.	Wormwood, Herb	135
		1000

Powder each ingredient and then roast to a brownish colour. Macerate altogether for 1 week with .

11.	Ethyl Alcohol 95%	1000
12.	Distilled Water	1000

Filter and to the residue add:

13.	Ethyl Alcohol 95%	1000
14.	Distilled Water	1000

Macerate again for another week. Filter. Distill altogether

Yield 4 liters
Concentration. 60 ml/gal

FIG, ESSENCE (NATURAL)

1.	Figs, Chopped	10 kg
2.	Alcohol 95%	20 kg

Macerate for 3 days. Add:

3.	Distilled Water	20 kg

Express.To the residue add:

4.	Ethyl Alcohol 95%	20 kg

Macerate for another 3 days Add:

5.	Ethyl Acetate	60 ml

Distill altogether
Yield 60 liters.

FISH, ODOUR (NATURAL)

1.	Fish, Fresh and Chopped	1 kg
2.	Propylene Glycol	2 1
3.	Distilled Water	1 1
4.	Ethyl Alcohol 95%	2 1

Express and filter

FONDANT-ORGEAT-PRALINE

Fondant-----A soft creamy compound of sugar, water, and flavorings, used as a basis for cadies or icing.

Orgeat-----From the French word "orge" meaning "barley," a sweet almond flavored, nonalcoholic syrup used as a cocktail ingredient or food flavoring.

Praline------Generally a confection of nut kernels, especially almonds roasted in boiling sugar untill brown and crispy; a patty of creamybrown sugar and pecan meats.

1.	Benzaldehyde (pure)	2
2.	Cherry Laurel Water (pure)	50
3.	Condensed Milk	825
4.	Fruit Essence (any type)	100
5.	Rose, Water	15
6.	Vanillin	2
7.	Ethyl Alcohol 95%	6
		1000

Note: Minimal amount of alcohol in fondants.

FORTIFIED EXTRACTS FROM VEGETABLES

1.	Any vegetable (crushed in small pieces)	10 kg
2.	Ethyl Alcohol 95%	20 l
3.	Distilled Water	20 l

Macerate for 1 week-Express To the 40 1 of expressed juice add:

4.	Anise, Oil	5 ml
5.	Calamus, Oil	5 ml
6.	Cardamom, Oil	5 ml
7.	Ginger, Oil	5 ml
8.	Juniper Berries, Oil	5 ml
9.	Mece, Oil	5 ml
10.	Nutmeg, Oil	5 ml
11.	Pepper (Black or White), Oil	5 ml

Stir and filter.

FRUIT EXTRACT, NATURAL FLAVOUR

Base:

1.	Ethyl Alcohol 95%	70
2.	Glycerin (neutral)	5
3.	Distilled Water	25

1.	Fresh Fruit Juice (any single)	4 l
2.	Base	4 l
3.	Ethyl Alcohol 95%	2 l

Stir. Filter
Yield: 10 liters.

FRUIT SODA

1.	Champagne Cedar Essence	125
2.	Cherry, Imitation No. 1*	175
3.	Grenadine, Imitation No. 1*	175
4.	Pineapple, Imitation No. 1*	175
5.	Raspberry, Imitation No. 1*	175
6.	Strawberry, Imitation No. 1*	175
		1000

FUNGI EXTRACT (NATURAL)

1.	Dried Fungi (Champignons, Morels, Mushrooms, or Truffles, single type)	1
2.	Ethyl Alcohol 95%	1
3.	Distilled Water	1

Macerate for 1 week. Separate the liquid without pressure. To the residue add:

4.	Distilled Water	1
		1000

* Formulas which appear in this book

Let stand for another day Express Blend the two liquids and filter.

Yield 3 liters

GARLIC, EXTRACT (NATURAL)

Use garlic, well peeled and finely cut. Press well. Discard the juice (no value).

1.	Garlic	1 kg
2.	Ethyl Alcohol 95%	4 l

Let stand for 3 days. Express. To the residue add:

3.	Ethyl Alcohol 95%	2 l
4.	Distilled Water	2 l

Let stand for another 3 days Express. Put the liquid together. Add:

5.	Mustard Oil	16 ml

Filter

Yield 8 Liters

GIN, IMITATION

1.	Angelic, Root, Oil	8
2.	Anise, Oil	4
3.	Coriander, Oil	12
4.	Juniper, Oil	930
5.	Lemon, Oil	30
6.	Orange, Oil	16
		1000

GINGER, ESSENCE (NATURAL)

1.	Cinnamon, Oil	60
2.	Clove, Oil	40
3.	Ginger, Oil	850
4.	Lemon, Oil	50
		1000

GINGER, EXTRACT (NATURAL) "GINGERINE"

1.	Ginger Roots (unpeeled)	10 kg

(Previously washed in 12 1 of water and 1 kg of sodium bicarbonate. Discard dirty water after 1 day wash the roots again 3 times.)

2.	Ethyl Alcohol 95%	10 l

Let stand for another 3 days Percolate Add to the residue (roots)

3.	Ethyl Alcohol 95%	4 l
4.	Distilled Water	4 l

Let stand for another 3 days Percolate. Put together the two percolates Distill.

Yield 18 liters.

GINGER, IMITATION NO. 1

1.	Amyl Butyrate	250
2.	Cardamom, Oil	12
3.	Clove, Oil	10
4.	Ethyl Acetate	350
5.	Ethyl Oenanthate	150
6.	Galange, Oil	16

7.	Ginger, Oil	200
8.	Petitgrain, Oil	12
		1000

GINGER, IMITATION NO. 2

1.	Ginger, Oil	700
2.	Lemon, Oil	25
3.	Orange, Oil	50
4.	Lemon, Oil Imitation No.1*	225
		1000

GINGER, IMITATION NO. 3

1.	Cinnamon, Oil	60
2.	Clove, Oil	40
3.	Ginger, Oil	850
4.	Lemon, Oil (terpeneless)	50
		1000

GINGER, IMITATION NO. 4

1.	Camphene	50
2.	Ginger, Imitation No. 1*	300
3.	Methylheptenone	100
4.	Phellandrene	200
5.	Pinene, Imitation No. 1*	100
6.	Terpineol	250
		1000

GINGER, IMITATION NO. 5

1.	Ginger, Imitation No. 1*	400
2.	Ginger, Imitation No. 2*	400
3.	Ginger, Oil	200
		1000

GINGER GRASS (PALMAROSA)

1.	Clove, Oil (10% solution)	500
2.	Geraniol	300
3.	Geranium, Palmarosa	200
		1000

GIROFLE (CLOVE), TINCTURE

1.	Eugenol	90
2.	Ethyl Alcohol 95%	910
		1000

GLACE CAKE MIX

(Candied for fruit cakes and desserts encrusted or coated with sugar or baked with sugar or syrup intill translucent)

(1). Drained Fruits

1. Cherries, Creshed
2. Grapefruits, Peels
3. Lemon, Peels
4. Orange, Peels
5. Pineapples, Pulp (cut) (Ananas)
6. Any Other Fruits

(2). Syrup

1. Corn Syrup
2. Sugar Syrup

(3). Preservatives

1. Citric Acid (1% solution)
2. Sodium Benzoate (1% solution)

3. Sulfur Dioxide (trace)

. Synthetic Flavour
. Colour FD&C Yellow No. 5

GOOSEBERRY, EXTRACT (NATURAL)

. Gooseberries, Red or Yellow (not green) 10 kg

Express the juice (7kg). To he residue (3kg) add:

2. Ethyl Alcohol 95% 3 l

Macerate for 3 days. Express Mix all juice and add:

3. Amyl Acetate 25 ml
4. Ethyl Acetate 25 ml
5. Ethyl Butyrate 45 ml

Filter.
Yield 10 liters

GOOSEBERRY, IMITATION NO.1

1.	Aldehyde C-14	10
2.	Ethyl Acetate	50
3.	Ethyl Benzoate	10
4.	Ethyl Oenanthate	10
5.	Gooseberry, Extract (Natural)*	425
6.	Orange, Oil	70
7.	Ethyl Alcohol 95%	425
		1000

GOOSEBERRY, IMITATION NO. 2

1.	Anethole	10
2.	Ethyl Acetate (10% solution)	340
3.	Ethyl Benzoate	50
4.	Ethyl Butyrate (10% solution)	275
5.	Isoamyl Acetate (10% solution)	275
6.	Phenyl Ethyl Alcohol	1
7.	Safrole	10
8.	Vanillin	39
		1000

GOOSEBERRY, IMITATION NO. 3

1.	Amyl Acetate	15
2.	Buchu, Leaves Extract	50
3.	Currant, Juice	28
4.	Ethyl Acetate	13
5.	Ethyl Benzoate	17
6.	Ethyl Butyrate	50
7.	Fennel, Oil	4
8.	Orris, Juice	3
9.	Raspberry, Juice	300
10.	Rose, Oil (10% solution)	6
11.	Safrole, Oil	10
12.	Vanillin	2
13.	Ethyl Alcohol 95%	502
		1000

GOOSEBERRY, IMITATION NO. 4

1.	Anethole	4
2.	Bromelia	1
3.	Ethyl Acetate (10% solution)	400
4.	Ethyl Benzoate	30

5.	Ethyl Butyrate (10% solution)	270
6.	Isoamyl Acetate (10% solution)	265
7.	Vanillin (10% solution)	30
		1000

GOOSEBERRY, IMITATION NO. 5

1.	Anethole	13
2.	Ethyl Acetate (10% solution)	350
3.	Ethyl Butyrate (10% solution)	275
4.	Isoamyl Acetate (10% solution)	275
5.	Isoamyl Butyrate	50
6.	Phenyl Ethyl Alcohol	1
7.	Safrole	6
8.	Vanillin (10% solution)	30
		1000

GOOSEBERRY, SYNTHETIC NO.1

1.	Acetaldehyde	1
2.	Aldehyde C-16	10
3.	Ethyl Acetate	10
4.	Ethyl Benzoate	10
5.	Ethyl Oenanthate	10
6.	Ethyl Alcohol 95%	480
7.	Distilled Water	479
		1000

GOOSEBERRY, SYNTHETIC NO. 2

1.	Anethole	2
2.	Anisaldehyde	1
3.	Ethyl Acetate	20
4.	Ethyl Benzoate	20
5.	Ethyl Butyrate	40
6.	Ethyl Oenanthate	2
7.	Isoamyl Acetate	4
8.	Isoamyl Butyrate	2
9.	Nerolin	1
10.	Phenyl Ethyl Alcohol	1
11.	Ethyl Alcohol 95%	447
12.	Distilled Water	460
		1000

GOOSEBERRY, SYNTHETIC NO. 3

1.	Benzoic Acid (1% solution)	100
2.	Ethyl Acetate (10% solution)	500
3.	Ethyl Benzoate	100
4.	Ethyl Oenanthate	100
5.	Succinic Acid (10% solution)	100
6.	Tartaric Acid (10% solution)	100
		1000

GOOSEBERRY, SYNTHETIC NO. 4

1.	Benzoic Acid (1% solution)	50
2.	Ethyl Acetate (10% solution)	250
3.	Ethyl Aldehyde	50
4.	Ethyl Benzoate	50
5.	Ethyl Pelargonate	50
6.	Glycerol	350
7.	Succinic Acid (10% solution)	50
8.	Tartaric Acid (10%	

solution)	150
	1000

GRAPE, EXTRACT (NATURAL) NO. 1

1.	Raisin, Seedless (unbleached)	2 kg
2.	Distilled Water	1 l

Let stand for 24 h and sieve expressing all juice. Add to the residue.

3.	Ethyl Alcohol 95%	1 l

Let stand for another 24 h and sieve expressing all juice. Add to the residue

4.	Distilled Water	1 l

Let stand for another 24 h had sieve expressing all juice Distill altogether.

Yield 3 liters

GRAPE, EXTRACT (NATURAL) NO. 2

1.	Raisins	10 kg
2.	Sweet Clear Wine (hot)	10 l

Let stand for 3 days. Express To the residue add:

3.	Ethyl Alcohol 95%	8 l
4.	Sweet Clear Wine	2 l

Let stand for another 3 days Express and add:

5.	Cognac	13 ml
6.	Ethyl Oenanthate	10 ml
7.	Mace, Oil	12 ml

Distill altogether the expressed juice

Yield 20 liters

Note: This type of grape extract is called "wine flavour" for fordants. Fondants are sweet creamy sugar paste eaten as a candy or employed for filling other candies.

GRAPE, IMITATION NO. 1

1.	Grape, Extract (Natural) No. 1*	250
2.	Grape, Extract (Natural) No. 2*	250
3.	Ethyl Alcohol 95%	250
4.	Distilled Water	250
		1000

GRAPE, IMITATION NO. 2

1.	Amyl Butyrate	6
2.	Cardamom, Oil	3
3.	Cognac, Oil	238
4.	Ethyl Acetate	25
5.	Ethyl Oenanthate	125
6.	Ethyl Pelargonate	175
7.	Mace, Oil	6
8.	Methyl Anthranilate	62
9.	Ethyl Alcohol 95%	180
10.	Distilled Water	180
		1000

GRAPE, SYNTHETIC NO. 1

1. Aldehyde C-14 (pure) 20
2. Chloroform (pure) 20
3. Ethyl Oenanthate 120
4. Glycerin (neutral) 180
5. Lees (dregs)** 10
6. Methyl Anthranilate 10
7. Ethyl Alcohol 95% 320
8. Distilled Water 320

1000

GRAPE, SYNTHETIC NO.2

1. Aldehyde C-14 (pure) 20
2. Choroform (pure) 20
3. Ethyl Formate 10
4. Ethyl Oenanthate 120
5. Glycerin (natural) 130
6. Ethyl Alcohol 95% 350
7. Distilled Water 350

1000

GRAPE, SYNTHETIC NO. 3

1. Butyl Anthranilate 24
2. Cinnamyl Anthranilate 29
3. Cinnamyl Formate 4
4. Cinnamyl Propionate 18
5. Diethyl Anthranilate 255
6. Dimethyl Anthranilate 113
7. Ethyl Butyrate 44
8. Ethyl Cinnamate 18
9. Ethyl Formate 35
10. Ethyl Lactate 141
11. Ethyl Oenanthete 37
12. Neroli 1
13. Propyl Cinnamate 18
14. Ethyl Alcohol 95% 263

1000

GRAPE, SYNTHETIC NO. 4

1. Cardamom, Oil 11
2. Ethyl Acetate 11
3. Ethyl Anthranilate 12
4. Ethyl Butyrate 2
5. Ethyl Cinnamate 4
6. Ethyl Formate 1
7. Ethyl Oenanthate 32
8. Ethyl Pelargonate 1
9. Isoamyl Acetate 1
10. Isoamyl Butyrate 3
11. Isoamyl Oenanthate 1
12. Isoamyl Valerianate 4
13. Mace, Oil 1
14. Methyl Anthranilate 12
15. Propyl Cinnamate 4
16. Ethyl Alcohol 95% 450
17. Distilled Water 450

1000

GRAPE, SYNTHETIC NO. 5

1. Ethyl Anthranilate (10% solution) 450
2. Ethyl Formate 100
3. Ethyl Oenanthate (10% solution) 450

1000

GRAPE, SYNTHETIC NO. 6

1. Ethyl Anthranilate 150
2. Ethyl Butyrate 40
3. Ethyl Cinnamate (10% solution) 220
4. Ethyl Oenanthate (10% solution) 370
5. Propyl Acetate (10% solution) 220

1000

** The setting of liquor during fermentation and aging.

GRAPE, SYNTHETIC NO. 7

1.	Cardamom, Oil	5
2.	Ethyl Acetate (10% solution)	550
3.	Ethyl Oenanthate (10% solution)	310
4.	Ethyl Pelargonate	30
5.	Isoamyl Butyrate	90
6.	Isoamyl Isovarlerate	3
7.	Mace, Oil	10
8.	Methyl Salicylate	2
		1000

GRAPE, SYNTHETIC NO. 8

1.	Ethyl Butyrate	30
2.	Ethyl Oenanthate (10% solution)	220
3.	Isoamyl Acetate	30
4.	Isoamyl Isovalerate	95
5.	Methyl Anthranilate (10% solution)	625
		1000

GRAPE, SYNTHETIC NO. 9

1.	Ethyl Formate	200
2.	Ethyl Oenanthate (10% solution)	400
3.	Ethyl Salicylate (10% solution)	10
4.	Succinic Acid (10% solution)	190
5.	Tartaric Acid (10% solution)	200
		1000

GRAPEFRUIT, SYNTHETIC

1.	Citral	5
2.	Ethyl Oenanthate (10% solution)	10
3.	Linalool	20
4.	Limonene	40
5.	Ethyl Alcohol 95%	463
6.	Distilled Water	462
		1000

GREEN GAGE, EXTRACT (NATURAL)

1. Green Gages (Blue) (crushed in small pieces) 5
2. Sugar

Let ferment for a few days Express the juice To the residue add.

3. Ethyl Alcohol 95% 15 1

Let macerate for another 3 days Add:

4. Amyl Valerianate 12 ml

Distill altogether
Yield 20 Liters

Note. Gage refers to any of the rather small rounded greenish greenish yellow cultivated Plums. The name gage is from the English botanist Sir William Gage.

GREEN GAGE, IMITATION

1. Amyl Alcohol 5

2.	Amyl Butyrate	30
3.	Benzaldehyde (pure)	30
4.	Cinnamon Oil	4
5.	Clove, Oil	2
6.	Cognac, Oil	5
7.	Ethyl Acetate	20
8.	Ethyl Butyrate	35
9.	Ethyl Oenanthate	60
10.	Ethyl Pelargonate	20
11.	Geranium, Oil	3
12.	Orange, (Sweet), Oil	15
13.	Rose, Oil	1
14.	Vanillin	6
15.	Ethyl Alcohol 95%	382
16.	Distilled Water	382
		1000

GUAVA, EXTRACT (NATURAL)

1.	Guava Fruits Crushed	10 kg
2.	Sugar	5 kg

Let ferment for 1 week Express all juice To the residue add:

3.	Ethyl Alcohol 95%	10 l

Let stand for 1 week Express and to the residue add:

4.	Distilled Water	10 l

Let stand for another 3 days Add:

5.	Vanilla Beans, Oil	2 ml

Distill altogether.
Yield 20 liters.

HAM, BAKED "GLAZE"

1.	Pineapple (Ananas) Extract (Natural)*	260
2.	Clove, Tincture	100
3.	Guar, Gum	5
4.	Sodium Benzoate	1
5.	Sorbic Acid	1
6.	Strawberry, Extract (Natural)*	260
7.	Sugar	300
8.	Vinegar	3
9.	Distilled Water	70
		1000

HAZELNUT, EXTRACT (NATURAL)

1.	Hazelnut Kernels (curshed near powder, fresh with good taste, not rancid)	10 kg
2.	Ethyl Alcohol 95%	30 1

Macerate for 10 days stirring each day for 1 h. Collect without pressure the extract (20 l). To the residue add:

3.	Distilled Water	20 l

Let stand for another 3 days.

4.	Amyl Formate	50 ml
5.	Ethyl Oenanthate	25 ml

Distill altogether.
Yield 40 liters.

* Formulas which appear in this book

HERBAL CREAM (CELERY OR ANY OTHER HERB)

1.	Celary, Oil	10
2.	Sugar	250
3.	Ethyl Alcohol 95%	495
4.	Distilled Water	245
		1000

HONEY, IMITATION NO. 1

1.	Ethyl Phenyl Acetate	1
2.	Farnesol, Oil	2
3.	Fennel, Oil	16
4.	Honey, Oil	480
5.	Rose, Oil	1
6.	Ethyl Alcohol 95%	500
		1000

HONEY, IMITATION NO. 2

1.	Cognac, Oil	10
2.	Honey, Imitation No. 1*	490
3.	Ethyl Alcohol 95%	500
		1000

HONEY, IMITATION NO.3

1.	Ethyl Pelargonate	50
2.	Farnesol, Oil	5
3.	Honey, Imitation No. 1*	200
4.	Honey, Imitation No. 2*	250
5.	Phenyl, Isobutyrate	100
6.	Ethyl Alcohol 95%	395
		1000

HONEY, IMITATION NO.4

1.	Ethyl Pelargonate	10
2.	Farnesol, Oil	2
3.	Honey, Oil	400
4.	Phenyl Isobutyrate	50
5.	Ethyl Alcohol 95%	538
		1000

HONEY, IMITATION NO. 5

1.	Ethyl Pelargonate	50
2.	Honey, Imitation No. 2*	500
3.	Honey, Oil	400
4.	Phenyl Ethyl Isobutyrate	50
		1000

HONEY, IMITATION NO. 6

1.	Celery, Oil	7
2.	Geranium, Oil	7
3.	Methyl Acetophenone	15
4.	Methyl Phenyl Acetate	240
5.	Phenyl Acetate Acid	240
6.	Propylene Glycol	371
7.	Vanillin	120
		1000

HONEY, IMITATION NO. 7

1.	Ethyl Acetate	21
2.	Ethyl Isovalerianate	63
3.	Ethyl Pelargonate	20
4.	Linalool	27
5.	Neroli, Oil	4
6.	Methyl Anthranilate	10
7.	Phenyl Ethyl Acetate	15
8.	Phenyl Ethyl Alcohol	10
9.	Propylene Glycol	820
10.	Rhodinyl Phenyl Acetate	10
		1000

HONEY, SYNTHETIC NO. 1

1.	Amyl Acetate	50
2.	Amyl Valerianate	200
3.	Ethyl Acetate	100
4.	Ethyl Oenanthate	175
5.	Propylene Glycol	300
6.	Rhodinyl Phenyl Acetate	175
		1000

* Formulas which appear in this book

HONEY, SYNTHETIC NO. 2 (FOR PERFUMES)

1.	Dimethyl Hydroquinone	110
2.	Geraniol	110
3.	Phenyl Acetate Acid	110
4.	Phenyl Acetate Aldehyde	110
5.	Phenyl Ethyl Acetate	110
6.	Phenyl Ethyl Alcohol	120
7.	Hydroxycitronellal	110
8.	Linalool	110
9.	Quinoline	110
		1000

HONEY, SYNTHETIC NO. 3 (FOR PERFUMES)

1.	Aldehyde C-14 (1% solution)	60
2.	Benzoic Acid	20
3.	Cinnamic Alcohol	50
4.	Dimethyl Hydroquinone	80
5.	Ethyl Naptholate	10
6.	Ethyl Phenyl Acetate	90
7.	Geraniol	90
8.	Hydroxycitronellal	80
9.	Indole (1% solution)	30
10.	Isoamyl Quinoline (10% solution)	20
11.	Methyl Cinnamate	30
12.	Methyl Naphtholate	10
13.	B Methyl Naphtholate	40
14.	Methyl Phenyl Acetate	90
15.	Musk Ketone	30
16.	Musk Xylene (10% solution)	50
17.	Phenoxy Ethanol	10
18.	Phenyl Acetic Acid	10
19.	Phenyl Ethyl Isobutyrate	40
20.	Phenyl Ethyl Alcohol	30
21.	Phenyl Ethyl Phenyl Acetate	70
22.	Skatole (1/1000 solution)	30
23.	Trichloromethyl Phenyl Carbinyl Acetate	30
		1000

HONEY, SYNTHETIC NO. 4

1.	Amyl Acetate (10% solution)	570
2.	Ethyl Acetate	160
3.	Ethyl Isovalerate (10% solution)	225
4.	Ethyl Pelargonate	25
5.	Isobutyl-α–Toluate	20
		1000

HONEY, SYNTHETIC NO. 5

1.	Ethyl Acetate (10% solution)	700
2.	Ethyl Butyrate	30
3.	Ethyl Isovalerate	200
4.	Ethyl Pelargonate	15
5.	Phenyl Ethyl Acetate	55
		1000

HOP, EXTRACT (NATURAL)

1. Hop, Flowers (freshly

	dried)	1 kg
2.	Ethyl Alcohol 95%	5 l
3.	Distilled Water	5 l

Macerate for 1 week Express all extract. Yield 9 liters.

HOP, IMITATION

1.	Amyl Acetate	20
2.	Amyl Butyrate	20
3.	Cinnamon, Oil	2
4.	Clove, Oil	8
5.	Ethyl Acetate	20
6.	Ethyl Oenanthate	20
7.	Ethyl Pelargonate	20
8.	Hop Extract (Natural)*	500
9.	Orange, Sweet, Oil	10
10.	Petitgrain, Oil	10
11.	Ethyl Alcohol 95%	185
12.	Distilled Water	185
		1000

HOP, SYNTHETIC NO. 1

1.	Anisaldehyde	1
2.	Butyric Acid	14
3.	Capraldehyde	2
4.	Cinnamic Aldehyde	1
5.	Ethyl Acetate	16
6.	Ethyl Oenanthate	12
7.	Ethyl Pelargonate	22
8.	Ethyl Isovalerianate	45
9.	Eugenol	2
10.	Heliotropin	1
11.	Isoamyl Acetate	29
12.	Isoamyl Butyrate	29
13.	Limonene	1
14.	Phenyl Ethyl Alcohol	1
15.	Ethyl Alcohol 95%	412
16.	Distilled Water	412
		1000

HOP, SYNTHETIC NO. 2

1.	Butyric Acid	5
2.	Capraldehyde	20
3.	Cinnamaldehyde	4
4.	Ethyl Acetate (10% solution)	500
5.	Ethyl Oenanthate	120
6.	Ethyl Pelargonate	45
7.	Eugenol	12
8.	Isoamyl Acetate	150
9.	Isoamyl Butyrate	130
10.	Limonene	14
		1000

HOP, SYNTHETIC NO. 3

1.	Anethole	12
2.	Butyric Acid	20
3.	Ethyl Acetate (10% solution)	400
4.	Ethyl Isovalerate	160
5.	Eugenol	10
6.	Heliotropin	13
7.	Isoamyl Acetate	200
8.	Isoamyl Butyrate	160
9.	Phenyl Ethyl Alcohol	25
		1000

HUCKLEBERRY, SYNTHETIC NO.1

1.	Anethole	10
2.	Ethyl Acetate (10% solution)	357
3.	Ethyl Benzoate (10% solution)	300
4.	Isoamyl Acetate	200
5.	Isoamyl Butyrate	130
6.	Linalool	3
		1000

HUCKLEBERRY, SYNTHETIC NO. 2

1.	Anethole	1
2.	Ethyl Acetate	35
3.	Ethyl Benzoate	30
4.	Isoamyl Acetate	20
5.	Isoamyl Butyrate	13
6.	Linalool	1
7.	Ethyl Alcohol 95%	450
8.	Distilled Water	450
		1000

JUICES, GENERAL

1.	Juice Concentrate (from any fruit)	1 l
2.	Distilled Water	1 l
3.	Potassium Sorbate (preservative, 20% solution)	1 g

KETCHUP (CATSUP), MUSHROOM FLAVOUR

1.	Acetic Acid	1 kg
2.	Cardamom, Seeds (ground)	1 kg
3.	Clove (ground)	1 kg
4.	Ginger, Root (ground)	1 kg
5.	Mushrooms (well crushed)	6 kg
6.	Pepper, Black (ground)	1 kl
7.	Pimienta (ground)	1 kg
8.	Salt (20% solution)	1 l
9.	Ethyl Alcohol 95%	10 l
10.	Distilled Water	10 l

Macerate for 10 days stirring for l h every day Express, and to the residue add:

11.	Ethyl Alcohol 95%	10 l
12.	Distilled Water	10 l

Let stand for another 3 days. Boil gently for 1 h Cool and express. Put all juice together and filter.

Yield 40 liters.

KETCHUP (CATSUP), TOMATO FLAVOUR

1.	Cassia, Oil	10
2.	Celery, Seeds, Oil	5
3.	Clove, Oil	50
4.	Mace, Oil	10
5.	Mustard, Oil	5
6.	Nutmeg,Oil	10
7.	Piments, Oil	10
8.	Ethyl Alcohol 95%	900

KETCHUP (CATSUP), TOMATO FLAVOR

1.	Basil, Oil	1 ml
2.	Cinnamon, Oil	1 ml
3.	Clary Sage, Oil	1 ml
4.	Clove, Oil	1 ml
5.	Corn Syrup	31
6.	Laurel Leaves, Oil	1 ml
7.	Mace, Oil	1 ml
8.	Marjoram, Oil	1 ml
9.	Nutmeg, Oil	1 ml
10.	Onion, Extract (Natural)*	500 ml
11.	Oregano, Oil	1 ml
12.	Paprika, Oil	1 ml
13.	Parsley, Oil	1 ml
14.	Pepper, Oil	1 ml
15.	Tomato, juice (from ripe crushed tomatoes)	1 ml
16.	Vinegar	1 ml
17.	Ethyl Alcohol 95%	5 ml

18. Distilled Water 5 ml

Macerate altogether for 10 days. Express and separate the residue To the residue add:

19. Ethyl Alcohol 95% 5 1
20. Distilled Water 5 L

Let stand for another 3 days. Express and put the juice together. Filter.

Yield 20 liters

KUMMEL

1.	Badian (Star Anise), Oil (terpeneless)	3
2.	Chamomile, German, Oil	5
3.	Carvi (Caraway), Oil (terpeneless)	25
4.	Cognac, Oil	175
5.	Coriander, Oil (terpeneless)	10
6.	Ethyl Propionate	10
7.	Maraschino, Imitation No. 1*	100
8.	Ethyl Alcohol 95%	672
		1000

LAVENDER,FLAVOUR

1.	Bergamot, Oil	150
2.	Clove, Oil	7
3.	Lavender, Oil (10% solution)	600
4.	Neroli, Oil	3
5.	Patchouli	3
6.	Rose, Oil	10
7.	Ethyl Alcohol 95%	227
		1000

LEMON, EXTRACT (NATURAL)

1. Lemon, Peels (fresh) 10kg
2. Ethyl Alcohol 95% 10 1
3. Distilled Water 10 1

Macerate for 3 days Express To the residue add:

4. Ethyl Alcohal 95% 10 l
5. Distilled Water 10 l

Let stand for another 3 days. Distill to separate the terpenes and the residue Mix the juice and the distillate. Redistill altogether. Filter.

Yield : 40 ltr.

LEMON, IMITATION NO. 1

1.	Citral	13
2.	Ethyl Acetate	6
3.	Ethyl Butyrate	3
4.	Isoamyl Acatate	8
5.	Isoamyl Butyrate	9
6.	Lemon, Oil	44
7.	Orange, Oil	3
8.	Tartaric Acid (10% solution)	10
9.	Ethyl Alcohol 95%	452
10.	Distilled Water	452
		1000

LEMON, IMITATION NO. 2

1.	Aldehyde C-8	20
2.	Chloroform (pure)	10
3.	Citral	10

4. Citronellal 1
5. Ethyl Acetate 100
6. Ethyl Nitrate 10
7. Glycerin (neutal) 50
8. Linalyl Acetate 50
9. Methyl Anthranilate 25
10. Lemon, Oil 50
11. Rhodinyl Acetate 10
12. Tartaric Acid (10% solution) 10
13. Ethyl Alcohol 95% 327
14. Distilled Water 327

1000

1. Aldehyde C-8 5
2. Aldehyde C-10 20
3. Ethyl Aceatate 50
4. Ethyl Nitrate 10
5. Glycerin (natural) 50
6. Lemon Extrant (Natural)* 500
7. Tartaric Acid (10% solution) 10
8. Ethyl Alcohol 95% 178
9. Distilled Water 177

1000

LEMON, IMITATION NO. 4

1. Amyl Acetate 15
2. Amyl Butyrate 35
3. Citral 5
4. Ethyl Acetate 30
5. Lemon Oil (terpeneless) 457
6. Ethyl Alcohol 95% 458

1000

LEMON, IMITATION NO. 5

1. Lemon Imitation No. 1* 550
2. Lemon, Oil 140
3. Lime, Oil 10
4. Ethyl Alcohol 95% 300

1000

LEMON, IMITATION NO. 6

1. Citral 50
2. Lemon Imitation No. 2* 300
3. Lemon, Oil (terpeneless) 50
4. Lime, Oil (terpeneless) 25
5. Orange, Sweet, Oil 10
6. Ethyl Alcohol 95% 565

1000

LEMON, IMITATION NO. 7

1. Citral 25
2. Lemon, Imitation No. 3* 325
3. Ethyl Alcohol 95% 650

1000

LEMON, IMITATION NO. 8

1. Lemon, Oil 500
2. Lemon, Oil (terpeneless) 50
3. Lime, Oil 25
4. Ethyl Alcohol 95% 425

1000

LEMON, IMITATION NO. 9

1. Ethyl Acetate (10% solution) 720
2. Lemon, Oil 140
3. Tartaric Acid (10% solution) 140

1000

LEMON, IMITATION NO. 10

1.	Ethyl Acetate	70
2.	Isoamyl Acetate	100
3.	Isoamyl Butyrate (10% solution)	280
4.	Lemon, Oil (10% solution)	400
5.	Orange, Oil	150
		1000

LEMON, IMITATION NO.11

1.	Ethyl Acetate	200
2.	Ethyl Butyrate	170
3.	Isoamyl Acetate (10% solution)	340
4.	Lemon, Oil	60
5.	Tartaric Acid (10% solution)	60
6.	Isoamyl Butyrate	170
		1000

LEMON, IMITATION NO. 12

1.	Citral	18
2.	Lemon, Oil (terpeneless)	8
3.	Ethyl Alcohol 95%	974
		1000

LEMON, IMITATION NO. 13

1.	Citral (10 % solution)	680
2.	Lemon, Oil (terpeneless, 10% solution)	320
		1000

LEMON, IMITATION NO. 14

1.	Ethyl Acetate (10% solution)	320
2.	Lemon, Oil (10% solution)	320
3.	Succinic Acid (10% solution)	40
4.	Tartaric Acid (10% solution)	320
		1000

LEMON, IMITATION NO. 15

1.	Citral (10% solution)	500
2.	Geraniol	50
3.	Lemon, Oil	100
4.	Linalool	150
5.	Methylheptenone	20
6.	Terpineol	180
		1000

LEMON, IMITATION NO. 16

1.	Citral	40
2.	Lemon, limtation No.1*	800
3.	Limonene	160
		1000

LEMON, POWDERED (CONCENTRATE)

1.	Colour, Certified	1
2.	Lemon, Oil	250
3.	Malic Acid (powdered)	249
4.	Sugar (granulated)	500
		1000

LEMON, SYNTHETIC NO. 1

1.	Acetaldehyde	2
2.	Amyl Valerianate	20
3.	Chloroform	1
4.	Citric Acid	10
5.	Ethyl Acetate	30
6.	Tartaric Acid	1
7.	Glycerin (neutral)	15
8.	Ethyl Alcohol 95%	461
9.	Disitilled Water	460
		1000

LEMON, SYNTHETIC NO. 2

1.	Aldehyde C-9 (10% solution)	2
2.	Citral	40
3.	Geraniol	25
4.	Geranyl Acetate	2
5.	Linalyl Acetate	25
6.	Linalool	25
7.	Terpineol	35
8.	Ethyl Alcohol 95%	423
9.	Distilled Water	423
		1000

LEMON, SYNTHETIC NO.3

1.	Amyl Butyrate	10
2.	Citral	25
3.	Chloroform	10
4.	Ethyl Acetate	20
5.	Ethyl Nitrate	10
6.	Glycerin (neutral)	50
7.	Ethyl Alcohol 95%	438
8.	Distilled Water	437
		1000

LICORICE, ROOT, EXTRACT (NATURAL)

1.	Licorice, Root (well ground)	5 kg
2.	Distilled Water	20 l

Let stand for 3 days stirring for l h each day. Percolate To the residue add:

3.	Distilled Water	10 1
4.	Ethyl Alcohol 95%	10 1

Let stand for another 3 days Heat to the boiling point. Cool and filter Evaporate to a viscid point Add while stirring:

5.	Sodium Benzoate (10% solution)	1 ml

Note: The desired coloration as well as the amount of essence could be increased or decreased.

LIME, EXTRACT (NATURAL)

1.	Lime, Peels (fresh)	10 kg
2.	Ethyl Alcohol 95%	10 l
3.	Distilled Water	10 l

Let stand for 3 days. Express off all juice (20 l) To the residue add;

4.	Ethyl Alcohol 95%	10 l
5.	Distilled Water	10 l

Let stand for another 3 days Distill altogether separating all terpenes. Filter.
Yield 40 liters.

LIME, IMITATION

1.	Ethyl Acetate	25
2.	Isoamyl Acetate	15
3.	Isoamyl Butyrate	12
4.	Lemon, Oil	30
5.	Lime, Oil	30
6.	Menthol	1
7.	Ethyl Alcohol 95%	444
8.	Distilled Water	443
		1000

LIME, SYNTHETIC NO. 1

1.	Benzoin	10
2.	Benzyl Acetate	30
3.	Geraniol	30
4.	Linalool	30
5.	Methyl Anthranilate	30
6.	Musk Ketone	10
7.	Peru Balsam	10
8.	Ethyl Alcohol 95%	425
9.	Distilled Water	425
		1000

LIME, SYNTHETIC NO. 2

1.	Lime, Oil (terpeneless)	500
2.	Orange, Sweet, Oil (terpeneless)	100
3.	Ethyl Alcohol 95%	400
		1000

LIME, SYNTHETIC NO. 3

1.	Lemon, Oil (terpeneless)	150
2.	Lime, Imitation No.1*	175
3.	Lime, Oil (terpeneless)	175
4.	Ethyl Alcohol 95%	500
		1000

LIME, SYNTHETIC NO.4

1.	Isoamyl Acetate	100
2.	Isoamyl Butyrate	95
3.	Lemon, Oil (10% solution)	400
4.	Lime, Oil (10% solution)	400
5.	Menthol	5
		1000

LIME, SYNTHETIC NO. 5

1.	Ethyl Acetate (10% solution)	250
2.	Isoamyl Acetate	200
3.	Isoamyl Butyrate	145
4.	Lemon, Oil	200
5.	Lime, Oil	200
6.	Menthol	5
		1000

MALT, EXTRACT (NATURAL)

1.	Malt (slightly dried and well crushed)	10 kg
2.	Cardamom, Seeds	300 g
3.	Distilled Water	24 l

Heat at 60°C and let stand for 2 h at this temperature. Cool and add:

4.	Ethyl Alcohol 95%	5 l
5.	Distilled Water	5 l

Distill slowly Dissolve into it.

6.	Maltol	2 kg

Filter.
Yield 25 liters.

MALT, IMITATION NO.1

1.	Ethyl Acetate	52
2.	Ethyl Formate	25
3.	Ethyl Oenanthate	13
4.	Ginger, Oil	1
5.	Isoamyl Alcohol	2
6.	Linalool	6
7.	Orange, Sweet, Oil	3
8.	Phenyl Ethyl Acetate	1
9.	Ethyl Alcohol 95%	449
10.	Distilled Water	448
		1000

MALT, IMITATION NO. 2

1.	Ethyl Acetate (10% solution)	525
2.	Ethyl Formate (10% solution)	250
3.	Ethyl Oenanthate	100
4.	Ginger, Oil	10
5.	Isoamyl Alcohol	20
6.	Linalool	60
7.	Orange, Sweet, Oil	30
8.	Phenyl Ethyl Acetate	5
		1000

MANDARIN, IMITATION NO. 1

1.	Mandarin, Oil (terpeneless)	500
2.	Orange, Sweet, Oil (terpeneless)	500
		1000

MANDARIN, IMITATION NO. 2

1.	Mandarin, Oil (terpeneless)	150
2.	Mandarin, Imitation No. 1*	100
3.	Orange, Bitter, Oil (terpenetess)	75
4.	Ethyl Alcohol 95%	675
		1000

MANDERIN, IMITATION NO. 3

1.	Mandarin, Imitation No. 2*	500
2.	Orange, Sweet, Oil (terpeneless)	100
3.	Ethyl Alcohol 95%	400
		1000

MANDARIN, IMITATION NO. 4

1.	Mandarin, Imitation No.1*	250
2.	Mandarin, Imitation No.2*	250
3.	Mandarin, Imitation No.3*	250
4.	Mandarin, Oil (terpeneless)	250
		1000

MANDARIN, IMITATION NO. 5

1.	Citral	40
2.	Grapefruit, Oil	20
3.	Lime, Oil	20
4.	Limonene (10% solution)	500
5.	Methyl Anthranilate	20
6.	Orange, Oil	400
		1000

MANDARIN, IMITATION NO. 6

1.	Citral (10% solution)	320
2.	Decyl Aldehyde	10
3.	Limonene	150
4.	Dipentene	100
5.	Linalool	150
6.	Methyl Anthranilate	50
7.	Nonyl Aldehyde	20
8.	Orange, Oil	200
		1000

MANDARIN, IMITATION NO. 7

1.	Aldehyde C-9	5
2.	Aldehyde C-10	5
3.	Citral	20
4.	Grapefruit, Oil	100
5.	Lemon, Oil	100
6.	Lime, Oil	55
7.	Limonene (10% solution)	240
8.	Mandarin, Oil	400
9.	Methyl Anthranilate	20
10.	Orange, Oil	55
		1000

MANDARIN, IMITATION NO. 8

1.	Citral	20
2.	Lime, Oil	10
3.	Limonene	70
4.	Mandarin, Oil	850
5.	Orange, Oil	50
		1000

MANDARIN, IMITATION NO. 9

1.	Aldehyde C-8 (10% solution)	20
2.	Aldehyde C-9	5
3.	Aldehyde C-14 (pure)	20
4.	Amyl Acetate	10
5.	Chloroform	20
6.	Citral	2
7.	Ethyl Benzoate	10
8.	Ethyl Formate	10
9.	Ethyl Butyrate	20
10.	Glycerin (neutral)	50
11.	Linalool	1
12.	Mandarin, Oil	75
13.	Methyl Anthranilate	1
14.	Neroli, Oil	1
15.	Tartaric Acid (10% solution)	10
16.	Ethyl Alcohol 95%	373
17.	Distilled Water	372
		1000

MANDRIN, SYNTHETIC NO. 1

1.	Aldehyde C-9	20
2.	Aldehyde C-10	10
3.	Dipenten	250
4.	Limonene	600
5.	Linalool	10
6.	Methyl Aethranilate	40
7.	Terpineol	10
		1000

MANGO, EXTRACT (NATURAL)

1.	Mango Fruits (ripe, freshly cut, separated from the stone, and crushed)	10 kg
2.	Ethyl Alcohol 95%	10 l
3.	Distilled Water	10 l

Macerate for 3 days. Express To the residue add:

4.	Ethyl Alcohol 95%	10 l
5.	Distilled Water	10 l

Let stand for another 3 days Add:

6.	Cinnamon, Oil	1 ml
7.	Clove, Oil	1 ml

Distill altogether.
Yield 40 liters

MANGO, IMITATION

1.	Aldehyde C-14 (pure)	1

2. Pineapple (Ananas) Extract (Natural)* 249
3. Mango, Extract (Natural)* 500
4. Peach, Extract (Natural)* 250

1000

MAPLE

1.	Cacao, Extract	15
2.	Coffee, Extract	15
3.	Fenugreek, Extract	120
4.	Glycerin	150
5.	Malta, Syrup	120
6.	Maple, Syrup	150
7.	Vanilin (10% solution)	30
8.	Ethyl Alcohol 95%	200
9.	Distilled Water	200
		1000

MAPLE, FLAVOUR

1.	Angelic, Tincture	15
2.	Coffee, Tincture	75
3.	Ethyl Oenanthate	4
4.	Fenugreek, Tinture	371
5.	Peru Balsam	28
6.	Vanillin	45
7.	Ethyl Alcohol 95%	462
		1000

MAPLE, SYRUP

1.	Maple, Flavour	300
2.	Sugar, Dark Brown	600
3.	Distilled Water	100
		1000

MARASCHINO, IMITATION NO. 1

1.	Almond, Bitter, Oil (cyanidefree)	40
2.	Cardamom, Oil	10
3.	Jasmine, Oil	1
4.	Mace, Oil	33
5.	Neroli, Oil	66
6.	Orange, Sweet, Oil	100
7.	Raspberry Imitation No. 1*	200
8.	Rose, Oil	6
9.	Ethyl Alcohol 95%	544
		1000

MARASCHINO, IMITATION NO. 2

1.	Cardamom, Oil	5
2.	Cinnamon, Ceylon, Oil	30
3.	Clove, Oil (terpeneless)	35
4.	Mace, Oil (terpeneless)	20
5.	Maraschino, Imitation No.	100
6.	Neroli, Oil	20
7.	y-Nonyl Lactone	10
8.	Orange, Sweet, Oil (terpeneless)	150
9.	Petitgrain, Oil (terpeneless)	35
10.	Rose, Oil	1
11.	Ethyl Alcohol 95%	594
		1000

MARASCHINO, IMITATION NO. 3

1.	Almond, Oil (pure)	300
2.	Cinnamon, Oil	30
3.	Lemon, Oil	350
4.	Neroli, Oil	10
5.	Orange, Oil	300
6.	Rose, Oil	10
		1000

MARSHMALLOW

1. Marshmallow Roots 300
2. Ethyl Alcohol 95% 700

Macerate warm for 3 days Filter and add:

3. Malt, Extract 30
4. Distilled Water (boiling) 30

Let cool and mix with:

5. Ethyl Formate 235
6. Peach, Imitation No. 1* 235
7. Pear, Imitation No. 1* 235
8. Pineapple, Imitation No. 1*235

Blend altogether and distill recovering 1800 cc.

MAYONNAISE

1. Eggs (whole or just yolk) 200
2. Lemon, Juice 200
3. Oil, Edible 380
4. Pepper 9
5. Slat 1
6. Saugar 200
7. Vinegar 10

1000

MAYONNAISE, REAL

1. Basil, Oil 1
2. Calcium Disodium EDTA 1
3. Clary Sage, Oil 1
4. Eggs (whole or just yolk) 200
5. Garlic (dehydrated) 50
6. Laurel Leaves, Oil 1
7. Lemon, Juice 150
8. Marjoram, Oil 1
9. Onion (dehydrated) 50
10. Oregano, Oil 1
11. Paprika, Oil 1
12. Parsley, Oil 1
13. Rosemary, Oil 1
14. Salt 1
15. Soybeans, Oil 380
16. Sugar 150
17. Vinegar 10

1000

MAYONNAISE, SPICE

1. Celary, Oil 100
2. Lemon, Oil 300
3. Mustard, Oil 400
4. Nutmeg, Oil 100
5. Pepper, Black, Oil 100

1000

MEAT, FLAVOUR

1. Meat

Boil in water until dissolved to the maximum. Freeze to separate from the water Dissolve in proplyene glycol.

MELON, EXTRACT (NATURAL)

1. Melon (fresh peeled and crushed) 100 kg

Remove the seeds with a sieve

2. Ethyl Alcohol 95% 10 l
3. Distilled Water 10 l

Macerate the pulp for 3 days Add:

4. Ethyl Butyrate 45 ml

Distill.
Yield: 20 liters.

MELON, IMITATION NO. 1

1.	Apple, Essence (Natural)	150
2.	Ethyl Pelargonate	50
3.	Lemon, Oil	50
4.	Orange, Oil	50
5.	Pear, Extract (Natural)*	150
6.	Pineapple (Ananas) Extract (Natural)	150
7.	Raspberry, Extract (Natural)*	250
8.	Ethyl Alcohol 95%	150
		1000

MELON, IMITATION NO. 2

1.	Apple, Extract (Natural)*	150
2.	Ethyl Pelargonate	50
3.	Lemon, Extract (Natural)*	50
4.	Orange, Extract (Natural)*	100
5.	Pear, Extract (Natural)*	50
6.	Pineapple (Ananas) Extract (Natural)*	150
7.	Raspberry, Extract (Natural) No.1*	250
8.	Vanillin	35
9.	Ethyl Alcohol 95%	165
		1000

MELON, IMITATION NO. 3

1.	Apple, Imitation No. 1*	45
2.	Ethyl Pelargonate	11
3.	Lemon, Oil	12
4.	Orange, Oil	10
5.	Pear, Imitation No. 1*	37
6.	Pineapple, Imitation No.1*	50
7.	Raspberry, Imitation No.1*	25
8.	Vanillin	5
9.	Ethyl Alcohol 95%	805
		1000

MELON, SYNTHETIC NO. 1

1.	Citral	10
2.	Ethyl Butyrate (10% solution)	300
3.	Ethyl Formate	100
4.	Ethyl Isovalerate (10% solution)	400
5.	Isoamyl Butyrate	165
6.	Vanillin (10% solution)	25
		1000

MELON, SYNTHETIC NO. 2

1.	Butyric Acid	15
2.	Citral	10
3.	Ethyl Acetate	150
4.	Ethyl Isovaterate	180
5.	Ethyl Pelargonate	40
6.	Isoamyl Acetate	120
7.	Isoamyl Butyrate	180
8.	Isoamyl Isovalerate (10% solution)	280
9.	Vanillin (10% solution)	25
		1000

MELON, SYNTHETIC NO. 3

1.	Ethyl Butyrate	200
2.	Ethyl Fromate	50
3.	Ethyl Isovalerate (10% solution)	250

4. Ethyl Sebacate (10% solution)	500
	1000

MELON, SYNTHETIC NO. 4

1. Ethyl Butyrate (10% solution)	300
2. Ethyl Formate	170
3. Ethyl Isovalerate (10% solution)	300
4. Ethyl Salicylate	10
5. Ethyl Sebacate (10% solution)	220
	1000

MELON, SYNTHETIC NO. 5

1. Aldehyde C-14 (myristic)	10
2. Aldehyde C-14 (pure)	20
3. Ethyl Butyrate	40
4. Ethyl Formate	10
5. Ethyl Sebacate	100
6. Ethyl Valerianate	45
7. Glycerin (neutral)	40
8. Ethyl Alcohol 95%	370
9. Distilled Water	365
	1000

MELON, SYNTHETIC NO. 6

1. Acetaldehyde	3
2. Chloroform	10
3. Clove, Oil	10
4. Glycerin (neutral)	157
5. Ethyl Acetate	10
6. Ethyl Formate	20
7. Ethyl Butyrate	90
8. Ethyl Sabacate	20
9. Ethyl Valerianate	70
10. Ethyl Alcohol 95%	305
11. Distilled Water	305
	1000

MELON, SYNTHETIC NO. 7

1. Aldehyde C-14 (pure)	20
2. Ethyl Butyrate	75
3. Ethyl Formate	10
4. Ethyl Sebacate	10
5. Ethyl Valerianate	50
6. Glycerin (neutral)	185
7. Ethyl Alcohol 95%	325
8. Distilled Water	325
	1000

MELON, SYNTHETIC NO. 8

1. Butyric Acid	1
2. Citral	1
3. Ethyl Acetate	3
4. Ethyl Butyrate	27
5. Ethyl Formate	5
6. Ethyl Isovalerianate	25
7. Ethyl Pelargonate	1
8. Ethyl Sebacate	15
9. Isoamyl Acetate	3
10. Isoamyl Butyrate	8
11. Isoamyl Isovalerianate	7
12. Vanillin	1
13. Ethyl Alcohol 95%	452
14 Distilled Water	451
	1000

MENTHA, CREAM

1. Menthol	5
2. Menthone	15
3. Menthol Acetate	15
4. Menthyl Isovalerianate	15
5. Ethyl Alcohol 95%	475

6.	Distilled Water	475
		1000

MILK, CARAMEL

1.	Amyl Butyrate	60
2.	Benzaldehyde (pure)	1
3.	Butyrate Acid	4
4.	Cardamom, Oil	5
5.	Cinnamom, Oil	1
6.	Ethyl Acetate	40
7.	Coriander, Oil	12
8.	Ethyl Butyrate	50
9.	Geranium, Oil	8
10.	Honey (natural)	10
11.	Thymol	1
12.	Ethyl Alcohol 95%	404
13.	Distilled Water	404
		1000

MINT

1.	Eucalyptol	50
2.	Menthol	200
3.	Menthyl Acetate	150
4.	Peppermint	500
5.	Phellandrene	50
6.	Terpineol	50
		1000

MIRABELLE

1.	Benzaldehyde (pure 10% solution)	75
2.	Cinnamaldehyde	15
3.	Citral	15
4.	Decyl Acetate	5
5.	Ethyl Acetate (10% solution)	290
6.	Ethyl Butyrate (10% solution)	220
7.	Ethyl formate	140
8.	Ethyl Oenanthate	175
9.	Isoamyl Alcohol	15
10.	Vanillin (10% solution)	20
11.	Eugenol	30
		1000

MIRABELLE (PLUM), EXTRACT (NATURAL)

1.	Mirabelles, Yellow (separated from the stones and well crushed)	100 kg
2.	Sugar	5 kg

Let ferment for 1 week or more until flavour and odor develop. Express the juice and to the residue add:

3.	Ethyl Alcohol 95%	10 l
4.	Distilled Water	10 l

Let stand for another 3 days Add:

5.	Amyl Valerate	12 ml

Distill altogether Redistill to rectify.
Yield 20 liters

MIRABELLE (PLUM), IMITATION

1.	Amyl Alcohol	65
2.	Benzaldehyde (pure)	5
3.	Cinnamon, Oil	60
4.	Clove, Oil	10
5.	Ethyl Acetate	90
6.	Ethyl Butyrate	150
7.	Ethyl Formate	60
8.	Ethyl Oenanthate	65

9. Geranium, Oil 10
10. Vanilla Benas, Tincture 65
11. Lemon, Oil 60
12. Ethyl Alcohol 95% 180
13. Distilled Water 180

1000

MIRABELLE (PLUM), SYNTHETIC

1. Benzaldehyde (pure) 1
2. Cinnamic Aldehyde 3
3. Citral 2
4. Ethyl Acetate 22
5. Ethyl Butyrate 29
6. Ethyl Formate 14
7. Ethyl Oenanthate 17
8. Eugenol 6
9. Isoamyl Butyrate 1
10. Linalool 3
11. Vanilin 2
12. Ethyl Alcohol 95% 450
13. Distilled Water 450

1000

MUGUET, FOR CREAM

1. Bergamot (terpeneless) 50
2. Cinnami Alcohol 50
3. Citronellol 50
4. Coriander, Oil 30
5. Dimethyl Benzyl Carbinol 30
6. Jasmine Absolute 10
7. Linlool, Oil (10% solution) 500
8. Orange Flower, Absolute 10
9. Rose Absolute 20
10. Terpineol, Extra 50
11. Trichlorophenyl methyl Carbinyl Acetate (rose crystale) 20
12. Vanillin (10% solution) 10
13. Ylang Ylang, Oil 170

1000

MULBERRY, EXTRACT (NATURAL)

1. Mulberries, Black or Red (crushed) 1 kg
2. Suger 2 kg

Let ferment for 1 week Express the juice and to the residue add:

3. Ethyl Alcohol 95% 10 l
4. Distilled Water 10 l

Let stand for another 3 days and add:

5. Distilled Water 20 l
6. Coriander, Oil 3 ml
7. Ethyl Acetate 24 ml
8. Fennel, Oil 5 ml

Distill altogother. Redistill to rectify
Yield 40 liters.

MULBERRY, IMITATION

1. Ethyl Acetate 150
2. Ethyl Butyrate 300
3. Mulberry Extract (Natural)* 530
4. Orris, Tincture 20

1000

* Formulas which appear in this book

MULBERRY, SYNTHETIC NO. 1

1. Benzaldehyde (pure) 2
2. Benzyl Acetate 10
3. Ethyl Acetate 22
4. Ethyl Butyrate 27
5. Ethyl Formate 13
6. Ethyl Oenanthate 37
7. Ethyl Pelargonate 61
8. Isoamyl Acetate 25
9. Ethyl Alcohol 95% 402
10. Distilled Water 401

1000

MULBERRY, SYNTHETIC NO. 2

1. Benzaldehyde (pure) 1
2. Benzyl Acetate 23
3. Ethyl Acetate (10% solution) 280
4. Ethyl Butyrate (10% solution) 550
5. Ethyl Formate 70
6. Ethyl Oenanthate 15
7. Ethyl Pelargonate 5
8. Isoamyl Acetate 56

1000

MULBERRY, SYNTHETIC NO. 3

1. Benzaldehyde (pure 10% solution) 4
2. Benzyl Acetate 100
3. Ethyl Acetate 170
4. Ethyl Formate 200
5. Ethyl Oenanthate 60
6. Ethyl Pelargonate 15
7. Isoamyl Acetate (10% solution) 450
8. Ionone 1

1000

MUSHROOM, IMITATION NO. 1

1. Basil, Oil 20
2. Chamomile, Oil 20
3. Carrot, Oil 30
4. Celery, Oil 20
5. Copaiba, Oil 20
6. Cotton Seeds, Oil 750
7. Isobutyl Phenyl Acetate 20
8. Marjoram, Oil 20
9. Nonyl Acetate 10
10. Oregano, Oil 20
11. Parsley, Oil 30
12. Sage, Oil 20
13. Thyme, Oil 20

1000

MUSHROOM, IMITATION NO. 2

1. Isobutyl Phenyl Acetate 100
2. Nonyl Acetate 100
3. Phenyl Propyl Aldehyde 100
4. Ethyl Alcohol 95% 350
5. Distilled Water 350

1000

NECTARINE

1. Aldehyde C-14 (pure) 2
2. Pineapple (Anans) Extract (Natural)* 500
3. Lemon Extract (Natural)* 200
4. Vanilla Beans, Tincture 298

1000

NOISETTE

1. Hazelnuts (roasted and powdered) 10 kg
2. Sugar 6 kg

Blend and totally pulverize Add:

3. Cocoa 200 g
4. Ethyl Alcohol 95% 5 l
5. Distilled Water 5 l

Note: The amount of cocoa, alcohol, and distilled water can be either reduced or increased per individual taste preference.

NOUGATINE

1. Almond or Peanuts 3 kg
2. Hazelnuts (chopped) 3 kg
3. Sugar (melted) 10 kg

Melt the sugar together with other ingredients.

NUTMEG, IMITATION NO. 1

1. Camphene, Oil 80
2. Limonene 20
3. Nutmeg, Oil 640
4. Pinene 240
5. Terpineol 20

1000

NUTMEG, IMITATION NO. 2

1. Camphene (10% solution) 250
2. Guaiacwood 50
3. Limonene (10% solution) 350
4. Pinene (10% solution) 250
5. Terpineol 100

1000

NUTMEG, IMITATION NO. 3

1. Isoeugenol 50
2. Nutmeg, Imitation No. 1* 700
3. Nutmeg, Imitation No. 2* 250

1000

NUTMEG, IMITATION NO. 4

1. Camphene (10% solution) 270
2. Guaiacwood 50
3. Limonene 100
4. Pinene (10% solution) 300
5. Terpineol (10% solution) 280

1000

NUTMEG, IMITATION NO. 5

1. Nutmeg, Imitation No. 3* 375
2. Nutmeg, Imitation N0. 4* 375
3. Nutmeg, Oil 250

1000

NUTS, FLAVOUR FOR PASTRY

1. Noisette* 200
2. Vanilla Beans, Tincture 200
3. Ethyl Alcohol 95% 350
4. Distilled Water 250

1000

NUTS, KERNELS (GENERAL METHOD OF FLAVOUR EXTRACTION)

(Kernels of fresh nuts of any type such as hazel, walnut, peanuts, macadamia, pistachio, etc, not rancid, well rasped or crushed, almost pulverized).

1. Nuts 10 kg
2. Ethyl Alcohol 95% 15 l
3. Distilled Water 15 l

Macerate for 10 days, stirring for 1 h each day Collect, without any pressure, 201 of extract. To the residue add:

4. Amyl Formate 45 ml
5. Ethyl Oenanthate 25 ml
6. Distilled Water 20 l

Distill altogether
Yeild 40 liters

ONION

1. Asafetida (10% solution in water) 100
2. Ethyl Alcohol 95% 900

1000

Note: This may be modified with traces of allyl sulfide. ** If it is cloudy filter with magnesium carbonate.

ONION, EXTRACT (NATURAL)

(Onions, well peeled and finely cut with its juice totally discarded since it has no value For every kilogram of residue add 2 l of ethyl alcohol 95%).

1. Onions, Residue 10 kg
2. Ethyl Alcohol 95% 20 1

Let stand for 3 days. Express. To the residue add:

3. Ethyl Alcohol 95% 10 l
4. Distilled Water 10 l

Let stand for another 3 days add:

5. Mustard Oil (1 ml for every kilogram of juice) 40 ml

Put all juice together and filter. Yield 40 liters.

ONION, IMITATION

1. Allyl Sulfide ** 1 drop
2. Asafetida 253
3. Ethyl Alcohol 95% 493
4. Distilled Water 253

Filter with magnesium carbonate .

Note. Mixed with water it makes a milky emulsion.

ORANGE, EXTRACT(NATURAL)

1. Orange, Peels (fresh) 10 kg
2. Ethyl Alcohol 95% 20 l

Macerate for 3 days Express 20 1 of extract To the residue add:

3. Distilled Water 20 1

Let stand for another 3 days Distill to separate the terpenes. Distill the extract altogether and add:

FOR ORANGE BITTER TYPE.

1.	Petitgrain Oil	500 ml
2.	Orange Bitter Oil	500 ml

Distill Filter

FOR SWEET ORANGE TYPE:

1.	Cinnamon Oil	60 ml
2.	Orange Sweet Oil	10 1

Distill Filter.
Yield 50 liters

ORANGE, IMITATION NO. 1

1.	Capraldehyde	10
2.	Ethyl Acetate	30
3.	Ethyl Benzoate	30
4.	Ethyl Butyrate	100
5.	Ethyl Formate	30
6.	Isoamyl Acetate	160
7.	Isoamyl Butyrate	150
8.	Lemon, Oil	200
9.	Linalool	10
10.	Orange, Oil	260
11.	Pimenta, Oil	10
12.	Tartaric Acid	10
		1000

Note. 25 cc is sufficient for 100 1 of orange liquor.

ORANGE, IMITATION NO. 2

1.	Aldehyde C-8	30
2.	Aldehyde C-14 (pure)	29
3.	Amyl Acetate	10
4.	Chloroform (pure)	20
5.	Ethyl Formate	10
6.	Glycerin (neutral)	50
7.	Linalool	13
8.	Methyl Anthranilate	25
9.	Neroli, Oil	2
10.	Orange, Oil	50
11.	Tartaric Acid	1
12.	Ethyl Alcohol 95%	380
13.	Distilled Water	380
		1000

Note. 25 cc is sufficient for 100 1 of orange liquor.

ORANGE, IMITATION NO. 3

1.	Citral	350
2.	Decyl Aldehyde (10%)	10
3.	D Limonene	250
4.	Linalool (Ex Bois De Rose)	150
5.	Nonyl Alcohol (10%)	20
6.	Orange, Sweet	100
7.	Terpineol Extra	120
		1000

Note: 25 cc is sufficient for 100 1 of orange liquor.

ORANGE, IMITATION NO. 4

1.	Ethyl Butyrate	15
2.	Mandarin, Oil (terpeneless)	20
3.	Orange, Bitter, Oil (terpeneless)	300
4.	Orange, Sweet, Oil	

(terpeneless) 300
5. Ethyl Alcohol 95% 365

1000

Note: 25 cc is sufficient for 100 1 of orange liquor.

ORANGE, IMITATION NO. 5

1. Lemon, Oil (terpeneless) 15
2. Mandarin, Oil (terpeneless) 12
3. Orange, Imitation No. 1* 473
4. Ethyl Alcohol 95% 500

1000

Note: 25 cc is sufficient for 100 1 of orange liquor.

ORANGE, IMITATION NO. 6

1. Lemon, Oil (terpeneless) 75
2. Orange, Imitation No. 2* 250
3. Orange, Sweet, Oil (terpeneless) 225
4. Ethyl Alcohol 95% 450

1000

Note: 25 cc is sufficient for 100 1 of orange liquor.

ORANGE, IMITATION NO.7

1. Lemon, Oil (terpeneless) 25
2. Lemon, Imitation No. 1* 25
3. Orange, Bitter, Oil (terpeneless) 50
4. Orange, Imitation No.3* 175
5. Orange, Sweet, Oil (terpeneless) 125
6. Ethyl Alcohol 95% 600

1000

Note: 25 cc is sufficient for 100 1 orange liquor.

ORANGE, IMITATION NO. 8

1. Mandarin, Oil 10
2. Orange, Sweet, Oil (terpeneless) 240
3. Orange Imitation No. 4* 250
4. Ethyl Alcohol 95% 500

1000

ORANGE, IMITATION NO. 9

1. Capraldehyde 25
2. Ethyl Acetate 110
3. Isoamyl Acetate (10% solution) 420
4. Isoamyl Butyrate (10% solution) 420
5. Orange, Oil 25

1000

ORANGE, IMITATION NO. 10

1. Ethyl Acetate 60
2. Isoamyl Acetate 120
3. Isoamyl Butyrate (10% solution) 350
4. Lemon, Oil 120
5. Orange, Oil 350

1000

ORANGE, IMITATION NO. 11

1.	Ethyl Acetate (10% solution)	250
2.	Ethyl Benzoate	50
3.	Ethyl Butyrate	50
4.	Ethyl Formate	50
5.	Isoamyl Acetate	50
6.	Orange, Oil (10% solution)	500
7.	Tartaric Acid (10% solution)	50
		1000

ORANGE, IMITATION NO. 12

1.	Ethyl Acetate	45
2.	Isoamyl Acetate	120
3.	Isoamyl Butyrate (10% solution)	310
4.	Linalool	60
5.	Orange, Oil (10% solution)	460
6.	Pimenta, Oil	5
		1000

ORANGE, IMITATION NO. 13

1.	Orange, Bitter, Oil (terpeneless)	250
2.	Orange, Imitation No. 5*	250
3.	Ethyl Alcohol 95%	500
		1000

ORANGE, IMITATION NO. 14

1.	Mandarin, Oil	75
2.	Lemon, Oil	75
3.	Orange, Imitation No.6*	250
4.	Ethyl Alcohol 95%	600
		1000

ORANGE, SYNTHETIC NO. 1

1.	Alcohol C-8	30
2.	Aldehyde C-8	20
3.	Aldehyde C-10	20
4.	Aldehyde C-12, MNA	50
5.	Amyl Acetate	150
6.	Citral	5
7.	Cuminic Aldehyde	25
8.	Ethyl Acetate	10
9.	Ethyl Butyrate	85
10.	Ethyl Formate	20
11.	Isobutyl Anthranilate	25
12.	Linalyl Acetate	50
13.	Rhodinyl Acetate	150
14.	Ethyl Alcohol 95%	180
15.	Distilled Water	180
		1000

ORANGE, SYNTHETIC NO. 2

1.	Acetaldehyde	2
2.	Amyl Acetate	70
3.	Chloroform	20
4.	Citric Acid	10
5.	Ethyl Acetate	20
6.	Ethyl Benzoate	20
7.	Ethyl Butyrate	150
8.	Ethyl Oenanthate	40
9.	Ethyl Formate	20
10.	Glycerin (neutral)	200
11.	Vanillin	10
12.	Tartaric Acid	10
13.	Ethyl Alcohol 95%	214
14.	Distilled Water	214
		1000

ORANGE, SYNTHETIC NO. 3

1.	Capraldehyde	20
2.	Ethyl Acetate (10%	

	solution)	500
3.	Ethyl Benzoate	100
4.	Ethyl Butyrate	100
5.	Ethyl Formate	100
6.	Isoamyl Acetate	100
7.	Tartaric Acid (10% solution)	80
		1000

ORANGE, SYNTHETIC NO. 4

1.	Amyl Butyrate	100
2.	Ethyl Acetate	50
3.	Ethyl Aldehyde	20
4.	Ethyl Benzoate	100
5.	Ethyl Butyrate	100
6.	Ethyl Formate	100
7.	Ethyl Salicylate (10% solution)	10
8.	Ethyl Alcohol 95%	520

OREGANO, TYPE

1.	Bergamot	40
2.	Ethyl Vanillin (10% solution)	120
3.	Jasmine, Absolute (10% solution)	240
4.	Heliotropin (10% solution)	300
5.	Mandarin, Oil	60
6.	Orange, Sweet, Oil	150
7.	Tonka, Resinoid	60
8.	Verbena, Oil	30
		1000

PEACH, EXTRACT (NATURAL)

1.	Peaches (dried, without stones well crushed)	10 kg
2.	Ethyl Alcohol 95%	10 l
3.	Distilled Water	10 l

Macerate for 3 days Express all the juice To the residue add:

4.	Distilled Water	20 l

Let stand for another 3 days Add:

5.	Amyl Valerate	5 ml
6.	Ethyl Valerate	3 ml

Distill altogether
Yeild 40 liters

PEACH, IMITATION NO. 1

1.	Peaches (crushed or sliced, with kernels broken)	1000
2.	Ethyl Alcohol 95%	500
3.	Distilled Water	486

Distill and add:

4.	Amyl Valerate	7
5.	Ethyl Valerate	5
6.	Phenyl Ethyl Acetate	1
7.	y-Undecalactone	1
		2000

Redistill over 1250 cc.

PEACH, IMITATION NO. 2

1.	Peach, Fruit Pulp	500
2.	Ethyl Alcohol 95%	250
3.	Distilled Water	250
		1000

PEACH, IMITATION NO. 3

1.	Acetaldehyde	30
2.	Almond, Oil (pure)	50
3.	Amyl Acetate	120
4.	Amyl Butyrate	100
5.	Anisaldehyde	20
6.	Cardamom, Oil	10
7.	Ethyl Acetate	150
8.	Ethyl Butyrate	50
9.	Ethyl Valerate	20
10.	Eugenol	10
11.	Lemon, Oil	50
12.	Nerol, Oil	10
13.	Orange, Oil	20
14.	y-Undelactone	10
15.	Vanillin (10% solution)	40
16.	Ethyl Alcohol 95%	310
		1000

Macerate for 3 days Distill over 1800 cc.

PEACH, IMITATION NO. 4

1.	Amyl Acetate (10% solution)	225
2.	Amyl Butyrate	24
3.	Benzaldehyde (pure 10% solution)	14
4.	Cardamom, Oil	6
5.	Ethyl Acetate (10% solution)	225
6.	Ethyl Butyrate	115
7.	Isoamyl Butyrolactone	25
8.	Lemon, Oil	24
9.	Orange, Sweet, Oil	12
10.	Peach Kernel Extract	100
11.	Petitgrain, Oil	3
12.	Pimento, Oil	3
13.	y-Undecalactone	3
14.	Vanillin	10
15.	Ethyl Alcohol 95%	211
		1000

Add Peach Imitation No. 1* and distill over 1800 cc.

PEACH, IMITATION NO. 5

1.	Almond, Bitter, Oil (cyanide free)	6
2.	Ethyl Methylphenylglycidate	10
3.	Ethyl Pelargonate	25
4.	y-Nonyl Lactone	10
5.	Peach, Imitation No. 1*	722
6.	y-Undecalactone	2
7.	Ethyl Alcohol 95%	225
		1000

PEACH, IMITATION NO. 6

1.	Apricot, Imitation No.1*	500
2.	Peach, Imitation No. 2*	500
3.	Ethyl Alcohol 95%	500
4.	Distilled Water	500
		1000

Distill over 1800 cc.

PEACH, IMITATION NO. 7

1.	Acetaldehyde	1
2.	Aldehyde C-14 (pure)	1
3.	Almond, Oil	15
4.	Amyl Acetate	12
5.	Amyl Butyrate	10
6.	Anisaldehyde	5
7.	Cardamon, Oil	1
8.	Ethyl Acetate	15
9.	Ethyl Butyrate	15
10.	Ethyl Valerianate	2

11.	Eugerol	1
12.	Lemon, Oil	5
13.	Neroli, Oil	1
14.	Orange, Sweet, Oil	2
15.	Vanillin	4
16.	Ethyl Alcohol 95%	455
17.	Distilled Water	455
		1000

PEACH, IMITATION NO. 8

1.	Aldehyde C-14 (10% solution)	50
2.	Amyl Acetate	130
3.	Amyl Butyrate	10
4.	Amyl Valerate	15
5.	Benzaldehyde (pure 10% solution)	8
6.	Ethyl Butyrate	15
7.	Ethyl Cinnamate	20
8.	Ethyl Oenanthate	10
9.	Ethyl Vanillin (10% solution)	22
10.	Orange, Sweet, Oil	100
11	Phenyl Acetic Acid	20
12.	Wine Residue (green)	10
13.	Ethyl Alcohol 95%	590
		1000

PEACH, IMITATION NO. 9

1.	Almond, Bitter, Oil (cyanide free)	5
2.	Amyl Acetate	80
3.	Amyl Butyrate	10
4.	Cardamom, Oil	6
5.	Ethyl Acetate	25
6.	Ethyl Butyrate	25
7.	Lemon, Oil	10
8.	Methyl Heptyne Carbonate	10
9.	Methyl Phenyl Acetate	25
10.	Methyl Pelargonate	25
11.	Orange, Sweet, Oil	6
12.	Peach, Imitation No. 1*	100
13.	Peach, Imitation No. 2*	100
14.	Peach, Imitation No. 3*	100
15.	Peach, Imitation No. 4*	100
16.	Peach, Imitation No. 5*	100
17.	Peach, Imitation No. 6*	100
18.	Petitgrain, Oil	4
19.	Phenyl Ethyl Acetate	50
20.	Pimenta, Oil	4
21.	Raspberry, Imitation No. 1*	100
22.	y-Undelactone	10
23.	Vanillin	5
		1000

PEACH, IMITATION NO. 10

1.	Aldehyde C-14 (10% solution)	100
2.	Apple	30
3.	Cherry	20
4.	Orange, Oil (10% solution)	100
5.	Pine, Siberian, Oil (10% solution)	50
6.	Ethyl Alcohol 95%	350
7.	Distilled Water	350
		1000

PEACH, IMITATION NO. 11

1.	Almond, Bitter, Oil (cyanide free)	10
2.	Amyl Butyrate	100
3.	Amyl Valerianate	100
4.	Ethyl Formate	25
5.	Peach, Imitation No. 7*	762
6.	y-Undecalactone	3
		1000

PEACH, IMITATION NO. 12

1.	Benzaldehyde (pure, 10% solution)	40
2.	Ethyl Butyrate	200
3.	Ethyl Isovalerate	140
4.	Isoamyl Acetate (10% solution)	280
5.	Isoamyl Alcohol	20
6.	Isoamyl Butyrate	70
7.	Lemon, Oil	70
8.	Linalool	70
9.	Orange, Sweet, Oil	70
10.	Pimenta, Oil	20
11.	Vanillin (10% solution)	20
		1000

PEACH, SYNTHETIC NO. 1

1.	Aldehyde C-14 (pure)	35
2.	Benzaldehyde (pure)	10
3.	Benzyl Butyrate	140
4.	Ethyl Acetate	25
5.	Ethyl Cinnamate	140
6.	Ethyl Isobutyrate	25
7.	Ethyl Isovalerianate	20
8.	Geranyl Formate	10
9.	Isoamyl Acetate	15
10.	Isoamyl Butyreta	70
11.	Isoamyl Salicylate	10
12.	Vanillin	10
13.	Ethyl Alcohol 95%	245
14.	Distilled Water	245
		1000

PEACH, SYNTHETIC NO. 2

1.	Aldehyde C-14 (pure)	20
2.	Ethyl Acetate	50
3.	Ethyl Butyrate	50
4.	Ethyl Formate	50
5.	Ethyl Oenanthate	50
6.	Ethyl Salicylate	20
7.	Ethyl Valerianate	50
8.	Glycerin (neutral)	50
9.	Sabacic Acid	1
10.	Ethyl Alcohol 95%	330
11.	Distilled Water	329
		1000

PEACH, SYNTHETIC NO. 3

1.	Aldehyde C-14 (pure, 10% solution)	840
2.	Benzaldehyde (pure)	10
3.	Ethyl Isobutyrate	30
4.	Ethyl Isovalerianate	20
5.	Isoamyl Acetate	10
6.	Vanillin	90
		1000

PEACH, SYNTHETIC NO. 4

1.	Aldehyde C-14	70
2.	Amyl Acetate	45
3.	Amyl Butyrate	250
4.	Amyl Isovalerianate	230
5.	Benzaldehyde (pure)	27
6.	Ethyl Acetate	120
7.	Ethyl Butyrate	90
8.	Ethyl Formate	70
9.	Ethyl Oenanthate	50
10.	Ethyl Salicylate	20
11.	Ethyl Sebacte	20
12.	Vanillin	8
		1000

PEACH, SYNTHETIC NO. 5

1.	Acetaldehyde	4
2.	Amyl Valerianate	10
3.	Ethyl Acetate	10
4.	Ethyl Butyrate	10
5.	Ethyl Formate	10
6.	Ethyl Alcohol 95%	478
7.	Distilled Water	478
		1000

PEACH, SYNTHETIC NO. 6

1.	Ethyl Acetate	140
2.	Ethyl Butyrate (10% solution)	600
3.	Ethyl Cinnamate	140
4.	Geranyl Formate	10
5.	Isoamyl Butyrate	70
6.	Isobutyl Salicylate	20
7.	y-Undecalactone (10% solution)	20
		1000

PEACH, SYNTHETIC NO. 7

1.	Benzaldehyde (pure 10% solution)	40
2.	Ethyl Acetate	100
3.	Isoamyl Butyrate (10% solution)	430
4.	Isoamyl Isovalerate (10% solution)	430
		1000

PEACH, SYNTHETIC NO. 8

1.	Benzaldehyde (pure, 10% solution)	40
2.	Ethyl Acetate	190
3.	Isoamyl Butyrate (10% solution)	360
4.	Isoamyl Isovalerate (10% solution)	385
		1000

PEACH, SYNTHETIC NO. 9

1.	Benzaldehyde (pure, 10% solution)	20
2.	Ethyl Acetate (10% solution)	360
3.	Ethyl Butyrate	125
4.	Geranyl Formate	10
5.	Isoamyl Acetate (10% solution)	360
6.	Lemon, Oil	30
7.	Linalool	5
8.	Isoamyl Butyrate	30
9.	Orange, Sweet, Oil	15
10.	Pimenta, Oil	5
11.	y-Undecalactone (10% solution)	25
12.	Vanillin (10% solution)	15
		1000

PEACH, SYNTHETIC NO. 10

1.	Aldehyde C-14 (pure)	100
2.	Jasmine, Oil	1
3.	Phenyl Ethyl Acetate	4
4.	Ethyl Alcohol 95%	448
5.	Distilled Water	447
		1000

PEACH, SYNTHETIC NO. 11

1.	Benzaldehyde (pure 10% solution)	30
2.	Ethyl Acetate	50
3.	Ethyl Oenanthate	50
4.	Ethyl Sebacate	125
5.	Isoamyl Butyrate (10% solution)	350
6.	Isoamyl Isovalerate (10% solution)	350
7.	Vanillin (10% solution)	45
		1000

PEACH, SYNTHETIC NO. 12

1.	Ethyl Acetate	150

2.	Ethyl Butyrate (10% solution)	270
3.	Ethyl Isobutyrate	180
4.	Ionone	1
5.	Methyl Heptyne Carbonate	140
6.	Methyl Phenyl Acetate	180
7.	y-Nonyl Lactone	9
8.	y-Undecalactone (10% solution)	45
9.	Vanilin (10% solution)	25
		1000

PEAR, EXTRACT (NATURAL)

1.	Pears (sliced and well crushed)	10 kg
2.	Ethyl Alcohol 95%	10 l
3.	Distilled Water	10 l

Macerate for 3 days. Express and to the residue add:

4. Distilled Water 20 l

Let stand for another 3 days and add:

5.	Amyl Acetate	25 ml
6.	Amyl Valerate	5 ml
7.	Bergamot, Oil	5 ml
8.	Coriander, Oil	5 ml

Distill altogether.
Yield 40 liters.

PEAR, IMITATION NO. 1

1.	Pears (crushed or sliced)	500
2.	Ethyl Alcohol 95%	250
3.	Distilled Water	250
		1000

Macerate for 8 days and distill over 800 cc.

PEAR, IMITATION NO. 2

1.	Pears (crushed or sliced)	500
2.	Amyl Acetate	90
3.	Coriander, Oil	4
4.	Ethyl Acetate	7
5.	Ethyl Butyrate	14
6.	Ethyl Nitrate	14
7.	Ginger, Oil	3
8.	Vanillin	5
9.	Ethyl Alcohol 95%	182
10.	Distilled Water	181
		1000

Macerate for 3 days and distill over 800 cc.

PEAR, IMITATION NO. 3

1.	Amyl Acetate	440
2.	Amyl Butyrate	50
3.	Bergamot, Oil	50
4.	Clary Sage, Oil	20
5.	Cognac, Oil	10
6.	Ethyl Acetate	120
7.	Eugenol	10
8.	Geranyl Butyrate	20
9.	Isobutyl Acetate	100
10.	Lemon, Oil	50
11.	Orange, Oil	100
12.	Petitgrain, Oil	10
13.	Vanillin	20
		1000

PEAR, IMITATION NO. 4

1.	Amyl Acetate	150
2.	Amyl Valerate	100

3.	Ethyl Acetate	5
4.	Ethyl Butyrate	150
5.	Ethyl Nitrate	50
6.	Ethyl Valerate	10
7.	Eugenol	3
8.	Ginger, Oil (terpeneless)	3
9.	Lemon, Oil (terpeneless)	3
10.	Vanillin (10% solution)	10
11.	Petitgrain, Oil	5
12.	Ethyl Alcohol 95%	511
		1000

PEAR, IMITATION NO. 5

1.	Amyl Acetate	150
2.	Amyl Butyrate	50
3.	Bergamot, Oil	50
4.	Clary Sage, Oil	20
5.	Coganc, Oil	5
6.	Eugenol	5
7.	Geranyl Butyrate	7
8.	Isobutyl Acetate	100
9.	Lemon, Oil	3
10.	Orange, Oil	10
11.	Petitgrain, Oil	10
12.	Vanillin (10% solution)	20
13.	Ethyl Alcohol 95%	570
		1000

PEAR, IMITATION NO. 6

1.	Ethyl Acetate	210
2.	Eugenol	1
3.	Isoamyl Acetate (10% solution)	700
4.	Linalool	9
5.	Linalyl Acetate	20
6.	Orange, Oil	50
7.	Vanillin (10% solution)	10
		1000

PEAR, IMITATION NO.7

1.	Ethyl Acetate	160
2.	Eugenol	5
3.	Isoamyl Acetate (10% solution)	600
4.	Linalool	15
5.	Linalyl Acetate	70
6.	Orange, Oil	120
7.	Vanillin (10% solution)	30
		1000

PEAR, INITATION NO. 8

1.	Amyl Acetate	50
2.	Ethyl Acetate	50
3.	Ethyl Butyrate	50
4.	Ethyl Nitrate	50
5.	Ginger, Oil	5
6.	Vanillin	5
7.	Ethyl Alcohol 95%	790
		1000

PEAR, IMITATION NO. 9

1.	Amyl Acetate (10% solution)	315
2.	Ethyl Acetate	75
3.	Ethyl Butyrate	125
4.	Ethyl Nitrate	50
5.	Ginger, Oil	5
6.	Vanillin	5
7.	Ethyl Alcohol 95%	25
		1000

PEAR, IMITATION NO. 10

1.	Amyl Valerianate	100
2.	Bergamot, Oil	10
3.	Ethyl Valerianate	150

4. Isobutyl Valeriante 150
5. Pear, Imitation No. 1* 295
6. Ethyl Alcohol 95% 295

1000

PEAR, SYNTHETIC NO. 1

1.	Ethyl Acetate	50
2.	Glycerin (neutral)	190
3.	Sebacic Acid (10% solution)	10
4.	Ethyl Alcohol 95%	375
5.	Distilled Water	375
		1000

PEAR, SYNTHETIC NO.2

1.	Amyl Acetate	300
2.	Ethyl Nitrate	150
3.	Glycerin (neutral)	300
4.	Ethyl Alcohol 95%	250
		1000

PEAR, SYNTHETIC NO. 3

1.	Amyl Acetate	330
2.	Ethyl Acetate	166
3.	Ethyl Nitrate	166
4.	Ethyl Alcohol 95%	338
		1000

PEAR, SYNTHETIC NO. 4

1.	Amyl Acetate	100
2.	Ethyl Acetate	50
3.	Ethyl Nitrate	50
4.	Glycerin (neutral)	100
5.	Ethyl Alcohol 95%	350
6.	Distilled Water	350
		1000

PEAR, SYNTEHTIC NO. 5

1.	Amyl Acetate	310
2.	Amyl Butyrate	10
3.	Ethyl Acetate	160
4.	Glycerin (neutral)	110
5.	Vanillin (10% solution)	10
6.	Ethyl Alcohol 95%	200
7.	Distilled Water	200
		1000

PEAR, SYNTHETIC NO. 6

1.	Amyl Acetate	150
2.	Ethyl Acetate	50
3.	Ethyl Cinnamate	120
4.	Ethyl Nitrate	150
5.	Glycerin (neutral)	350
6.	Isoamyl Butyrate	20
7.	Isoamyl Pelargonate	150
8.	Sebacic Acid (10% solution)	10
		1000

PEAR, SYNTHETIC NO. 7

1.	Ethyl Acetate	160
2.	Ethyl Butyrate	160
3.	Ethyl Isovalerate	100
4.	Ginger, Oil	5
5.	Isoamyl Acetate(10% solution)	500
6.	Isobutyl Isovalerate	60
7.	Linalyl Acetate	5
8.	Vanillin (10% solution)	10
		1000

PEAR, SYNTHETIC NO. 8

1.	Benzoic Acid (1% in ethylalcohol 95%)	50
2.	Ethyl Acetate (10% solution)	250
3.	Ethyl Benzoate (10% solution)	250
4.	Ethyl Pelargonate	50
5.	Ethyl Alcohol 95%	400
		1000

PEAR, SYNTHETIC NO. 9

1.	Ethyl Acetate (10% solution)	450
2.	Isoamyl Acetate (10% solution)	450
3.	Isoamyl Butyrate	100
		1000

PEAR, SYNTHETIC NO. 10

1.	Ethyl Acetate (10% solution)	300
2.	Isoamyl Acetate (10% solution)	700
		1000

PEAR, SYNTHETIC NO. 11

1.	Ethyl Acetate	140
2.	Ethyl Butyrate (10% solution)	240
3.	Isoamyl Acetate (10% solution)	600
4.	Ginger, Oil	10
5.	Vanillin (10% solution)	10
		1000

PEAR, SYNTHETIC NO. 12

1.	Buty Acetate	120
2.	Ethyl Cinnamate (10% solution)	525
3.	Geraniol	55
4.	Geranyl Butyrate (10% solution)	220
5.	Isoamyl Formate	55
6.	Propyl Propionate	25
		1000

PEAR, SYNTHETIC NO. 13

1.	Ethyl Acetate	200
2.	Isoamyl Acetate (10% solution)	800
		1000

PEAR, SYNTHETIC NO. 14

1.	Butyl Acetate	13
2.	Ethyl Acetate	17
3.	Ethyl Butyrate	44
4.	Ethyl Cinnamate	58
5.	Ethyl Isovalerianate	11
6.	Eugenol	1
7.	Geraniol	6
8.	Geranyl Butyrate	24
9.	Ginger, Oil	2
10.	Isoamyl Acetate	59
11.	Isoamyl Butyrate	11
12.	Isoamyl Formate	5
13.	Isoamyl Isovalerianate	6
14.	Isobutyl Isovalerianate	6
15.	Linalool	2
16.	Linalyl Acetate	10
17.	Orange, Oil	18
18.	Propyl Propionate	2
19.	Vanillin	6
20.	Ethyl Alcohol 95%	350

21. Distilled Water 349

1000

PEA, SWEET, IMITATION NO. 1

1. Anisic Aldehyde 100
2. Bergamot, Oil 230
3. Ethyl Phenly Acetate 100
4. Isobutyl Benzoate 100
5. Musk Ambrette 20
6. Petitgrain, Oil 100
7. Phenylacetic Aldehyde 50
8. Terpineol 300

1000

PEA, SWEET, IMITATION NO. 2

1. Benzylidene Acetone 180
2. Ethyl Phthalate (10% solution) 100
3. Methyl Heptyne Carbonate 10
4. Pea, Sweet, Imitation No. 1* 710

1000

PEA, SWEET, IMITATION NO. 3

1. Pea, Sweet, Imitation No. 1* 500
2. Pea, Sweet, Imitation No. 2* 500

1000

PEA, SWEET, SYNTHETIC NO. 1

1. Alcohol C-10 2
2. Aldehyde C-9 4
3. Aldehyde C-10 2
4. Bergamot, Oil 180
5. Cinnamic Alcohol 80
6. Heliotropin 60
7. Hydroxycitronellal 60
8. Ionone 45
9. Jasmine, Absolute 10
10. Linalool 120
11. Methey Anthranilate 60
12. Musk Ambrette 40
13. Neroli, Oil 20
14. Phenyl Ethyl Alcohol 120
15. Rhodinol 60
16. Rose, Oil 60
17. Terpineol 65
18. Vanillin 2
19. Ylang Ylang, Oil 10

1000

PEA, SWEET, SYNTHETIC NO. 2

1. Benzophenone 75
2. Benzylidene Acetone 200
3. Heliotropin 115
4. Isobutyl Phenyl Acetate 115
5. Musk Ambrette 85
6. Petitgrain, Oil 85
7. Phenyl Acetaldehyde 75
8. Rose, Absolute 80
9. Terpineol 85
10. Violet Leaves, Absolute 85

1000

PEPPERMINT, IMITATION NO. 1

1. Camphor, Oil 130
2. Menthol 700
3. Mint, Sweet (10% solution) 150
4. Terpinyl Acetate 20

1000

PEPPERMINT, IMITATION NO. 2

1.	Camphor, Oil	200
2.	Menthol	100
3.	Peppermint, Imitation No. 1*	700
		1000

PEPPERMINT, IMITATION NO. 3

1.	Camphor, Oil	100
2.	Eucalyptol	80
3.	Menthol (10% solution)	370
4.	Menthone (10% solution)	250
5.	Menthyl Acetate	80
6.	Phellandrene	120
		1000

PEPPERMINT, IMITATION NO. 4

1.	Anethole	10
2.	Lemon, Oil	5
3.	Peppermint, Oil (10% solution)	485
4.	Peppermint, Imitation No.1*	125
5.	Peppermint, Imitation No.2*	125
6.	Peppermint, Imitation No.3*	125
7.	Peppermint, Oil	125
		1000

PEPERMINT, IMITATION NO. 5

1.	Anethole	20
2.	Lemon, Oil	10
3.	Menthol	250
4.	Menthone	175
5.	Menthyl Acetate	60
6.	Menthyl Isovalerianate	15
7.	Peppermint, Oil	270
8.	Ethyl Alcohol 95%	200
		1000

PEPPERMINT, IMITATION NO. 6

1.	Menthol (10% solution)	300
2.	Menthone	200
3.	Menthyl Acetate	50
4.	Peppermint	50
5.	Ethyl Alcohol 95%	400
		1000

"PERSICOT," (PEACH KERNEL IMITATION)

1.	Aldehyde C-16	15
2.	Benzaldehyde (pure)	15
3.	Laurel Leaves Oil (pure)	1
4.	Parsely, Oil	10
5.	Ethyl Alcohol 95%	480
6.	Distilled Water	479
		1000

PICKLE SPICE SALTS

1.	Capsicum, Oil	140
2.	Celery, Oil	88
3.	Dill, Oil	88
4.	Mustard, Oil	44
5.	Pepper, Oil	70
6.	Pimenta, Oil	39
7.	Table Salt (refined sodium chioride)	45
8.	Tarragon, Oil	26
9.	Ethyl Alcohol 95%	230
10.	Distilled Water	230
		1000

PINEAPPLE (ANANAS) EXTRACT (NATURAL) NO. 1

PEELED PINEAPPLE:

1. Pineapple (Ananas) (fresh, peeled, and ground) 10 kg
2. Ethyl Alcohol 95% 10 l

Let macerate for 3 days Express, and to the residue add:

3. Ethyl Alcohol 95% 10 l

Let stand for another 3 days Add:

4. Vanillin 15 g

Distill

Yield :20 liters

PINEAPPLE PEELS :

1. Pineapple Peels (well ground) 10 kg
2. Ethyl Alcohol 95% 10 l

Let stand for another three days Express, and to the residue add:

3. Ethyl Alcohol 95% 10 l

Let stand for three days Add:

4. Amyl Butyrate 12 ml

Distill

Yield 20 liters

Put together the two distillates (from the peeled pineapple and the peels of pineapple). Redistill.

Yield 40 liters.

PINEAPPLE, (ANANAS) EXTRACT IMITATION NO. 2

1. Pineapple (grated) 500
2. Ethyl Alcohol 95% 250
3. Distilled Water 250

Macerate for 5 days Distill over 800 cc. Add:

4. Pineapple (grated) 500
5. Ethyl Butyrate 3

Macerate for 5 days Distill over 1200 cc.

PINEAPPLE (ANANAS), IMITATION NO. 1

1.	Acetaldehyde	1
2.	Amyl Acetate	16
3.	Amyl Butyrate	3
4.	Chloroform	3
5.	Citric Acid	1
6.	Ethyl Acetate	2
7.	Ethyl Butyrate	8
8.	Ethyl Pelargonate	1
9.	Glycerin (neutral)	313
10.	Lime, Oil	9
11.	Orange, Oil	10
12.	Vanillin	1
13.	Ethyl Alcohol 95%	316
14.	Distilled Water	316
		1000

PINEAPPLE (ANANAS), IMITATION NO. 2

1. Amyl Acetate 4
2. Amyl Butyrate 4

3. Butyl Acetate 7
4. Butyraldehyde 2
5. Butyric Acid 1
6. Ethyl Acetate 2
7. Ethyl Butyrate 2
8. Ethyl Palargonate 1
9. Ethyl Sebacate 4
10. Isoamyl Acetate 6
11. Isoamyl Isovalerianate 11
12. Lemon, Oil 1
13. Orange, Oil 1
14. Vanillin 1
15. Ethyl Alcohol 95% 477
16. Distilled Water 476

1000

PINEAPPLE (ANANAS), IMITATION NO. 3

1. Amyl Acetate 5
2. Amyl Butyrate 50
3. Amyl Isobutyrate 50
4. Ethyl Butyrate 25
5. Ethyl Pelargonate 2
6. Ethyl Valerianate 3
7. L-Ionone 1
8. Isoethyl Acetate 10
9. Lemon, Oil 2
10. Orange, Oil 1
11. Vanillin 1
12. Ethyl Alcohol 95% 425
13. Distilled Water 425

1000

PINEAPPLE (ANANAS), IMITATION NO. 4

1. Amyl Acetate 10
2. Amyl Butyrate 25
3. Ethyl Acetate 30
4. Ethyl Butyrate 35
5. Ethyl Vanillin 20
6. Lemon, Oil (terpeneless) 2
7. Orange, Oil (terpeneless) 1
8. Ethyl Alcohol 95% 877

1000

PINEAPPLE (ANANAS), IMITATION NO. 5

1. Butyric Acid 2
2. Ethyl Acetate 64
3. Ethyl Butyrate 170
4. Ethyl Pelargonate 120
5. Ethyl Sebacate 60
6. Isoamyl Acetate (10% solution) 320
7. Isoamyl Butyrate (10% solution) 260
8. Lemon, Oil 2
9. Vanillin 2

1000

PINEAPPLE (ANANAS), IMITATION NO. 6

1. Orris, Roots (granulated) 50
2. Pineapple (grated) 450
3. Ethyl Alcohol 95% 250
4. Distilled Water 250

1000

Macerate,cool for 20 days Shake often. Press and filter. Distill over 800 cc.

PINEAPPLE (ANANAS), IMITATION NO. 7

1. Pineapple, Imitation No. 2* 250
2. Pineapple, Imitation No. 3* 250
3. Wine, White 250
4. Ethyl Alcohol 95% 250

1000

PINEAPPLE (ANANAS), IMITATION NO. 8

1. Pineapple (Ananas), Extract (Natural) No. 1* 500
2. Pineapple (Ananas), Extract (Natural) No. 2* 500

1000

PINEAPPLE (ANANAS), IMITATION NO. 9

1.	Butyric Acid	2
2.	Ethyl Acetate	64
3.	Ethyl Butyrate	170
4.	Ethyl Pelargonate	120
5.	Ethyl Sebacate	60
6.	Isoamyl Acetate (10% solution)	320
7.	Isoamyl Butyrate (10% solution)	260
8.	Lemon, Oil	2
9.	Vanillin	2
		1000

PINEAPPLE (ANANAS), SYNTHETIC NO. 1

1.	Aldehyde C-14	10
2.	Amyl Acetate	10
3.	Amyl Butyrate	90
4.	Chloroform	10
5.	Ethyl Butyrate	50
6.	Glycerin (neutral)	330
7.	Ethyl Alcohol 95%	250
8.	Distilled Water	250
		1000

PINAPPLE (ANANAS), SYNTHETIC NO. 2

1.	Acetaldehyde	1
2.	Amyl Butyrate	150
3.	Chloroform	9
4.	Ethyl Butyrate	150
5.	Glycerin (neutral)	230
6.	Ethyl Alcohol 95%	230
7.	Distilled Water	230
		1000

PINEAPPLE (ANANAS), SYNTHETIC NO. 3

1.	Amyl Butyrate	5
2.	Chloroform	5
3.	Ethyl Butyrate	2
4.	Glycerin (neutral)	170
5.	Ethyl Alcohol 95%	408
6.	Distilled Water	410
		1000

PINEAPPLE (ANANAS), SYNTHETIC NO. 4

1.	Aldehyde C-10	4
2.	Allyl Caproate	2
3.	Ethyl Formate	4
4.	Ethyl Hepthylate	4
5.	Ethyl Valerianate	4
6.	Geraniol	20
7.	Isoamyl Butyrate	10
8.	Phenyl Ethyl Alcohol	30
9.	Ethyl Alcohol 95%	461
10.	Distilled Water	461
		1000

PINEAPPLE (ANANAS), SYNTHETIC NO. 5

1.	Ethyl Butyrate	190
2.	Isoamyl Isovalerate	162
3.	Ethyl Alcohol 95%	648
		1000

PINEAPPLE (ANANAS), SYNTHETIC NO. 6

1.	Amyl Butyrate	100
2.	Chloroform	10
3.	Ethyl Aldehyde	100
4.	Ethyl Butyrate (10% solution)	290
5.	Ethyl Alcohol 95%	500
		1000

PINEAPPLE (ANANAS), SYNTHETIC NO. 7

1.	Ethyl Acetate	75
2.	Ethyl Butyrate (10% solution)	550
3.	Ethyl Sebacate	150
4.	Isoamyl Acetate	75
5.	Isoamyl Butyrate	150
		1000

PINEAPPLE (ANANAS), SYNTHETIC NO. 8

1.	Ethyl Butyrate	190
2.	Isoamyl Isovalerate (10% solution)	810
		1000

PINEAPPLE (ANANAS), SYNTHETIC NO. 9

1.	Ethyl Butyrate (10% solution)	330
2.	Isoamyl Butyrate (10% solution)	670
		1000

PINEAPPLE (ANANAS), SYNTHETIC NO. 10

1.	Ethyl Butyrate (10% solution)	300
2.	Isoamyl Acetate	85
3.	Isoamyl Butyrate (10% solution)	600
4.	Lemon, Oil	5
5.	Orange, Oil	10
		1000

PINEAPPLE (ANANAS), SYNTHETIC NO.11

1.	Ethyl Acetate	50
2.	Ethyl Butyrate (10% solution)	820
3.	Ethyl Sebacate	130
		1000

PISTACHIO NUT, EXTRACT (NATURAL)

1.	Pistachio Nuts (rasped and totally ground) a	10 kg
2.	Ethyl Alcohol 95%	15 l
3.	Distilled Water	15 l

Macerate for 10 days, stirring for 1 h each day. Collect, Without any pressure, .01 of extract. To the residue add:

4. Distill Water 20 l

Let stand for another 3 days. Add:

5. Amyl Formate 5 ml
6. Ethyl Oenanthate 25 ml

Distill Altogether.
Yeild 30 liters.

PISTACHIO NUT, IMITATION NO. 1

1.	Almond Extract (Natural)	200
2.	Neroli, Oil	1
3.	Vanilla Beans, Tincture	400
4.	Ethyl Alcohol 95%	200
5.	Distilled Water	199
		1000

PISTACHIO NUT, IMITATION NO. 2

1.	Almond, Bitter, Oil (pure)	30
2.	Calamus, Oil	30
3.	Cinnamon, Oil	2
4.	Cloves, Oil	60
5.	Mangnesium Carbonate	6
6.	Nutmeg, Oil	2
7.	Orange, Oil	10
8.	Ethyl Alcohol 95%	550
9.	Distilled Water	310
		1000

PISTACHIO NUT, IMITATION NO. 3

1.	Aldehyde C-14 (pure)	2
2.	Benzaldehyde (pure)	12
3.	Benzyl Benzoate	12
4.	Butyric Acid	1
5.	Ethyl Acetate	17
6.	Ethyl Butyrate	33
7.	Ethyl Oenanthate	5
8.	Heliotropin	1
9.	Isoamyl Acetate	10
10.	Mandarin, Oil	1
11.	Nutmeg, Oil	2
12.	Orange, Sweet, Oil	12
13.	Pimento, Oil	2
14.	Ethyl Alcohol 95%	445
15.	Distilled Water	445
		1000

PISTACHIO NUT, IMITATION NO. 4

1.	Peach, limtation No. 1*	199
2.	Peach, Imitation No. 2*	199
3.	Peach, Imitation No. 3*	199
4.	Peach, Imitation No. 4*	199
5.	Raspberry, Imitation No. 1*	199
6.	y-Undelactone	5
		1000

PISTACHIO NUT, IMITATION NO. 5

1.	Almond, Oil	100
2.	Almond, Bitter, Oil (cyanidefree)	30
3.	Calamus, Oil	30
4.	Cinnamon, Oil	2
5.	Clove, Oil	60
6.	Neroli, Oil	2
7.	Nutmeg, Oil	4
8.	Vanilla, Oil	20
9.	Orange, Oil	6
10.	Ethyl Alcohol 95%	373

11.	Distilled Water	373
		1000

PISTACHIO NUT, IMITATION NO. 6

1.	Almond, Bitter, Oil (cyanidefree)	20
2.	Calamus, Oil	30
3.	Cassia, Oil	20
4.	Clove	20
5.	Nerol, Oil	1
6.	Nutmeg, Oil	1
7.	Orange, Oil	4
8.	Vanilla, Oil	4
9.	Ethyl Alcohol 95%	450
10.	Distilled Water	450
		1000

PISTACHIO NUT, IMITATION NO. 7

1.	Benzaldehyde (pure 10% solution)	80
2.	Benzyl Benzoate	15
3.	Butyric Acid	10
4.	Ethyl Acetate (10% solution)	350
5.	Ethyl Butyrate	180
6.	Ethyl Oenanthate	100
7.	Heliotropin	30
8.	Isoamyl Acetate	80
9.	Mandarin, Oil	15
10.	Nutmeg, Oil	40
11.	Orange, Sweet, Oil	40
12.	Pimenta, Oil	40
13.	y-Undelactone	20
		1000

PISTACHIO NUT, IMITATION NO. 8

1.	Benzaldehyde (pure 10% solution)	70
2.	Ethyl Acetate (10% solution)	310
3.	Ethyl Butyrate	170
4.	Isoamyl Acetate	150
5.	Orange, Sweet, Oil (10% solution)	300
		1000

PLUM, EXTRACT (NATURAL)

1.	Plums Fruits (without stones)	10 kg
2.	Ethyl Alcohol 95%	10 l
3.	Distilled Water	10 l

Macerate for 3 days. Express and to the residue add:

4.	Distilled Water	20 l

Let stand for another 3 days and add:

5.	Amyl Valerianate	5 ml

Distill altogether.
Yield 40 liters.

PLUM, IMITATION NO. 1

1.	Aldehyde C-14 (pure)	4
2.	Benzaldehyde (pure)	8
3.	Benzyl Acetate	15
4.	Cinnamic Aldehyde	2
5.	Cineol	1
6.	Citral	6
7.	Ethyl Acetate	10
8.	Ethyl Butyrate	26

9. Ethyl Caprate 5
10. Ethyl Benzoate 3
11. Ethyl Formate 6
12. Ethyl Heptyne Carbonate 7
13. Ethyl Oenanthate 5
14. Ethyl Pelargonate 13
15. Eugenol 7
16. Ionone 1
17. Geraniol 1
18. Isoamyl Acetate 3
19. Isoamyl Alcohol 17
20. Isoamyl Butyrate 19
21. Isoamyl Formate 6
22. Linalool 2
23. Methyl Anthranilate 2
24. Nerolin 1
25. Orange, Oil 6
26. Phenyl Ethyl Alcohol 1
27. Vanillin 2
28. Ethyl Alcohol 95% 411
29. Distilled Water 410

1000

PLUM, IMITATION NO. 2

1. Aldehyde C-14 (pure) 50
2. Ethyl Acetate 20
3. Ethyl Butyrate 50
4. Ethyl Formate 10
5. Parsley, Oil 30
6. Glycerin (nurtral) 280
7. Ethyl Alcohol 95% 280
8. Distilled Water 280

1000

PLUM, IMITATION NO. 3

1. Benzaldehyde (pure 10% solution) 45
2. Benzyl Acetate 60
3. Bromelia 1
4. Cinnamaldehyde 5
5. Ethyl Acetate (10% solution) 280
6. Ethyl Butyrate 190
7. Ethyl Caprate 5
8. Ethyl Formate 80
9. Ethyl Oenanthate 80
10. Ethyl Pelargonate 30
11. Eugenol 2
12. Geraniol 2
13. Isoamyl Alcohol 5
14. Isoamyl Butyrate 190
15. Orange, Oil 15
16. Vanillin (10% solution) 10

1000

PLUM, IMITATION NO. 4

1. Benzaldehyde (pure 10% solution) 40
2. Benzal Acetate 20
3. Cinnamaldehyde 5
4. Ethyl Butyrate 180
5. Ethyl Acetate 150
6. Ethyl Caprate 5
7. Ethyl Oenanthate 150
8. Ethyl Pelargonate 50
9. Eugenol 20
10. Gerniol 2
11. Isoamyl Alcohol 20
12. Isoamyl Butyrate (10% solution) 300
13. Orange, Oil 20
14. Phenyl Ethyl Alcohol 30
15. Vanillin (10% solution) 8

1000

PLUM, IMITATION NO. 5

1. Benzaldehyde (pure 10% solution) 45

2.	Benzal Acetate	60
3.	Cinnamaldehyde	10
4.	Ethyl Acetate (10% solution)	271
5.	Ethyl Butyrate	170
6.	Ehtyl Caprate	9
7.	Ethyl Oenanthate	100
8.	Ethyl Pelargonate	25
9.	Eugenol	5
10.	Geraniol	5
11.	Isoamyl Alcohol	15
12.	Isoamyl Butyrate (10% solution)	240
13.	Orange, Oil	20
14.	Phenyl Ethyl Alcohol	10
15.	Vanillin (10% solution)	15
		1000

PLUM, IMITATION NO. 6

1.	Almond, Bitter, Oil (cyanide free)	10
2.	Amyl Alcohol	15
3.	Amyl Butyrate	75
4.	Amyl Formate	50
5.	Clove, Oil	10
6.	Coriander, Oil	10
7.	Ethyl Acetate	100
8.	Ethyl Butyrate	40
9.	Ethyl Formate	20
10.	Ethyl Methylphenylglycidate	5
11.	Lemon, Oil	25
12.	Mandarin, Oil	25
13.	y-Nonyl Lactone	10
14.	Pineapple, Imitation No. 1*	50
15.	Raspberry, Imitation No.1	100
16.	Ethyl Alcohol 95%	455
		1000

PLUM, SYNTHETIC NO. 1

1.	Benzaldehyde (pure 10% solution)	20
2.	Ethyl Acetate	140
3.	Ethyl Butyrate	160
4.	Ethyl Formate	80
5.	Ethyl Alcohol 95%	600
		1000

PLUM, SYNTHETIC NO. 2

1.	Benzaldehyde (pure 10% solution)	90
2.	Citral	5
3.	Ethyl Acetate	90
4.	Ethyl Formate	180
5.	Eugenol	15
6.	Isoamyl Alcohol	40
7.	Isoamyl Butyrate (10% solution)	270
8.	Isoamyl Formate (10% solution)	270
9.	Linalool	20
10.	Methyl Anthranilate	20
		1000

PLUM, SYNTHETIC NO. 3

1.	Ethyl Acetate (10% solution)	350
2.	Ethyl Butyrate (10% solution)	350
3.	Ethyl Caprylate	60
4.	Eugenol	2
5.	Ionone	1
6.	Isoamyl Butyrate	200
7.	y-Nonyl Lactone	17
8.	Vanillin (10% solution)	20
		1000

PLUM, SYNTHETIC NO. 4

1.	Benzaldehyde (pure 10% solution)	40
2.	Cineol	5
3.	Cinnamaldehyde	10
4.	Ethyl Acetate (10% solution)	400
5.	Ethyl Benzoate (10% solution)	280
6.	Ethyl Oenanthate	140
7.	Eugenol	10
8.	Isoamyl Acetate	30
9.	Isoamyl Alcohol	50
10.	Isoamyl Butyrate	30
11.	Vanillin	5
		1000

PLUM, SYNTHETIC NO. 5

1.	Benzaldehyde (pure 10% solution)	60
2.	Cinnamaldehyde	5
3.	Ethyl Acetate	140
4.	Ethyl Formate	200
5.	Eugenol	5
6.	Isoamyl Alcohol	8
7.	Isoamyl Butyrate (10% solution)	300
8.	Isoamyl Formate (10% solution)	250
9.	Methyl Anthranilate	1
10.	Phenyl Ethyl Alcohol (10% solution)	31
		1000

PLUM, SYNTHETIC NO. 6

1.	Acetaldehyde	2
2.	Aldehyde C-14 (pure)	50
3.	Ethyl Acetate	20
4.	Ethyl Butyrate	50
5.	Ethyl Formate	10
6.	Ethyl Nitrate	10
7.	Ethyl Oenanthate	10
8.	Ethyl Salicylate	8
9.	Glycerin (neutral)	280
10.	Ethyl Alcohol 95%	280
11.	Distilled Water	280
		1000

POMEGRANATE (GRENADINE), IMITATION NO. 1

1.	Lemon, Imitation No.1*	245
2.	Orange, Imitation No.1*	245
3.	Pineapple, Imitation No.1*	245
4.	Raspberry ,Imitation No.1*	245
5.	Vanillin	20
		1000

POMEGRANATE (GRENADINE), IMITATION NO. 2

1.	Pineapple, Imitation No. 2*	250
2.	Pomegranate (Grenadine) Imitation No. 1*	750
		1000

POMEGRANATE (GRENADINE), IMITATION NO. 3

1.	Benzyl Benzoate	100
2.	Bromelia	12
3.	Cinnamaldehyde	8
4.	Ethyl Acetate (10% solution)	450
5.	Eugenol	5
6.	Isoamyl Acetate	200
7.	Isoamyl Isovalerate	180

8. Isoamyl Propionate 5
9. Limonene 20
10. y-Undelactone 20

1000

POMEGRANATE (GRENADINE), IMITATION NO.4

1. Benzaldehyde (pure 10% solution) 80
2. Benzal Benzoate 160
3. Cinnamaldehyde 10
4. Ethyl Acetate (10% solution) 300
5. Eugenol 10
6. Isoamyl Acetate 160
7. Isoamyl Isovalerate (10% solution) 240
8. Limonene 20
9. y-Undelactone 20

1000

POMEGRANATE (GRENADINE), IMITATION NO. 5

1. Ethyl Acetate (10% solution) 250
2. Ethyl Benzoate (10% solution) 250
3. Ethyl Butyrate 200
4. Ethyl Salicylate 10
5. Isoamyl Acetate 200
6. Isoamyl Butyrate 80
7. Vanillin (10% solution) 10

1000

POMEGRANATE (GRENADINE), IMITATION NO. 7

1. Pineapple (Ananas), Extract (Natural)* 170
2. Lemon, Oil 100
3. Raspberry, Extract (natural) No. 1* 325
4. Orange, oil 105
5. Orris Root, Tincture 150
6. Vanilla, Beans, Tincture 150

1000

POMEGRANATE (GRENADINE), IMITATION NO. 8

1. Amyl Acetate 10
2. Amyl Valerianate 10
3. Benzyl Benzoate 4
4. Cinnamon, Oil 6
5. Clove, Oil 4
6. Ethyl Acetate 10
7. Hoeny, Natural 30
8. Nerolin 2
9. Peach, Extract (Natural)* 220
10. Petitgrain, Oil 4
11. Ethyl Alcohol 95% 355
12. Distilled Water 345

1000

POMEGRANATE (GRENADINE), SYNTHETIC

1. Aldehyde C-14 (pure) 1
2. Benzaldehyde 1
3. Benzal Benzoate 8
4. Cinnamic Aldehyde 1
5. Ethyl Acetate 11
6. Ethyl Benzoate 8

7. Ethyl Butyrate 4
8. Eugenol 1
9. Isoamyl Acetate 17
10. Isoamyl Butyrate 4
11. Isoamyl Valerianate 15
12. Isobutyl α–Toluate 1
13. Limonene 1
14. Nerolin 1
15. Vanillin 1
16. Ethyl Alcohol 95% 470
17. Distilled Water 455

1000

POTATO, FLAVOUR

1. Potaloes (peeled)
2. Propylene Glycol

Add propylene glycol to potatoes. Boil at 187 F for 15 min. Drain by pressing (gravity) or by centrifuge.

Note: This procedure could be applied to other natural products.

POUND CAKE, FLAVOUR

1. Almond, Bitter, Oil (pure) 175
2. Cardamom, Oil 120
3. Cinnmon, Oil 120
4. Clove, Oil 120
5. Lemon, Oil 200
6. Nutmeg, Oil 120
7. Vanillin 145

1000

POWDERED FLAVOURS

1. Colour, Certified 1
2. Essence (Any Extract of Synthetic) 247
3. Malic Acid 2
4. Sugar (granulated) 750

1000

Note: The amount of certified colour could be increased or decreased to suit. The amount of sugar could be reduced adding arabic gum *(Acacia senegal)*. The amount of essence could be redused or increased.

PRALINE ** FLAVOUR (CRYSTALS)

1. Almond (blanched) 10 kg
2. Hazelnuts 10 kg
3. Sugar 18 kg

Roast the almonds and hazelnuts at 143-149 C. Dissolve the sugar with the minimum amount possible of distilled water. Heat altogether at 158C. Pour all on a water cooled table. Pulverize.

PROTEINIC BASIC FLAVOUR

1. Raw Meterial
2. Propylene Glycol
3. Ethyl Alcohol 95%

Use raw material from any plant or animal substance. Separate off solids. Boil in water until dissolved to the maximum. Freeze. Separate water. Dissolve in proPylene glycol. Add alcohol to 10% the entire amount.

PRUNELLE, EXTRACT (NATURAL)

1.	Prunelles (chopped)	10 kg
2.	Ethyl Alcohol 95%	10 1
3.	Distilled Water	10 1

Let macerate for 3 days. Express. To the residue add:

4.	Distilled Water	20 l

Let stand for another 3 days. Add:

5.	Amyl Valerianate	5 ml

Distill Altogether.
Yield 40 liters

QUINCE, EXTRACT (NATURAL)

1.	Quinces (well ripe crushed)	100 kg
2.	Ethyl Alcohol 95%	20 l

Macerate for 3 days Express To the residue add:

3.	Ethyl Alcohol	10 l
4.	Distilled Water	10 l

Let stand for another 3 days. Add:

5.	Amyl Acetate	24 ml
6.	Ethyl Pelargonate	24 ml
7.	Ethyl Valerianate	12 ml

Distill altogether.
Yeild 40 liters.

QUINCE, IMITATION

1.	Benzaldehyde (pure)	15
2.	Ethyl Butyrate	40
3.	Ethyl Isobutyrate	310
4.	Ethyl Oenanthate	08
5.	Ethyl Pelargonate	60
6.	Eugenol	15
7.	Isoamyl Acetate	310
8.	Isoamyl Isovalerianate	180
9.	Linalyl Acetate	2
10.	Orange, Sweet, Oil	60
		1000

QUINCE, SYNTHETIC NO. 1

1.	Amyl Acetate	5
2.	Ethyl Butyrate	150
3.	Ethyl Oenanthate	1
4.	Ethyl Pelargonate	50
5.	Ethyl Alcohol 95%	397
6.	Distilled Water	397
		1000

QUINCE, SYNTHETIC NO. 2

1.	Alcohol C-11 (undecylenic)	100
2.	Amyl Valerianate	2
3.	Ethyl Acetate	20
4.	Ethyl Caprate	35

** Confection of nut kernels (almond, hazel, pecen, etc.) roasted in boiling sugar until brown colored.

Alcohol C-11 (undecylenic) is obtained by heating undecylenic acid (from destructive distillation of castor oil) with alcohol in presence of sulfuric acid (as a catalyst) washing it with alkaline water (as a catalyst) washing it with alkaline water (sodium bicarbonate) and distilling.It has the quince fruit aroma.

5.	Ethyl Formate	5
6.	Ethyl Pelargonate	15
7.	Glycerin (neutral)	411
8.	Ethyl Alcohol 95%	412
		1000

QUINCE, SYNTHETIC NO.3

1.	Benzaldehyde (pure, 10% solution)	15
2.	Ethyl Butyrate	60
3.	Ethyl isobutyrate (10% solution)	310
4.	Ethyl Oenanthate	8
5.	Eugenol	15
6.	Isoamyl Acetate (10% solution)	370
7.	Isoamyl Isovalerate	180
8.	Linalyl Acetate	2
9.	Orange, Sweet, Oil	40
		1000

RAISIN, SYNTHETIC

1.	Aldehyde C-14 (pure)	20
2.	Chloroform (pure)	10
3.	Ethyl Formate	20
4.	Ethyl Oenanthate	92
5.	Glycerin (neutral)	140
6.	Methyl Anthranilate	10
7.	Succinic Acid	3
8.	Tartaric Acid	5
9.	Ethyl Alcohol 95%	700
		1000

RASPBERRY, EXTRACT (NATURAL) NO. 1

1.	Respberries	100 kg
2.	Sugar	5 kg

Let ferment for 1 week or more until the flavour is well developed Add:

3.	Ethyl Alcohol 95%	24 l

Let stand for another week. Express and to the residue add:

4.	Ethyl Alcohol 95%	12 l
5.	Distilled Water	12 l

Let stand for another 3 days. Add:

6.	Anisaldehyde	12 ml
7.	Cognac, Oil	8 ml
8.	Ethyl Acetate	24 ml
9.	Ethyl Benzoate	24 ml
10.	Ethyl Pelargonate	12 ml
11.	Vanillin	12 g

Distill altogether Resdistill for rectification. Yield 50 liters.

RASPBERRY, EXTRACT (NATURAL) NO. 2

1.	Raspberry Juice (fresh)	40 l
2.	Ethyl Alcohol 95%	4 l

Distill
Yield 8 liters.

RASBERRY, EXTRACT (NATURAL) NO. 3

1.	Raspberry, Extract (Natural) No. 1*	10 l

2.	Raspberry, Extract (natural) No. 2*	10 l
3.	Sugar Syrup (60%)	40 l
4.	Ethyl Alcohol 95%	20 l
5.	Distilled Water	20 l
		1000

Filter Yield : 100 litrs

RASPBERRY, IMITATION NO. 1

1.	Acetaldehyde	2
2.	Aldehyde C-20	1
3.	Amyl Acetate	5
4.	Amyl Butyrate	25
5.	Amyl Isobutyrate	25
6.	Cinnamon, Oil	1
7.	Clove, Oil	3
8.	Ethyl Acetate	5
9.	Ethyl Butyrate	15
10.	Ethyl Formate	5
11.	Ethyl Isobutyrate	15
12.	Ethyl Salicylate	1
13.	α–Ionone	2
14.	Isobutyl Acetate	15
15.	Lemon, Oil	2
16.	Neroli, Oil	2
17.	Orris, Oil	2
18.	Vanillin	5
19.	Ethyl Alcohol 95%	435
20.	Distilled Water	434
		1000

RASPBERRY, IMITATION NO. 2

1.	Aldehyde C-16	10
2.	Amyl Acetate	10
3.	Benzoic Acid	1
4.	Ethyl Acetate	50
5.	Ethyl Benzoate	10
6.	Ethyl Butyrate	10
7.	Ethyl Formate	10
8.	Ethyl Nitrate	10
9.	Ethyl Oenanthate	10
10.	Ethyl Salicylate	10
11.	Glycerin (neutral)	106
12.	Orange, Oil	62
13.	Sebacic Acid	1
14.	Ethyl Alcohol 95%	350
15.	Distilled Water	350
		1000

RASBERRY, IMITATION NO. 3

1.	Aldehyde C-20	30
2.	Amyl Acetate	60
3.	Benzyl Butyrate	12
4.	Benzyl Formate	10
5.	Benzyl Propionate	10
6.	Butyl Acetate	60
7.	Ethyl Acetate	60
8.	Isobutyl Acetate	20
9.	Isocinnamic Acetate	40
10.	Phenyl Ethyl Butyrate	80
11.	Orris, Oil	12
12.	Vanillin	6
13.	Ethyl Alcohol 95%	300
14.	Distillled Water	300
		1000

RASPBERRY, IMITATION NO. 4

1.	Orris, Roots (granulated)	100
2.	Amyl Acetate	175
3.	Amyl Butyrate	25
4.	Ethyl Acetate	80
5.	Ethyl Butyrate	150
6.	Ethyl Nitrate	25
7.	Ethyl Oenanpthate	15

8. Isobutyl Formate 5
9. Orange, Oil 20
10. Raspberry Juice 400
11. Vanillin 5

1000

Macerate for 1 days and Distill over 800 cc.

RASPBERRY, IMITATION NO. 5

1.	Almond, Bitter, Oil (cyanide free)	8
2.	Benzyl Acetate	100
3.	Cinnamon, Ceylon, Oil	15
4.	Civette, Tincture (3%)	1
5.	Clove, Oil	15
6.	Neroli, Oil	4
7.	Orris, Root, Extract (10%)	5
8.	Phenyl Ethyl Alcohol	75
9.	Propyl Acetate	30
10.	Peru Balsam	15
11.	Raspberry, Imitation No. 1*	346
12.	Rose, Oil	7
13.	Tolu, Extract (10% solution)	15
14.	Vanillin (10% solution)	18
15.	Ethyl Alcohol 95%	346
		1000

RASPBERRY, IMITATION NO. 6

1.	Aldehyde C-12	10
2.	y-Nonyl Lactone	20
3.	Raspberry Imitation No. 1*	485
4.	Ethyl Alcohol 95%	485
		1000

RASPBERRY, IMITATION NO. 7

1.	Aldehyde C-20	10
2.	y-Nonyl Lactone	10
3.	Raspberry, Imitation No.2*	490
4.	Ethyl Alcohol 95%	490
		1000

RASPBERRY, IMITATION NO. 8

1.	Almond, Bitter, Oil (cyanide free)	3
2.	Benzal Acetate	40
3.	Cinnamon, Ceylon, Oil	5
4.	Civette, Tincture (10%)	1
5.	Clove, Oil	5
6.	Neroli, Oil	2
7.	Orris, Extract (10%)	1
8.	Phenyl Ethyl Alcohol	50
9.	Peru, Balsam, Oil	10
10.	Propyl Acetate	10
11.	Raspberry, Imitation No. 3*	432
12.	Rose, Oil	3
13.	Vanillin	5
14.	Ethyl Alcohol 95%	433
		1000

RASPBERRY, IMITATION NO. 9

1.	y-Nonyl Lactone	10
2.	Raspberry, Imitation No.1*	165
3.	Raspberry, Imitation No.2*	165
4.	Raspberry, Imitation No.3*	165
5.	Raspberry, Imitation No.4*	165
6.	Raspberry, Imitation No.5*	165
7.	Ethyl Alcohol 95%	165
		1000

RASPBERRY, IMITATION NO. 10

1.	Acetaldehyde	50
2.	Aldehyde C-20	3
3.	Amyl Acetate	50
4.	Amyl Butyrate	150
5.	Amyl Isobutyrate	150
6.	Cinnamon Ceylon Oil	15
7.	Clove, Oil	15
8.	Ethyl Acetate	50
9.	Ethyl Butyrate	150
10.	Ethyl Formate	50
11.	Ethyl Isobutyrate	100
12.	α–Ionone	15
13.	Lsobutyl Acetate	150
14.	Lemon, Oil (terpeneless)	12
15.	Methyl Salicylate	5
16.	Neroli, Oil	15
17.	Orris, Oil	15
18.	Vanillin	5
		1000

RASPBERRY, SYNTHETIC NO. 1

1.	Aldehyde C-20	40
2.	Amyl Acetate	10
3.	Amyl Valerianate	10
4.	Ethyl Acetate	5
5.	Ethyl Benzoate	10
6.	Ethyl Formate	10
7.	Ethyl Nitrate	10
8.	Glycerin (neutral)	100
9.	Tartaric Acid	5
10.	Ethyl Alcohol 95%	400
11.	Distillled Water	400
		1000

RASPBERRY, SYNTHETIC NO. 2

1.	Acetaldehyde	2
2.	Aldehyde C-20	30
3.	Amyl Acetate	10
4.	Amyl Butyrate	20
5.	Amyl Valerianate	20
6.	Ethyl Acetate	10
7.	Ethyl Benzoate	10
8.	Ethyl Butyrate	20
9.	Ethyl Formate	10
10.	Ethyl Nitrate	10
11.	Ethyl Oenanthate	20
12.	Ethyl Salicylate	1
13.	Ethyl Sebacate	4
14.	Ethyl Succinate	1
15.	Ethyl Valerianate	10
16.	Glycerin (neutral)	120
17.	Succinic Acid	1
18.	Tartaric Acid	1
19.	Ethyl Alcohol 95%	350
20.	Distilled Eater	350
		1000

RASPBERRY, SYNTHETIC NO. 3

1.	Aldehyde C-20	15
2.	Amyl Acetate	10
3.	Amyl Butyrate	5
4.	Amyl Valerianate	25
5.	Ethyl Acetate	15
6.	Ethyl Benzoate	10
7.	Ethyl Formate	10
8.	Ethyl Nitrate	10
9.	Glycerin (neutral)	293
10.	Tartaric Acid	5
11.	Vanillin	2
12.	Ethyl Alcohol 95%	300
13.	Distilled Water	300
		1000

RASPBERRY, SYNTHETIC NO. 4

1.	Amyl Acetate	45
2.	Amyl Butyrate	220
3.	Ethyl Acetate	45
4.	Ethyl Formate	45
5.	Ethyl Pelargonate	45
6.	Glycerin (neutral)	160
7.	Ethyl Alcohol 95%	220
8.	Distilled Water	220
		1000

RASPBERRY, SYNTHETIC NO. 5

1.	Benzyl Acetate	1
2.	Benzyl Benzoate	35
3.	Ethyl Acetate	200
4.	Ethyl Formate	20
5.	Eugenol	5
6.	Ionone	2
7.	Geraniol	2
8.	Isoamyl Acetate	200
9.	Isobutyl Acetate	400
10.	Linalool	120
11.	Nerolin	10
12.	Vanillin	5
		1000

RASPBERRY, SYNTHETIC NO.6

1.	Aldehyde C-18	4
2.	Amyl Butyrate	140
3.	Benzaldehyde (pure)	2
4.	Benzyl Acetate	68
5.	Benzyl Benzoate	12
6.	Butyl-ß-Naphthyl Ether	36
7.	Cinnamic Aldehyde	8
8.	Ethyl Acetate	44
9.	Ethyl Benzoate	62
10.	Ethyl Butyrate	146
11.	Ethyl Cinnamate	10
12.	Ethyl Formate	54
13.	Ethyl Oenanthate	60
14.	Ethyl Salicylate	36
15.	Ethyl Sebacate	36
16.	Eugenol	10
17.	Geraniol	4
18.	Ionone	8
19.	Isoamyl Acetate	24
20.	Isoamyl Butyrate	74
21.	Isoamyl Isovalerianate	10
22.	Isobutyl Acetate	18
23.	Isobutyl Formate	8
24.	Linalool	4
25.	Nerolin	4
26.	Phenyl Ethyl Alcohol	90
27.	Propyl Acetate	14
28.	Succinic Acid	2
29.	Tartaric Acid	4
30.	Vanillin	8
		1000

RASPBERRY, SYNTHETIC NO. 7

1.	Ethyl Acetate	50
2.	Ethyl Benzoate	3
3.	Ethyl Butyrate	5
4.	Ethyl Formate	3
5.	Ethyl Heptanoate	3
6.	Ethyl Nitrate	10
7.	Ethyl Salicylate	5
8.	Ethyl Sebacate	10
9.	y-Nonyl Lactone	10
10.	Raspberry, Synthetic No. 1*	260
11.	Raspberry, Synthetic No. 2*	100
12.	Ethyl Alcohol 95%	541
		1000

RASPBERRY, SYNTHETIC NO. 8

1.	Ethyl Benzoate	120
2.	Ethyl Butyrate	120
3.	Isoamyl Acetate	25
4.	Isoamyl Formate	20
5.	Ionone	10
6.	Vanillin	5
7.	Ethyl Alcohol 95%	700
		1000

RASPBERRY, SYNTHETIC NO. 9

1.	Ethyl Acetate (10% solution)	550
2.	Ethyl Benzoate	110
3.	Ethyl Butyrate	110
4.	Ionone	10
5.	Isoamyl Acetate	110
6.	Isoamyl Butyrate	110
		1000

RASPBERRY, SYNTHETIC NO. 10

1.	Benzaldehyde (pure 10% solution)	20
2.	Benzyl Acetate (10% solution)	350
3.	Bromelia	2
4.	Cinnamaldehyde	40
5.	Ethyl Acetate (10% solution)	350
6.	Eugenol	40
7.	Geraniol	20
8.	Ionone	10
9.	Isoamyl Acetate	20
10.	Phenyl Ethyl Acetate (10% solution)	50
11.	Propyl Acetate	80
12.	Vanillin (10% solution)	18
		1000

RASPBERRY, SYNTHETIC NO. 11

1.	Benzyl Acetate	1
2.	Benzyl Benzoate	50
3.	Cinnamaldehyde	5
4.	Ethyl Acetate	200
5.	Ethyl Formate	60
6.	Eugenol	15
7.	Geraniol	1
8.	Ionone	3
9.	Isoamyl Acetate (10% solution)	250
10.	Isobutyl Acetate (10% solution)	380
11.	Linalool	15
12.	Vanillin (10% solution)	20
		1000

RASPBERRY, SYNTHETIC NO. 12

1.	Benzyl Acetate	2
2.	Benzyl Benzoate	20
3.	Bromelia	15
4.	Ethyl Acetate	200
5.	Ethyl Formate	35
6.	Eugenol	6
7.	Geraniol	1
8.	Ionone	1
9.	Isoamyl Acetate (10% solution)	275
10.	Isobutyl Acetate (10% solution)	425
11.	Linalool	10
12.	Vanillin (10% solution)	10
		1000

RASPBERRY, SYNTHETIC NO. 13

1.	Ethyl Acetate	120
2.	Ethyl Oenanthate	180
3.	Isoamyl Acetate (10% solution)	300
4.	Isobutyl Acetate (10% solution)	240
5.	Isoamyl Formate	45
6.	Linalool	10
7.	ß-Naphthyl Ethyl Ethyl (10% solution)	80
8.	y-Nonyl Lactone (10% solution)	25
		1000

RATAFIA

Ratafias are liqueurs made with extract from fresh fruits macerated with alcohol and synthetic flavour.

Liqueurs are flavoured with fruit kernels and bitter almonds.

Sweet biscuits are made with almond paste.

Note: Liqueur is a sweet alcoholic beverage flavoured with fruits or aromatics.

Liquor is a distilled, rather than fermented alcoholic beverage.

RHODIUM

1.	Bois De Rose, Oil	200
2.	Geranium Bourbon, Oil	200
3.	Rhodium, Oil	200
4.	Triacetin	400
		1000

ROOT BEER, IMITATION

1.	Amyl Butyrate	45
2.	Anise, Oil	2
3.	Cassia, Oil	90
4.	Clove, Oil	10
5.	Ethyl Salicylate	110
6.	Lemon, Oil	90
7.	Nutmeg, Oil	5
8.	Vanillin Beans, Oil	113
9.	Ethyl Alcohol 95%	535
		1000

ROSE, FLAVOUR

1.	Citral	1
2.	Geraniol	100
3.	Geranium Rose (10% solution)	250
4.	Orange, Sweet	47
5.	Rhodinol	150
6.	Rose, Turkish, Oil	2
7.	Ethyl Alcohol 95%	450
		1000

ROSE, LIQUOR

1.	Cardamom, Oil	35
2.	Cedar, Oil	15
3.	Cinnamon, Oil	20
4.	Clove, Oil	15
5.	Iris, Florentine	15
6.	Lemon, Oil	50
7.	Melissa, Oil	25
8.	Mint, Oil	15
9.	Nutmeg, Oil	25

10.	Orange Flower, Oil	135
11.	Orange, Oil	100
12.	Rose, Oil	25
13.	Rosemary, Oil	25
14.	Storax	3
15.	Vanilla	25
16.	Ethyl Alcohol 95%	236
17.	Distilled Water	236
		1000

ROSEMARY, CHILI

1.	Rosemary, Leaves	30 kg
2.	Vinegar, Natural	240 l

Let stand for 1 week. Sieve, and Add:

3.	Vinegar, Natural	1600

Let stand several months. Filter.

RUM, ETHER FLAVOUR

1.	Acetic Acid	3
2.	Ethyl Alcohol 95%	624
3.	Manganese Dioxide	5
4.	Pyroligneous Acid (tar free)	150
5.	Charcoal	3

Distill slowly with low flame under cap. Add:

6.	Peru Balsam, Oil	210
7.	Charcoal	5
		1000

Redistill Filter.

RUM, IMITATION NO. 1

1.	Angelic, Root, Extract	25
2.	Catechu, Extract	25
3.	Cinnamon, Ceylon, Oil	30
4.	Ethyl Acetate	110
5.	Ethyl Butyrate	120
6.	Ethyl Formate	50
7.	Neroli, Oil	5
8.	Vanilla, Oil (10% solution)	35
9.	Ethyl Alcohol 95%	600
		1000

RUM, IMITATION NO.2

1.	Ethyl Formate	100
2.	Ethyl Nitrate	150
3.	Rum Imitation No. 1*	745
4.	Vanillin	5
		1000

RUM, IMITATION NO. 3

1.	Birch Tar, Oil (10% solution)	50
2.	Ethyl Acetate	50
3.	Rum Imitation No.2*	450
4.	Ethyl Alcohol 95%	450
		1000

RUM, IMITATION NO. 4

1.	Rum, Imitation No. 2*	488
2.	Rum, Imitation No. 3*	487
3.	Saffron, Extract	25
		1000

RUM, IMITATION NO. 5

1.	Rum, Imitation No. 4*	500
2.	Sugar, Syrup	500
		1000

RUM "JAMAICA," NO. 1

1. Acetic Acid (10% solution) 30 ml
2. Butyric Acid (2% solution) 1 ml
3. Kino, Tincture 45 ml
4. Ethyl Alcohol 95% 10 l
5. Distilled Water 10 l

Colour with burnt sugar (caramel). Lat stand 5 days stirring for 1 h every day. Filter.

RUM "JAMAICA," NO. 2

1. Amyl Acetate 100
2. Amyl Butyrate 100
3. Amyl Formate 100
4. Birch Tar (rectified) 20
5. Clove, Oil 35
6. Ethyl Acetate 28
7. Ethyl Butyrate 58
8. Ethyl Formate 56
9. Ethyl Oenanthate 58
10. Ethyl Propionate 72
11. Peru Balsam Oil 50
12. Styrax, Resinoid 68
13. Vanillin 133
14. Ethyl Alcohol 95% 122

1000

RUM, OIL

1. Birch Tar, Oil 3
2. Ethyl Acetate 42
3. Ethyl Butyrate 14
4. Ethyl Formate 12
5. Lemon, Oil 4
6. Peru Balsam, Oil 75
7. Vanillin 15
8. Ethyl Alcohol 95% 418
9. Distilled Water 417

1000

RUM, SYNTHETIC NO. 1

1. Amyl Butyrate 100
2. Amyl Isobutyrate 100
3. Caramel 249
4. Ethyl Formate 100
5. Furfural 1
6. Isobutyl Acetate 100
7. Isobutyl Butyrate 100
8. Ethyl Alcohol 95% 250

1000

RUM, SYNTHETIC NO. 2

1. Acetic Acid (10% solution) 80
2. Amyl Butyrate 60
3. Butyric Acid 28
4. Ethyl Acetate 86
5. Ethyl Butyrate 118
6. Heliotropin 38
7. Rum Ether 62
8. Vanillin 28
9. Ethyl Alcohol 95% 500

1000

RUM, SYNTHETIC NO. 3

1. Amyl Acetate 10
2. Angelica, Oil (terpeneless) 1
3. Birch Tar, Oil (10% solution) 1
4. Cinnamon, Ceylon, Oil (terpeneless) 1
5. Ethyl Acetate 10
6. Ethyl Butyrate 100
7. Ethyl Formate 200
8. Ethyl Nitrate 100
9. Neroli, Oil 1
10. Rum, Synthetic No. 1* 571
11. Vanillin 5

1000

SAINT JOHN'S BREAD (CAROB) TINCTURE

1.	St. John's Bread (Carob) (roasted and powdered)	457
2.	Ethyl Alcohol 95%	355
3.	Distilled Water	188
		1000

SARSAPARILLA, IMITATION NO. 1

1.	Anise	200
2.	Caraway	50
3.	Cinnamon	50
4.	Fennel	50
5.	Sassafras	25
6.	Wintergreen	50
7.	Ethyl Alcohol 95%	288
8.	Distilled Water	287
		1000

SARSAPARILLA, IMITATION NO. 2

1.	Anise, Oil	4
2.	Fennel, Oil	2
3.	Sweet Birch, Oil	35
4.	Wintergreen, Oil	92
5.	Ethyl Alcohol 95%	434
6.	Distilled Water	433
		1000

SASSAFRAS, IMITATION NO. 1

1.	Benzyl Benzoate (10% solution)	300
2.	Limonene	60
3.	Sassafras, Oil	100
4.	Ocotea Cymbarum, Oil (10% solution)	540
		1000

SASSAFRAS, IMITATION NO. 2

1.	Benzyl Benzoate (10% solution)	300
2.	Limonene	30
3.	Sassafras, Oil	120
4.	Ocotea Cymbarum, Oil (10% solution)	550
		1000

SASSAFRAS, IMITATION NO.3

1.	Benzyl Benzoate (10% solution)	280
2.	Citral	10
3.	Fenchone	110
4.	Lemongrass	70
5.	Limonene (10% solution)	250
6.	Pine, Oil	110
7.	Terpineol	170
		1000

SASSAFRAS, IMITATION NO. 4

1.	Camphene	50
2.	Phellandrene	150
3.	Pinene	50
4.	Sassafras, Imitation No.1*	250
5.	Sassafras, Imitation No.2*	250
6.	Sassafras, Oil	250
		1000

SASSAFRAS, SYNTHETIC NO. 1

1.	Camphene	100
2.	Maple, Lactone	1
3.	Musk	10
4.	Ocotea Cymbarum	200
5.	Phellandrene	150
6.	Pine, Oil	50
7.	Sassafras, Oil	489
		1000

SASSAFRAS, SYNTHETIC NO. 2

1.	Citral	10
2.	Benzyl Benzoate	280
3.	Fenchone, Oil	110
4.	Lemongrass	70
5.	Limonene	250
6.	Pine, Oil	110
7.	Terpineol	170
		1000

SAUCE FLAVOURS

Note: Sauces can be made with either fruits or vegetables e, g, apple date mango or onion, garlic, etc. These formulas can be applied to any type of fruit or vegetable.

SAUCE, FLAVOUR BASE

1.	Anyl Fruit or Vagetable	25 kg
2.	Distilled Water	35 l
3.	Sugar Syrup	55 l
4.	Vinegar, Natural	35 l

Let macerate for 10 days and then add:

5.	Acetate Acid (10% solution)	5 l
6.	Caramel (10% solution)	2 l
7.	Cinnamon (ground)	187 g
8.	Cloves (ground)	120 g
9.	Paprika (ground)	200 g
10.	Pepper (ground)	120 g
11.	Pimienta (ground)	200 g
12.	Tragacanth, Gum	16 g

Let macerate for another 10 days. Sieve and percolate.

SAUCE, SOY FLAVOUR

1.	Soy Beans (roasted powdered @ 250 F)	2 kg
2.	Propylene Glycol	1 l
3.	Ethyl Alcohol 95%	5 l
4.	Distilled Water	1 l

SAVORY, OIL NO. 1

1.	Cinnamic Aldehyde	400
2.	Geraniol	10
3.	Ocotea Cymbarum	100
4.	Propylene Glycol	480
5.	Vetiver, Oil	10
		1000

SAVORY, OIL NO. 2

1.	Cassia, Oil	750
2.	Ocotea Cymbarum	150
3.	Vetiver, Oil	100
		1000

SCOTCH, SMOKE TYPE TASTE

1. Barley, Malted (dried on peat fuel instead of coal) 250
2. Rye or Oats (unmalted and with no smoke taste) 250
3. Ethyl Alcohol 95% 250
4. Distilled Water 250

SMOKE, FLAVOUR

1. Hardwoods (Hickory or Maple) Burning

Introduce smoke to a liquid:

2. Glycerin (neutral), or Propylene Glycol, or Triethylene Glycol, or Tween

3. Ethyl Alcohol 95% 25% *of total amount*

SMOKE, FLAVOUR FOR FISH (SEASONING)

1.	Cassia, Oil	40
2.	Capsicum, Oil	30
3.	Clove, Oil	80
4.	Ginger, Oil	10
5.	Pimenta Berries, Oil	140
6.	Propylene Glycol	210
7.	Tween 80	490
		1000

SMOKE, FLAVOUR FOR MEAT

1.	Cade, Oil (rectified)	687
2.	Capsicum, Oleoresin	187
3.	Pepper, Black, Oil	126
		1000

SPEARMINT- WINTERGREEN- PEPPERMINT NO. 1

1.	Benzyl Alcohol	200
2.	Camphora	50
3.	Eucalyptol	170
4.	Menthol	120
5.	Menthone	60
6.	Menthyl Acetate	40
7.	Phellandrene (10% solution)	360
		1000

SPEARMINT- WINTERGREEN- PEPPERMINT NO. 2

1.	Benzyl Alcohol	200
2.	Methyl Salicylate (10% solution)	25
3.	Phellandrene (10% solution)	375
4.	Spearmint Wintergreen Peppermint No.1*	400
		1000

SPICE, IMITATION NO. 1

1.	Calamus, Oil	150
2.	Capsicum, Oil	150
3.	Cardamom, Oil	150
4.	Cassia, Oil	25
5.	Cinnamon, Oil	40
6.	Clove, Oil	60
7.	Coriander, Oil	30
8.	Nutmeg, Oil	80
9.	Pepper, Oil	150
10.	Pimento, Oil	15
11.	Tarragon, Oil	150
		1000

SPICE, IMITATION NO. 2

.	Cassia, Oil (10% solution)	250
.	Cinnamon, Oil (10% solution)	400
.	Clove, Oil	60
.	Coriander, Oil	30
.	Nutmeg, Oil	80
.	Orange, Oil	30
.	Pimento, Oil	150
		1000

STRAWBERRY, EXTRACT (NATURAL) NO. 1

. Strawberries (freshly harvested) 100 kg

Express and to the residue add:

2. Ethyl Alcohol 95% 30 l

Let stand for 3 days Distill altogether Add:

3.	Allspice, Oil	10 ml
4.	Cognac, Oil	5 ml
5.	Ethyl Acetate	8 ml
6.	Ethyl Salicylate	8 ml

Redistill to rectify
Yield 50 liters.

STRAWBERRY, EXTRACT (NATURAL) NO. 2

1.	Strawberry Fruits	500
2.	Ethyl Alcohol 95%	250
3.	Distilled Water	250
		1000

Macerate for 5 days and distill over 750 cc.

STRAWBERRY, IMITATION NO. 1

1.	Aldehyde C-16	210
2.	Almond, Bitter (pure)	2
3.	Amyl Butyrate	25
4.	Amyl Formate	4
5.	Amyl Valerianate	3
6.	Benzyl Acetate	5
7.	Benzyl valerianate	3
8.	Cinnamon, Oil	2
9.	Cognac, Oil	5
10.	Ethyl Acetate	15
11.	Ethyl Butyrate	35
12.	Ethyl Cinnamate	206
13.	Ethyl Fomate	4
14.	Ethyl Phenyl Glycidate	206
15.	Eugenol	2
16.	Isoamyl Butyrate	25
17.	Isoethyl Butyate	35
18.	NerethylOil	2
19.	Methyl Cinnamate	206
20.	Orange, Oil	1
21.	Orris, Oil	2
22.	Vanillin	2
		1000

STRAWBERRY, IMITATION NO. 2

1.	Acetaldehyde	2
2.	Acetic Acid	2
3.	Aldehyde C-9	5
4.	Aldehyde C-10	5
5.	Aldehyde C-14 (pure)	16
6.	Aldehyde C-16	25
7.	Almond Bitter Oil (pure)	1
8.	Amyl Acetate	20
9.	Amyl Butyrate	30
10.	Amyl Formate	9

11.	Amyl Valerianate	6
12.	Anethole	5
13.	Anisaldehyde	10
14.	Benzyl Acetate	8
15.	Benzyl Butyrate	6
16.	Benzyl Propionate	30
17.	Butyric Acid	1
18.	Cinnamon Oil	2
19.	Cinnamyl Butyrate	4
20.	Citral	4
21.	Citronellol	2
22.	Citronellyl Acetate	2
23.	Citronellyl Formate	1
24.	Ethyl Acetate	15
25.	Ethyl Cinnamate	20
26.	Ethyl Formate	10
27.	Ethyl Oenanthate	1
28.	Ethyl Phenyl Glycidate	25
29.	Ethyl Salicylate	10
30.	Eugenol	2
31.	Geraniol	30
32.	Hexyl Cinnamic Aldehyde	20
33.	Glycerin (neutral)	235
34.	ß-Ionone	20
35.	Isoethyl Butyrate	26
36.	Isojasmone	2
37.	Isovaleric Acid	2
38.	Lactic Acid	2
39.	Methyl Anthranilate	10
40.	Methyl Cinnamate	20
41.	Methyl Heptyne Carbonate	20
42.	Neroli, Oil	3
43.	Orange, Oil	1
44.	Orris, Oil	2
45.	Phenyl Ethyl Acetate	10
46.	Phenyl Ethyl Alcohol	20
47.	Phenyl Ethyl Butyrate	20
48.	Phenyl Ethyl Propionate	30
49.	Rhiodinol	1
50.	Rhodianyl Butyrate	2
51.	Vanillin	10
52.	Ethyl Alcohol 95%	235
		1000

STRAWBERRY, IMITATION NO. 3

1.	Aldehyde C-16	50
2.	Aldehyde C-20	50
3.	Ethyl Phenyl Glycidate	50
4.	Strawberry, Extract	175
5.	Ethyl Alcohol 95%	175
6.	Distillled Water	175
		1000

STRAWBERRY, IMITATION NO. 4

1.	Ethyl Methylphenylglycidate	25
2.	ß-Naphthyl Ethyl Ether	15
3.	Strawberry, Imitation No. 2*	480
4.	Ethyl Alcohol 95%	480
		1000

STRAWBERRY, IMITATION NO. 5

1.	Ethyl Methylphenylglycidate	15
2.	ß-Naphthyl Ethyl Ether	5
3.	Pineapple, Imitation No. 1*	150
4.	Raspberry, Imitation No. 1*	330
5.	Strawberry, Imitation No. 1*	500
		1000

STRAWBERRY, IMITATION NO. 6

1.	Ethyl Methylphenylglycidate	25
2.	Pineapple, Imitation No.2*	325
3.	Raspberry, Imitation No.2*	325
4.	Strawberry, Imitation No.3*	325
		1000

STRAWBERRY, IMITATION NO. 7

1. Ethyl Methylphenylglycidate 10
2. Pineapple, Imitation No.3* 248
3. Pineapple, Imitation No.4* 248
4. Raspberry, Imitation No.3* 248
5. Strawberry, Imitaton No.4* 246

1000

STRAWBERRY, IMITATION NO. 8

1. Ethyl Methylphenylglycidate 3
2. ß-Naphthyl Ethyl Ether 2
3. Pineapple, Imitation No. 4* 335
4. Raspberry, Imitation No. 4* 330
5. Strawberry, Imitation No. 5* 330

1000

STRAWBERRY, IMITATION NO. 9

1. Ethyl Methylphenylglycidate 2
2. ß-Naphthyl Ethyl Ether 3
3. Pineapple, Imitation No. 5* 100
4. Pineapple, Imitation No. 6* 50
5. Raspberry ,Imitation No. 5* 95
6. Strawberry, Imitation No. 6* 750

1000

STRAWBERRY, IMITATION NO.10

1. Amyl Acetate 30
2. Amyl Butyrate 10
3. Amyl Formate 10
4. Amyl Valerianate 20
5. Ethyl Acetate 15
6. Ethyl Methylphenylglycidate 10
7. Orris, Roots, Extract 50
8. Strawberry, Imitation No. 7* 100
9. Ethyl Alcohol 95% 755

1000

STRAWBERRY, IMITATION NO. 11

1. ß-Naphthyl Ethyl Ether 50
2. Strawberry, Imitation No. 8* 300
3. Ethyl Alcohol 95% 650

1000

STRAWBERRY, SYNTHETIC NO. 1

1. Almond, Oil (pure) 20
2. Amyl Butyrate 100
3. Amyl Formate 50
4. Amyl Valerate 3
5. Benzyl Acetate 100
6. Benzyl Valerate 3
7. Cinnamon, Oil 15
8. Cognac, Oil 20
9. Ethyl Acetate 100
10. Ethyl Butyrate 150
11. Ethyl Cinnamate 2
12. Ethyl Formate 50
13. Eugenol 20
14. Isoamyl Butyrate 100
15. Isoethyl Butyrate 150
16. Methyl Ethylphenylglycidate 2
17. Neroli, Oil 20
18. Orange, Oil (terpeneless) 50
19. Orris, Oil 15
20. Vanillin (10% solution) 30

1000

STRAWBERRY, SYNTHETIC NO. 2

1.	Amyl Acetate	30
2.	Amyl Butyrate	10
3.	Amyl Formate	10
4.	Amyl Valerianate	20
5.	Ethyl Acetate	15
6.	Ethyl Methylphenylglycidate	10
7.	Orris, Root, Oil	50
8.	Strawberry, Imitation No. 9*	428
9.	Ethyl Alcohol 95%	427
		1000

STRAWBERRY, SYNTHETIC NO. 3

1.	Aldehyde C-16	15
2.	Amyl Acetate	240
3.	Amyl Butyrate	120
4.	Ethyl Acetate	300
5.	Ethyl Benzoate	10
6.	Ethyl Butyrate	45
7.	Ethyl Formate	45
8.	Ethyl Nitrate	10
9.	Ethyl Salicylate	10
10.	Vanillin	5
11.	Glycerin (nautral)	200
		1000

STRAWBERRY SYNTHETIC NO. 4

1.	Acetate Acid, Glacial	10
2.	Aldehyde C-14	4
3.	Aldehyde C-16	22
4.	Anethole	1
5.	Benzyl Acetate	20
6.	Ethyl Salicylate	3
7.	ß-Ionone	3
8.	Methyl Anthranilate	20
9.	Methyl Cinnamate	5
10.	Vanillin	10
11.	Methyl Heptyne Carbonate	2
12.	Propylene Glycol	450
13.	Ethyl Alcohol 95%	450
		1000

STRAWBERRY, SYNTHETIC NO.5

1.	Acetic Acid	3
2.	Aldehyde C-16	35
3.	Amyl Formate	42
4.	Benzyl Butyrate	8
5.	Benzyl Propionate	15
6.	Butyric Acid	2
7.	Cinnamyl Butyrate	2
8.	Ethyl Butyrate	15
9.	Ethyl Acetate	95
10.	Ethyl Cinnmate	30
11.	Isopropyl Butyrate	43
12.	Isovaleric Acid	5
13.	Methyl Heptyne Carbonate	5
14.	Phenyl Butyl Ketone	4
15.	Phenyl Ethyl Butyrate	21
16.	Phenyl Ethyl Formate	5
17.	Phenyl Ethyl Propionate	15
18.	Vanillin	5
19.	Ethyl Alcohol 95%	325
20.	Distilled Water	325
		1000

STRAWBERRY, SYNTHETIC NO. 6

1.	Amyl Butyrate	200
2.	Amyl Formate	48
3.	Benzyl Acetate	200
4.	Ethyl Acetate	200

5. Ethyl Benzoate 85
6. Ethyl Butyrate 135
7. Ethyl Phenyl Glycidate 20
8. Ethyl Salicylate 6
9. Nerolin 2
10. Vanillin 4
11. Ethyl Alcohol 95% 100

1000

STRAWBERRY, SYNTHETIC NO. 7

1. Aldehyde C-14 (pure) 18
2. Aldehyde C-16 12
3. Benzaldehyde (pure) 3
4. Benzyl Acetate 45
5. Benzyl Benzoate 11
6. Cinnamic Aldehyde 2
7. Ethyl Acetate 17
8. Ethyl Benzoate 15
9. Ethyl Butyrate 24
10. Ethyl Cinnamate 40
11. Ethyl Formate 5
12. Ethyl Pelargonate 20
13. Ethyl Phenyl Glycidate 20
14. Ethyl Salicylate 3
15. Geraniol 10
16. Isoamyl Acetate 11
17. Isoamyl Butyrate 40
18. Isoamyl Formate 25
19. Isoamyl Isovalerianate 18
20. Isobutyl Isovalerianate 1
21. Nerolin 5
22. Vanillin 5
23. Ethyl Alcohol 95% 325
24. Distilled Water 325

1000

STRAWBERRY, STNTHETIC NO. 8

1. Amyl Acetate 90
2. Amyl Butyrate 60
3. Ethyl Acetate 150
4. Ethyl Butyrate 150
5. Ethyl Formate 30
6. Ethyl Nitrate 30
7. Ethyl Salicylate 30
8. Glycerin (nautral) 60
9. Ethyl Alcohol 95% 400

1000

STRAWBERRY, SYNTHETIC NO. 9

1. Aldehyde C-16 20
2. Amyl Acetate 30
3. Amyl Butyrate 20
4. Ethyl Acetate 50
5. Ethyl Butyrate 50
6. Ethyl Formate 10
7. Ethyl Nitrate 10
8. Ethyl Salicylate 10
9. Ethyl Alcohol 95% 400
10. Distilled Water 400

1000

STRAWBERRY, SYNTHETIC NO. 10 "GENERAL BASE"

1. Aldehyde C-16 300
2. Ethyl Phenyl Glycidate 200
3. Methyl Cinnamate 200
4. Methyl Heptyne Carbonate 5
5. Nerolin 20
6. Ethyl Alcohol 95% 138
7. Distilled Water 137

1000

STRAWBERRY, SYNTHETIC NO. 11

1. Alcohol C-7 50
2. Aldehyde C-14 25

3.	Aldehyde C-16	25
4.	Cinnamyl Isobutyrate	25
5.	Cinnamyl Isovalerate	35
6.	Ethyl Lactate	10
7.	Ethyl Valerate	25
8.	Propylene Glycol	400
9.	Vanillin	5
10.	Ethyl Alcohol 95 %	400
		1000

STRAWBERRY, SYNTHETIC NO. 12

1.	Aldehyde C-16 (10% solution)	20
2.	Ethyl Butyrate	200
3.	Ethyl Pelargonate	75
4.	Ethyl Phenyl Glycidate (10% solution)	250
5.	Glycerol	125
6.	Methyl Anthranilate	10
7.	Methyl Cinnamate	10
8.	Vanillin (10% solution)	10
9.	Ethyl Alcohol 95%	300
		1000

STRAWBERRY, SYNTHETIC NO. 13

1.	Aldehyde C-16 (10% solution)	20
2.	Borneol	5
3.	Bornyl Acetate	5
4.	Ethyl Butyrate	100
5.	Ethyl Caproate	25
6.	Ethyl Phenyl Glycidate	200
7.	Ionone	10
8.	Methyl Cinnamate	50
9.	Vanillin (10% solution)	10
10.	Ethyl Alcohol 95%	575
		1000

SYRUP, BASE FOR FLAVOUR (PANCAKE)

1.	Caramel ** (Quantity depending on desired colour)	
2.	Citric Acid (10% solution)	1
3.	Corn Sweetener (syrup)	300
4.	Flavour, Natural (10% solution)	10
5.	Flavour, Synthetic (10% solution)	5
6.	Potassium Sorbate (10% solution)	1
7.	Sodium Benzoate (10% solution)	1
8.	Distilled Water	70
		1000

SYRUP, SIMPLE, BASE FOR FLAVOUR

1.	Sugar	3000 g
2.	Distilled Water	700 ml

TAMARIND, EXTRACT (NATURAL)

1.	Tamarind, Fruit Pulp	10 kg
2.	Ethyl Alcohol 95%	10 l
3.	Distilled Water	10 l

Let stand for 10 days, stirring for 1 h each day. Collect the juice without any pressure. Add to the residue:

4.	Ethyl Alcohol 95%	10 l
5.	Distilled Water	10 l

Let stand for 10 days, stirring for 1 h each day. Collect the juice without any pressure. Add to the residue.

6.	Ethyl Alcohol 95%	10 l
7.	Distilled Water	10 l

Let stand for 10 days, stirring for 1 h each day. Put altogether and distill.

Yield 60 liters.

Note: The pulp of the tamarind fruit is the most useful for beverages. The pulp is about 75% of the fruit with 30-40% sugar and 9-15% tartaric acid. The tartaric acid is useful for effervescent beverages.

Sugar can be added according to personal taste to make the beverage sweeter or more pleasent.

In large quantities, the beverage has a slightly purgative action.

The leaves of tamarind must not be used due to their acidic content.

The seeds of tamarind if pounded and boiled form adhesives.

TANGERINE, EXTRACT (NATURAL)

1.	Tangerine Peels (fresh well ground)	10 kg
2.	Ethyl Alcohol 95%	20 l

Let stand for 3 day. Express and to the residue add:

3.	Distilled Water Let stand for aNother 3 days and add :	20 l
4.	Orange, Sweet, Oil	6 l
5.	Tangerine, Oil	4 l
6.	Thyme, Oil	3 ml

Distill altogether.
Yield 50 liters.

TANGERINE, IMITATION NO. 1

1.	Ethyl Acetate	150
2.	Isoamyl Acetate	100
3.	Isoamyl Butyrate	350
4.	Orange, Bitter, Oil	100
5.	Tangerine, Oil	200
6.	Lemon, Oil	100
		1000

TANGERINE, IMITATON NO. 2

1.	Ethyl Acetate	150
2.	Ethyl Butyrate (10% solution)	350
3.	Isoamyl Acetate	100
4.	Lemon, Oil	100
5.	Orange, Bitter, Oil	100
6.	Tangerine, Oil	200
		1000

TARRAGON

1.	Tarragon	30 kg

Bland with:

2. Vinegar, Natural 240 l

Let stand for 1 week. Sieve and add:

3. Vinegar, Natural 1600 l

Filter.

TEA, IMITATION NO.1

1.	Benzyl Acetate	50
2.	Ethyl Acetate	400
3.	Ethyl Formate	100
4.	Ethyl Oenanthate	10
5.	Ethyl Pelargonate	60
6.	Isoamyl Butyrate	200
7.	Lamon, Oil	10
8.	Nerolin	2
9.	Phenyl Ethyl Alcohol	158
10.	Vanillin	10
		1000

TEA, IMITATION NO. 2

1.	Benzyl Acetate	50
2.	Bromelia	2
3.	Ethyl Acetate (10% solution)	420
4.	Ethyl Formate	140
5.	Ethyl Oenanthate	7
6.	Ethyl Pelargonate	60
7.	Isoamyl Butyrate (10% solution)	280
8.	Lemon, Oil	10
9.	Phenyl Ethyl Alcohol	1
10.	Vanillin (10% solution)	30
		1000

TEA, NATURAL NO. 1

1.	Tea, Leaves (dry)	3 kg
2.	Ethyl Alcohol 95%	10 l
3.	Distilled Water	10 l

Let stand for 3 days. Filter.

TEA, NATURAL NO. 2

1.	Rose, Flower Petals	1 kg
2.	Tea, Leaves (dry)	2 kg
3.	Ethyl Alcohol 95%	10 l

Let stand for 1 day and then add:

4. Water, Boiling 8 l

Let cool and express. Add:

5.	Pineapple (Ananas) Extract (Natural) No. 1*	1 l
6.	Lemon, Oil	24 ml
7.	Orange Flowers, Oil	8 ml

Filter.
Yield 10 liters.

TEA, NATURAL NO. 3

1.	Pineapple (Ananas), Extract (Natural) No. 1*	1500 ml
2.	Arrack	1 kg
3.	Lemon, Oil	150 ml
4.	Orange Flowers, Oil	15 ml
5.	Rose, Petals (dry)	150 g
6.	Tea Ceylon (black)	3 kg
7.	Ethyl Alcohol 95%	2 l
8.	Distilled Water	2 l

Let stand for 3 days

Percolate and then add:

9. Distilled Water q.s. 20 l

Concentration: 60 ml/gal

TOBACCO FORMULAS FOR IMPROVING FLAVOUR AND ODOUR

Family: Solanaceae
Genus: Nicotiana

SPECIES OF
NATURAL TOBACCO

1. *N. acuminata*, Northern Syria
2. *N. latakia,* Turkey, Syria
3. *N. multivalis*
4. *N. nepansa,* Havana
5. *N. persica,* Iran, Shiraz
6. *N. quadrivalis*
7. *N. rustica,* southtern Europe, Turkey
8. *N. tabacum,* South America

These formulas can be used to improve the natural flavour and odour of tobacco for cigarettes, cigars, chewing tobacco, snuff tobacco, pipe tobacco, etc.

TOBACCO, CHEWING, FLAVOUR NO. 1

1.	Cascarilla, Oil	50
2.	Cassia, Oil	50
3.	Clove, Oil	50
4.	Heliotropin	20
5.	Nutmeg, Oil	80
6.	Orange, Sweet, Oil	150
7.	Rhodinyl Valerianate	50
8.	Rose, Oil	30
9.	Tonka Beans, Tincture	500
10.	Vanillin	20
		1000

TOBACCO, CHEWING, FLAVOUR NO. 2

1.	Anise Seeds, Oil	150
2.	Caraway, Oil	150
3.	Cascarilla, Oil	100
4.	Clove, Oil	150
5.	Nutmeg, Oil	100
6.	Valerian, Oil	200
7.	Vanilla Beans, Tincture	150
		1000

TOBACCO, CIGARETTE, FLAVOUR NO. 1

1.	Bergamot, Oil	40
2.	Clove, Oil	10
3.	Cascarilla, Oil	100
4.	Geranium, Oil	400
5.	Isobutyl Valerianate	50
6.	Lavender, Oil	80
7.	Menthol	40
8.	Orange, Sweet, Oil	100
9.	Rose Otto, Oil	20
10.	Tonka Beans, Oil	60
11.	Orris Tincture	100
		1000

TOBACCO, CIGARETTE, FLAVOUR NO. 2

1.	Bergamot, Oil	30
2.	Cassia, Oil	5
3.	Clove, Oil	15

4.	Geranium, Oil	50
5.	Lemon, Oil	30
6.	Orange, Sweet, Oil	70
7.	Orris, Tincture	500
8.	Phenyl Ethyl Valerianate	20
9.	Tonka Beans, Tincture	30
10.	Vanilla, Tincture	250
		1000

TOBACCO, CIGARETTE, FLAVOUR NO. 3

1.	Angelica Roots, Oil	8
2.	Cardamom, Oil	2
3.	Coriander Seeds, Oil	125
4.	Mace, Oil	15
5.	Tonka Beans, Oil	125
6.	Ethyl Alcohol 95%	363
7.	Distilled Water	362
		1000

TOBACCO FLAVOUR GENERAL

1.	Bergamot, Oil	50
2.	Clary Sage, Oil	10
3.	Cascarilla, Oil	50
4.	Castoreum, Resinoid	50
5.	Labdanum, Resinoid	50
6.	Licorice, Extract	200
7.	Methyl Ionone	50
8.	Phenyl Acetic Acid	100
9.	Rum, Ether Flavour*	350
10.	Sandalwood or Cedarwood, Oil	50
11.	y-Valerolactone	20
12.	Vetiver, Oil	20
		1000

TOBACCO FLAVOUR NO. 2

1.	Cedar, Oil	350
2.	Mastic *(Pistacia lentiscus)*, Resinoid	60
3.	Methyl Eugenol	340
4.	Storax, Resinoid	250
		1000

TOBACCO FLAVOUR NO. 3

1.	Cascarilla, Oil	300
2.	Cedar, Oil	250
3.	Clove, Oil	350
4.	Vanillin	100
		1000

TOBACCO FLAVOR NO. 4

1.	Amyl Valerianate	25
2.	Cascarilla, Oil	13
3.	Castor, Tincture	48
4.	Butyric Acid	36
5.	Ethyl Valerianate	13
6.	Ethyl Butyrate	135
7.	Geranium, Oil	25
8.	Lavender, Oil	15
9.	Peru Balsam	36
10.	Rum, Ether Flavour*	140
11.	Sandalwood, Oil	32
12.	St. John's Bread, Tincture	96
13.	Valerian, Oil	7
14.	Vanillin	25
15.	Ethyl Alcohol 95%	177
16.	Distilled Water	177
		1000

TOBACCO FLAVOUR NO.5

1.	Butyl Butyrate	275
2.	Cardamom, Oil	50
3.	Cinnamon, Oil	150
4.	Clove, Oil	125
5.	Ginger, Oil	250
6.	Isoeugenol	125
7.	Vanillin	25
		1000

TOBACCO FLAVOUR NO. 6

1.	Bergamot, Oil	175
2.	Clove, Oil	50
3.	Cinnamon, Oil	50
4.	Ethyl Valerianate	50
5.	Geranium, Oil	175
6.	Lemon, Oil	175
7.	Methyl Ionone	50
8.	Orange, Oil	50
9.	Tonka Beans, Resinoid	175
10.	Vanillin	50
		1000

TOBACCO FLAVOUR NO. 7

1.	Bergamot, Oil	40
2.	Cascarilla, Oil	40
3.	Clove, Oil	40
4.	Ethyl Valerianate	40
5.	Geranium, Oil	180
6.	Lavender, Oil	180
7.	Methyl Ionone	40
8.	Orange, Oil	180
9.	Rose, Oil	40
10.	Tonka Beans, Resinoid	180
11.	Vanillin	40
		1000

TOBACCO FLAVOUR NO. 8

1.	Geranium, Oil	9
2.	Jasmine, Absolute	2
3.	Lavender, Oil	8
4.	Methyl Phenyl Acetate	1
5.	Orange Blossom, Absolute	5
6.	Orris, Tincture	800
7.	Patchouli, Oil	2
8.	Rose Otto, Oil	5
9.	Tonka Absolute	5
10.	Tuberose, Absolute	3
11.	Vanilla Beans, Tincture	160
		1000

TOBACCO FLAVOUR NO. 9

1.	Honey, Imitation No. 1*	20
2.	Lovage, Oil	20
3.	Peru Balsam	85
4.	Phenyl Ethyl Valerianate	20
5.	Propylene Glycol	238
6.	Rhodinol Acetate	20
7.	Rum, Oil*	245
8.	Rose, Otto, Oil	2
9.	Snakeroot, Oil	20
10.	Styrax	85
11.	Tolu Balsam	85
12.	Valerian, Oil	20
13.	Vanillin	140
		1000

TUTTI FRUTTI

1.	Pineapple (Ananas) Extract (Natural) No. 1*	360
2.	Lemon, Extract (Natural)	240
3.	Raspberry, Extract (Natural) No.1 *	130
4.	Rum, Ether Flavour*	130

5.	Strawberry, Extract (Natural) *	140
		1000

VALERIAN, ROOT, EXTRACT (NATURAL)

1.	Valerian, Roots (well Powdered)	300
2.	Ethyl Alcohol 95%	350
3.	Distilled Water	350
		1000

Macerate and let stand for 8 days. Distill.

VANILLA

1.	Vanilla, Oil	100
2.	Ethyl Alcohol 95%	900
		1000

VANILLA, CONCENTRATED FLAVOUR

1.	Caramel Colouring (10% solution)	100
2.	Glycerol	500
3.	Sugar	100
4.	Vanillin (10% solution)	100
5.	Ethyl Alcohol 95%	200
		1000

VANILLA, FLAVOUR NO. 1

1.	Caramel Colouring	10
2.	Glycerol	100
3.	Vanillin (10% solution)	20
4.	Ethyl Alcohol 95%	870
		1000

VANILLA, FLAVOUR NO. 2

1.	Bourbonal (Ethyl Vanillin) (10% solution)	100
2.	Heliotropin Piperonal	100
3.	Tonka, Oil	100
4.	Vanilla Beans, Oil	200
5.	Ethyl Alcohol 95%	500
		1000

VANILLA, FLAVOUR NO. 3

1.	Vanilla, Beans Bourbonal	20
2.	Vanillin (10% solution)	83
3.	Ethyl Alcohol 95%	897
		1000

VANILLA, IMITATION NO. 1

1.	Cascara Sagrada, Bark	100
2.	Chicory, Seeds	45
3.	Prune Juice	55
4.	Ethyl Alcohol 95%	385
5.	Vanillin	30
6.	Distilled Water	385
		1000

Boil and distill.

VANILLA, IMITATION NO. 2

1.	Furfuryl Alcohol	125
2.	Propylene Glycol	250
3.	Tolu Balsam	25
4.	Vanillin	600
		1000

VANILLA BEANS, EXTRACT (NATURAL) NO. 1

1. Vanillin Beans (well crushed) 10 kg
2. Ethyl Alcohol 95% 20 l
3. Distilled Water 20 l

Macerate for 10 days. Express and to the residue add:

4. Ethyl Alcohol 95% 20 l
5. Distilled Water 20 l

Macerate for 10 days Express and to the residue add:

6. Ethyl Alcohol 95% 20 l
7. Distilled Water 20 l

Let stand for another 10 days Distill altogether.

Yield 120 liters.

VANILLA BEANS, EXTRACT (NATURAL) NO. 2

1. Sugar 100
2. Vanilla Beans (cut very fine) 100
3. Ethyl Alcohol 95% 400
4. Distilled Water 400

1000

VANILLA BEANS, IMITATION

1. Caramel (per desied colour)
2. Sugar 2 kg
3. Vanilla Beans, Extract (Natural) No. 1* 6 l
4. Vanillin 200 g
5. Ethyl Alcohol 95% 6 l
6. Distilled Water 6 l

Yield 20 liters.

VANILLA BEANS, TINCTURE NO. 1

1. Vanilla Beans (finely cut) 10 g
2. Ethyl Alcohol 95% 990 ml

VANILLA BEANS, TINCTURE NO. 2

1. Vanilla Beans (finely cut) 10 g
2. Vanillin 10 g
3. Ethyl Alcohol 95% 980 ml

VANILLA, CRYSTAL (PARTIAL)

1. Anisic Aldehyde 10
2. Benzyl Benzoate 550
3. Cinnamic Alcohol 40
4. Heliotropin 100
5. Vanillin 200
6. Ethyl Alcohol 95% 100

1000

VANILLIN, FLAVOURED MIXTURE

1. Cardamom, Oil 15
2. Cinnamaldehyde 30
3. Ethyl Acetate (10% solution) 500
4. Ethyl Oenanthate 85
5. Eugenol 40
6. Isoamyl Acetate (10% solution) 250
7. Vanillin (10% solution) 80

1000

VANILLA NO. 1

1.	Glycerin (neutral)	50 ml
2.	Heliotropin	50 g
3.	Vanillin	450 g
4.	Ethyl Alcohol 95%	250 ml
5.	Distilled Water	200 ml

VANILLIN NO.2 (ESTER MIXTURE)

1.	Cinnamic Aldehyde	30
2.	Ethyl Acetate	500
3.	Ethyl Oenanathate	85
4.	Eugenol	40
5.	Isoamyl Acetate	250
6.	Vanillin	95
		1000

VANILLIN, SUPER ODOUR

1.	Anisic Aldehyde	10
2.	Benzyl Alcohol	200
3.	Benzyl Benzoate	200
4.	Cinnamic Alcohol	20
5.	Heliotropin	50
6.	Vanillin	100
7.	Ethyl Alcohol 95%	210
8.	Distilled Water	210
		1000

VANILLIN, WATER SOLUBLE

1.	Anisic Aldehyde	10
2.	Cinnamic Alcohol	20
3.	Heliotropin	50
4.	Propylene Glycol	300
5.	Vanillin	100
6.	Ethyl Alcohol 95%	260
7.	Distilled Water	260
		1000

VERMOUTH

1.	Agaric, White	8
2.	Aloe	18
3.	Angelica, Roots	13
4.	Anise, Seeds	5
5.	Balm	8
6.	Benzoin	5
7.	Calamus, Roots	16
8.	Chamomile, Flowers	2
9.	Cardamom	2
10.	Cantaury	8
11.	Cinchona, Bark (Peruvian or Bolivian)	18
12.	Cinnamon, Ceylon, Quills	13
13.	Cloves	8
14.	Coriander, Seeds	18
15.	Dittany (Origanum leaves of Creta)	38
16.	Elder	18
17.	Elecampane, Roots	13
18.	Galangal, Roots	10
19.	Gentian, Roots	18
20.	Germander	13
21.	Hops, Flowers	13
22.	Hyssop	18
23.	Marjoram	2
24.	Nutmeg	23
25.	Orange, Bitter, Peels	10
26.	Orris, Roots and Powdered Flowers	10
27.	Pimento	3
28.	Quassia, Bitter, Wood	8
29.	Rhubarb, Roots	18
30.	Saffron, Thread	2
31.	Sage, Flowers and Leaves	10
32.	Star Anise, Seeds	5
33.	Sugar	50
34.	Thistle	13
35.	Thyme	18
36.	Vanilla	2
37.	Wine, White	500

38.	Wormwood	20
39.	Wort, Roots	13
40.	Zedoary	10
		1000

Macerate for 20 days in a double amount of ethyl alcohol 95% (2000 cc). Blend every day. Press and filter. Add Caramel 2% Filter.
Use: 1 liter for 100 liters of wine.

VERMOUTH, ITALIAN TYPE NO. 1

1.	Absinthe (Artemisia), Wormwood Oil	1
2.	Angelica, Root	10
3.	Cardamom, Seeds	35
4.	Cardo Benedict, Herb	20
5.	Calamus, Root	20
6.	Centaury	20
7.	Elecampane, Root	20
8.	Gentian, Root	10
9.	Germander	2
10.	Nutmeg	2
11.	Orange, Peels (dried)	1
12.	Ethyl Alcohol 95%	439
13.	Distilled Water	420
		1000

Let macerate for 10 days Press and filter. Use: 1 liter for 100 liters of wine.

VERMOUTH, ITALIAN TYPE NO. 2

1.	Absinthe	1 kg
2.	Angelica, Root	240 g
3.	Calamus, Root	1 kg
4.	Cardamom	150 g
5.	Cardo Santo (Blessed Thistle)	1 kg
6.	Cantaury	1 kg
7.	Cinnamon, Bark	109 g
8.	Elecampane, Root	1 kg
9.	Gentian, Root	40 g
10.	Germander	1 kg
11.	Nutmeg	60 g
12.	Wine, White Sweet	375 1
13.	Ethyl Alcohol 95%	20 1

Let stand for 8 days. Press. Filter. Bottle. Concentration: 1 liter for 1000 liters of wine.

VINEGAR, SPICED

1.	Chilies, Hot Pepper	22 kg
2.	Cloves	14 kg
3.	Coriander	25 kg
4.	Ginger	15 kg
5.	Mustard Seeds	15 kg
6.	Pepper, Black	14 kg
7.	Pimiento	15 kg
8.	Vinegar Natural (boiling)	280 gal

Let stand for 1 week for maceration. Sieve and blend with:

9.	Vinegar, Natural	600 gal

Filter.

Yield 1000 gal

VIOLET, FLAVOUR

1.	Bergamot, Oil	50
2.	Eugenol	20
3.	Heliotropin	40

4.	Hydroxycitronellal	30
5.	L-Ionone	200
6.	ß-Ionone	150
7.	Lauric Aldehyde	2
8.	Methyl Ionone	100
9.	Musk	10
10.	Rose, Oil	30
11.	Sandalwood	10
12.	Vanillin (10% solution)	20
13.	Ylang Ylang, Oil	40
14.	Ethyl Alcohol 95%	298
		1000

WALNUT, EXTRACT (NUTURAL)

1.	Walnut Kernels (fresh without rancid taste, very well rasped or totally pulverized)	10 kg
2.	Ethyl Alcohol 95%	15 l
3.	Distilled Water	15 l

Macerate for 10 days, stirring for 1 h every day. Collect 20 l without any pressure and to the residue add:

4.	Distilled Water	20 l

Let stand for another 3 days and then add:

5.	Amyl Formate	45 ml
6.	Ethyl Oenanthate	25 ml

Distill altogether

Yield 30 liters.

WALNUT, FLAVOUR FOR KETCHUP

1.	Acetic Acid	1 ml
2.	Cardamom, Seeds (ground)	1 kg
3.	Cloves (ground)	1 kg
4.	Ginger, Root	1 kg
5.	Pepper, Black (ground)	1 kg
6.	Pimenta (ground)	1 kg
7.	Salt (20% solution)	1 l
8.	Walnut Kernels (fresh, without rancid taste, well pulverized)	6 kg
9.	Ethyl Alcohol 95%	10 l
10.	Distilled Water	10 l

Macerate for 10 days, stirring for l h every day. Express and to the residue add:

11.	Ethyl Alcohol 95%	10 l
12.	Distilled Water	10 l

Let stand for another 3 days. Boil gently for 1 h. Cool and express. Put all juices together and filter.

Yield 40 liters.

WALNUT, IMITATION NO. 1

1.	Ethyl Valerianate	77
2.	Maple Flavour*	248
3.	Methyl-p-Cresol	38
4.	Valerian Root, Extract (Natural)*	637
		1000

WALNUT, IMITATION NO. 2

1.	Amyl Valerianate	57

2.	Anisaldehyde	23
3.	Benzaldehyde (pure)	21
4.	Butyric Acid	23
5.	Cardamom, Oil	7
6.	Clove, Oil	26
7.	Ethyl Acetate	45
8.	Ethyl Oenanthate	57
9.	Lemon, Oil	115
10.	Mace, Oil	100
11.	Orange, Sweet, Oil	50
12.	Vanillin	21
13.	Ethyl Alcohol 95%	455
		1000

WALNUT, IMITATION NO. 3

1.	Anisaldehyde	9
2.	Benzaldehyde (pure)	28
3.	Butyric Acid	6
4.	Cardamom, Oil	20
5.	Ethyl Acetate	34
6.	Ethyl Oenanthate	23
7.	Eugenol	10
8.	Isoamyl Isovalerianate	24
9.	Lemon, Oil	31
10.	Mace, Oil	45
11.	Nutmeg, Oil	6
12.	Orange, Oil	8
13.	Vanillin	21
14.	Ethyl Alcohol 95%	368
15.	Distilled Water	367
		1000

WALNUT, IMITATION NO. 4

1.	Anisaldehyde	12
2.	Benzaldehyde (pure, 10% solution)	25
3.	Butyric Acid	10
4.	Cardamom, Oil	3
5.	Ethyl Acetate (10% solution)	320
6.	Ethyl Oenanthate	190
7.	Eugenol	15
8.	Isoamyl Isovalerate (10% solution)	220
9.	Lemon, Oil	75
10.	Mace, Oil	75
11.	Orange, Oil	25
12.	Vanillin (10% solution)	30
		1000

WALNUT, IMITATION NO. 5

1.	Anisaldehyde	10
2.	Benzaldehyde (pure, 10% solution)	20
3.	Butyric Acid	3
4.	Cardamom, Oil	2
5.	Ethyl Acetate (10% solution)	300
6.	Ethyl Oenanthate (10% solution)	300
7.	Eugenol	5
8.	Isoamyl Isovalerate (10% solution)	300
9.	Lemon, Oil	10
10.	Nutmeg, Oil	20
11.	Orange, Oil	20
12.	Vanillin (10% solution)	10
		1000

WALNUT, IMITATION NO. 6

1.	Anisaldehyde	5
2.	Benzaldehyde (pure 10% solution)	40
3.	Butyric Acid	7
4.	Cardamom, Oil	3
5.	Ethyl Acetate (10% solution)	400
6.	Ethyl Oenanthate	200

7. Eugenol 10
8. Isoamyl Isovalerante 200
9. Lemon, Oil 10
10. Mace, Oil 60
11. Orange, Oil 40
12. Vanillin (10% solution) 25

1000

WINTERGREEN

1. Ethyl Salicylate (10% solution) 30
2. Ethyl Alcohol 95% 970

1000

WINTERGREEN, SYNTHETIC NO. 1

1. Methyl Salicylate 50
2. Ethyl Alcohol 95% 750
3. Distilled Water 200

1000

Stir. Filter.

WINTERGREEN, SYNTHETIC NO. 2

1. Methyl Salicylate 30
2. Ethyl Alcohol 95% 570
3. Distilled Water 400

1000

Stir. Filter.

WINTERGREEN, SYNTHETIC NO. 3

1. Methyl Salicylate (10% solution) 20
2. Ethyl Alcohol 95% 980

1000

WOODRUFF, EXTRACT (NATURAL)

1. Pineapple (Ananas) Extract (Natural) No.1* 1 l
2. Grape, Extract (Natural) N0.1* 2 l
3. Orange Flower, (Natural)* 120 ml
4. Tonka Beans Extract (ground) 120 g
5. Wine (Brandy) 1 l
6. Woodruff Flowering Tops (fresh, crushed, and expressed**) 8 kg
7. Ethyl Alcohol 95% 4 l

Let stand for 3 days Express 10 l.

WOODRUFF, IMITATION

1. Tonka Beans, Tincture (1:5) 1 l
2. Vanillin 30 g
3. Ethyl Alcohol 95% (hot) 450 ml
4. Ethyl Alcohol 95% 4 l
5. Distilled Water 5 l

Yield 10 liters

WOODRUFF, SYNTHETIC NO. 1

1. Benzyl Acetate 75
2. Ethyl Acetate 240
3. Ethyl Oenanthate 170
4. Ethyl Pelargonate 100
5. Isoamyl Butyrate 280

6.	Vanillin	135
		1000

WOODRUFF, SYNTHETIC NO.2

1.	Benzyl Acetate	75
2.	Ethyl Acetate (10% solution)	280
3.	Ethyl Oenanthate	170
4.	Ethyl Pelargonate	100
5.	Isoamyl Butyrate (10% solution)	240
6.	Vanillin (10% solution)	135
		1000

WORCESTERSHIRE SAUCE NO. 1

1.	Brandy	7 l
2.	Cherry Essence (Natural)*	5 l
3.	Coriander (ground)	1 kg
4.	Mace (ground)	1 kg
5.	Mushroom (dried and ground)	10 kg
6.	Pepper, Cayenne (pulverized)	1 kg
7.	Pimenta (ground)	1 kg
8.	Sugar	3 kg
9.	Tamarind, Extract (Natural)*	10 1
10.	Vinegar Natural	70 l
11.	Walnut, Flavour for Ketchup*	10 l

Percolate after 10 days of stirring for I h each day. Filter.

Yield 100 liters

Note: Well chopped garlic or onion may be added (1 kg).

WORCESTERSHIRE SAUCE NO. 2

1.	Clove (ground)	3 kg
2.	Lemon, Peels (ground)	6 kg
3.	Nutmeg (ground)	3 kg
4.	Pepper, Cayenne (ground)	4 kg
5.	Soy Sauce, Flavour	4 l
6.	Vinegar Natural	70 l
7.	Sugar	3 kg
8.	Walnut Flavour for Ketchup*	8 l

Percolate after 10 days of stirring for I h each day. Filter.

Yield : 75 liters

Note: Well chopped garlic or onion may be added (1 kg).

Chapter-4

CHEMICAL SPECIFICATIONS FOR PERFUME AND FLAVOUR COMPONENTS

NOTE ON SOLVENTS:

An exlanation is offered regarding the solvents listed for each ingredient of the formules:

1. Fixed Oil-A nonvolatile fatty oil from a plant distinguished from the essential oil.

2. Mineral Oil-Any of various oils of mineral origin especially the distillate from petroleum (petrolatum). Naphtha derives from a crude petroleum used as a solvent and is considered a mineral spirit.

3. Vegetable Oil-Any of the various oils obtained from plants and used industrially and in food products. Major vegetable oils include: linseed, cottonseed, soybean, castor, corn, sesame.

4. Volatile Oil-An oil that volatilizes with a distinctive flavour and odour of the original plant and which is called an essential oil. It is used for flavour and perfume compositions.

5. Tincture-An alcoholic or aqueous alcoholic solution of plants or minerals. Tincture is more diluted than fluid extract and less volatile. than spirit.

ACETALDEHYDE

SYNONYMS: Acetic aldehyde; Aldehyde; Ethanal; Ethyl aldehyde
CAS NUMBER: 75-07-0
MOLECULAR FORMULA: C_2H_4O
MOLECULAR WEIGHT: 44.05
CHARACTERISTICS: *Form Liquid; Colour: Colorless; Odor:* Fruity pungent
PHYSICAL PROPERTIES: *Specific gravity:0783 (18 C); Refractive index:* 1.3316

(20 C); Boiling point: 20.2 C; Freezing point:-123.5 C;Flash point: 40 F (Open Cup); Solubility: Soluble in benzene gasoline, naphtha, toluene, xylene, turpentine, acetone

DERIVATION: Oxidation of ethylene; vapour-phase oxidation of propane and butane; direct conversion of ethylene

WARNING AND CAUTION: Highly flammable and toxic; dangerous fire and explosion risk

ACETATE C-8

SYNONYMS: Octyl acetate
MOLECULAR FORMULA: $C_{10}H_{20}O_2$
MOLECULAR WEIGHT: 172.27
CHARACTERISTICS: Form : Liquid; Colour : Colourless; odour : Orange. Jasmine physical properties Specific gravity: 0.865-0.868(25/25 C); Refractive index: 1.4180-1.4210(20 C); Flash point: 185 F(TCC); Solubility: Soluble in 4 parts 70% ethyl alcohol 95%
DERIVATION: From oil of green tea and Heracleum giganteum L.

ACETATE C-9

SYNONYMS: Nonyl acetate
MOLECULAR FORMULA: $C_{11}H_{22}O_2$
MOLECULAR WEIGHT: 186.30
CHARACTERISTICS: Form: Liquid; Color: Colorless; Odor: Fruity floral, strong
PHYSICAL PROPERTIES: Secific gravity: 0.864-0.868 (25/25 C); Refractive index: 1.4220-1.4260 (20 C); Flash point:>212 F(TCC)

ACETATE C-10

SYNONYMS: Decyl acetate
MOLECULAR FORMULA: $C_{12}H_{24}O_2$
MOLECULAR WEIGHT: 200.32
CHARACTERISTICS: Form: Liquid; Colour: Colorless; Odor: Flora orange rose
PHYSICAL PROPERTIES: Specific gravity: 0.862-0.866 (25/25 C Refractive index: 1.4250-1.4300 (20 C); Boiling Point: 187-190C; Flas point:>212 F(TCC); Solubility: Soluble in ethylalcohal 95% (2 par 80%), ether, glacial acetic acid, benzene; insoluble in water

ACETATE C-11

SYNONYMS: 10 Undecen 1 yl acetate
MOLECULAR FORMULA: $C_{13}H_{24}O_2$
MOLECULAR WEIGHT: 212.33
CHARACTERISTICS: Form: Liquid; Color: Colorless; Odor: Flor fatty
PHYSICAL PROPERTIES : Specific gravity: 0.876-0.880 (25/2 C); Refractive index: 1.4380-1.4420 (20 C); Flash point: 212 (TCC); Solubility: Soluble in ethyl alcohol 95% (2 parts 80%)

ACETATE C-12

SYNONYMS: Lauryl acetate; Dodecyl acetate
MOLECULAR FORMULA $C_{14}H_{28}O_2$
MOLECULAR WEIGHT: 228.37
CHARACTERISTICS: Form: Liquid; Color: Colorless; Odor: Ligh citrus rose
PHYSICAL PROPERTIES:Specific gravity: 0.860-0.865(25/25 C Refractive index:
1.4320-14360 (20C); Flash point:>212 F(TCC);Sollubility: Solub in ethyl alcohol 95% (4 parts 80%)

ALDEHYDE C-14 PURE

SYNONYMS: 4 Hydroxyundecanoic acid lactone;y Undelacton Peach aldehyde; y-n-Heptylbutyrolactone; Undecanolide 1, Persicol; y- Undecalactone
CAS NUMBER: 710-04-3
MOLECULAR FORMULA: $C_{11}H_{20}O_2$
MOLECULAR WEIGHT: 184.28

CHARACTERISTICS: Form: Liquid Color Slightly yellow to yellowish; Odor: Strong peach Taste: Peach
PHYSICAL PROPERTIES: Specific gravity: 0.940-0.944 (25/25 C); Refractive index: 1.4500-1.4540 (20C); Flash Point: 212 F (TCC); Solubility: Soluble in ethyl alcohol 95% (5 parts 60%) benzyl alcohol, benzyl benzoate, organic solvents
DERIVATION : From ß ionone and methyl or ethyle hloroacetate

ALDEHYDE C-16 PURE

SYNONYMS: Ethyl α–,ß-epoxy-ß-methylhydrocinnamte; Strawberry aldehyde;
Ethyl methylphenylglycidate
MOLECULAR FORMULA : $C_{12}H_{14}O_2$
MOLECULAR WEIGHT: 206.24
CHARACTERSITICS: Form, Liquid, Color, Colorless to yellowish, Odor: Strong strawberry; Taste, Strawberry
PHYSICAL PROPERTIES, Specific gravity, 1.0887-1.0920 (25/25 C); Refractive index: 1.5040-1.5090 (20C); Solubility, soluble clear in ethyl alcohol 95% (4 parts 70%)
WARNING AND CAUTION: Low tocicity

ALDEHYDE C-18

SYNONYMS: 4 Hydroxynonanoic acid lactone; y Nonalactone, Prunolide: y n Amylbutyrolactone; Nonanolide 1, 4, Coconut aldehyde
MOLECULAR FORMULA: $C_9H_{16}O_2$
MOLECULAR WEIGHT: 156.23
CHARACTERISTICS: Form, Liquid, Color, Slightly yellow to yellow Odor, Strong coconut like
PHYSICAL PROPERTIES: *Specific gravity:* 0.958-0.965 (25/25 C), *Refractive index*: 1.4460-1.4500 (20C), Flash Point, 212 F (TCC); Solubility: Soluble in ethyl alcohol 95% (2 parts 60%)

ALLYL SULFIDE

SYNONYMS: Diallyl sulfide,Thioallyl ether, Garlic Oil 3.3 Thiobis (1-propene)
MOLECULAR FORMULA: $C_6H_{10}S$
MOLECULAR WEIGHT: 114.20
CHARACTERISTICS: *Form: Liquid, Color,* Colorless, Odor, Garlic
PHYSICAL PROPERTIES: Specific gravity, 0.888(27/4C),

Refractive index: 1.4877 (27C), Boiling point: 139 C, Solubilty, Soluble in alcohol, chloroform ether, carbon tetrachloride, insoluble in water
DERIVATION: Form allyl bromide and sulfur in solution with sodium
WARNING AND CAUTION: Highly toxic

AMYL ACETATE

SYNONYMS: Amyl acetate ester Banana Oil Pear Oil Pentyl acetate, Amyl acetic ester
CAS NUMBER 628-63-7
MOLECULAR FORMULA. $C_7H_{14}O_2$
MOLECULAR WEIGHT . 130.13
CHARACTERISTICS: Form Liquid; Color; Colorless; Odor: Banana
PHYSICAL PROPERTIES: Flash point: 651- 95F (CC); Solubility; Soluble in alcohol; slightly soluble in water.
DERIVATION: From amyl alcohol with acetic acid and a small amount of sulfuric acid as a catalyst.

WARNING AND CAUTION: Flammable; moderately toxic

AMYL ALCOHOL

SYNONYMS: (a) Primary (normal) n- Butylcarbinol, h- Amyl alcohol;1 Pentanol; (b) Secondary (iso) 1-Methylbutanol; 2-Pentanol; (C) Tertiary Amylene hydrate; Dimethythyl Carbinol; 1-Dimethylpropyl alcohol
CAS NUMBER: (a) 71-41-0 (primary); (b) 6032-29-7 (secondary); (C) 75-85-4 (tertiary)
MOLECULAR FORMULA: $C_5H_{12}O$
MOLECULAR WEIGHT :88.11
CHARACTERISTICS: *Form: Liquid, Color, Colorless, Odor, Camphor; Taste:* Burning
PHYSICAL PROPERTIES: *Specific gravity*: 0.825 (20C); *Refractive index*: 1.0425 (20C); Boiling point: (a) 137 C (primary); (b) 118 C (secondary); (C) 102 C (tertiary); Flash Point 70 F(TOC) Solubility Soluble in alcohol; slightly soluble in water
DERIVATION : Fractional distillation of mixed alcohol from chlorination and alkaline hudrolysis of pentane

WARNING AND CAUTION : Flammable; moderately toxic

AMYL BUTYRATE

SYNONYMS: Butanoic acid pentyl ester1, Isoamyl n butyrate, Isoamyl butyric ester
CAS NUMBER: 106-27-4
MOLECULAR FORMULA : $C_9H_{18}O_2$
MOLECULAR WEIGHT 158.23
CHARACTERISTICS: *Form:* Liquid, *Color;* Colorless; *Odor,* Apricot
PHYSICAL PROPERTIES: *Specific gravity:* 0.8832-0.866(15C); *Refractive index:* 1.4110 (20C); *Boiling point:* 150-180 C; *Freezing point* 73.2 C; *Solubility:* Soluble in alcohol ether; slightly soluble in water
DERIVATION : By treating isoamyl alcohol with butyric acid
WARNING AND CAUTION : Combustible low toxicity

AMYL FORMATE

MOLECULAR FORMULA: $C_6H_{12}O_2$
MOLECULAR WEIGHT: 116.13
CHARACTERISTICS : *Form:* Liquid; *Color,* Colorless; *Odor:* Plum
PHYSICAL PROPERTIES: *Specific gravity:* 0.880-0.885 (25/25 C); *Boiling point:* 123.5 C; *Flash point:* 80F (TCC), *Solubility,* Soluble in alcohol oils, hydrocarbons, ketones; slightly soluble in water
WARNING AND CAUTION: Flammable, moderately toxic

AMYL VALERATE

SYNONYMS: Isoamyl valerate; Apple essence, Apple oil; Isoamyl isovalerate; Amyl valrianate;, Amyl isovalerate, Isoamyl valerianate
MOLECULAR FORMELA: $C_{10}H_{20}O_2$
MOLECULAR WEIGHT: 172.26
CHARACTERISTICS: *Form:* Liquid; *Color;* Clear, Colorless; *Odor:* Apple when diluted with alcohol
PHYSICAL PROPERTIES: *Specific gravity:* 0.8812 (25/25 C); *Refractive index:* 1.413 (19 C); *Boiling point:* 203.7 C; *Solubility,* Soluble in alcohol; ether, slightly soluble in water
DERIVATION: By adding sulfuric acid to a mixture of amyl alcohol and valeric acid further distilling
WARNING AND CAUTION: Combustible, low toxicity

ANETHOLE

SYNONYMS: *Isoestragole,* p-Propenylphenyl methyl ether, 1-Methoxy-4-(1-propenyl) benzene, p-Propenyl anisole, Anise camphor

MOLECULAR FORMULA: $C_{10}H_{12}O$

MOLECULAR WEIGHT: 148.20

CHARACTERISTICS: *Form: Liquid, Colour,* Colorless; *Odor,* Anise

PHYSICAL PROPERTIES: *Specific gravity,* 0.984-0.987 (25/25 C); *Refractive index,* 1.5570-1.5610 (20C); *Optical rotation* 0.15°; *Freezing point,* 20 C; *Flash point.* 212 F (TCC); *Solubility.* Soluble in 2 parts of 90% ethyl alcohol

DERIVATION: From aniseed star anise, fennel oils, from leaves of Clausene anisata hook, Backhousia anisata and Magnolia salicifolia maxim

ANISALDEHYDE

SYNONYMS. Anisyl aldehyde, p-Methoxybenzaldehyde; 4-Methoxybenzaldehyde; Anisic aldehyde

CAS NUMBER. 123-11-5

MOLECULAR FORMULA. $C_8H_8O_2$

MOLECULAR WEIGHT. 136.14

CHARACTERISTICS. *Form:* Liquid; *Color,* Colorless, to yellowish; *Odor,* Hawthorn

PHYSICAL PROPERTIES: *Specific gravity:* 1.119-1.122 (25/25 C); *Refractive index.* 1.572-1.5764 (20C); *Boiling point,* 245C; *Freezing point.* 0 C; *Solubility.* Soluble in 5 parts 50% ethyl alcohol 95%

DERIVATION. Form anethole or anisole by oxidation

WARNING AND CAUTION. Combustible

BENZALDEHYDE

SYNONYMS: Benzoic aldehyde; Artificial essential oil of almond

CAS NUMBER: 100-52-7

MOLECULAR FORMULA: C_7H_6O

MOLECULAR WEIGHT: 106.12

CHARATERISTICS. Form: Liquid; Color, Colorless, Odor, Bitter almod; Taste: Burning aromatic

PHYSICAL PROPERTIES: *Specific gravity;* 1.041-1.0446 (25/25 C); *Refractive index.* 1.5440-1.5456 (20C), *Boiling point.* 178C; *Freezing point:* 56C; *Flash point.* 145F (TCC), *Solubility.*

Soluble in 3 parts 60% ethyl alcohol 95%

DERIVATION. Occurs in kernels of bitter almond, synthetically made from benzyl chloride and lime, or by oxidation of toluene

WARNING AND CAUTION. Narcotic in high concentration, causes dermatitis by contact

BENZOIC ACID

SYNONYMS: Carboxybenzene; Benzenecarboxylic acid; Dracylic acid; Phenylformic acid

CAS NUMBER: 65-85-0

MOLECULAR FORMULA: $C_7H_6 0_2$

MOLECULAR WEIGHT. 122.12

CHARACTERISTICS. *Form,* Scales, needle crystals; *Color,* White; *Odor:* Benzoin or benzaldehyde

PHYSICAL PROPERTIES. *Specific gravity:* 1.2659 (25/25 C); *Boiling point:* 249.2 C; *Freezing point.* 121.25C

DERIVATION. Occurs naturally in benzoin resin; decarboxylation of phthalic acid by steam in the presence of catalyst; chlorination of toluene to yield benzotrichloride which is hydrolyzed to benzoic acid; oxidation of toluene; from benzoin resin

WARNING AND CAUTION: May cause nausea and gastroenteric disturbance allergic reactions

BENZYL ACETATE

SYNONYMS: Phenylmethyl acetate; Acetic acid phenylmethyl ester; Acetic acid benzyl ester

MOLECULAR FORMULA: $C_9 H_{10} O_2$

MOLECULAR WEIGHT: 150.17

CHARACTERISTICS: *Form:* Liquid; *Colour;* White; *Odor:* Floral, pear

PHYSICAL PROPERTIES: *Specific gravity:* 1.059-1.062 (15C); *Refractive index:* 1.5015-1.5035 (20C); *Flash Point*: 216F (TCC); *Solubility.* Soluble in alcohol, ether

DERIVATION. From benzyl chloride with sodium acetate in a solvent; by esterification of benzyl alcohol with acetic anhydride or acetic acid triethylamine, naturally in jasmine and other plants

WARNING AND CAUTION. Moderately toxic; irritant of the skin

BENZYL ALCOHOL

SYNONYMS. α–Hydroxytoluene; Phenyl methanol; Phenyl carbinol;
Benzene methanol
CAS NUMBER: 100-51-6
MOLECULAR FORMULA: $C_7 H_8 O$
MOLECULAR WEIGHT: 108. 13
CHARACTERISTICS: *Form:* Liquid, *Colour:* White; *Odour:* Slight; *Taste;* Sharp burning
PHYSICAL PROPERTIES. *Specific gravity.* 1.040-1.050 (25 /25C), *Refractive index:* 1.5385-1.5405; *Boiling point.* 206 C; *Flash Point:* 213 F (TCC); *Solubility:* Soluble in alcohol cheoroform, ether, water
DERIVATION. By hydrolysis of benzyl chloride; from benzaldehyde by catalystic reduction or Cannizaro reaction
WARNING AND CAUTION: Combustible;low toxicity

BENZYL FORMATE

SYNONYMS: Formic acid phenylmethyl ester. Formic acid benzyl ester
MOLECULAR FORMULA: $C_8 H_8 O_2$
MOLECULAR WEIGHT: 136.14
CHARACTERISTICS: *Form:* Liquid; *Odor,* Fruity, spicy
PHYSICAL PROPERTIES: *Specific gravity:* 1.083- (25/25 C); *Refractive index:* 1.511-1.513 (20C); *Boiling point:* 203C; *Solubility:* Soluble in alcohol; in soluble in water,
DERIVATION: From formic acid and benzyl alcohol
WARNING AND CAUTION: Combustible

BORNEOL

SYNONYMS: endo- 1,7,7 - Trimethylbicyclo (2,2,1) heptane- 2-ol; endo- 2- Bornanol; endo-2- Camphanol; endo- 2-Hydrocamphane; Bornyl alcohol; Baros camphor; Sumatra camphor; Dryobalanops camphor; Bhimsaim Camphor; Malayan camphor; Camphol, Broneo camphor
CAS NUMBER: 507-70-0
MOLECULAR FORMULA: $C_{10} H_{18} O$
MOLECULAR WEIGHT: 154.24
CHARACTERSTICS: *Form,* Lumps; *Color,* White, translucent, *Odor:* Camphor
PHYSICAL PROPERTIES: *Specific gravity,* 1.011 (25/25C);

Boiling point. 212C; *Freezing point.* 203C; *Flash Point:* 150F (TCC); *Solubility:* Soluble in alcohol ether; insoluble in water.

DERIVATION. By reduction of camphor; from wood of *Dyrobalanops camphora,* a tree of Sumatra and Borneo (solid Crystalline mass deposited in the trunks)

WARNING AND CAUTION: Moderately toxic; flammable

BORNYL ACETATE

SYNONYMS: 1,7,7- Trimethy!bicyclo (2,2,1) heptan -2-ol acetate; Borneol acetate, Bornyl acetic ether, Bornyl acetate pure laevo

MOLECULAR FORMULA: $C_{12} H_{20} O_2$

MOLECULAR WEIGHT: 196.28

CHARACTERISTICS: *Form:* Crystals; *Color:* Colorless; *Odor:* Camphoraceous

PHYSICAL PROPERTIES: *Specific gravity:* 0.980-0.984 (25/25 C), *Refractive index:* 1.463-1.465 (20C); *Solubility,* Soluble in 3 parts 70% ethyl alcohol, ether

DERIVATION: Interaction of borneol and acetic anhydride in presence of formic acid

WARNING AND CAUTION: Moderately toxic. flammable

n-BUTYL ACETATE

SYNONYMS: Acetic acid butyl ester

CAS NUMBER: 123-86-4

MOLECULAR FORMULA: $C_6 H_{12} O_2$

MOLECULAR WEIGHT: 116.16

CHARACTERISTICS: *Form:* Liquid; *Color:* Colorless; *Odor:* Fruity

PHYSICAL PROPERTIES. *Specific gravity:* 0.8826 (20/20C); *Refractive index.* 1. 3951 (20C); *Boiling point:* 126.3 C; *Freezing point:* 75C; *Flash point:* 92F (TOC); *Solubility.* Soluble in alcohol, ether, hydrocarbons; slightly soluble in water

DERIVATION: Esterification and distillation after contact of butyl alcohol in the presence of a catalyst such as sulfuric acid

WARNING AND CAUTION: Flammable; moderately toxic, skin irritant

n- BUTYL BUTYRATE

SYNONYMS: Butyl butanoate; Butanoic acid butyl ester; Butyric acid butyl ester; *n*-Butyl *n*-butyrate

CAS NUMBER: 109-21-7

MOLECULAR FORMULA: $C_8 H_{16} O_2$

MOLECULAR WEIGHT: 144.21
CHARACTERISTICS: *Form,* Liquid
PHYSICAL PROPERTIES: *Specific gravity:* 0.8692 (20/20C); *Refractive index:* 1.4064 (20C); *Boiling point:* 165C; *Freezing point:-* 91.5C; *Flash point:* 128 F (OC); *Solubility:* Soluble in alcohol, ether, insoluble in water
WARNING AND CAUTION: Moderately toxic; irritant and narcotic; flammable

BUTYRIC ACID

SYNONYMS: *n*-Butyric acid: Butanoic acid; Ethylacetic acid; Propylformic acid
CAS NUMBER: 107-92-6
MOLECULAR FORMULA: $C_4 H_8 O_2$
MOLECULAR WEIGHT: 88.10
CHARACTERISTICS: *Form:* Liquid; *Color:* Colorless; *Odor:* Rancid; Taste, Unpleasant
PHYSICAL PROPERTIES: *Specific gravity.* 0.9583 (20/4C), *Refractive index.* 1.3981 (20C), *Boiling point.* 163.5C, *Freezing Point.* 5 to 8C, *Flash point.* 170F (TCC) *Solubility.* Soluble in alcohol, ether, water
DERIVATION. Occurs as glyceride in animal fats, produced as a by product in hydrocarbon synthesis, by oxidation of butyraldehyde, and by fermentation of molasses or starch
WARNING AND CAUTION. Combustible, low toxicity

CAPRALDEHYDE

SYNONYMS: n-Decanal; Capric aldehyde; n-Decyl aldehyde; Aldehyde C-10
MOLECULAR FORMULA: $C_{10} H_{20} O$
MOLECULAR WEIGHT: 156.27
CHARATERISTICS: *Form:* Liquid; *Color:* Colorless, to light yellow; *Odor:* Floral fatty
PHYSICAL PROPERTIES: *Specific gravity:* 0.831-0.838 (15C); *Rafractive index:* 1.427-1.431 (20C); *Solubility:* Soluble in 80% alcohol, fixed oils, volatile oils, mineral oils; insoluble in water and glycerol
DERIVATION: Lemongrass; citronella; orange, sunthetically by oxidation of the alcohol or reduction of the acid
WARNING AND CAUTION: Combustible; low toxicity

CARAMEL, COLOURING

CHARACTERISTICS: *Form:* Powder or thickliquid; *ColoUr,* Dark brown, *Odor:* Burnt sugar, *Taste:* Bitter taste

PHYSICAL PROPERTIES: *Specific gravity:* 1.35 (25/25 C); *Solubility.* Soluble in diluted alcohol, water, insoluble in chloroform, ether, organic solvents

DERIVATION: Heating sugar or glucose, adding small quantities of alkali, alkaline carbonate, or trace of mineral acid during the heating; sucrose, adding small quantities of sodium carbonate during heating

CHLOROFORM

SYNONYMS: Trichloromethane

CAS NUMBER: 67-66-3

MOLECULAR FORMULA: $CHCL_3$

MOLECULAR WEIGHT: 119.-39

CHARACTERISTICS: *Form:* Liquid; *Color,* Colorless, *Odor:* Characteristic, *Taste:* Sweet

PHYSICAL PROPERTIES: *Specific gravity:* 1.485 (20/20C), *Refractive index:* 1.4476 (20C); *Boiling point:* 61.2 C; *Freezing point:* 63.5C; *Solubility.* Soluble in alcohol, ether, benzene, naphtha, fixed volatile oils; slightly soluble in water

DERIVATION: Chlorinated lime with acetone, acetaldehyde, or ethyl alcohol; by product from chlorination of methane; purification with concentrated sulfuric acid and rectification; from acetone and bleaching powder by addition of sulfuric acid, methane chlorination

WARNING AND CAUTION: Highly toxic, narcotic, prolonged inhalation or ingestion may be fatal

CINEOL

SYNONYMS: Eucalyptol; Cajeputol; Cineole

CAS NUMBER: 470-82-6

MOLECULAR FORMULA: $C_{10} H_{18} O$

MOLECULAR WEIGHT: 154.25

CHARACTERISTICS: *Form:* Liquid; *Color:* Colorless; *Odor:* Camphor, Pungent; *Taste:* Spicy

PHYSICAL PROPERTIES: *Specific gravity:* 0.921-0.923 (25/25C), *Refractive index.* 1.4550-1.4600 (20C); *Boiling point:* 174-177 C;*Freezing point:* O C; *Solubility;* Soluble in alcohol, chloroform, ether, glacial, acetic, acid, and fixed or volatile oils; slightly in water

DERIVATION: By fractional distillation of eucalyptus oil, followed by freezing

WARNING AND CAUTION: Combustible; moderatey toxic

CINNAMIC ALDEHYDE

SYNONYMS: Cinnamaldehyde; 3-Phenylpropenal; Cinnamyl aldehyde

CAS NUMBER: 104-55-2

MOLECULAR FORMULA: $C_9 H_8 O$

MOLECULAR WEIGHT: 132.16

CHARACTERISTICS: *Form:* Oil; *Color:* Yellowish; *Odor:* Cinnamon; *Taste:* Sweet

PHYSICAL PROPERTIES: *Specific gravity:* 1.048- 1.052 (25/25 C); *Refractive index:* 1.618-1.623 (20C); *Boiling point.* 248 C; *Freezing point:* 8 C; *Solubility:* Soluble in 5 volumes 60% alcohol; slightly soluble in water

DERIVATION: From. Ceylon and Chinese cinnamon oils; by condensation of benzaldehyde and acetaldehyde

WARNING AND CAUTION: Combustible

CITRAL

SYNONYMS: Geranial; Geranialdehyde; 3,7-Dimethyl-2-6 octadienal

CAS NUMBER: 5392-40-.5

MOLECULAR FORMULA: $C_{10} H_{16} O$

MOLECULAR WEIGHT: 152.24

CHARACTERISTICS: *Form:* Liquid; *Color:* Pale yellow; *Odor:* Strong lemon

PHYSICAL PROPERTIES: *Specific gravity:* 0.891-0.897 (15 C); *Refractive index;* 1.4860-1.4900 (20C); *Solubility:* Soluble in alcohol, benzyl benzoate, diethyl phthalate, glycerin, propylene glycol, mineral oils, fixed oils

DERIVATION: Lemongrass Oil by fractional distillation, synthetically by oxidation of geraniol, nerol, or linalool by chromic acid

WARNING AND CAUTION: Combustible

CITRONELLAL

SYNONYMS: 3-1,7- Dimethyl1-6-octen1-1- al, 3,7-

Dimethyloct-6 (or7)-enal
MOLECULAR FORMULA: $C_{10} H_{18} O$
MOLECULAR WEIGHT: 154.25
CHARACTERISTICS: *Form:* Liquid, *Color:* Colorless, to slightly yellow; *Odor:* Strong and intense lemon
PHYSICAL PROPERTIES: *Specific gravity:* 0.848-0.856 (25/25 C); *Refractive index:* 1.4460-1.4520 (20C); Optical rotation. 8-11°, *Boiling point:* 205 C; *Flash point:* 178 F(TCC); *Solubility:* Soluble in 5 parts 70% alcohol, ether, slightly soluble in water
DERIVATION: Found as a main constituent in oils of citronella, lemongrass, and other oils

CITRONELLOL

SYNONYMS: 3,7-Dimethyl -6 octen- ol, 2,6-Dimethyl-2-octen-8-ol; Cephrol
CAS NUMBER. 106-22-9
MOLECULAR FORMULA. $C_{10} H_{20} O$
MOLECULAR WEIGHT. 156.27
CHARACTERISTICS: *Form:* Liquid; *Color:* Colorless; *Odor:* Light rosy
PHYSICAL PROPERTIES: *Specific gravity:* 0.852-0.860 (25/25C), *Refractive index.* 1.4530-1.4600 (20C); Optical rotation: 1.30 to 3-, *Boiling point:* 108.4 C; *Solubility:* soluble in alcohol,° ether, slightly soluble in water
DERIVATION: Constituent of rose, geranium, Eucalyptus citriodora, Ceylon and Java citronella oils, verbena, savin, oakmoss, palmarosa

DECYL ACETATE

See Acetate C-10

DIACETYL

SYNONYMS: 2,-3-Butanedione; Butanedione; Biacetyl; Dimethyl diketone, Dimethyl glyoxal, 2,-3-Diketobutane
CAS NUMBER: 431-03-8
MOLECULAR FORMULA: $C_4 H_6 O_2$
MOLECULAR WEIGHT: 86.09
CHARACTERISTICS: *Form.* Liquid; *Color:* Yellowish-green, *Odor:* Quinone
PHYSICAL PROPERTIES: *Specific gravity:* 0.990 (15/15 C); *Refractive index.* 1.3933 (18C); *Boiling point:* 88-91 C; *Freezing Point:* 80F (TCC); *Solubility:* soluble in ether, 4 parts water

DERIVATION: Found in bay and other oils and in butter; made from methyl ethyl ketone by converting to the isonitroso compound, then with HCL, decomposing to diacetyl by hydrolysis and by special fermentation of glucose viamethylacetylcarbinol

WARNING AND CAUTION: Flammable

ETHYL ACETATE

SYNONYMS: Acetic ether, Acetic ester; Acetic acide ethyl ester; Vinegar naphtha

CAS NUMBER: 141-78-6

MOLECULAR FORMULA: $C_4 H_8 O_2$

MOLECULAR WEIGHT: 88.10

CHARACTERISTICS: *Form:* Liquid; *Color:* Colorless; *Odor:* Fragrant

PHYSICAL PROPERTIES: *Specific gravity* 0.8945 (25/25C); *Boiling Point:* 77C; *Freezing point:* 83.6C; *Flash point:* 24F (TCC); *Solubility:* Soluble in alcohol, Chloroform, ether; slightly soluble in water

DERIVATION: By heating acetic acid and ethyl alcohol in presence of sulfuric acid and distilling

WARNING AND CAUTION: Flammable; moderately toxic by inhalation and skin absorption

ETHYL ACETOACETATE

SYNONYMS: Diacetic ester; Acetoacetic ester; 3-Oxobutanoic acid ethyl ester; Acetoacetic acid ethyl ester; Ethyl 3-oxobutanoate

MOLECULAR FORMULA: $C_6 H_{10} O_2$

MOLECULAR WEIGHT: 130.14

CHARACTERISTICS: *Form:* Liquid; *Color:* Colorless; *Odor:* Fruity

PYHSICAL PROPERTIES: *Specific gravity:* 1.0250 (20/4C); *Boiling Point.* 180-181 C; *Flash point.* 185F (TCC); *Solubility:* Soluble in alcohol, water

DERIVATION: Action of metallic sodium on ethyl acetate and distillation.

WARNING AND CAUTION: Moderately toxic by ingestion and inhalation, irritant to skin and eyes

ETHYL ALCOHOL

SYNONYMS: Alcohol; Grain alcohol; Ethanol; Spirit of wine; Absolute alochol; Ethyl hydrate; Spirit

CAS NUMBER. 64-17-5
MOLECULAR FORMULA: $C_2 H_6 O$
MOLECULAR WEIGHT: 46. 046
CHARACTERSTICS: *Form:* Liquid; volatile; *Color:* Colorless; *Odor:* Ethereal, vinous
PHYSICAL PROPERTIES: Specific gravity: 0.816 (15.56C); Rafractive index: 1.3651 (15 C); Boiling point: 78C; Freezing point: 117.3 to 114 C; Flash point: 55 F; Solubility: Miscible with chloroform, ether, water, other solvents
WARNING AND CAUTION: Flammable

ETHYL ALDEHYDE

See Acetaldehyde

ETHYL ANTHRANILATE

SYNONYMS: Ethyl o-aminobenzoate
CAS NUMBER: 87-25-2
MOLECULAR FORMULA: $C_9 H_{11} O_2$
MOLECULAR WEIGHT: 165.20
CHARACTERISTICS: *Form:* Liquid; *Color:* Slightly yellow to brownish; *Odor:* Fruity
PHYSICAL PROPERTIES: *Specific gravity:* 1.115-1.120 (25/25C), *Refractive index:* 1.5630-1.5660 (20C); *Boiling point;* 260 C; *Solubility:* Soluble in alcohol, propylene glycol

ETHYL BENZOATE

SYNONYMS: Banzoic acid ethyl ester
CAS NUMBER. 93-89-0
MOLECULAR FORMULA: $C_9 H_{10} 0_2$
MOLECULAR WEIGHT: 150. 18
CHARACTERISTICS. *Form:* Liquid; *Color:* Colorless; *Odor:* Aromatic, suggestive of wintergreen
PHYSICAL PROPERTIES: *Specific gravity:* 1.043-1.046 (25/25C); *Refractive index:* 1.5030-1.5060 (20C); *Boiling point:* 212.9 C; *Freezing Point:* -32.7 C; *Flash point:* 190F (TCC); *Solubility:* soluble in alcohol, Chloroform, ether
DERIVATION: By heating ethyl alcohol and benzoic acid in presence of sulfuric acid

ETHYL BUTYRATE

SYNONYMS: Ethyl butanoate; Butanoic acid ethyl, Butyric acid ethyl ester, Ethyl n-butyrate
CAS NUMBER: 105-54-4
MOLECULAR FORMULA: $C_6 H_{12} O_2$
MOLECULAR WEIGHT: 116.16
CHARACTERISTICS: *Form:* Liquid; *Color:* Colorless; *Odor:* Pineapple
PHYSICAL PROPERTIES: *Specific gravity:* 0.8788 (25/25C); *Refractive index:* 1.400 (20C); *Boiling Point:* 120.6C; *Freezing point:* -93.3C; *Flash point:* 78F(TCC); *Solubility:* Soluble in alcohol, ether; insoluble in water, glycerin
DERIVATION: From ethyl alcohol and butyric acid heated in presence of sulfuric acid, and distillation
WARNING AND CAUTION: Flammable; irriting to eyes; narcotic in high concentration

ETHYL CAPRATE

SYNONYMS: Ethyl decanoate, Decanoic acid ethyl ester
CAS NUMBER: 110-38-3
MOLECULAR FORMULA: $C_{12} H_{24} O_2$
MOLECULAR WEIGHT: 200.31
CHARACTERISTICS: *Form:* Liquid; *Color:* Colorless; *Odor:* Fragrant
PHYSICAL PROPERTIES: *Specific gravity:* 0.862 (25/25C); *Boiling point:* 243 C; *Solubility.* Soluble in alcohol, ether; insoluble in water
DERIVATION: By heating capric acid, absolute alcohol, sulfuric acid, and distilling
WARNING AND CAUTION: Combustible; low toxicity

ETHYL CAPRYLATE

SYNONYMS: Ethyl
CAS NUMBER: 106-32-1
MOLECULAR FORMULAL: $C_{10} H_{20} 0_2$
MOLECULAR WEIGHT: 172.17
CHARACTERISTICS: *Form:* Liquid; *Color:* Colorless; *Odor:* Pineapple
PHYSICAL PROPERTIES: Specific gravity: 0.865-0.869 (25/25C); Boiling point: 207-209C; Freezing point: 48C; Solubility:-Soluble in alcohol;ether,insoluble in water, glycerin
DERIVATION: Heating caprylic acid, alcohol, sulfuric acid, and distilling

WARNING AND CAUTION: Combustible, low toxicity

ETHYL CARBONATE

SYNONYMS: Diethyl carbonate; Carbonic acid diethyl ester
CAS NUMBER: 105-58-8
MOLECULAR FORMULA: $C_5 H_{10} O_2$
MOLECULAR WEIGHT: 118. 30
CHARACTERISTICS: *Form:* Liquid; *Color:* Colorless; *Odor:* Mild
PHYSICAL PROPERTIES: *Specific gravity:* 0.975 (20.4C); *Boiling point:* 126C; *Freezing point:* 43 C; *Flash point:* 77F (OC); *Solubility:* Soluble in alcohol, ketones, esters, aromatic hydrocarbons, aliphatic solvents; insoluble in water
DERIVATION: Reacting chlorine and carbon monoxide to produce phosgene ($COCl_2$); reacting phosgene with ethyl alcohol to make ethyl chlorocarbonate ($ClCO_2 C_2 H_5$); reacting ethyl chlorocarbonate with anhydrous ethyl alcohol to produce diethyl carbonate
WARNING AND CAUTION: Flammable; moderately toxic; strong irritant

ETHYL CINNAMATE

SYNONYMS: Ethyl phenyl acrylate, Cinnamylic ether
MOLECULAR FORMULA: $C_{11} H_{12} O_2$
MOLECULAR WEIGHT: 176.22
CHARACTERISTICS: *Form:* Liquid; *Color:* Colorless; *Odor:* Sweet, balsamic honey note
PHYSICAL PROPERTIES: *Specific gravity:* 1.045-1.048 (25/25C); *Refractive index:* 1.5590-1.5610 (20C); *Boiling point:* 271 C; *Freezing point:* 7C; *Flash point:* >212 F; *Solubility:* Soluble in alochol; ether; insoluble in water
DERIVATION: Heating ethyl alcohol and cinnamic acid in presence of sulfuric acid; found in storax oil and Kavempferia galanga
WARNING AND CAUTION: Low toxicity

ETHYL FORMATE

SYNONYMS: Ethyl formic ester
CAS NUMBER: 109-94-4
MOLECULAR FORMULA: $C_3 H_6 O_2$
MOLECULAR WRIGHT: 74.07
CHARACTIERISTICS: *Form.* Unstable; *Color:* Colorless; *Odor:*

Pleasant aromatic

PHYSICAL PROPERTIES: Specific gravity: 0.9236 (20/20C); *Refractive index:* 1.35975 (20C), *Boiling point.* 54.3C; *Freezing point.* 80.5C; *Flash point:* 4F (TCC); *Solubility:* Soluble in alcohol, ether, benzene; slightly soluble in water with gradual decomposition

DERIVATION: Heating ethyl alcohol with formic acid in presence of sulfuric acid

WARNING AND CAUTION: Highly flammable; narcotic; irritating to skin and eyes

ETHYL ISOBUTYRATE

SYNONYMS: Methyl propanoic acid ethyl ester

CAS NUMBER: 97-62-1

MOLECULAR MOLEMULA: $C_6 H_{12} O_2$

MOLECULAR WEIGHT: 116.6

CHARACTERISTICS: *Form:* Liquid; volatile; *Color:* Colorless

PHYSICAL PROPERTIES: Specific gravity: 0.870 (25/25C); *Refractive index:* 1.3903 (20C); *Boiling point.* 110-111 C; *Freezing Point.* -88C, *Solubilty:* Soluble in alcohol, ether; silghtly soluble in water

DERIVATION: Heating isobutyric acid and ethyl alcohol and distilling

WARNING AND CAUTION: Moderately toxic

ETHYL ISOVALERATE

SYNONYMS: Ethyl valerate, Ethyl valeriate, Ethyl 2-methyl butyrate; 3-Methyl butanoic acid ethyl ester; Pentanoic acid ethyl ester

CAS NUMBER: 108-64-5

MOLECULAR FORMULA: $C_7 H_{14} O_2$

MOLECULAR WEIGHT: '130.18

CHARACTERISTICS: *Form:* Liquid; oily; *Color:* Colorless; *Odor:* Fruity

PHYSICAL PROPERTIES: *Specific gravity:* 0.864 (20/20C); *Refractive index:*1.3950-1.3990 (20C); *Boiling point.* 135C; *Freezing point:* 99 C; *Solubility:* Soluble in alcohol, ether, benzene; slightly soluble in water

DERIVATION: Heating sodium valerate and ethyl alcohol in presence of sulfuric acid, or hydrochloric acid, and distilling

WARNING AND CAUTION: Low toxicity

ETHYL MALONATE

SYNONYMS; Propanechoic acid diethyl ester, Diethyl malonate, Malonic ester
CAS NUMBER: 105-53-3
MOLECULAR FORMULA: $C_7 H_{12} O_4$
MOLECULAR WEIGHT: 160.17
CHARACTERISTICS: *Form:* Liquid; *Color,* Colorless; *Odor: Aromatic, Pleasant*
PHYSICAL PROPERTIES. *Specific gravity:* 1.055 (25/25); Refrective index : 1.4143 (20c), Boiling Peel Point : 198-199 C; Freezing Point: 50C; Flash Point : 200 F; Solubility Soluble in alcohol, eather; slightty Soluble in water
DERIVATION : - From chloroacetic acid and sodium cyanid; casterifiction with cthnol and sulfuric acid
WARNING AND CAUTION : Combustible ; low foxicity.

ETHYL METHYL PHENYL GLYCIDATE

See Aldehyde C-16 Pure

ETHYL MYRISTATE

SYNONYMS: Ethyl tetradecanoate; Tetradecanoic acid ethyl ester
MOLECULAR FORMULA: $C_{16} H_{32} O_2$
MOLECULAR WEIGHT: 256.44
CHARACTERISTICS: *Form:* Liquid; *Color:* Colorless; *Odor:* Orris, fatty
PHYSICAL PROPERTIES: *Specific gravity.* 0.856-0.860 (25 25C), *Refractive index:* 1.4340-1.4380 (20C); *Freezing point.* 4C; *Flash point.* > 212 F(TCC); *Solubility:* Soluble in 2 parts 90% ethyl alcohol; slightly soluble in ether; insoluble in water
WARNING AND CATION: Combustible; low toxicity

ETHYL NITRATE

SYNONYM: Aether nitricus
CAS NUMBER: 625-58-1
MOLECULAR FORMULA: $C_2 H_5 NO_3$
MOLECULAR WEIGHT: 91.09
CHARACTERISTICS: *Form:* Liquid; *Color:* Colorless; *Odor:* Pleasant; *Taste:* Sweet
PHYSICAL PROPERTIES. *Specific gravity:* 1.116 (25/25C); *Boiling point:* 87.6 C; *Freezing point:*- 112 C; *Flash point.* 50F (CC); *Solubility:* Soluble in alcohol, ether; insoluble in water

DERIVATION: Heating alcohol, urea nitrate, and nitric acid, and distilling
WARNING AND CAUTION: Flammable; explodes at 185 F

ETHYL OENANTHATE

SYNONYMS: Ethyl enanthate; Ethyl heptanoate; Ethyl n heptoate; Oenanthic ether; Heptanoic acid ethyl ester; Cognac oil synthetic; Oil of grapes; Aether oenanthicus; Oleum vitis viniferae
MOLECULAR FORMULA: $C_9 H_{18} O_2$
MOLECUALR WEIGHT: 158.23
CHARACTERISTICS: *Form:* Liquid; *Color;* Colorless; *Odor:* Fruity
PHYSICAL PROPERTIES: *Specific gravity:* 0.87 (25/25 C), *Boiling point:* 187 C; *Solubility:* Soluble in alcohol, chloroform, ether; insoluble in water
DERIVATION: Heating oenanthic acid and ethyl alcohol in presence of sulfuric acid, and distilling
WARNING AND CAUTION. Low toxicity; combustible

ETHYL PELARGONATE

SYNONYMS: Ethyl nonoate; Wine ether; Nonanoic acid ethyl ester
MOLECULAR FORMULA: $C_{11} H_{22} O_2$
MOLECULAR WEIGHT: 186.29
CHARACTERISTICS: *Form:* Liquid; *Color:* Colorless; *Odor:* Fruity
PHYSICAL PROPERTIES: *Specific gravite:* 0.863-0.865 (25 25C); *Refractive index:* 1.4210-1.4260 (20C); *Boiling point:* 220C; *Freezing point:* 44C; *Solubility:* Insoluble in water; soluble in alcohol and ether
WARNING AND CAUTION: Low toxicity

ETHYL PHENYL ACETATE

SYNONYMS: Ethyl toluate α–Benzeneacetic acid ethyl ester α–Toluic acid ethyl ester
CAS NUMBER: 101-97-3
MOLECULAR FORMULA: $C_{10} H_{12} O$
MOLECULAR WEIGHT: 164.21
CHARACTERISTICS: *Form:* Liquid; *Color;* Colorless, *Odor,* Sweet hoeny-rose
PHYSICAL PROPERTIES: *Specific gravity.* 1.027-1.032 (25/25C), *Refractive index.* 1.4960-1.4980 (20C); *Boiling point:* 276C, *Flash point:* >212 F(TCC); *Solubility:* Soluble in 10 parts

60% ethyl alcohol, 3 parts 70% ethyl alcohol

ETHYL PHENYL GLYCIDATE

SYNONYMS: Ethyl ß-phenyl glycidate
MOLECULAR: FORMULA: $C_{11} H_{12} O_3$
MOLECULAR WEIGHT: 192.13
CHARACTERISTICS: *Form:* Liquid: *Color:* Colorless to slightly yellow: *Odor:* Strong strawberry
PHYSICAL PROPERTIES: *Specific gravity:* 1.120-1.125 (25 25C); *Refractive index:* 1.5160 1.5210 (20C); *Flash point:* >212 F(TCC); *Solubility:* Soluble in 6 parts 70% ethyl alcohol, 1 part 80% ethyl alcohol

ETHYL SALICYLATE

SYNONYMS: Ethyl hydroxybenzoate; Salicylic acid ethyl ester; Salicylic ether; Sal ethyl
CAS NUMBER: 118-61-6
MOLECULAR FORMULA: $C_9 H_{10} O_2$
MOLECULAR WEIGHT: 166.18
CHARACTERISTICS: *Form:* Liquid; *Color;* Colorless; *Odor:* Faint methyl salicylate
PHYSICAL PROPERTIES: *Specific gravity:* 1.126-1.129 (25 25C), *Refractive index:* 1.5210-1.5230 (20C); *Boiling point:* 231-234 C; *Solubility:* Insoluble in water
WARNING AND CAUTION: Combustible

ETHYL SEBACATE

SYNONYMS: Decanedioic acid diethyl ester; Diethyl sebacate
MOLECULAR FORMULA: $_{C14} H_{26} O_4$
MOLECULAR WEIGHT: 258.35
CHARACTERISTICS: *Form:* Liquid; *Color;* Colorless, to yellowish
PHYSICAL PROPERTIES: *Specific gravity:* 0.965 (20C), *Refractive index.* 1.4369 (20C); *Boiling point:* 307C; *Solubility.* Soluble in alcohol, ether, organic solvents

ETHYL VALERATE

See Ethyl isovalerate

ETHYL VANILLIN

SYNONYMS: Bourbonal; 3 Ethoxy 4 hydroxybenzaldehyde; Ethyl protal; Ethovan; Ethyl protocatechuic aldehyde, Vanillal

CAS NUMBER: 121-32-4

MOLECULAR FORMULA: $C_9 H_{10} O_3$

MOLECULAR WEIGHT: 166.17

CHARACTERISTICS: *Form:* Crystals; *Color:* White, affected by light, *Odor,* Intense vanillin, *Taste,* Vanilla

PHYSICAL PROPERTIES: *Melting point:* 76.5C, *Solubility;* Soluble in alcohol, chloroform, ether, glycerol, propylene: glycol; slightly: soluble in water

WARNING AND CAUTION: Low toxicity; combustible

EUGENOL

SYNONYMS: 4- Allyl-2- methoxyphenol; Eugenic acid; 4-Allylguaiacol; 2- Methoxy- 4- (2- porpenyl); phenol; Caryophyllic acid

CAS NUMBER: 97-53-0

MOLECULAR FORMULA: $C_{10} H_{12} O_2$

MOLECULAR WEIGHT: 164.21

CHARACTERISTICS: *Form:* Liquid; *Color:* Light yellow; *Odor:* Pungent, spicy, cloves, characteristic

PHYSICAL PROPERTIES. *Specific gravity.* 1.064-1.068 (25 25C), *Refractive index:* 1.5400-1.5420(20C); *Boiling point.* 253.5 C; *Freezting point:* 9.2 to 9.1 C; *Flash point:* 230 F(TCC); *Solubility:* Soluble in 2 parts 60% ethyl alcohol

DERIVATION: Found mainly in oil of clove, cinnamon leaf, pimento, and in minor quantity in many other oils such as ylang ylang, cananga, patchouli, rose, violet, hyacinth, tuberose, orange flower, acacia

WARNING AND CAUTION: Low toxicity. combustible

GERANIOL

SYNONYMS: trans- 3, 7 Dimethyl- 2,6- octadien- 1 ol; (E) 3,7-Dimethyl- 2,6- octadien- 1- ol; 2,6- Dimethyl- 2,6- octadien- 8-ol; Lemonol

MOLECULAR FORMULA: $C_{10} H_{18} O$

MOLECULAR WEIGHT: 154.25

CHARACTERISTICS: *Form:* Liquid; *Color;* Colorless; *Odor;* Rosy

PHYSICAL PROPERTIES: *Specific gravity:* 0.870-0.880 (25 25C); *Refractive index:*1.4710-1.4760 (20C); *Optical rotation:* 2. *Boiling point.* 229-230 C; *Flash point:* 217 F(TCC); *Solubility:*

Soluble in 2 parts 70% ethyl alcohol; insoluble in water

DERIVATION: Main constituent of oils of palmarosa, rose geranium, citronella, and in lesser amounts in verbena, lemongrass, rosewood, linaloe, petitgrain, and many other oils

GERANYL ACETATE

SYNONYMS: trans- 3, 7- Dimethyl-2,6- octadienyl acetate; Geraniol acetate

CAS NUMBER: 105-87-3

MOLECULAR FORMULAL: $C_{12} H_{20} O_2$

MOLECULAR WEIGHT: 196.29

CHARACTERISTICS: *Form:* Liquid; *Color:* Colorless to slightly yellow; *Odor:* Sweet rose- lavender note

PHYSICAL PROPERTIES: *Specific gravity:* 0.900-0.910 (25 25C); *Refractive index:* 1.4570-1.4620 (20C); *Optical rotation:* 2 to 2; *Boiling point.* 128-129 C; *Flash point:* 228 F(TCC); *Solubility:* Soluble in 2 parts 80% ethyl alcohol

DERIVATION: Found in citronella, lemongrass, palmarosa, geranium, coriander, lavender, neroli, petitgrain, and others, and in greater amounts in Eucalyptus staigeriana, E. macarthurii, Dancus carota; by heating geraniol and sodium acetate with acetic anhydride

WARNING AND CAUTION: Combustible; nontoxic

GERANYL BENZOATE

SYNONYMS: *trans-* 3, 7 Dimethyl- 2, 6- octadienyl benzoate

MOLECULAR FORMULA: $C_{17} H_{22} O_2$

MOLECULAR WEIGHT: 258.37

CHARACTERISTICS: *Form:* Liquid; *Color;* Slightly yellow; *Odor:* Sweet, suggestive of ylang ylang

PHYSICAL PROPERTIES: *Specific gravity:* 0.978-0.984 (25/25C); *Refractive index:* 1.5130-1.5180 (20C); *Optical rotation:* 1; *Flash point:* 212 F(TCC); *Solubility:* Soluble in 4 parts 90% ethyl alcohol

GERANYL BUTYRATE

SYNONYMS: Geraniol butyrate; trans- 3, 7- Dimethyl- 2, 6 octadienyl butyrate

MOLECULAR FORMULA: $C_{14} H_{24} O_2$

MOLECULAR WEIGHT: 224.34

CHARACTERISTICS: *Form:* Liquid; *Color;* Colorless, to slightiy yellow; *Odor,;* Fruity- rosy-

PHYSICAL PROPERTIES: *Specific gravity:* 0.891-0.896 (25/25C); *Refractive index:* 1.4560-1.4620 (20C); *Optical rotation:* 1; *Boiling point:* 151 C; *Flash point:* 200 F(TCC); *Solubility:* Soluble in 7 parts 80% parts 80% ehtyl alcohol, 1 part 90% ethyl alcohol, ether; insoluble in water and glycerin
DERIVATION: Occurs in several essential oils
WARNING AND CAUTION: Combustible; nontoxic

GERANYL FORMATE

SYNONYMS: trans- 3, 7- Dimethyl- 2, 6- octadienyl formate; Geraniol formate
CAS NUMBER: 105-86-2
MOLECULAR FORMULA: $C_{11} H_{18} O_2$
MOLECULAR WEIGHT: 182.26
CHARACTERISTICS: *Form:* Liquid; *Color:* Colorless, to slightly yellow; *Odor:* Fresh, light / leafy rose-
PHYSICAL PROPERTIES: *Specific gravity:* 0.906-0.914 (25/25C); *Refractive index:* 1.4580-1.4640 (20C); *Flash Point:* 186F (TCC); *Solubility:* Soluble in 3 parts 80% ethyl alcohol, ether; insoluble in water and glycerin
DERIVATION: Found in oil of geranium
WARNING AND CAUTION: Combustible; nontoxic

GERANYL PHENYLACETATE

SYNONYMS: trans- 3, 7- Dimethyl- 2, 6- octadientyl phenylacetate
MOLECULAR FORMULA: $C_{18} H_{24} O_2$
MOLECULAR WEIGHT: 272.39
CHARACTERISTICS: *Form:* Liquid; *Color:* Yellow; *Odor:* Soft honey- rose-
PHYSICAL PROPERTIES: *Specific gravity:* 0.971-0.978 (25/25C), *Refractive index.* 1.5070-1.5110 (20C); *Opitcal rotation.* 1, *Flash point:* 210F(TCC); *Solubility:* soluble in 4 parts 90% ethyl alcohol

GERANYL PROPIONATE

SYNONYMS: trans- 3, 7- Dimethyl- 2, 6- octadienyl propionate; Geraniol propionate
MOLECULAR FORMULA: $C_{13} H_{22} O_2$
MOLECULAR WEIGHT: 210.32
CHARACTERISTICS: *Form:* Liquid; *Color;* Silghtly yellow; *Odor,* Fruity- rose
PHYSICAL PROPERTIES: *Specific gravity:* 0.896-0.909 (25/25C); *Refractive index:* 1.4570-1.4620 (20C); *Optical rotation.*

1, *Flash point:* 210F(TCC); *Solubility:* Soluble in 3 parts 80% ethyl alcohol, most oils; insoluble in glycerol

WARNING AND CAUTION: Combustible; nontoxic

GLYCEROL

SYNONYMS: Glycerin; Glycerinum; 1, 2, 3- Propanetriol; Propenyl hydrate; Glycerol alcohol; Trihydroxypropane; Trihydric (polyhydric) alcohol

CAS NUMBER: 56-81-5

MOLECULAR FORMULA: $C_3 H_8 O_3$

MOLECULAR WEIGHT: 92.09

CHARACTERISTICS: *Form:* Liquid, syrup; *Color:* Colorless; *Odor;* Odorless; *Taste:* Sweet, warm

PHYSICAL PROPERTIES: *Specific gravity:* 1.2653 (25/25C); *Boiling point:* 290C; *Freezing point:* 17C (solidifies at lower temperature); *Flash point:* 320F (TCC); *Solubility:* Soluble in water and alcohol; insoluble in chloroform, ether, benzene, fixed and valatile oils, organic solvents

DERIVATION: By saponification of fats and oils; from propylene and chlorine with hydrochlorous acid

WARNING AND CAUTION: Combustible, low toxicity

HELIOTROPIN

SYNONYMS: Piperonal; Piperonyl aldehyde; 3, 4-(Methylenedioxy) benzaldehyde; 1, 3- Benzodioxole- 5-carboxaldehyde; Dioxymethyleneprotocatechuic aldehyde; Protocatechuic aldehyde methylene ether

CAS NUMBER: 120-57-0

MOLECULAR FORMULA: $C_8 H_6 O_3$

MOLECUALR WEIGHT: 150.13

CHARACTERISTICS: *Form:* Crystals; *Color:* White, lustrous; turns red brown; *Odor:* Sweet heliotrope

PHYSICAL PROPERTIES: *Boiling point:* 263 C; *Freezing point,* 35.5-37 C; *Solubility:* Soluble in alcohol, ether; slightly soluble in water and glycerol

DERIVATION: By oxidation of isosafrole; found in oils of Vanilla tahitiana

WARNING AND CAUTION: Combustible; low toxicity

HEXYL ACETATE

CAS NUMBER: 142-92-7

MOLECULAR FORMULA: $C_8 H_{16} O_2$
MOLECULAR WEIGHT: 144.2
CHARACTERISTICS: *Form:* Liquid; *Color;* Colorless; *Odor:* Sweet ester
PHYSICAL PROPERTIES: *Specific gravity:* 0.890 (25/25C); *Boiling point:* 169.2C; *Solubility:* Soluble in alcohol, ether; insoluble in water
DERIVATION: From primary and secondary hexyl alcohol
WARNING AND CAUTION: Combustible

HEXYL ALCOHOL

SYNONYMS: 1-Hexanol; Amyl carbinol; n-Hexyl alcohol; Pentylcarbinol; 1-Hydroxyhexane
CAS NUMBER: 111-27-3
MOLECULAR FORMULA: $C_6 H_{14} O$
MOLECULAR WEIGHT: 102.17
CHARACTERISTICS: *Form:* Liquid; *Color;* Colorless
PHYSICAL PROPERTIES: *Specific gravity:* 0.886 (25/25 C); *Refractive index:* 1.469 (25C); *Boiling point:* 157C; *Freezing point:* 149F (TCC); *Solubility:* Soluble in alcohol, ether; silghtly in water
DERIVATION: By reducing ethyl caproate with sodium in absolute alcohol; from olefins by the oxo process
WARNING AND CAUTION: Combustible; low toxicity

HYDROXYCITRONELLAL

SYNONYMS: Citronellal hydrate; 3, 7 Dimethyl- 1-7/ hydroxyoctanal; Laurine; 7-Hydroxy 3, 7 dimethyloctan 1-al
CAS NUMBER: 107-75-5
MOLECULAR FORMULA: $C_{10} H_{20} 0_2$
MOLECULAR WEIGHT: 172.27
CHARACTERISTICS: *Form:* Liquid; viscous; *Color;* Colorless or faint yellow; *Odor;* Sweet and intense odor of linden blossom
PHYSICAL PROPERTIES: *Specific gravity:* 0.97-0.921 (25/25C); Refractive index : 1.4470-1.4500 (20C); optical rolation: 9-10; Boiling point: 94-96 C; Flash point : 270 F (TCC); Solubility Soluble in 1 part 50% ethyl alcohol, fixed oils; slightly soluble in water, glycerol, mineral oils
DERIVATION: From citronella or Eucalyptus citriodora
WARNING AND CAUTION: Combustible; nontoxic

IONONE

SYNONYMS: α– or ß-Cyclocitrylidenacetone; Irisone; 4-(2,6,6-Trimethyl-2-cyclohexenyl)-2-buten-2-one; α–or ß-Ionone; 4-(2,6,6-Trimethyl-1-cyclohexenyl)-3-buten-2-one
CAS NUMBER: 8013-90-9
MOLECULAR FORMULA: $C_{13}H_{20}O$
MOLECULAR WEIGHT: 193.30
CHARACTERISTICS: *Form:* Liquid; *Color;* Light yellow; *Odor:* Violet
PHYSICAL PROPERTIES: *Specific gravity:* 0.927-0.933 (25\25C); *Refractive index:* 1.4970-1.5020 (20C); *Boiling point:* 126-128C; *Flash point:* >212 F (TCC); *Solubility:* Soluble in 2-3 parts 70% alcohol, chloroform, ether, mineral oils, propylene glycol, benzene; insoluble in water and glycerin
DERIVATION: Condensing citral with acetone; reaction of acetylene with acetone, followed by hydrogenation, condensation with diketone, and further reaction with acetylene

ISOAMYL ACETATE

CAS NUMBER: 123-92-2
MOLECULAR FORMULA: $C_7H_{14}O_2$
MOLECULAR WEIGHT: 130.18
CHARACTERISTICS: *Form:* Liquid; *Color;* Colorless; *Odor;* Banana, pear
PHYSICAL PROPERTIES: *Specific gravity:* 0.876(15.4C); *Refractive index:* 1.400 (20C); *Boiling point:* 142C; *Freezing point:* -78.5C; *Flash point:* 80F (TCC); *Solubility:* Soluble in alcohol, ether, slightly soluble in water
DERIVATION: Rectification of commercial amyl acetate
WARNING AND CAUTION: Flammable; moderately toxic and irritating

ISOAMYL ALCOHOL

SYNONYMS: 3-Methyl- 1-butanol; Isobutyl carbinol
CAS NUMBER: 123-51-3
MOLECULAR FORMULA: $C_5H_{12}O$
MOLECULAR WEIGHT: 88.11
CHARACTERISTICS. *Form:* Liquid; *Color;* Colorless; *Odor:* Disagreeable; *Taste:* Pungent
PHYSICAL PROPERTIES: *Specific gravity:* 0.813 (15.4C); *Refractive index:* 1.4075 (20C); *Boiling point:* 132 C; *Freezing point:* 117.2C; *Flash point:* 109 F (CC); *Solubility:* Soluble in alcohol, ether; slightly soluble in water

DERIVATION: Distillation of fusel oil or the mixed alcohol resulting from chloriantion and hydrolysis of pentane (amyl hydride)

WARNING AND CAUTION: Flammable; moderately toxic and irritating

ISOAMYL BUTYRATE

CAS NUMBER: 106-27-4

MOLECULAR FORMULA: $C_9H_{18}O_2$

MOLECULAR WEIGHT: 158.23

CHARACTERISTICS: *Form:* Liquid; *Color;* White; *Odor:* Aromatic, Pear

PHYSICAL PROPERTIES: *Specific gravity:* 0.866-0.868 (15-5C); Boiling Point : 150-180C; Solubility: Soluble in alcohol, ether; very slightly soluble in water.

DERIVATION : By treating ISoamye alcohol with butyric acid and distilling.

WARNING AND CAUTION : Combustible; low roxi city.

ISOAMYL ISOVALERATE

See Amyl valerate

ISOAMYL PROPIONATE

SYNONYMS: Amyl propionate

MOLECULAR FORMULA: $C_8H_{16}O_2$

MOLECULAR WEIGHT: 144.42

CHARACTERISTICS: *Form:* Liquid; *Color;* Colorless; *Odor;* Apple

PHYSICAL PROPERTIES: *Specific gravity:* 0.869-0.873 (20C); *Refractive index:* 1.4065(20C); *Boiling point:* 160-161C; *Flash point:* 106 F(TCC); *Solubility:* Soluble in alcohol, ether; insoluble in water

DERIVATION: From amyl alcohol with propionic acid in presence of sulfuric acid as a catalyst and distilling

WARNING AND CAUTION: Flammable; moderately toxic

ISOAMYL SALICYLATE

SYNONYMS: Amyl salicylate

CAS NUMBER: 87-20-7

MOLECULAR FORMULA: $C_{12}H_{16}O$

MOLECULAR WRIGHT: 208.25

CHARACTERISTICS. *Form:* Liquid; *Color;* Colorless, to faint

yellow; *Odor:* Pleaseant, orchid like
PHYSICAL PROPERTIES: *Specific gravity:* 1.053-1.059 (15C); *Refractive index:* 1.5050-1.5080 (20C); *Optical rotation:* 0\2.30\ *Boiling point:* 280 C; *Solubility:* Soluble in alcohol, ether; insoluble in water and glycerol
DERIVATION: By esterifying salicylic and with amyl alcohol, and distilling
WARNING AND CAUTION: Combustible; low toxicity

ISOBUTYL ACETATE

CAS NUMBER: 110-19-0
MOLECULAR FORMULA: $C_6H_{12}O$
MOLECULAR WEIGHT: 116.16
CHARACTERISTICS: *Form:* Liquid; *Color;* Colorless; *Odor;* Fruit-like
PHYSICAL PROPERTIES: *Specific gravity:* 0.8685 (15C); *Refractive index:* 1.392 (20C); *Boiling point:* 116-117C; *Freezing point:* 99 C; *Flash point:* 88 F(OC); *Solubility:* Soluble in alcohol, ether, hydrdocarbons; insoluble in water
DERIVATION: Treating isobutyl alcohol with acetic in presence of catalysts
WARNING AND CAUTION: Flammable; moderately toxic by ingestion and inhalation

ISOBUTYL ISOBUTYRATE

SYNONYMS: Isobutyl n- butyrate
CAS NUMBER: 97-85-8
MOLECULAR FORMULA: $C_8H_{16}O_2$
MOLECULAR WEIGHT: 144.21
CHARACTERISTICS: *Form:* Liquid; *Color;* Colorless; *Odor;* Fruity
PHYSICAL PROPERTIES: *Specific gravity:* 0.853-0.857 (20 20C); *Refractive index:* 1.3999 (20C); *Boiling point:* 148.7C; *Freezing point:* 80.7C; *Solubility:* Soluble in alcohol, ether; insoluble in water
WARNING AND CAUTION: Combustible; may be toxic

SOBUTYL FORMATE

SYNONYMS: Tetryl formate
MOLECULAR FORMULA: $C_5H_{10}O_2$
MOLECULAR WEIGHT: 102.13
CHARACTERISTICS. *Form:* Liquid
PHYSICAL PROPERTIES: *Specific gravity:* 0.885 (25/25C); *Refractive index:* 1.3858 (20C); *Boiling point:* 98C; *Freezing*

point: 95C; *Solubility:* Soluble in alcohol, ether; slightly soluble in water

ISOBUTYL ISOVALERATE

SYNONYMS: Isobutyl valerate
MOLECULAR FORMULA: $C_9H_{18}O_2$
MOLECULAR WEIGHT: 158.23
CHARACTERISTICS. *Form:* Liquid; *Color;* Colorless; *Odor;* Ethereal
PHYSICAL PROPERTIES: *Specific gravity:* 0.853 (25/25C); *Refractive index:* 1.4064 (20C); *Boiling point;* 170-172; *Solubility:* Soluble in alcohol, ether; insoluble in water

ISOBUTYL PROPIONATE

CAS NUMBER: 540-42-1
MOLECULAR FORMULA: $C_7H_{14}O_2$
MOLECULAR WEIGHT: 130.18
CHARACTERISTICS: *Form:* Liquid; *Odor;* Ethereal, agreeable
PHYSICAL PROPERTIES: *Specific gravity:* 0.8600-0.8635 (20 20C); *Refractive index:* 1.3975 (20C); *Boiling point:* 138C; *Freezing point:* 71.4 C; *Solubility:* Soluble in alcohol, insoluble in water

ISOBUTYL SALICYLATE

SYNONYMS: Isobutyl o- hydroxybenzoate
CAS NUMBER: 87-19-4
MOLECULAR FORMULA: $C_{11}H_{14}O_3$
MOLECULAR WEIGHT: 194.23
CHARACTERISTICS: *Form:* Liquid; *Color;* Colorless to slightly yellow; *Odor:* Cloveorchid, and salicylate
PHYSICAL PROPERTIES: *Specific gravity:* 1.061-1.065 (25 25C); *Refractive index:* 1.5070-1.5100 (20C); *Boiling point* 259C; *Flash point:* >212F(TCC); *Solubility:* Soluble in 9 parts 80% ethyl alcohol, 2 parts 90% ethye alcohol, mineral oils insoluble in water and glycerol.
WARNING AND CAUTION · Combustible; low toxicity.

ISOBUTYL α–TOLUATE

SYNONYMS: Isobutyl phenyl acetate
MOLECULAR FORMULA: $C_{12}H_{16}O_2$

MOLECULAR WEIGHT: 192.26

CHARACTERISTICS. *Form:* Liquid; *Color;* Colorless; *Odor;* Musk, honey, rose

PHYSICAL PROPERTIES: *Specific gravity:* 0.984-0.986 (25 25C); *Refractive index:* 1.4860-1.4875 (20C); *Flash point:* 212F(TCC); *Solubility:* Soluble in 8 parts 70% ethyl alcohol, 2 parts 80% ethyl alcohol

ISOEUGENOL

SYNONYMS: 2 Methoxy-4- propenylphenol; 4 Hydroxy- 3- methoxy -1-propenyl benzene; 4 Propenyl guaiacol; 1-Hydroxy\ 2-methoxy -4- propenyl benzene

CAS NUMBER: 97-54-1

MOLECULAR FORMULA : $C_{10}H_{12}0_2$

MOLECULAR WEIGHT: 164.20

CHARACTERISTICS. *Form: oily; Color;* Pale yellow; *Odor:* Spicy clove

PHYSICAL PROPERTIES: *Specific gravity:* 1.081-1.084 (25\ 25C); *Refractive index:* 1.5739(19C); *Boiling point:* 268C; *Freezing point:* 19C; *Solubility:* Soluble in alcohol, ether, oreganic solvents; slightly soluble in water

DERIVATION: Occurs in ylang ylang and other essential oils, from eugenol by isomerization with caustic potash

WARNING AND CAUTION: Combustible; low toxicity

LAURIC ALDEHYDE

SYNONYMS: Lauryl aldehyde; Dodecylaldehyde; Aldehyde C-12 lauric; Dodecanal; Lauraldehyde; n- Dodecylic aldehyde

CAS NUMBER: 112-54-9

MOLECULAR FORMULE; $C_{12}H_{24}O$

MOLECULAR WEIGHT: 184.32

CHARACTERISTICS. *Form:* Crystale, powder, leaflet; *Color;* White or colorless; *Odor:* Bay oil, slight

PHYSICAL PROPERTIES: *Specific gravity:* 0.828-0.836 (25 25C); *Refractive index:* 1.433-1.440 (20C); *Boiling Point:* 225 C; *Melting point:* 44 C; *Flash point:* 212 F(TCC); *Solubility:* Soluble in 90% alcohol, insoluble in water

DERIVATION: Small constituent in oils of sweet orange, petitgrain, and several species of pinus

WARNING AND CAUTION: Combustible, low toxicity

LIMONENE

SYNONYMS: 1- Methyl- 4- (1 methylethenyl) cyclohexene; p Mentha\ 1,8\ diene; Cinene; Cajeputene; Kautschin
CAS NUMBER: 138-86-3
MOLECULAR FORMULA: $C_{10}H_{16}$
MOLECULAR WEIGHT: 136.23
CHARACTERISTICS. *Form:* Liquid; *Color;* Colorless; *Odor:* Pleasant, Lemon-like
PHYSICAL PROPERTIES: *Specific gravity:* 0.8422 (20C); *Refractive index:* 1.4744 (20C); *Boiling point:* 176-176.4 C; *Solubility:* Soluble in alcohol, insoluble in water
DERIVATION: Occurs in various ethereal oils, particularly in oils of lemon,orange, caraway, dill, bergamot, peppermint, and spearmint

LINALOOL

SYNONYMS: 3, 7 Dimethyl- 1,6- octadien- 3 ol; 2,6- Dimethyl- 2,7 octadien- 6- ol; Linalol
CAS NUMBER: 78-70-6
MOLECULAR FORMULA: $C_{10}H_{18}0$
MOLECULAR WEIGHT: 154.25
CHARACTERISTICS. *Form:* Liquid; *Color;* Colorless; *Odor;* Sweet, intense floral
PHYSICAL PROPERTIES: *Specific gravity:* 0.859-0.867(25/25C); *Refractive index:* 1.4610-1.4640 (20C); *Optical rotation:* +2; *Flash point:* 175F (TCC); *Solubility:* Soluble in alcohol, ether; insoluble in water
DERIVATION: Occurs in oils of Ceylon cinnamon, sassafras, orange flower, bergamot, ylang ylang, rosewood, petitgrain, linalol wood; synthetically made from geraniol; made synthetically form geraniol
WARNING AND CAUTION: Combustible; nontoxic

LINALYL ACETATE

SYNONYMS: 3, 7- Dimethyl 1, 6 octadien -3yl acetate; Beramol
CAS NUMBER: 115-95-7
MOLECULAR FORMULA: $C_{14}H_{24}O_2$
MOLECULAR WEIGHT: 196.28
CHARACTERISTICS: *Form:* Liquid; *Color;* Colorless; *Odor;* Bergamot
PHYSICAL PROPERTIES: *Specific gravity:* 0.908-0.920 (25\

25C); *Refractive index:* 1.450-1.458 (20C); *Optical rotation-* 1 to +1°.; *Boiling point:* 108-110 C; *Solubility:* Soluble in alcohol, ether, diethyl phthalate, benzyl benzoate, mineral oils, slightly soluble in propylene glycol; insoluble in water, glycerin

DERIVATION: Action of acetic anhydride on linalool in presence of sulfuric acid

WARNING AND CAUTION: Combustible; low toxicity

LINALYL BENZOATE

SYNONYMS: 3,7- Dimethyl- 1, 6 octadien- 3- yl benzoate

MOLECULAR FORMULA: $C_{17}H_{22}O_2$

MOLECULAR WEIGHT: 258.37

CHARACTERISTICS: *Form:* Liquid; *Color;* Yellow- brownish; *Odor:* Heavy tuberose

PHYSICAL PROPERTIES: *Specific gravity:* 0.980-0.999 (25/25C); *Refractive index:* 1.5050-1.200 (20C); *Flash point:* 208 F(TCC); *Solubility:* Soluble in 1 part 90% ethyl alcohol

LINALYL BUTYRATE

SYNONYMS: 3, 7- Dimethyl- 1, 6- octadien- 3- yl butyratre Linaly isobutyrate

CAS NUMBER: 78-35-3

MOLECULAR FORMULA: $C_{14}H_{24}O_2$

MOLECULAR WEIGHT: 224.34

CHARACTERISTICS: *Form:* Liquid; *Color;* yellow; *Odor;* Fruity

PHYSICAL PROPERTIES: *Specific gravity:* 0.893-0.904 (25/25C); *Refractive index:* 1.4510-1.4560 (20C); *Flash point:* >212 F(TCC); *Solubility:* Soluble in 3 parts 80% ethyl alcohol

DERIVATION: Found in lavender oil; synthetically from acetone

LINALYL FORMATE

SYNONYMS: 3, 7- Dimethyl- 1, 6 octadien- 3- yl formate

MOLECULAR FORMULA: $C_{11}H_{18}O_2$

MOLECULAR WEIGHT: 182.26

CHARACTERISTICS. *Form:* Liquid; *Color;* Slightly yellow; *Odor;* Fruity, rose, bergamot

PHYSICAL PROPERTIES: *Specific gravity:* 0.915-0.924 (25/25 C); *Refractive index:* 1.4550-1.4580 (20C); *Boiling Point:* 100-103 C; *Flash point:* 190 F (TCC); *Solubility:* Solubly in 6 parts 70% ethyl alcohol, 1 part 80% ethyl alcohol; insoluble in water

DERIVATION: Synthetically from acetone

WARNING AND CAUTION: Combustible; low toxicity

LINALYL PROPIONATE

SYNONYMS: 3, Dimethyl- 1, 6 octadium- 3- yl propionate
MOLECULAR FORMULA: $C_{13}H_{22}O_2$
MOLECULAR WEIGHT: 210.32
CHARACTERISTICE: *Form:* Liquid; *Color;* Colorless; to slightly yellow; *Odor;* fresh bergamot, lily of the valley
PHYSICAL PROPERTIES: *Specific gravity:* 0.895-0.902 (25/25C); *Refractive index:* 1.4500-1.4550 (20C); *Flash Point:* 196F(TCC); *Solubility:* Soluble in 8 parts 70% ethyl alcohol,2 parts 80% ethyl alcohol, most fixed oils, mineral oils, propylene glycol; insoluble in glycerin
DERIVATION: Found in lavender oil; synthetically form acetone
WARNING AND CAUTION: Combustible; low toxicity

MAGNESIUM CARBONATE

MOLECULAR FORMULA: $MgCO_3$
MOLECULAR WEIHGT: 485
CHARACTERISTICS: *From :* Powder, light bulk; Color : White; Odor : Odorless
PHYSICAL PROPERTIES : Specific gravity : 3.0 (25/25C); Refreative index : 1.52 (20C); Solubility; Soluble in water and indiluted acids with effervescence; in soluble in alcohol.
DERIVATION: By mixing solution of magnesium sulfate and sodium carbonate; and filtering
WARNING AND CANTION: Low toxicity

MALIC ACID

SYNONYMS: Hydroxybutatenedioic acid; Hydroxysuccinsic acid, Apple acid
CAS NUMBER: 6915-15-7
MOLECULAR FORMULA: $C_4H_6O_5$
MOLECULAR WEIGHT: 134.09
CHARACTERISTICS : From : Crystals; Color: Colorless; odor: sour
PHYSCIAL PROPERTIES : *Specific gravity:* 1.601 (dl), (20.4C) (d or l); *Boiling point:* 150C (dl), 140 C(d or l); *Melting point:* 128 C (dl); 100 C(dor l); *Solubility:* Soluble in alcohol, water; slightly soluble in ether; insoluble in benzene
DERIVATION: From natural unripe apple and other fruits; synthetically by catalytic oxidation of benzene, by catalytic

oxidation of benzene, by heating with steam under pressure
WARNING AND CAUTION: Combustible; low toxicity

MALONIC ACID

SYNONYMS: Methanedicarbonic acid; Propanedioic acid; Methanedicarboxylic acid
CAS NUMBER: 141-82-2
MOLECULAR FORMULA: $C_3H_4O_4$
MOLECULAR WEIGHT: 104.06
CHARACTERISTICS: *Form:* Crystals, triclinic small; *Color:* White
PHYSICAL PROPERTIES: *Specific gravity:* 1.63(25/25C); *Melting point:* 132-134 C; *Solubility:* Soluble in alcohol, ether, water
DERIVATION: From monochloroacetic acid with potassium cyanide and hydrolysis; from malic acid; from diethyl malonate; from lignous wastes
WARNING AND CAUTION: Highly toxic; strong irritant

MALTOL

SYNONYMS: 3- Hydroxy- 2- methyl- 4- pyrone; 3- Hydroxy- 2- methyl 4H- pyran 4- one; 3- Hydroxy- 2- methyl -y- pyrone; Larixinic acid; Palatone; Veltol
CAS NUMBER: 118-71-8
MOLECULAR FORMULA: $C_6H_6O_3$
MOLECULAR WEIGHT: 126.11
CHARACTERISTICS: *Form:* Crystalline powder; *Color:* White; *Odor:* Caramel, butterscotch, fruity, strawberry
PHYSICAL PROPERTIES: *Solubility:* Soluble in alcohol, propylene glycol; slightly soluble in water
DERIVATION: Found and isolated from bark of young larch tress (Larix decidua mill.); in pine needles (Abies alba mill. pinaceae); in chicory, wood tars and oils, roasted malt

MENTHOL

SYNONYMS: Isopropyl- 4- methylcyclohexan- 2- ol; Hexahydrothymol; 3- p- Menthanol; Peppermint camphor; 3- Hydroxymenthane; Mentha camphor; 5- Methyl 2- (1 methylethyl) cyclohexanol; p- Menthanol; 1- Menthol; Methylhydroxyisopro pylcyclohexane; p- Menthan- 3- ol
CAS NUMBER: 89-78-1
MOLECULAR FORMULA: $C_{10}H_{20}O$

MOLECULAR WEIGHT: 156.27
CHARACTERISTICS: *Form:* Crystals or granules; *Color;* Colorless; *Odor;* Peppermint; *Taste:* Peppermint
PHYSICAL PROPERTIES: *Specific gravity:* 0.890 (25/25C); *Refractive index:* 1.458 (25C); *Optical rotation:* 50⁰ (10% alcohol solution); *Boiling point:* 212 C; *Freezing point:* 41-43C; *Flash point:* 200F (TCC); *Solubility:* Soluble in 3 parts 70% alcohol, chloroform, ether, glacial acetic acid; slightly soluble in water
DERIVATION: From peppermint oil and other mint oils; synthetically by hydrogenation of thymol
WARNING AND CAUTION: Moderate irritant

MENTHONE

SYNONYMS: 1- p- Menthan- 3-one; 5- Methyl- 2- (1 methylethyl) cyclohexanone; 1- Methyl- 4- isopropylcyclohexan -3- one; 4- Isopropyl -1- methylcyclohexan-3-one; -3- p- Menthanone; Terpinene; 3-Hydroxymenthene
CAS NUMBER: 1074-95-9
MOLECULAR FORMULA: $C_{10}H_{18}O$
MOLECULAR WEIGHT: 154.25
CHARACTERISTICS: *Form:* Oily liquid; *Colour:* Colorless; *Odor:* Slightly peppermint; *Taste:* Bitter
PHYSICAL PROPERTIES: *Specific gravity:* 0.888-0.895 (25 25C); *Refractive index:* 1.4480-1.4530 (20C); *Optical rotation:* - 15 to + 15⁰ *Boiling point:* 207 C; *Flash point:* 170F (TCC); *Solubility:* Soluble in 3 parts 70% ethyl alcohol, oranic solvents; slightly soluble in water
DERIVATION: Found in oils of peppermint, Japanese mint, pennyroyal, geranium, and many other oils
WARNING AND CAUTION: Combustible; low toxicity

MENTHYL ACETATE

SYNONYMS: 5- Methyl- 2- (1- methyl) cyclohexanol acetate; Menthol acetic ester; 1/ Isopropyl- 4- methylcyclohex 2 yl acetate
CAS NUMBER: 89-48-5
MOLECULAR FORMULA: $C_{12}H_{22}O_2$
MOLECULAR WEIGHT: 198.31
CHARACTERISTICS: *Form:* Liquid; *Color;* Colorless; *Odor;* Menthol
PHYSICAL PROPERTIES: *Specific gravity:* 0.922-0.927(25/25C);

Refractive index: 1.447 (20C); *Optical rotation:* 72.47 to 72.18; *Boiling point:* 227 C; *Flash point:* 198F(TCC); *Solubility:* Soluble in alcohol, ether, slightly soluble in water

DERIVATION: From peppermint oil; by boiling menthol with acetic anhydride in presence of sodium acetate

WARNING AND CAUTION: Combustible; low toxicity

METHYL ACETATE

CAS NUMBER: 79-20-9

MOLECULAR FORMULA: C_3H_6O

MOLECULAR WEIGHT: 74.08

CHARACTERISTICS: *Form:* Liquid, volatile; *Color:* Colorless; *Odor;* Fragrant, apple

PHYSICAL PROPERTIES: *Specific gravity:* 0.92428 (25/25C); *Refractive index:* 1.3619 (20C); *Boiling point:* 54.05C; *Freezing point:* 98.05C; *Flash point:* 15 F(TCC); *Solubility:* Soluble in alcohol, ether, water

DERIVATION: By heating methyl alcohol and acetic acid in presence of sulfuric acid, and distilling

WARNING AND CAUTION: Flammable; explosive

METHYL ANTHRANILATE

SYNONYMS: 2- Aminobenzoic acid methyl ester; Methyl 2-aminobenzoate; Neroli oil, artificial; Methyl o-aminobenzoate

CAS NUMBER: 134-20-3

MOLECULAR FORMULA: $C_8H_9NO_2$

MOLECULAR WEIGHT: 151.16

CHARACTERISTICS: *Form:* Liquid; *Colour;* Pale yellow with bluish florescence; *Odor;* Grape

PHYSICAL PROPERTIES: *Specific gravity:* 1.167-1.175 (15C); *Refractive index:* 1.5820-1.5840 (20C); *Boiling point:* 135 C; *Freezing point:* 23.8 C; *Solubility:* Soluble in 60% alcohol, propylene glycol; slightly soluble in water

DERIVATION: Occurs in neroli, ylang ylang, bergamot, jasmine, grape juice; by heating anthranilic acid and methyl alcohol in presence of sulfuric acid, and distilling

WARNING AND CAUTION: Combustible

METHYL BENZOATE

SYNONYMS: Niobe oil; Benzoic acid methyl ester; Essence of

niobe; Oil of niobe
CAS NUMBER: 93-58-3
MOLECULAR FORMULA: $C_8H_8O_2$
MOLECULAR WEIGHT: 136.15
CHARACTERISTICS: *Form:* Liquid; *Colour;* Colorless; *Odor;* Fruity, ylang ylang
PHYSICAL PROPERTIES: *Specific gravity:* 1.085-1.088 (25 25C); *Refractive index:* 1.5150-1.5180(20C); *Boiling point:* 98-200C; *Freezing point:* 12.3 C; *Flash point:* 181F(TCC); *Solubility:* Soluble in 4 parts 60% ethyl alcohol, ether, methanol, fixed oils, insoluble in water
DERIVATION: Found in oils of clove, ylang ylang, jonquil, tuberose; heating methyl alcohol and benzoic acid in presence of sulfuric acid; passing dry hydrogen chloride through a solution of benzoic acid in methanol
WARNING AND CAUTION: Combustible

METHYL BUTYRATE

SYNONYME. Butanoic acid methyl ester
CAS NUMBER: 623-42-7
MOLECULAR FORMULA: $C_5H_{10}O_2$
MOLECULAR WEIGHT: 102.13
CHARACTERISTICS: *Form:* Liquid; *Color;* Colorless
PHYSICAL PROPERTIES: *Specific gravity:* 0.898 (20C); *Refractive index:* 1.3879 (20C); *Boiling point:* 102C; *Freezing point:* 95C; *Flash point:* 14 F(TCC); 57 C (CC); *Solubility:* Soluble in alcohol, ether, slightly soluble in water
WARNING AND CAUTION: Flammable; moderately toxic

METHYL CINNAMATE

SYNONYMS: Methyl 3- phenyl propionate; Methyl cinnamylate
CAS NUMBER: 103-26-4
MOLECULAR FORMULA: $C_{10}H_{10}O_2$
MOLECULAR WEIGHT: 162.19
CHARACTERISTICS: *Form:* Crystals; *Color;* White; *Odor;* Strawberry
PHYSICAL PROPERTIES: *Specific gravity:* 1.0415; *Boiling point:* 259.6C; *Freezing point:* 34C; *Solubility:* Soluble in 1 parts 80% alcohol, ether, mineral oil; insoluble in water
DERIVATION: Found as constituent in oil of galanga; by heating methyl alcohol, cinnamic acid, and sulfuric acid, and distilling
WARNING AND CAUTION: Combustible; low toxicity

METHYL HEPTENONE

SYNONYMS: 6- Methyl- 5- heptene- 2- one
CAS NUMBER: 409-02-9
MOLECULAR FORMULA: $C_8H_{14}O$
MOLECULAR WEIGHT: 126.20
CHARACTERISTICS: *Form:* Liquid; *Color;* Colorless; *Odor;* Sharp citrus lemon grass
PHYSICAL PROPERTIES: *Specific gravity:* 0.846-0.851 (25 25C); *Refractive index:* 1.4380-1.4420 (20C); *Boiling point:* 173-174C; *Freeszing point:* 67.1 C; *Solubility:* Soluble in alcohol, ether, insoluble in water
WARNING AND CAUTION: Combustible; low toxicity

METHYL HEPTYNE CARBONATE

SYNONYMS: Methyl 2- octynoate; Heptyne carboxylic acid methyl ester; Folione
CAS NUMBER: 111-12-6
MOLECULAR FORMULA: $C_9H_{14}O_2$
MOLECULAR WEIGHT: 154.21
CHARACTERISTICS: *Form:* Liquid; *Color;* Colorless; *Odor;* Strong violet
PHYSICAL PROPERTIES: *Specific gravity:* 0.919-0.924 (25 25C); *Refractive index:* 1.446-1.490 (20C); *Flash point:* 192F (TCC); *Solubility:* Soluble in 6 parts 70% ethyl alcohol, 2 parts 80% ethyl alcohol, most fixed oils, mineral oils
DERIVATION: From heptaldehyde
WARNING AND CAUTION: Combustible; low toxicity

METHYL IONONE

SYNONYMS: α–Methyl ionone; ß-Methyl ionone; Methyl ionone; Irone; Raldeine; Cyclocitrylidene methyl ethyl ketone
MOLECULAR FORMULA: $C_{14}H_{22}O$
MOLECULAR WEIGHT: 206.33
CHARACTERISTICS: *Form:* Liquid; *Color;* Colorless to amber yellow; *Odor:* Floral
PHYSICAL PROPERTIES: *Specific gravity:* 0.926-0.939 (25/ 25C); *Refractive index:* 1.501-1.504 (20C); *Boiling point:* 144C; *Flash point:* 217 F (TCC); *Solubility:* Soluble in alcohol, insoluble in water
DERIVATION: Oil of orris; several isomers are available α–ß- and mixtures. The constants are approximately as above specified

METHYL ISOEUGENOL

SYNONYMS: Propenylveratrole; Isoeugenol methyl ether; 1, 2/ Dimethoxy- 4- propenylbenzene; Propenyl guaiacol
CAS NUMBER: 93-16-3
MOLECULAR FORMULA: $C_{11}H_{14}O_2$
MOLECULAR WEIGHT: 178.23
CHARACTERISTICS: *Form:* Liquid; *Color;* Colorless to slightly yellow; *Odor:* Spicy, carnation, sweeter than eugenol
PHYSICAL PROPERTIES: *Specific gravity:* 1.047-1.053 (25/ 25C); *Refractive index:* 1.5650-1.5690 (20C); *Boiling point:* 262-264 C; *Flash point:* >212F (TCC); *Solubility:* Soluble in 2 parts 70% ethyl alcohol; insoluble in mineral oil, glycerol
WARNING AND CAUTION: Combustible; low toxicity

METHYL ISOVALERATE

SYNONYMS: 3- Methylbutanoic acid methyl ester
MOLECULAR FORMULA: $C_6H_{12}O_2$
MOLECULAR WEIGHT: 116.16
CHARACTERISTICS: *Form:* Liquid; *Color;* Colorless; *Odor;* Valerian
PHYSICAL PROPERTIES: *Specific garvity:* 0.881 (20C); *Boiling point*: 116-117C; *Solubility:* Soluble in alcohol, ether, slightly soluble in water

METHYL NAPHTHYL KETONE

SYNONYMS: α–and ß-Naphthyl methyl ketone;a and ß-Acetonaphthylene; 1 and 2-acetonaphtone; Oranger liquid (trademark)
MOLECULAR FORMULA: $C_{12}H_{10}O$
MOLECULAR WEIGHT: 170.21
CHARACTERISTICS: *Form:* Liquid; *Color;* Amber; *Odor;* Sweet neroli, grape
PHYSICAL PROPERTIES: Specific gravity: 1.110-1.116 (25/25C); Flash point: >212F (TCC); Solubility: Soluble in 7 parts 70% ethyl alcohol, 2 parts 80% ethyl alcohol
DERIVATION: A mixture of α–and ß-naphthyl methyl ketone, in which the α–isomer predominates

METHYL PHENYL ACETATE

SYNONYME: α–Methyl toluate
MOLECULAR FORMULA: $C_9H_{10}O_2$

MOLECULAR WEIGHT: 150.18

CHARACTERISTICS: *Form:* Liquid; *Color;* Colorless; *Odor;* Musky, honey

PHYSICAL PROPERTIES: *Specific gravity:* 1.062-1.066 (25/25C); *Refractive index:* 1.5050-1.5080 (20C); *Flash point:* 193F (TCC); *Solubility:* Soluble in 7 parts 60% ethyl alcohol, 2 parts 70% ethyl alcohol, fixed, oils, insoluble in water

METHYL SALICYLATE

SYNONYMS: Methyl o- hydroxybenzoate; Oil of wintergreen synthetic; Gaultheria oil; Wintergreen oil; Betula oil; Sweet birch oil; Teaberry oil; 2- Hydroxybenzoic acid methyl ester

CAS NUMBER: 119-36-8

MOLECULAR FORMULA: $C_8H_8O_3$

MOLECULAR WEIGHT: 152.15

CHARACTERISTICS: *Form:* Oily liquid; *Color;* Colorless; yellowish, reddish; *Odor:* Wintergreen, sharp

PHYSICAL PROPERTIES: *Specific gravity:* 1.180-1,185 (25 25C); *Refractive index:* 1.5350-1.5380(20C); *Boiling point:* 222C; *Freezing point:*- 8 C; *Flash point:* 210F(TCC); *Solubility:* Soluble in 7 parts 70% ethyl alcohol, glacial acetic acid, slightly soluble in water

DERIVATION: From wintergreen oil leaves of Gaultheria; by heating methanol and salicylic acid in presence of sulfuric acid; by esterification of salicylate acid with methanol; by distillation of gaultheria or bark of Betula lenta; it is a constituent of many fruit juices, e,g, apple grape, raspberry cherry

WARNING AND CAUTION: Combustible; highly toxic; restricted by FDA for food use

NEROL

SYNONYMS: cis- 3, 7 Dimethyl- 2, 6- octadien- 1- ol; 2, 6 Dimethyl- 2-
6- octadien- 8- ol

CAS NUMBER: 106-25-2

MOLECULAR FORMULA: $C_{10}H_{18}O$

MOLECULAR WEIGHT: 154.24

CHARACTERISTICS: *Form:* Liquid; *Color;* Colorless; *Odor;* Sweet rose, neroli

PHYSICAL PROPERTIES: *Specific gravity:* 0.875-0.880 (25/25C); *Refractive index:* 1.4730-1.4780 (20C); *Boiling point:*

224-225 C; *Flash point:* 198 F (TCC); *Solubility:* Soluble in 9 parts 50% ethyl alcohol

DERIVATION: Found in many essential oils, mostly in neroli oil; indization of geraniol with hydriodic acid and alcoholic soda

NEROLIN

SYNONYMS: ß-Naphthyl ethyl ether; Naphthol ethyl ether; Ethyl 2-naphthyl ether; 2- Ethoxynaphthalene; Bromelia; Nerolin 11

MOLECULAR FORMULA: $C_{12}H_{12}O$

MOLECULAR WEIGHT: 172.23

CHARACTERISTICS: *Form:* Crystals; *Color;* White; *Odor;* Neroli, orange blossom

PHYSICAL PROPRETIES: *Freezing point:* 35C; *Solubility:* Soluble in 5 parts 95% ethyl alcohol; insoluble in water

DERIVATION: From ß-naphthol and ethyl alcohol in presence of sulfuric acid

WARNING AND CAUTION: Combustible

y-NONYL LACTONE

See Aldehyde C-18

y-OCTALACTONE

SYNONYMS : y Hydroxyoctanoic acid lactone

MOLECULAS FORMULA: $C_8H_{14}O_2$

MOLECULAS WEIGHT: 142.20

CHARACTERISTICS: *Form:* Liquid; *Color;* Colorless; to slighthly yellow; *Odor;* Strong coconut-like

PHYSICAL PROPERTIES: *Specific gravity:* 0.970-0.980 (25/25C); *Refractive index:* 1.4430-1.4470; *Flash point:* >212F(TCC); *Solubility:* Soluble in 3 parts 50% ethyl alcohol, 2 parts 60% ethyl alcohol, 1 part 70% ethyl alcohol

PHENYL ACETATE

SYNONYMS: d-Acetylphenol; Acetic acid phenyl ester

CAS NUMBER: 122-79-2

MOLECULAR FORMULA: $C_8H_8O_2$

MOLECULAR WEIGHT: 136.14

CHARACTERISTICS: *Form:* Liquid; *Color;* Colorless; *Odor;* Phenolic

PHYSICAL PROPERTIES: *Specific gravity:* 1.073(25/25C);

Refractive index: 1.5030 (20C); *Boiling point:* 195-196C; *Flash point:* 176F (TCC); *Solubility:* Soluble in alcohol, chlorofrom, ether, glacial acetic acid; slightly soluble in water.

DERIVATION : From phenol and acctyl chloride; by heating triphenye phoshate with potasium acctete and alcohol.

WARNING AND CAUTION: Combustiblel low toxicity

PHENYLACETIC ACID

SYNONYMS: α–Toluic acid; Benzeneacetic acid

CAS NUMBER: 103-82-2

MOLECULAR FORMULA: $C_8H_8O_2$

MOLECULAR WEIGHT: 136.14

CHARACTERISTICS: *Form:* Crystals; *Color;* White; *Odor;* Floral

PHYSICAL PROPERTIES: *Specific gravity:* 1.0809 (25/25C); *Boiling point:* 262 C; *Freezing point:* 74C; *Solubility:* Soluble in alcohol, ether, slighthly soluble in water

DERIVATION: Found in oil of rose, neroli, and tobacco leaf; from benzyl cyanide refluxing with sulfuric acid; leaflets on distillation in vacuo

WARNING AND CAUTION: Combustible; toxic

PHENYL ETHYL ACETATE

SYNONYMS: Phenethyl acetate; ß-Phenethyl acetate; 2-Phenylethyl acetate; Benzylcarbinyl acetate

CAS NUMBER: 103-45-7

MOLECULAR FORMULA: $C_{10}H_{12}O_2$

MOLECULAR WEIGHT: 164.21

CHARACTERISTICS: *Form:* Liquid; *Color;* Colorless; *Odor;* Rose, peach-like

PHYSICAL PROPERTIES: *Specific gravity:* 1.030-1.034 (25/25C); *Refractive index:* 1.4970-1.5010 (20C); *Boiling point:* 226C; *Flash point:* >212F(TCC); *Solubility:* Soluble in 2 parts 70% ethyl alcohol, ether, fixed oils

DERIVATION: Interaction of ethyl acetate and aluminum phenyl ethylate; interaction of acetic anhydride and phenylethyl alcohol in the presence of sodium acetate

WARNING AND CAUTION: Combustible

PHENYL ETHYL ALCOHOL

SYNONYMS: Phenethyl alcohol; 2- Phenylethanol; Benzyl

carbinol; Phenyl ethyl alcohol; Hydroxyethyl benzene
CAS NUMBER: 60-12-8
MOLECULAR FORMULA: $C_8H_{10}O$
MOLECULAR WEIGHT: 122.16
CHARACTERISTICS: *Form:* Liquid; *Color;* Colorless; *Odor;* Floral odor, rose, characteristic; *Taste;* Burning
PHYSICAL PROPERTIES: *Specific gravity:* 1.017-1.020 (25/25C); *Refractive index:* 1.5310-1.5330 (20C); *Boiling point:* 219C; *Freezing point:* /27C; *Solubility:* Soluble in 50% ethyl alcohol, fixed oils, glycerol; soluble 1 part in 50 parts of water
DERIVATION: By reduction of phenylacetic ethyl ester by sodium in absolute alcohol; by action of ethylene oxide on phenyl magnesium bromide, with hydrolysis
WARNING AND CAUTION: Highly toxic by inhalation

PHENYL ETHYL ANTHERNILATE

SYNONYMS: Phenethyl anthranilate; Benzylcarbinyl anthranilate; Phenylethyl o- aminobenzoate
CAS NUMBER: 133-18-6
MOLECULAR FORMULA: $C_{15}H_{15}H_2$
MOLECULAR WEIGHT: 241.29
CHARACTERISTICS: *Form:* Liquid; *Color;* Colorless; yellowish with time; *Odor;* Grape- orange
PHYSICAL PROPERTIES: *Specific gravity:* 1.14 (25/25C); *Solubility:* Soluble in alcohol
WARNING AND CAUTION: Combustible; nontoxic

PHENYL ETHYL PROPIONAEE

SYNONYMS: Phenethyl propionate; ß-Phenethye propionate; ßenzye carbinye propionate
CAS NUMBER: 120-45-6
MOLECULAR FORMULA: $C_{11}H_{14}O$
MOLECULAR WEIGHT: 178.23
CHARACTERISTICS: *Form:* Liquid; *Color;* Colorles to slightly yellow; *Odor;* Fruity, lily rose
PHYSICAL PROPERTIES: Specfic gravity: 1.010-1.014 (25/25C); Refractive index: 1.493-1.496 (20C); Flash point: >212 F(TCC); Solubility: Soluble in 4 parts 70% ethyl alcohol, ether
WARNING AND CAUTION: Combustible; low toxicity

PROPYL ACETATE

SYNONYMS: Acetic acid n- propyl ester
CAS NUMBER: 109-60-4
MOLECULAR FORMULA: $C_5H_{10}O_2$
MOLECULAR WEIGHT: 102.13
CHARACTERISTICS: *Form:* Liquid; *Color;* Colorless; *Odor;* Pear
PHYSICAL PROPERTIES: *Specific gravity:* 0.836 (20C); *Refractive index:* 1.3844 (20C); *Boiling point:* 101.6 C; *Flash point:* 14C; *Solubility:* Soluble in alcohol, ether
DERIVATION: From acetic acid and n- propyl alcohol in the presence of sulfuric acid; from acetic and mixture of propene in the presence of zine chloride catalyst
WARNING AND CAUTION: Flammable; moderately toxic

PROPYL PROPIONATE

SYNONYMS: Propanoic acid propyl ester
CAS NUMBER: 106-36-5
MOLECULAR FORMULA: $C_6H_{12}O_2$
MOLECULAR WEIGHT: 116.16
CHARACTERISTICS: *Form:* Liquid; *Color;* Colorless
PHYSICAL PROPERTIES: *Specific gravity:* 0.883 (20C); *Refractive index:* 1.3935 (20C); *Boiling point:* 122-124 C; *Freezing point:* 76C; *Flash point:* 174F (OC); *Solubility:* Soluble in alcohol, ether, most organic solvents; slightly soluble in water
WARNING AND CAUTION: Combustible

RHODINOL

SYNONYMS:3, 7 Dimethyl- 7- octen- 1- ol; l-Citronellol; Reuniol; Roseol
CAS NUMBER: 6812-78-8
MOLECULAR FORMULA: $C_{10}H_{20}O$
MOLECULAR WEIGHT: 156.26
CHARACTERISTICS: *Form:* Oily Liquid; *Color;* Slightyl yellow; *Odor;* Rose, warm
PHYSICAL PROPERTIES: *Specific gravity:* 0.860-0.880 (25/25C); *Refractive index:* 1.4630-1.4730 (20C); *Optical rotation:* 5 to 9_0 *Boiling point:* 114-115C; *Flash point:* >212 F(TCC); *Solubility:* Soluble in 5 parts 60% ethyl alcohol, ether, mineral oils; slightly soluble in water; insoluble in glycerin
DERIVATION: A mixture of i citronellol and geraniol from

geranium; from Reunion geranium oil
WARNING AND CAUTION: Combustible; low toxicity

SAFROLE

SYNONYMS: 4- Allyl 1, 2 methylenedioxybenzene; Methylene ether ally-dioxybenzene; Methylene ether m allylprocatechin; 5-(2 Propenyl) -1, 3 benzodioxole; Allyl catechol methylene ether; Allyldioxybenzene methylene ester; m Allylpyrocatechin- methylene ether, Allyl pyrocatechol methylene ether; Shikimol; 1- Allyl- 3, 4 methylenedioxybenzene
CAS NUMBER: 94-59-7
MOLECULAS FORMULA: $C_{10}H_{10}O_2$
MOLECULAR WEIGHT: 162.18
CHARACTERISTICS: *Form:* Oily liquid; *Color;* Colorless to pale yellow; *Odor;* Sassafras, camphor
PHYSICAL PROPERTIES: Specific gravity: 1.100-1.107 (15C); Refractive index: 1.5365-1.5385 (20C); Freezing point: 11C; Flash point: >212 F (TCC); Solubility: Soluble in alcohol,Chloroform, ether, slightly soluble in propylene glycol; insoluble in water, glycerin
DERIVATION: From oil of sassafras or camphor oil 75%; constituent of many essential oils
WARNING AND CAUTION: Highly toxic by ingestion; strong irritant

SUCCINIC ACID

SYNONYMS: Butanedioic acid; Amber acid; Ethylenesuccinic acid; Ethylenecarboxylic acid
CAS NUMBER: 110-15-6
MOLECULAR FORMULA: $C_4H_6O_4$
MOLECULAR WEIGHT: 118.09
CHARACTERISTICS: *Form:* Crystals; *Color;* Colorless; *Odor;* Odorless; Taste: Acid
PHYSICAL PROPERTIES: *Specific gravity:* 1.552 (25/25C); *Boiling point:* 235C; *Melting point:* 185C; *Solubility:* Soluble in alcohol, ether, methanol, acetone, glycerol; slightly in water; insoluble in benzene, carbon disulfide, carbon tetrachloride, petroleum ether
DERIVATION: Fermentation of ammonium tartrate; occurs in amber and other resins as a colorless monoclinic prism
WARNING AND CAUTION: Combustible;low toxicity

SUGAR

SYNONYMS: Sweet carbohydrate; Sucrose; Glucose (from grape); Cane (Saccharum officinarum)
CHARACTERISTICS: *Form:* Crystalline; *Taste;* Sweet
PHYSICAL PROPERTIES: *Solubility:* Soluble in water
DERIVATION: The sugar cane is from a bamboo in tropical and subtropical regions around the world: juice from the cane is boiled to remove the water and produce grains of sugar

TARTARIC ACID

SYNONYMS: Dihydroxysuccinic acid; 2,3- Dihydroxybutanedioic acid
CAS NUMBER: 133-37-9
MOLECULAR FORMULA: $C_4H_6O_6$
MOLECULAR WEIGHT: 150.1
CHARACTERISTICS: *Form:* Crystals or crystalline powder; *Color;* Colorless;
PHYSICAL PROPERTIES: *Specific gravity:* 1.7598 (25/25C); *Melting point:* 170C; *Solubility:* Soluble in alcohol, ether, water, glycerol; insoluble in chloroform.
DERIVATION: From maleic anhydride and hydrogen peroxide; from wine residues; occurs in many fruits, free and combined with potassium, calcium, or magnesium
WARNING AND CAUTION: Low toxicity

TERPINEOL

SYNONYMS: Lilacin: Terpinelol; p- 1- Menthene- 8- ol; 1- Methyl- 4-isopropyl- 1- cyclohexen- 8- ol; ßp 8 Menthen- 1- ol; 1- Methyl- 4-ispropenyl cyclohexan- 1- ol
CAS NUMBER: 98-55-5 d
MOLECULAR FORMULA: $C_{10}H_{18}O$
MOLECULAR WEIGHT: 154.25
CHARACTERISTICS: Form: and Color; Colorless liquid or transparent crystals of low melting point; Odor; Sweet lilac
PHYSICAL PROPERTIES: *Specific gravity:* 0.931-0.936 (25/25C); *Refractive index:* 1.4825-1.4850(20C); *Optical rotation:* -10 to $+10_0$ *Boiling point:* 214-224 C; *Freezing point:* 6-12 C; *Flash point:* 195F (TCC); *Solubility:* Soluble in 2 parts 70% ethyl alcohol, 3 parts 60% ethyl alcohol; slightly soluble in water, glycerin
DERIVATION: Found in several essential oils; by heating terpin

hydrate with phosphoric acid and distilling or with dilute sulfuric acid using an azeotropin separation; fractional distillation of pine oil

WARNING AND CAUTION: Combustible

TERPINYL ACETATE

CAS NUMBER:80-26-2

MOLECULAR FORMULA: $C_{12}H_{20}O_2$

MOLECULAR WEIGHT: 196.29

CHARACTERISTICS: *Form:* Liquid; *Color;* Colorless

PHYSICAL PROPERTIES: *Specific gravity:* 0.955-0.962 (25/25C); *Refractive index:* 1.4640-1.4660 (20C); *Flash point:* 212 F (TCC); *Solubility:* Soluble in 3-5 parts 70% ethyl alcohol

DERIVATION: From cajeput oil, melaleuca, cardamom, Siberian pine needle

THEOBROMA OIL

SYNONYMS: Cacao butter; Cocoa butter

CHARACTERISTICS: *Form:* Solid; *Color;* Yellowish- white; *Odor;* Chocolate; *Taste:* Chocolate

PHYSICAL PROPERTIES: *Specific gravity:* 0.858-0.864 (100/25C); *Refractive index:* 1.4537-1.4585 (40C); *Melting point:* 30-35 C; *Solubility:* Soluble in chlorofrom, ether, slightly soluble in ethyl alcohol; insoluble in water

DERIVATION: From roasted seeds of theobroma cacoa, sterculaceae; from the cacao bean by expression, decoction, or extraction by solvent

WARNING AND CAUTION: Combustible; low toxicity

y-UNDECALACTONE

See Aldehyde C-14 pure

VALILLIN

SYNONYMS: 4- Hydroxy- 3- methoxybenzaldehyde; Methoxyprotocatechuic aldehyde; Protocatechualdehyde- 3-methyl ether; Methylprotocatechuc aldehyde; Vanillic aldehyde; Methoxy 4 hydroxybenzaldehyde

CAS NUMBER: 121-33-5
MOLECULAR FORMULA: $C_8H_8O_3$
MOLECULAR WEIGHT: 152.15
CHARACTERISTICS: *Form:* Crystalline needles; *Color;* White; *Odor;* Sweetish
PHYSICAL PROPERTIES: *Specific gravity:* 1.056 (25/25C); *Boiling point:* 285C; *Melting point:* 81-83 C; *Solubility:* Soluble in 2 parts 95% ethyl alcohol, chloroform, ether, carbon disulfide, glacial acetic acid, pyridine, water
DERIVATION: It occurs in vanilla bean extract and in many balsams and resins; from lignin contained in sulfite waste pulp liquor; made also from eugenol or guaiacol
WARNING AND CAUTION: Combustible; low toxicity

WINE RESIDUE (GREEN PURE LEES, OIL)

CHARACTERISTICS: *Form:* A distinctive appearance, odor, and flavor is imparted by producers
PHYSICAL PROPERTIES: Naturally fermented grape juice contains 6-22% alcohol
DERIVATION: The fermented juice of grapes, and of other fruits or plants
WARNING AND CAUTION: Flammable; low toxicity

YARA YARA

SYNONYMS: 2- Methoxynaphthalene; ß-Naphthol methyl ether; Methyl ß-naphthyl ether; Naphthyl methyl ether; ß-Methoxynaphthalene

MOLECULAR FORMULA: $C_{11}H_{10}O$
MOLECULAR WEIGHT: 158.20
CHARACTERISTICS: *Form:* Power, crystals; *Color;* Colorless; to white; *Odor;* Fruity, acacia, orange
PHYSICAL PROPERTIES: Solubility: Soluble in alcohol, ether, insolble in water
DERIVATION: By heating ß-naphthol and methyl alcohol in presence of sulfuric acid; by methylating ß-naphthol with dimethyl sulfate
WARNING AND CAUTION: Combustible

Chapter-5

PLANT & EQUIPMENT SUPPLIERS

Danfoss Industries Pvt. Ltd.
Regd. Office: 296 Old Mahabalipuram Road, Sholinganallur, Chennai-600 119,
Ph. : 91-44-4963511-17
Fax : 91-11-6817668
Delhi: F-89/13 Okhla Industrial Area Phase I, New Delhi-110 020
Ph. : 91-11-6813692-96,
Fax : 91-11-6817668,
Mumbai : Unit No. II, Ground Floor, Corporate Park, Sion-Trombay Road, Chembur, Mumbai - 400 071.
Ph. : 91-22-5289091-95,
Fax : 91-22-5289098
Manufacturer of : Refrigeration Controls, Compressors for Refrigerators & Freezers Commercial Compressors & Condensing units, Thermostats, Industrial Control

Jitendrea Cooling Tower (Engs.)
Head Off. A-81, Jagatpuri Mandoli Road, Delhi-93
Ph. : 011-91-2283158, 2126592
Fax : 011-91-2283158, 2128056 2124844
Manufacturer of Cooling Towers

Swaraj Herbal Exports
Faizabad Road, Barabanki-1 (U.P.) India http://www.swaranjindia.com lucknow online.com/swarajindia
E-mail : herbal@ swaraj india.com
Ph. : +91-5248-22792, 23142
Fax : +91-5248-24444, 22569
Specialities in Manufacturing : Hydro and Steam Distillation Unit for Essential Oils, Extraction Unit for Herbal and Medicinal Plants.
Solvent Extraction Plant
Agitated Reaction Vessel
Vacuum Concentrator

Fractionating Column, Water Treatment Plant, Stainless Steel Storage Tank.

Kesar Steel Udyog
C-91/9, Wazirpur
Industrial Area, Delhi-52
Ph. : 7231285
7131470, 7231287
Fax : (011) 7249960
Manufacturer of : All Sizes Alluminium & Stainless Steel Containers for flex & Bold Crystals

Bhagsons Engineers
& Consultant P. Ltd.
9, Amar Park, Rohtak Road, Delhi - 110 035
Ph. : 5412707 Fax : 5110211
E-mail:bhagsons@bol.net.in.
Manufacturer of : Reaction & Pressure Vessels, heat Exchanger, Rotary Vacuum Extractor, Distillation Unit, Mixers-Planetary, Ribbon, Kneader Ball Mills, Filters, Tanks, Coating Pans Etc.

Ruchi Sales Pvt. Ltd.
4233/1 Ansari Road,
Darya Ganj,
New Delhi - 110 002
Ph. : 3272757 Fax : 3273173
E-mail: ruchisal@ mantraonline.com
Refrigeration & Air Conditioning Spares & Accessories

Sangeeta
Scientific Instruments
2847-B, Sant Nagar, Rani Bagh, New Delhi - 110034
Ph. : Off : 7016197
Manufacturer of : Distillation Column for Mint Products, Essential Oil, Aromatic Chemicals, Vacuum Stainless Steel Pump, Reaction Vessel, Column Packing Stainless Steel, Storage Tank, Heating Mentles Labs, Heat Exchanger.

Toshiba India
2/2, DSIDC Community Works Centre
J-Block Shakurpur, Delhi-34
Ph. : 7108890, 7184490
Fax : 011-7108890
E-mail : toshiba@del3. vsnl.net.in
Manufacturer of : Refractometer, Moisture Meter, Hardness Tester, Autoclave, Incubator, Oven, Deep Freezer, Cabinet, Etc.

Brintex
Sales Corporation
ED - 55, Tagore Garden,
New Delhi - 110 027
Ph. : 5460255
Manufacturer of : Elmach, Blister, Subnil Tube, Filling Alliance, Fluid Bed Dryer, Komal DM/RO Plants, Magumps/ Monita, Pharma M/Cs. Bifriends Vacuum Dryer, Flakers, Filters. EM Boiler, Thermic Heaters, Intech Lequid, Injectable M/cs.

Radhika
Containers Pvt. Ltd.
UG-7&8, Padma Tower - II,
22, Rajindra Place, New Delhi-110 008
Ph. : 5753877/78
5761074-75, 5772131
Fax : 011-5758817
Factory : 5476858
(Fibre Drums)

Premier
Refrigeration Limited
Unit 1-2, Akurli Indl.
Estate Akurli Road
Kandivli (E) Mumbai - 400 001
Ph. : 91-22-8870304/8870305
Fax : 91-22-8841275
E-mail : premierchiller @vsnl.com
(Cooler/freezer Etc.)

Prestair Systems P.I.C
H-43, Sector - 9 Noida 20301
Ph. : 91-914-4538824/4526777
Fax : 91-914-4526777
E-mail : 777@mantra online.com
(Water Coolers, Deep Freezers, Display Trays)

Pooja Steel & Alloys
11, Ardeshir Dady Cross Lane , Pathak Bldg.
Office No. 20 Nr. C.P. Tank
Mumbai - 400 004
Ph. : 91-22-3872562/3829630
Fax : 91-22-3829630
E-mail : jayantilal@ vsnl.net
(Distillation Plants, Deep Freezers, Etc.)

Shiva Udyog
Shiv Vihar, Sonepat
Road, Sampla
Distt. Rohtak - 124501
Ph. : 01262-63605, 63305
Fax : 01262-63180
(Mfrs. of : Steel Barrels & Cantainers)

K.G. Scientific
Engineering Works
Bawana Road, Near Rajdhani Properties
Prahladpur, Delhi
Ph. : 7894294, 7898001,
Fax : 011-7294598
A Name in Latest Technology Pharma, Chemicals & Mentha Peppermint industry Distillation Plants, High Grade Flake & Crystal Machines, Melting Tanks, Filtration Unit, Crystal Drying Machines, Storage Container, Aluminium Can, etc.

Kemitek Links
India (Pvt.) Ltd.
C-33, New Multan Nagar,
Rohtak Road,
New Delhi - 110 056
Ph. : 0091-11-5587989, 5583128
Fax : 0091-11-5675679
(High Fractional Distillation Units, Reaction Units in Glass & Stainless Steel, Laboratory Equipments for R & D Units)

Blue Star Limited
Blue Star house
9A Ghatkopar Link Road
Sakinaka, Mumbai - 400 072
Ph. : 91-22-8523600
Fax : 91-22-8522988
Website : www.bluestarindia.com
(Cooler/Freezer, Deep Freezers)

Kemitek Links India (P) Ltd.
C-33, New Multan Nagar
New Delhi- 110 056
Ph. : 0091-11-5587989, 5583128
Fax : 0091-11-5675679
Manufacturers of : Fabricator Designers of Glass Units for Essential Oils & Menthol Industries

U.S. Enterprises
487/108, Peeragarhi Indl.Area, Rohtak Road
Delhi- 110 041
Ph. : 5587989, 5583128
Manufacturer of : Menthol Plants, Menthol Essential Plants

Swaraj Fabricators
Faizabad Road
Barabanki - 225001 (U.P.)
Ph. : 22792, 24444, 23142
Fax : +91-5248-24444, 22569
E-mail : swarajindia@yahoo. com
Manufacturer of : Distillation and Extraction Plant, Dairy Equipment, Water Treatment & Solvent Extraction Plant

HCKL Barrel Container Works
11-A, Najafgarh Road,
Shivaji Marg
(Moti Nagar),
New Delhi - 110 015
Ph. : 5423803, 5937270
Fax : 91-11-5423803
Manufacturer of G.p., Double Liner, Open Top Grease, Lube Epoxy Coated, PU Insulated Tanks, Hot Dipped Galvanised Heavy Barrels

Ashok Kumar Jha
194, Suraj Apartment
Suraj Kund Road Pul Prahlad Pur,
New Delhi- 110 044
Ph. : 6418421
Fax : 011-6819209
Menthol Essential Oil & Aromatic Consultants at your Service, 17 Years Experience in this Field will help you with all your problems of Project

Chapter-6

Suppliers of Raw Materials

ABSOLUTES & HERBAL EXTRACTS

M/s. Mittal Aroma & Essential Oil Pvt. Ltd.
2279, 1st floor,
Gali Hinga Beg, Tilak Bazar,
Delhi - 110 006
Ph. : 3932141, 3920541, 2945735 Fax : 7212697

ABSOLUTES JASMINE, SAMBAC

M/s. Jasmine Concrete Exports Pvt. Ltd.
19, Josier Street,
Nangumbakkam,
Chennai - 600 034
Tamil Nadu Ph. : 8279451
Mr. A.K. Venkatasamy, Mr. S.Natarajan

ACETIC ACID GLACIAL

M/s. Indian Organic Chemicals Ltd. Chemtex
House, 2nd Floor
Main Street, Sector 12,
Hiranandani Gardens, Powai,
Mumbai - 400 076
Maharashtra
Ph. : (O) 5780625, 5780232
Fax : 5793924

ACETIC ANHYDRIDE

M/s. Indian Organic Chemicals Ltd.
Chemtex House, 2nd Floor Main Street, Sector 12, Hiranandani Gardens, Powai
Mumbai - 400 076
Ph. : (O) 5780625, 5780232
Fax : 5793924

ACETATE BENZYL ALCOHOL

M/s. Indian Organic Chemicals Ltd.
Chemtex House, 2nd Floor Main Street, Sector 12, Hiranandani Gardens, Powai, Mumbai - 400 076 Maharashtra
Ph. : (O) 5780625, 5780232
Fax : 5793924

AGARBATTI CHEMICALS LIKE DI ETHYL PHTHALATE

M/s. Agro Extracts Limited. Plot No. 6,
Phase - II,
Pennya Industrial Area
Bangalore - 560 001
Karnataka
Ph. : (O) 8394216, 8394922, 8395928 Fax : 8392134

AGARBATTI COMPOUNDS

M/s. Devson Organics
No. 38, 6th Cross,
Pipeline, Chelurpalya,
Vijaynagar, Magadi Road,
Bangalore - 560 023
Karnataka
Ph. : (O) 3300076, 3350104,
Fax : 3350562
C.P. : Mr. G.D. Kantharaj

AVETYL LONGIFOLENE

M/s. Prabhat General Agencies
154/6, Mittal Tower, 'B' Wing
Nariman Point, Mumbai - 400 021
Maharashtra
Ph. : (O) 2823680, 2825055, 2828182 Fax : 2842147
C.P.: Mr. V.T. Chudiwal, Mr. J.P. Singh

ALDEHYDE C-11

M/s. ACE Aromatics Pvt. Ltd.
108/109, Swiss Complex,
33, Race Cource Road
Bangalore - 560 001
Karnataka
Ph. : (O) 2205455, 2250118,
Fac : 3351626
Fax : 2202875

ALDEHYDE C- 16

M/s. Odochem Industries
C-71, II Stage,
Peenya Indl. Estate
Bangalore - 560 058
Karnataka
Ph. : (F) 8392229
Fax : 839229
C.P.: Mr. P. Annapumaiah, Mr. M.S. Raikar

M/s. R.C. Aromatic & Chemicals
69, Narayan Rao Koli Marg, (Bhansari Street,) Koliwada, Mandvi, Near Vadagadi, Mumbai - 400 003 Maharashtra
Ph. : (O) 3432235,
Fac : 6247635, 6246809

C.P.: Mr. Anil R. Shah
Mr. Vikram R. Shah

ALOE VEERA

M/s. Vaishali Aromatics India Pvt. Ltd.
Off. & Fact. : 30 M.I.D.C.,
Chilkal Thana,
Aurangabad - 431 001
Maharashtra
Ph. : (O) 484193
484120, 486744
Resi: 482807,486701
Fax : 0240-482078
C.P.: Mr. Mahesh Joshi, Mr. Vijay Joshi

ALDEHYDES

M/s. R.K. Shapurji & Co.
Prospect Chambers,
4th Floor, R.No. 8,
319, Dr. D. Naroji Rd.
Mumbai - 400 001
Maharashtra
Ph. : (O) 2047408
Fax : 3865951
C.P.: Miss.
Jinee R. Icewalla

ALLIED CHEMICALS

M/s. Devson Organics
No. 38, 6th Cross,
Pipeline, Chelurpalya,
Vijaynagar, Magadi Road,
Bangalore - 560 023
Karnataka
Ph. : (O) 3300076, 3350104,
Fax : 3350562
C.P. : Mr. G.D. Kantharaj

ALFA-PINENE

M/s. Kali Agro Chemicals Limited
F-35, Okhla Indl. Area
Ph-1, New Delhi - 110 020
Ph. : 0091-11-6819362
Fax : 0091-11-6812492

ALLYL PHENOXY ACETATE

M/s. IDL Chemicals Ltd.,
"Nirmal" 15th Floor,
Nariman Point
Mumbai - 400 021
Maharasthra
Ph. : (O) 2026946,
2025318, 2041267
Fax : 2041187
C.P.:
Mr. B.Sriniwas Reddy

AJOWAIN OIL

M/s. Aroma Industries
DSIDC Shed No. 111, Okhla Industrial Area
SCHEME -1, Phase - II,
New Delhi - 110 020
Ph. : 6914573,6841353
Fax : (91)(11)6841353
Website:www:gogia.com
E-mail:gcipl@vsnl.com

M/s. Sonic Biochem Extractions Pvt. Ltd.,
38, Patel Nagar,
Indore - 452001
Madhya Pradesh
Ph. : (O) 466546, 466458
Fax : 0731-462564

ASHWAGANDHA ROOTS & SEEDS

M/s. Save Earth Plantations Limited
11A/33, WEA Karol Bagh
New Delhi - 110 005
Ph. : 57897495, 5766899
Fax : 5766899

AMBRIENE OIL

M/s. Osom Extracts
Som Santi House, 152,
Patparganj Ind. Estate
Delhi - 110 092
Ph. : 91-11-2148207
2143195, 2153077
Fax : 91-11-2143066,2154284
E-mail :som@ndb.vsnl.net.in

ANETHOLE OIL

M/s. Aroma Industries
DSIDC Shed No. 111, Okhla Industrial Area
SCHEME -1, Phase - II,
New Delhi - 110 020
Ph. : 6914573,6841353
Fax : (91)(11)6841353
Website:www:gogia.com
E-mail gcipl@vsnl com

M/s. Aroma Chemicals
Siddhi Sadan, Tiraha
Tubewell Colony
Moradabad - 244 001
Ph. : 414365, 418960
Fax : 424408

M/s. Arihant Aromatics
Gali No. 1/3-A, C-36/2 Bhajanpura
(Behind Petrol Pump), Delhi - 53
Telefax : 2183876, 2265174

M/s. Evergreen Aromatics Pvt. Ltd.,
Fact. : 6-A, Industrial Estate,
Roshan Bagh,
Civil Lines, Rampur - 244 901
(U.P.)
Fax : (0595) 350184, 350190
E-mail : evergreen@del5.vsnl.net.in

M/s. Hindustan Mint & Agro Products Pvt. Ltd.,
Barehseni Street,
Chandausi - 202 412
Ph. : 91-5921-50540, 51900
Fax : 9105921-50074
Factory Deverkhera, Moradabad Road
Chandausi - 202 412
Ph. : 91-5921-51274, 51894
E-mail : hindustn@nde.vsnl.net.in

M/s. J.S. Traders
Dr. Ramswaroop Road, (Near State Bank of India)
Chandausi - 202 412 (U.P.)
Ph. : 05921-50777

M/s. K.K. Aromatics
Shree Ram Kunj (Behind Bankey

Behari Mandir) Indira Nagar
Bareilly (U.P.) 243122
Ph. : 91(0591) 448512, 448631
Fax : 91-(0581) 444188

M/s. Siddh Aromatic Chemicals
Dr. Ram Swaroop Road,
Chandausi - 202 412 (U.P.)
Ph. : (05921) 50792

ANISEED OIL

M/s. Indira Dinesh Chemicals
Factory : 131, HSIDC Industrial Estate,
Kundli (Sonepat)
Haryana - 131 028
Ph. : (01264) 70123, 70131
Fax : 91-11-6830158
(R) : 91-11-7860411
E-mail : idchem@vsnl.com
Webpage: http://dinesh.vsnl.com/menthol

AJOWAN OIL

M/s. LA Aromatics
BG-6/25B, Paschim Vihar
New Delhi - 110 063
Contact Person :
Umesh Jha

M/s. S.A.V. Aromatic
BG-6/25 B, Paschim Vihar,
New Delhi - 110 063
Ph. : 5672186, 5585022
Fax : 011-5672186

AROMATIC PRODUCTS

M/s. Indira Dinesh Chemicals
Factory : 131, HSIDC Industrial Estate,
Kundli (Sonepat)
Haryana - 131 028
Ph. : (01264) 70123, 70131
Fax : 91-11-6830158
(R) : 91-11-7860411
E-mail : idchem@vsnl.com
Webpage:http://dinesh.vsnl.com/menthol

AROMATIC COMPOUNDS

M/s. Devson Organics
No. 38, 6th Cross,
Pipeline, Chelurpalya,
Vijaynagar, Magadi Road,
Bangalore - 560 023
Karnataka
Ph. : (O) 3300076, 3350104,
Fax : 3350562
C.P. : Mr. G.D. Kantharaj

AROMATIC ESTERS

M/s. Maschmeijer Aromatics (India) Ltd.,
P.B. NO. 3, G.S.T. Road,
Chromepet
Chennai - 600 044
Tamil Nadu
Ph. : (O) 2368788, 2368789, 2368790
Fax : 2366808, 2341375
C.P.: Mr. S.A. Md. Shareef

A.L.D.C.

M/s. LA Aromatics
BG-6/25B, Paschim Vihar

New Delhi - 110 063
Contact Person :
Umesh Jha

M/s. S.A.V. Aromatic
BG-6/25 B, Paschim Vihar,
New Delhi - 110 063
Ph. : 5672186, 5585022
Fax : 011-5672186

AROMATHERAPY OILS

M/s. Ultra International Limited
304/M-3, Connaught Circus
New Delhi - 110 001
Ph. : (011) 3324100, 3352200
Fax : (011) 3712563, 3317776

ALPHA A.C.A.

M/s. Aroma Industries
DSIDC Shed No. 111, Okhla Industrial Area
SCHEME -1, Phase - II,
New Delhi - 110 020
Ph. : 6914573,6841353
Fax : (91)(11)6841353
Website:www:gogia.com
E-mail:gcipl@vsnl.com

AMYL BUTYRATE

M/s. Aroma Industries
DSIDC Shed No. 111, Okhla industrial Area
SCHEME -1, Phase - II
New Delhi - 110 020
Ph. : 6914573,6841353
Fax : (91)(11)6841353
Website:www:gogia.com
E-mail:gcipl@vsnl.com

ANISE

M/s. LA Aromatics
BG-6/25B, Paschim Vihar
New Delhi - 110 063
Contact Person :
Umesh Jha

M/s. S.A.V. Aromatic
BG-6/25 B, Paschim Vihar,
New Delhi - 110 063
Ph. : 5672186, 5585022
Fax : 011-5672186

ANETHOLE

M/s. Dee Kay Exports
Shakuntla Bhawan
Malgodan Road
Budaun, (U.P.) - 243 601
Ph. : 05832-24331, 24922
(R) : 24883, 24507
Fax : 91-5832-25085

ANISOLE, HERBALS

M/s. Malve Chemicals
"Shabri" Building,
Kapar Road, Ahead of Santoshi Mata Bldg.,
Dombivli (W) - 421 202
Maharashtra
Ph. : (O) 452336,
Fac : 590846
Fax : 452336
C.P.: Mr.Datta Malve, Mr.

Suhas Malve

A.P. ACETATE

M/s. LA Aromatics
BG-6/25B, Paschim Vihar
New Delhi - 110 063
Contact Person :
Umesh Jha

M/s. S.A.V. Aromatic
BG-6/25 B, Paschim Vihar,
New Delhi - 110 063
Ph. : 5672186, 5585022
Fax : 011-5672186

ANETHOLE

M/s. Arovision Industries
B-13, Industrial Estate,
Salarpur, Budaun - 243 601
(U.P.) Ph. : 05832-24250
(R) : 26126

M/s. Menthol & Allied Products
F-26/1, B.S. Road, Indl. Area,
Site - 1
Ghaziabad - 201 009 (U.P.)
Ph. : 0120-4700257, 4700442,
4701995
(R) : 4702693, 4750785
Fax : 0120-4700257
E-mail : menthol@satyam.net.in

M/s. Surya Aromatic & Essential Oils
D- 662, Saraswati Vihar,
Pitampura, Delhi - 110 034
Ph 7019930
Fax : 011-7028516, 7022396

M/s. LA Aromatics
BG-6/25B, Paschim Vihar
New Delhi - 110 063
Contact Person :
Umesh Jha

M/s. S.A.V. Aromatic
BG-6/25 B, Paschim Vihar,
New Delhi - 110 063
Ph. : 5672186, 5585022
Fax : 011-5672186

M/s. Virat Exports Pvt. Ltd.,
23/3, East Patel Nagar,
Delhi - 110 008
Ph. : 0091-011-5767182,
576183, 5730485
Fax : 0091-011-5755209
E-mail : viratexp@del2.vsnl.net.in

AROMATIC CHEMICALS

M/s. Kali Agro Chemicals Limited
F-35, Okhla Indl. Area
Ph-1, New Delhi - 110 020
Ph. : 0091-11-6819362
Fax : 0091-11-6812492

ASPARAGUS

M/s. Save Earth Plantations Limited
11A/33, WEA Karol Bagh
New Delhi - 110 005
Ph. : 57897495, 5766899
Fax 5766899

BALSAM TOLU

M/s. Pharm
Aromatic Chemicals
507, Nain Krupo
118/122, Kazi Syed Street
Mumbai - 400 003
Maharashtra
Ph. : (O) 3432526, 3448032
Resi: 362690, 3625386
Fax : 340805
C.P.: Mr. Madhu L. Thakkar

BALSAM PERU

M/s. Pharm
Aromatic Chemicals
507, Nain Krupo
118/122, Kazi Syed Street
Mumbai - 400 003
Maharashtra
Ph. : (O) 3432526, 3448032
Resi: 362690, 3625386
Fax : 340805
C.P.: Mr. Madhu L. Thakkar

BALSAM COPAIDA

M/s. Pharm
Aromatic Chemicals
507, Nain Krupo
118/122, Kazi Syed Street
Mumbai - 400 003
Maharashtra
Ph. : (O) 3432526, 3448032
Resi: 362690, 3625386
Fax : 340805
C.P. Mr. Madhu L. Thakkar

BASIL OIL

M/s. Aroma Chemicals
Siddhi Sadan, Tiraha
Tubewell Colony
Moradabad - 244 001
Ph. : 414365, 418960
Fax : 424408

M/s. Indira Dinesh
Chemicals
Factory : 131, HSIDC Industrial
Estate,
Kundli (Sonepat)
Haryana - 131 028
Ph. : (01264) 70123, 70131
Fax : 91-11-6830158
(R) : 91-11-7860411
E-mail : idchem@vsnl.com
Webpage: http://dinesh.vsnl.com/menthol

M/s. LA Aromatics
BG-6/25B, Paschim Vihar
New Delhi - 110 063
Contact Person :
Umesh Jha

M/s. Naini Essential
Oils & Chemicals
Vill. & P.O. Khod Sharif
Tehsil : SUAR
Distt. : Rampur
(U.P.) 244 924
Ph. : Maswasi (0595) 555527

M/s. S.A.V. Aromatic
BG-6/25 B, Paschim Vihar,
New Delhi - 110 063
Ph. : 5672186, 5585022

Fax : 011-5672186

M/s. Sandeep Chemicals
(Patiyali Sarai)
Near Nai Sarai Ki Chowki,
Budaun - 243 601 (U.P.)
Ph. : 05832-24341

BENZYL ACETATE - FFC

M/s. Omega Polycoats
'Nirmal' Near Khare Town,
P.O. Dharampeth
Nagpur - 440 010

BENZYL ALCOHOL

M/s. Gujarat Organic Chemicals
32, Vithal Udyognagar,
Anand Sijitra Road
Kaira - 388 121, Gujarat
Ph. : 46205 Fax : 46446

M/s. Sabari Chemicals P. Ltd.
A/2/236 GIDC Estate,
Nandesari,Baroda - 391340
Gujarat
Ph.(O) : 23081, 338334
Fac : 840429, 840143
Fax : 481265, 840890
C.P. : Mr. Ravi Nair Mr. Mohan Nair

BENZYL BENZOATE

M/s. Gujarat Organic Chemicals
32, Vithal Udyognagar,
Anand Sijitra Road
Kaira - 388 121, Gujarat
Ph. : 46205 Fax : 46446

M/s. Sabari Chemicals P. Ltd.
A/2/236 GIDC Estate,
Nandesari
Baroda - 391340, Gujarat
Ph.(O) : 23081, 338334
Fac : 840429, 840143
Fax : 481265, 840890
C.P. : Mr. Ravi Nair Mr. Mohan Nair

BENZYL CHLORIDE

M/s. Sabari Chemicals P. Ltd.
A/2/236 GIDC Estate,
Nandesari, Baroda - 391340
Gujarat
Ph.(O) : 23081, 338334
Fac : 840429, 840143
Fax : 481265, 840890
C.P. : Mr. Ravi Nair Mr. Mohan Nair

BENZYL FORMATE

M/s. LA Aromatics
BG-6/25B, Paschim Vihar
New Delhi - 110 063
Contact Person :
Umesh Jha

M/s. S.A.V. Aromatic
BG-6/25 B, Paschim Vihar,
New Delhi - 110 063
Ph. : 5672186, 5585022
Fax : 011-5672186

BENZALDEHYDE

M/s. Indian Organic Chemicals Ltd.
Chemtex House,
2nd Floor
Main Street, Sector 12,
Hiranandani
Gardens, Powai
Mumbai - 400 076
Maharashtra
Ph. : (O) 5780625, 5780232
Fax : 5793924

BETA-PINENE

M/s. Kali Agro Chemicals Limited
F-35, Okhla Indl.
Area Ph-I.
New Delhi - 110 020
Ph. : 0091-11-6819362
Fax : 0091-11-6812492

B.P. ACETATE

M/s. LA Aromatics
BG-6/25B, Paschim Vihar
New Delhi - 110 063
Contact Person :
Umesh Jha

M/s. S.A.V. Aromatic
BG-6/25 B, Paschim Vihar,
New Delhi - 110 063
Ph. : 5672186, 5585022
Fax : 011-5672186

BOLD CRYSTALS

M/s. Naini Essential Oils & Chemicals
Vill. & P.O. Khod Sharif
Tehsil : SUAR
Distt. : Rampur
(U.P.) 244 924
Ph. : Maswasi (0595) 555527

BOTANICALS

M/s. Indrag Pvt. Ltd.
S-913, Manipal Centre,
Dickenson Road,
Bangalore - 560 042
Karnataka
Ph. : (O) 5589521,
Fax : 5589521, 5560594
C.P.: Mr. Philip Samuel

BENZYL ACETATE

M/s. Iscon Research Laboratories Pvt. Ltd.,
16-B, (11), Heavy Indl. Area
Jodhpur - 342 003
Rajasthan
Ph. : 42582, 40418
Fac : 40468 Fax : 0291-41193
Mr. M.L.Jain
Mr. C.S. Bhandari

M/s. Sabari Chemicals P. Ltd.
A/2/236 GIDC Estate,
Nandesari
Baroda - 391340
Gujarat
Ph.(O) : 23081, 338334
Fac : 840429, 840143
Fax : 481265, 840890
C.P. : Mr. Ravi Nair
Mr. Mohan Nair

BENZYL ALCOHOL

M/s. Iscon Research Laboratories Pvt. Ltd.,
16-B, (11), Heavy Indl. Area
Jodhpur - 342 003
Rajasthan
Ph. : 42582, 40418
Fac : 40468 Fax : 0291-41193
Mr. M.L.Jain
Mr. C.S. Bhandari

BENZYL BENZOATE

M/s. Iscon Research Laboratories Pvt. Ltd.,
16-B, (11), Heavy Indl. Area
Jodhpur - 342 003
Rajasthan
Ph. : 42582, 40418
Fac : 40468
Fax : 0291-41193
Mr. M.L.Jain
Mr. C.S. Bhandari

BLENDED ROSE OIL

M/s. Haritwal Essential Oils Exports
272/273, Hind Rajasthan,
Shopping Centre, Block No. 113,
1st Floor, SION (West)
Mumbai - 400 022 Maharashtra
Ph. : (O) 4075865
Fax : 022-4015998
C.P.: Mr. Haritwal

BLACK PEPPER

M/s. Save Earth Plantations Limited
11A/33, WEA Karol Bagh
New Delhi - 110 005
Ph. : 57897495, 5766899
Fax : 5766899

CAMPHOR

M/s. Ishwarlal Jethalal
Mul Ratna, 3rd Floor,
No. 7, 334 Narsi Natha Street,
Katha Bazar
Mumbai - 400 009
Maharashtra
Ph. : (O) 3425632, 3446157
C.P.: Mr. Arvindbhai
Mr. Jitendrabhai

CALAMUS TAGETES

M/s. Aum Aromas
V.P.O. Galma - 175021
Distt. : Mandi (H.P.)
Himachal Pradesh

Ph. : 01905 - 42281, 23204

CARDAMOM OIL

M/s. Aroma Industries
DSIDC Shed No. 111, Okhla Industrial Area
SCHEME -1, Phase - II
New Delhi - 110 020
Ph. : 6914573,6841353
Fax : (91)(11)6841353
Website:www:gogia.com
E-mail:gcipl@vsnl.com

M/s. Devi Industries
2/176, Subbiah,
Naidu Ind. Complex
Y.Pudupatti, Arumpanur, Post
Madurai North 625107 Tamilnadu
Ph. : (O) 832731, 832823
Fac : 832631 Fax : 602455
C.P.: Mr. S.Rajagopal
Mr. Rajamannar

M/s. Osom Extracts
Som Santi House, 152,
Patparganj Ind. Estate
Delhi - 110 092
Ph. : 91-11-2148207
2143195, 2153077
Fax : 91-11-2143066,2154284
E-mail :som@ndb.vsnl. net.in

CEDARWOOD OIL

M/s. Arihant Aromatics
Gali No. 1/3-A, C-36/2 Bhajanpura
(Behind Petrol Pump), Delhi - 53
Telefax : 2183876, 2265174

M/s. Aum Aromas
V.P.O. Galma - 175021
Distt. : Mandi (H.P.)
Himachal Pradesh
Ph. : 01905 - 42281, 23204

M/s. H.P. International
Sec-23, H. No. 3673
Gurgaon - 122 001
Haryana Ph. : (O) 9810111447
Fax : (011)567-6386

M/s. Hindustan Mint & Agro Products Pvt. Ltd.,
Barehseni Street,
Chandausi - 202 412
Ph. : 91-5921-50540, 51900
Fax : 9105921-50074
Factory Deverkhera
Moradabad Road
Chandausi - 202 412
Ph. : 91-5921-51274, 51894
E-mail : hindustn@nde.vsnl.net.in

M/s. Osom Extracts
Som Santi House, 152,
Patparganj Ind. Estate
Delhi - 110 092
Ph. : 91-11-2148207,2143195, 2153077
Fax : 91-11-2143066,2154284

M/s. Surya Aromatic & Essential Oils
D- 662, Saraswati Vihar,
Pitampura, Delhi - 110 034
Ph. : 7019930
Fax : 011-7028516, 7022396

M/s. Virat Exports Pvt. Ltd.,
23/3, East Patel Nagar,
Delhi - 110 008
Ph. : 0091-011-5767182, 576183, 5730485
Fax : 0091-011-5755209
E-mail : viratexp@del2.vsnl.net.in

CELERY SEED OIL

M/s. Aroma Industries
DSIDC Shed No. 111, Okhla Industrial Area
SCHEME -1, Phase - II,
New Delhi - 110 020
Ph. : 6914573,6841353
Fax : (91)(11)6841353
Website:www:gogia.com
E-mail:gcipl@vsnl.com

CEDAR WOOD OIL TRIPPLE RECTIFIED

M/s. LA Aromatics
BG-6/25B, Paschim Vihar
New Delhi - 110 063
Contact Person :
Umesh Jha

M/s. S.A.V. Aromatic
BG-6/25 B, Paschim Vihar,
New Delhi - 110 063
Ph. : 5672186, 5585022
Fax : 011-5672186

CITRAL SUPER

M/s. Aroma Industries
DSIDC Shed No. 111, Okhla Industrial Area
SCHEME -1, Phase - II
New Delhi - 110 020
Ph. : 6914573,6841353
Fax : (91)(11)6841353
Website:www:gogia.com
E-mail:gcipl@vsnl.com

CHAMMOMILE OIL

M/s. Save Earth Plantations Limited
11A/33, WEA Karol Bagh
New Delhi - 110 005
Ph. : 57897495, 5766899
Fax : 5766899

COSTUS ROOT

M/s. Aum Aromas
V.P.O. Galma - 175021
Distt. : Mandi (H.P.)
Himachal Pradesh
Ph. : 01905 - 42281, 23204

CONCENTRATE

M/s. Rubin Chemicals
30 Hari Market, Khar (W)
Mumbai - 400 064
Maharashtra
Ph. : (O) 6491331, 6041691
Fax : 6464076
C.P.: Mr. P.H. Mehra, Mr. Ravi Mehra

CYCLOGALBANATA

M/s. IDL Chemicals Ltd.,
"Nirmal" 15th Floor,
Nariman Point
Mumbai - 400 021

Maharashtra
Ph. : (O) 2026946, 2025318, 2041267
Fax : 2041187
C.P.: Mr. B.Sriniwas Reddy

CITRONELYL ACETATE

M/s. LA Aromatics
BG-6/25B, Paschim Vihar
New Delhi - 110 063
Contact Person :
Umesh Jha

M/s. S.A.V. Aromatic
BG-6/25 B, Paschim Vihar,
New Delhi - 110 063
Ph. : 5672186, 5585022
Fax : 011-5672186

COMMOMILE FLOWERS

M/s. Save Earth Plantations Limited
11A/33, WEA Karol Bagh
New Delhi - 110 005
Ph. : 57897495, 5766899
Fax : 5766899

CITRONELLA OIL

M/s. Esthapanose Sons
Syrian Chruch Road,
Post Box No. 9
Alwaye - 683101 Kerala
Ph. : (O) 24044, 24344, 23330
C.P.: Mr. K.S. Tomy

M/s. Hindustan Mint & Agro Products Pvt. Ltd.,
Barehseni Street,
Chandausi - 202 412
Ph. : 91-5921-50540, 51900
Fax : 9105921-50074
Factory Deverkhera
Moradabad Road
Chandausi - 202 412
Ph. : 91-5921-51274, 51894
E-mail : hindustn@nde.vsnl.net.in

M/s. D.V. Deo
V/1084, Pandit Road, Corner,
Cochin - 682 002 Kerala
Ph. : (O) 224196, 226903, 373809
Fac : 422248, Fax : 373780,
Telex : 885-7041
C.P. : Mr. Dhanajai D.Deo
Mr. Bobby Gulati

M/s. Swastik Eucalyptus Oil Co.
166, Main Bazar,
Ootacamund - 643 001
Bangalore - 560 010
Karnataka Ph. : (O) 42527
Fac : 43489
C.P.: Mr. Shantilal B. Mehta

CITRIODORA OIL

M/s. Swastik Eucalyptus Oil Co. 166, Main Bazar,
Ootacamund - 643 001
Bangalore - 560 010
Karnataka
Ph. : (O) 42527
Fac : 43489

C.P.: Mr. Shantilal
B. Mehta

CITRONELLOL

M/s. Raj Woollen Industries
G.T. Road, P.O. Box 20,
Panipat - 132 103 (HR)
Ph. : (01742)-30050,
30347, 34176
Fax : (01742) 32346, 58346

M/s. Surya Aromatic & Essential Oils
D- 662, Saraswati Vihar,
Pitampura,
Delhi - 110 034 Ph. : 7019930
Fax : 011-7028516, 7022396

M/s. LA Aromatics
BG-6/25B, Paschim Vihar
New Delhi - 110 063
Contact Person :
Umesh Jha

M/s. S.A.V. Aromatic
BG-6/25 B, Paschim Vihar,
New Delhi - 110 063
Ph. : 5672186, 5585022
Fax : 011-5672186

CITRONELYL FORMATE

M/s. LA Aromatics
BG-6/25B, Paschim Vihar
New Delhi - 110 063
Contact Person :
Umesh Jha

M/s. S.A.V. Aromatic
BG-6/25 B, Paschim Vihar,
New Delhi - 110 063
Ph. : 5672186, 5585022
Fax : 011-5672186

CITRATA OIL

M/s. Naini Essential Oils & Chemicals
Vill. & P.O. Khod Sharif
Tehsil : SUAR
Distt. : Rampur
(U.P.) 244 924
Ph. : Maswasi (0595) 555527

M/s. Sandeep Chemicals
(Patiyali Sarai)
Near Nai Sarai Ki Chowki,
Budaun - 243 601 (U.P.)
Ph. : 05832-24341

CINNAMON OIL

M/s. Osom Extracts
Som Santi House, 152,
Patparganj Ind. Estate
Delhi - 110 092
Ph. : 91-11-2148207
2143195, 2153077
Fax : 91-11-2143066,2154284
E-mail :som@ndb.vsnl.net.in

CINNAMONLEAF OIL

M/s. D.V. Deo
V/1084, Pandit Road, Corner
Cochin - 682 002Kerala
Ph. : (O) 224196, 22690

373809
Fac : 422248, Fax : 373780
Telex : 885-7041
C.P. : Mr. Dhanajai D.Deo
Mr. Bobby Gulati

M/s. Esthapanose Sons
Syrian Chruch Road,
Post Box No. 9
Alwaye - 683101, Kerala
Ph. : (O) 24044, 24344, 23330
C.P.: Mr. K.S. Tomy

CLOVE OIL

M/s. Aroma Industries
DSIDC Shed No. 111
Okhla Industrial Area
SCHEME -1, Phase - II
New Delhi - 110 020
Ph. : 6914573,6841353
Fax : (91)(11)6841353
Website:www:gogia.com
E-mail:gcipl@vsnl.com

M/s. LA Aromatics
BG-6/25B, Paschim Vihar
New Delhi - 110 063
Contact Person :
Umesh Jha

M/s. Nova Menthochem
D-93, Phase VII,
Mohali Industrial Area,
Chandigarh
Haryana Ph. : 670798

M/s. Osom Extracts
Som Santi House, 152,
Patparganj Ind. Estate
Delhi - 110 092
Ph. : 91-11-2148207,2143195, 2153077
Fax : 91-11-2143066,2154284
E-mail :som@ndb.vsnl.net.in

M/s. S.A.V. Aromatic
BG-6/25 B, Paschim Vihar,
New Delhi - 110 063
Ph. : 5672186, 5585022
Fax : 011-5672186

CELERY SEED OIL

M/s. Singhal Export Corporation
Works : 6th KM, Nainital Road,
Rampur- 244 901 (U.P.)
Admin.Office : 7, Kailash
Colony, Civil Lines
Rampur - 244 901 (U.P.)
Ph. : (O) 91-595-350897, 352979
(W) : 91-595-325073, 325074
Fax : 91-595-350684
E-mail : sec@nde.vsnl.net.in

M/s. Sonic Biochem Extractions Pvt. Ltd.,
38, Patel Nagar,
Indore - 452001
Madhya Pradesh
Ph. : (O) 466546, 466458
Fax : 0731-462564

CUMIN SEED OIL

M/s. Aroma Industries
DSIDC Shed No. 111
Okhla Industrial Area
SCHEME -1, Phase - II
New Delhi - 110 020

Ph. : 6914573,6841353
Fax : (91)(11)6841353
Website:www:gogia.com
E-mail:gcipl@vsnl.com

M/s. Sonic Biochem Extractions Pvt. Ltd.,
38, Patel Nagar,
Indore - 452001
Madhya Pradesh
Ph. : (O) 466546, 466458
Fax : 0731-462564

CONCRETES & ABSOLUTES

M/s. Cigma Essence & Aromatics Pvt. Ltd.,
910/1, Thimmampalayam
Karamadai, Coimbatore - 641 104
Tamilnadu
Ph. : (O) 72480, 72001
Fax : 04267-72690
C.P.: Mr. S.R.Varadharajan

M/s. Jasmine Concrete Exports Pvt. Ltd.
19, Josier Street,
Nangumbakkam,
Chennai - 600 034
Tamilnadu Ph. : 8279451
Mr. A.K. Venkatasamy
Mr. S.Natarajan

CORRIANDER OIL

M/s. Aroma Industries
DSIDC Shed No. 111, Okhla Industrial Area
SCHEME -1, Phase - II
New Delhi - 110 020
Ph. : 6914573,6841353
Fax : (91)(11)6841353
Website:www:gogia.com
E-mail:gcipl@vsnl.com

CANDLE PERFUMES

M/s. Ultra International Limited
304/M-3, Connaught
Circus, New Delhi - 110 001
Ph. : (011) 3324100, 3352200
Fax : (011) 3712563, 3317776

CUSTOM BLENDS

M/s. Ultra International Limited
304/M-3, Connaught
Circus, New Delhi - 110 001
Ph. : (011) 3324100, 3352200
Fax : (011) 3712563, 3317776

CIS -3 HEXENOL

M/s. Evergreen Aromatics Pvt. Ltd.,
Fact. : 6-A, Industrial Estate,
Roshan Bagh,
Civil Lines,
Rampur - 244 901 (U.P.)
Fax : (0595) 350184, 350190
E-mail : evergreen@del5.vsnl.net.in

M/s. Kali Agro Chemicals Limited
F-35, Okhla Indl. Area
Ph-1, New Delhi - 110 020

Ph. : 0091-11-6819362
Fax : 0091-11-6812492

CIs -3 OCTANOL

M/s. Evergreen Aromatics Pvt. Ltd.,
Fact. : 6-A, Industrial Estate
Roshan Bagh, Civil Lines
Rampur - 244 901 (U.P.)
Fax : (0595) 350184, 350190
E-mail : evergreen@del5.vsnl.net.in

M/s. Kali Agro Chemicals Limited
F-35, Okhla Indl. Area
Ph-1, New Delhi - 110 020
Ph. : 0091-11-6819362
Fax : 0091-11-6812492

DAVANA & SPICE OILS

M/s. Vignesh Essential Oils
SKS Residency,
Cutchery Road,
Gobichettipalayam -
638 452, Distt. Erode (T.N.)
Tamilnadu
Ph. : (O) (91-4285) 22222, 22822, 23949
Fax : 91-4285-23333
C.P.: Mr. S. Subramaniam

DIHYDRO ISO JASMINE

M/s. Parekh Perfumery Works
128, Bhuleshwar Road,
Kabutarkhana
Mumbai - 400 002
Ph. : (O) 3739711, 3739712
Fac : 3727052
C.P.: Mr. Harkrishan R. Parekh

DILL OIL

M/s. Sonic Biochem Extractions Pvt. Ltd.,
38, Patel Nagar
Indore - 452001
Madhya Pradesh
Ph. : (O) 466546, 466458
Fax : 0731-462564

D.M.O.

M/s. Kali Agro Chemicals Limited
F-35, Okhla Indl. Area
Ph-1, New Delhi - 110 020
Ph. : 0091-11-6819362
Fax : 0091-11-6812492

M/s. Siddh Aromatic Chemicals
Dr. Ram Swaroop Road,
Chandausi - 202 412 (U.P.)
Ph. : (05921) 50792

DE-MENTHOLISED OIL

M/s. Naini Essential Oils & Chemicals
Vill. & P.O. Khod Sharif
Tehsil : SUAR
Distt. : Rampur
(U.P.) 244 924

Ph. : Maswasi (0595) 555527

DI-PHENYL OXIDE

M/s. Silver Sons
110, Narayan Chamber,
Nehru Bridge Corner,
Ashram Road
Ahmedabad - 380 009
Gujarat
Ph. : 6579314

DIMETHYL HYDROQUINONE

Ms. R.C. Aromatic & Chemicals
69, Narayan Rao
Koli Marg, (Bhansari Street,)
Koliwada,
Mandvi, Near Vadagadi
Mumbai - 400 003
Maharashtra
Ph. : (O) 3432235,
Fac : 6247635, 6246809
C.P.: Mr. Anil R. Shah, Mr. Vikram R. Shah

DIPHENYL OXIDE

M/s. Vikram Enterprises
202, Classic Avenue,
2nd Floor, Opp. Sales India,
Ashram Road
Ahmedabad - 380 009
Gujarat
Ph. : 6569269, 403745
Fax : 409562

DRY FLOWERS

M/s. Synthite Industrial Chemicals Ltd.
Ajay Vihar,, M.G. Road,
Cochin - 682 016,Kerala
Ph. : (O) 355794, 360698
Fac : 04853-60316, 60285
Fax : 370405
C.P. : Mr. C.V. Jacob, Mr. George Paul

DRY FRUIT EXTRACTS

M/s. Nat-Con
No. 490 (L), Phase,
Peenya Indl. Area,
Bangalore - 560 058
Karnataka
Ph. : (O) 8396545
Fax : 8392956
C.P.: Mr. Sujit Mukund

DIETHYL PHTHALATE BENZYL

M/s. Indian Organic Chemicals Ltd.
Chemtex House,
2nd Floor
Main Street, Sector 12,
Hiranandani Gardens, Powai,
Mumbai - 400 076
Ph. : (O) 5780625, 5780232
Fax : 5793924

EUCALYPTOL OIL

M/s. Osom Extracts
Som Santi House, 152,
Patparganj Ind. Estate
Delhi - 110 092
Ph. : 91-11-2148207,2143195
2153077
Fax : 91-11-2143066,2154284
E-mail :som@ndb.vsnl.net.in

EUCALYPTUS OIL

M/s. Hindustan Mint & Agro Products Pvt. Ltd.,
Barehseni Street,
Chandausi - 202 412
Ph. : 91-5921-50540, 51900
Fax : 9105921-50074
Factory Deverkhera
Moradabad Road
Chandausi - 202 412
Ph. : 91-5921-51274, 51894
E-mail : hindustn@nde.vsnl.net.in

M/s. Osom Extracts
Som Santi House, 152,
Patparganj Ind. Estate
Delhi - 110 092
Ph. : 91-11-2148207,2143195
2153077
Fax : 91-11-2143066,2154284
E-mail :som@ndb.vsnl.net.in

M/s. Surya Aromatic & Essential Oils
D- 662, Saraswati Vihar,
Pitampura,, Delhi - 110 034
Ph. : 7019930
Fax : 011-7028516, 7022396

M/s. Vinod Kumar Rakesh & Company
Gyanmalaya
32, Mount Plesant Road,
Coonor - 643102
Tamilnadu Ph. : (O) 20868
Fac : 21767
Fax : 04264-20868
C.P.: Mr. P.Vinod Kumar, Mr. P. Rakesh

M/s. Vignesh Essential Oils
SKS Residency, Cutchery Road,
Gobichettipalayam - 638 452,
Distt. Erode (T.N.)
Ph. : (O) (91-4285) 22222
22822, 23949
Fax : 91-4285-23333
C.P.: Mr. S. Subramaniam

EUGENOL OIL

M/s. LA Aromatics
BG-6/25B, Paschim Vihar
New Delhi - 110 063
Contact Person :
Umesh Jha

M/s. Nova Menthochem
D-93, Phase VII,
Mohali Industrial Area,
Chandigarh, Haryana
Ph. : 670798

M/s. Nova Menthochem
D-93, Phase VII,
Mohali Industrial Area,
Chandigarh - 122 017
Haryana Ph. : (O) 670798

M/s. Osom Extracts
Som Santi House, 152,
Patparganj Ind. Estate
Delhi - 110 092
Ph. : 91-11-2148207,2143195, 2153077
Fax : 91-11-2143066,2154284
E-mail :som@ndb.vsnl.net.in

M/s. Omega Polycoats
'Nirmal' Near Khare Town,
P.O. Dharampeth
Nagpur - 440 010
Maharashtra
Ph. : (O) 531006
Fac : 071104-36667
C.P.: Mr. Dilip Pandharpurkar

M/s. S.A.V. Aromatic
BG-6/25 B, Paschim Vihar
New Delhi - 110 063
Ph. : 5672186, 5585022
Fax : 011-5672186

M/s. Surya Aromatic & Essential Oils
D- 662, Saraswati Vihar,
Pitampura, Delhi - 110 034
Ph. : 7019930
Fax : 011-7028516, 7022396

ESSENTIAL OILS

M/s. Indira Dinesh Chemicals
Factory : 131, HSIDC
Industrial Estate
Kundli (Sonepat)
Haryana - 131 028
Ph. : (01264) 70123, 70131
Fax : 91-11-6830158
(R) : 91-11-7860411
E-mail : idchem@vsnl.com
Web: http:/dinesh.vsnl.com/menthol

M/s. Kali Agro Chemicals Limited
F-35, Okhla Indl.
Area Ph-1, New Delhi - 110 020
Ph. : 0091-11-6819362
Fax : 0091-11-6812492

M/s. Naini Essential Oils & Chemicals
Vill. & P.O. Khod Sharif
Tehsil : SUAR
Distt. : Rampur
(U.P.) 244 924
Ph. : Maswasi (0595) 555527

M/s. Ultra International Limited
304/M-3, Connaught Circus, New Delhi - 110 001
Ph. : (011) 3324100, 3352200
Fax : (011) 3712563, 3317776

EXOTIC NATURAL OILS

M/s. Ultra International Limited
304/M-3, Connaught Circus
New Delhi - 110 001
Ph. : (011) 3324100, 3352200
Fax : (011) 3712563, 3317776

ETHYL VANILLIN

M/s. Indo Vanillon Chemicals Ltd.
H.O. : 245, Sector - 17,
Gurgaon - 122 001,Haryana
Ph. : 343245, 343246, 341976
Fax : 343245

M/s. Indo Vanillin Chemicals Ltd.
H.O. : 245, Sector - 17,
Gurgaon - 122 001, Haryana
Ph. : (O) 343245
343246, 341976, Fax : 343245

FENNEL OIL

M/s. Osom Extracts
Som Santi House, 152,
Patparganj Ind. Estate
Delhi - 110 092
Ph. : 91-11-2148207,2143195, 2153077
Fax : 91-11-2143066,2154284
E-mail :som@ndb.vsnl.net.in

FLOWERS OIL

M/s. Ultra International Limited
304/M-3, Connaught Circus
New Delhi - 110 001
Ph. : (011) 3324100, 3352200
Fax : (011) 3712563, 3317776

FLAVOURING ESSENCES

M/s. Keva Fragrances Ltd.,
Devkaran Mansion, 36
Mangaldas Road
Mumbai - 400 002
Ph. : 2069609, 2019198
Fac : 5645273, 5645274
Fax : 5645271, 2081204

FINE FRAGRANCES

M/s. Ultra International Limited
304/M-3, Connaught
Circus, New Delhi - 110 001
Ph. : (011) 3324100, 3352200
Fax : (011) 3712563, 3317776

FRUIT OILS

M/s. Ultra International Limited
304/M-3, Connaught Circus,
New Delhi - 110 001
Ph. : (011) 3324100, 3352200
Fax : (011) 3712563, 3317776

FRAGRANCE

M/s. S.H. Kelkar & Co. Ltd.
Devkaran Mansion,
36, Mangaldas Road,
Mumbai - 400 002
Ph. : (O) 2069609, 2019130
Fax : 2081204
C.P.: Mr. G.D.Kelkar
Mr. S.V. Vaze

FOOD COLOUR

M/s. L. Liladhar & Company
257-259, Samuel Street,
Vadgadi, Mumbai - 400 003
Maharashtra
Ph. : (O) 3422988, 3447690
Fac : 7670396, 7671102
C.P.: Mr. Madhusudan Mody

M/s. Dayal Chemical Works
4/1, Jail Road
Indore - 452 001
Madhya Pradesh
Ph. : (O) 534307, 531962
Fac : 420515

FOOD FLAVOURS

M/s. L. Liladhar & Company
257-259, Samuel Street,
Vadgadi, Mumbai - 400 003
Maharashtra
Ph. : (O) 3422988, 3447690
Fac : 7670396, 7671102
C.P.: Mr. Madhusudan Mody

M/s. Natwar Lal Nathala & Co.
49, Balahnuman - Gandhi Road,
Ahmedabad - 380 001
Gujarat Ph. : 2140147
Fax : 2144807
C.P. : Mr. Mahendra Bhai N. Shah & Niren G. Shah

M/s. R.R. Gondal Wala & Co.
Tower Road
Surendranagar - 363 001
Gujarat Ph. : 20032, 23640

FLAVOURS

M/s. S.H. Kelkar & Co. Ltd.
Devkaran Mansion,
36, Mangaldas Road,
Mumbai - 400 002
Ph. : (O) 2069609, 2019130
Fax : 2081204
C.P.: Mr. G.D.Kelkar, Mr. S.V. Vaze

FLORAL CONCENTRATES

M/s. Synthite Industrial Chemicals Ltd.
Ajay Vihar, M.G. Road,
Cochin - 682 016, Kerala
Ph. : (O) 355794, 360698
Fac : 04853-60316, 60285
Fax : 370405
C.P. : Mr. C.V. Jacob, Mr. George Paul

FLORAL EXTRACTIVES

M/s. Vignesh Essential Oils
SKS Residency, Cutchery Road,
Gobichettipalayam - 638 452,
Distt. Erode (T.N.)
Tamilnadu
Ph. : (O) (91-4285) 22222
22822, 23949
Fax : 91-4285-23333
C.P.: Mr. S. Subramaniam

GERANYL ACETATE

M/s. LA Aromatics
BG-6/25B, Paschim Vihar
New Delhi - 110 063
Contact Person :
Umesh Jha

M/s. S.A.V. Aromatic
BG-6/25 B, Paschim Vihar,
New Delhi - 110 063
Ph. : 5672186, 5585022
Fax : 011-5672186

GERANIOL OIL

M/s. Kali Agro Chemicals Limited
F-35, Okhla Indl.
Area Ph-1,
New Delhi - 110 020
Ph. : 0091-11-6819362
Fax : 0091-11-6812492

M/s. Osom Extracts
Som Santi House, 152,
Patparganj Ind. Estate
Delhi - 110 092
Ph. : 91-11-2148207,2143195, 2153077
Fax : 91-11-2143066,2154284
E-mail :som@ndb.vsnl.net.in

M/s. Raj Woollen Industries
G.T. Road, P.O. Box 20,
Panipat - 132 103 (HR)
Ph. : (01742)-30050, 30347, 34176
Fax : (01742) 32346, 58346

GERANYL BUTRATE

M/s. LA Aromatics
BG-6/25B, Paschim Vihar
New Delhi - 110 063
Contact Person :
Umesh Jha

M/s. S.A.V. Aromatic
BG-6/25 B, Paschim Vihar
New Delhi - 110 063
Ph. : 5672186, 5585022
Fax : 011-5672186

GERANYL FORMATE

M/s. LA Aromatics
BG-6/25B, Paschim Vihar
New Delhi - 110 063
Contact Person :
Umesh Jha

M/s. S.A.V. Aromatic
BG-6/25 B, Paschim Vihar,
New Delhi - 110 063
Ph. : 5672186, 5585022
Fax : 011-5672186

GERANIUM OIL

M/s. Osom Extracts
Som Santi House, 152,
Patparganj Ind. Estate
Delhi - 110 092
Ph. : 91-11-2148207,2143195 2153077
Fax : 91-11-2143066,2154284
E-mail :som@ndb.vsnl.net.in

M/s. Vignesh Essential Oils
SKS Residency,
Cutchery Road,
Gobichettipalayam - 638 452
Distt. Erode (T.N.)
Ph. : (O) (91-4285) 22222
22822, 23949
Fax : 91-4285-23333
C.P.: Mr. S. Subramaniam

GERANIOL EX-PALMROSA

M/s. Odochem Industries
C-71, II Stage,
Peenya Indl. Estate
Bangalore - 560 058
Karnataka
Ph. : (F) 8392229
Fax : 839229
C.P.: Mr. P. Annapumaiah
Mr. M.S. Raikar

GUAJACWOOD OIL

M/s. Osom Extracts
Som Santi House, 152,
Patparganj Ind. Estate
Delhi - 110 092
Ph. : 91-11-2148207
2143195 2153077
Fax : 91-11-2143066,2154284
E-mail :som@ndb.vsnl.net.in

GUAR GUM

M/s. Singhal Export Corporation
Works : 6th km, Nainital Road
Rampur- 244 901 (U.P.)
Admin.Office : 7, Kailash Colony
Civil Lines, Rampur - 244 901 (U.P.)
Ph. : (O) 91-595-350897, 352979
(W) : 91-595-325073, 325074
Fax : 91-595-350684
E-mail : sec@nde.vsnl.net.in

GINGERGRASS OIL

M/s. Haritwal Essential Oils Exports
272/273, Hind Rajasthan,
Shopping Centre, Block No. 113
1st Floor, SION (West)
Mumbai - 400 022 Maharashtra
Ph. : (O) 4075865
Fax : 022-4015998
C.P.: Mr. Haritwal

ISOEUGENOL

M/s. Omega Polycoats
'Nirmal' Near Khare Town,
P.O. Dharampeth
Nagpur - 440 010
Maharashtra
Ph. : (O) 531006
Fac : 071104-36667
C.P.: Mr. Deillip
Pandharpurkar

HONEY

M/s. Save Earth Plantations Limited
11A/33, WEA Karol Bagh
New Delhi - 110 005
Ph. : 57897495, 5766899
Fax : 5766899

HYDRATROPIC ALDEHYDE

M/s. Parekh
Perfumery Works
128, Bhuleshwar Road,
Kabutarkhana
Mumbai - 400 002
Ph. : (O) 3739711, 3739712
Fac : 3727052
C.P.: Mr. Harkrishan R. Parekh

HYDROXY CITRONELLOL

M/s. Surya Aromatic
& Essential Oils
D- 662, Saraswati Vihar,
Pitampura, Delhi - 110 034
Ph. : 7019930
Fax : 011-7028516, 7022396

M/s. Suresh Chemicals
298/2, N.S. Palya,
Bannerghatta Road
Bangalore - 560 076
Karnataka Ph. : (F) 6634118,
Fax : 628912
C.P.: Mr. K.S. Suresh Babu

HERBAL EXTRACTS

M/s. Indrag Pvt. Ltd.
S-913, Manipal Centre,
Dickenson Road,
Bangalore - 560 042
Karnataka Ph. : (O) 5589521,
Fax : 5589521, 5560594
C.P.: Mr. Philip Samuel

M/s. Nat-Con
No. 490 (L), Phase,
Peenya Indl. Area,
Bangalore - 560 058
Karnataka Ph. : (O) 8396545
Fax : 8392956
C.P.: Mr. Sujit Mukund

ISO EUGENOL

M/s. Aroma Industries
DSIDC Shed No. 111
Okhla Industrial Area
SCHEME -1, Phase - II,
New Delhi - 110 020
Ph. : 6914573,6841353
Fax : (91)(11)6841353
Website:www:gogia.com E-mail:gcipl@vsnl.com

ISO LONGIFOLENE

M/s. Prabhat
General Agencies
154/6, Mittal Tower,
'B' Wing, Nariman Point
Mumbai - 400 021
Maharashtra
Ph. : (O) 2823680
2825055, 2828182
Fax : 2842147
C.P.: Mr. V.T. Chudiwal,
Mr. J.P. Singh

JASMINE

M/s. Cigma Essence & Aromatics Pvt. Ltd.
910/1, Thimmampalayam,

Karamadai,
Coimbatore - 641 104
Tamilnadu
Ph. : (O) 72480, 72001
Fax : 04267-72690
C.P.: Mr. S.R.Varadharajan

JASMINE CONCRETE

M/s. Natural & Essential Oils Pvt. Ltd.
No. 224, 8th Cross
Gokulam III Stage
Mysore - 570 002
Karnataka
Ph. : (O) 512021,
Fac : 77738, 77587
Fax : 512021
C.P.: Mr. Tyagarajan, Mr. T.Gowrishankar

M/s. Nesstate Flora
No. 4, Veerapandi
Coimbatore - 641 019
Tamilnadu
Ph. : (O) 892587
Fax : 892286
C.P.: Mr. K.Loganathan, Mr. T. Gowrishankar

M/s. Jasmine Concrete Exports Pvt. Ltd.
19, Josier Street,
Nangumbakkam,
Chennai - 600 034
Tamilnadu Ph. : 8279451
Mr. A.K. Venkatasamy
Mr. S.Natarajan

JASMINE ABSOLUTE

M/s. Natural & Essential Oils Pvt. Ltd.
No. 224, 8th Cross
Gokulam III Stage
Mysore - 570 002
Karnataka Ph. : (O) 512021,
Fac : 77738, 77587
Fax : 512021
C.P.: Mr. Tyagarajan, Mr T.Gowrishankar

M/s. Jasmine Concrete Exports Pvt. Ltd.
19, Josier Street,
Nangumbakkam,
Chennai - 600 034
Tamilnadu
Ph. : 8279451
Mr. A.K. Venkatasamy
Mr. S.Natarajan

JASMINE POWDER
M/s. LA Aromatics
BG-6/25B, Paschim Vihar
New Delhi - 110 063
Contact Person :
Umesh Jha

M/s. S.A.V. Aromatic
BG-6/25 B, Paschim Vihar,
New Delhi - 110 063
Ph. : 5672186, 5585022
Fax : 011-5672186

JASMINE SAMBAC

M/s. Cigma Essence & Aromatics Pvt. Ltd.,
910/1, Thimmampalayam,
Karamadai,
Coimbatore - 641 104
Tamilnadu
Ph. : (O) 72480, 72001
Fax : 04267-72690
C.P.: Mr. S.R.Varadharajan

M/s. Navrat Fragrances Pvt. Ltd.,
J.P. Tower, 8th Floor
7/2, Nugambakkam High Road,
Chennai - 600 034
Tamilnadu
Ph. : (O) 8260134
Fax : 8270346
C.P.: Mr. N. Peter Perianayagam

JASMINE SAMBAC CONCRETE

M/s. Nesstate Flora
No. 4, Veerapandi
Coimbatore - 641 019
Tamilnadu Ph. : (O) 892587
Fax : 892286
C.P.: Mr. K.Loganathan, Mr. T. Gowrishankar

JASMINE GRANDIFLORUM

M/s. Navrat Fragrances Pvt. Ltd.,
J.P. Tower, 8th Floor
7/2, Nugambakkam High Road,
Chennai - 600 034
Tamilnadu
Ph. : (O) 8260134
Fax : 8270346
C.P: Mr. N. Peter Perianayagam

JAMROSA OIL

M/s. Dee Kay Exports
Shakuntla Bhawan,
Malgodan Road,
Budaun, (U.P.) - 243 601
Ph. : 05832-24331, 24922
(R) : 24883, 24507
Fax : 91-5832-25085

M/s. Hindustan Mint & Agro Products Pvt. Ltd.,
Barehseni Street,
Chandausi - 202 412
Ph. : 91-5921-50540, 51900
Fax : 9105921-50074
Factory Deverkhera
Moradabad Road
Chandausi - 202 412
Ph. : 91-5921-51274, 51894
E-mail : hindustn@nde.vsnl.net.in

M/s. K.K. Aromatics
Shree Ram Kunj (Behind Bankey Behari Mandir) Indira Nagar
Bareilly (U.P.) 243122
Ph. : 91(0591) 448512, 448631
Fax : 91-(0581) 444188

M/s. Naini Essential Oils & Chemicals
Vill. & P.O. Khod Sharif
Tehsil : SUAR
Distt. : Rampur (U.P.) 244 924
Ph. : Maswasi (0595) 555527

M/s. Osom Extracts
Som Santi House, 152,
Patparganj Ind. Estate
Delhi - 110 092
Ph. : 91-11-2148207
2143195 2153077
Fax : 91-11-2143066,2154284
E-mail :som@ndb.vsnl.net.in

M/s. Sandeep Chemicals (Patiyali Sarai)
Near Nai Sarai Ki Chowki,
Budaun - 243 601 (U.P.)
Ph. : 05832-24341

JAVA CENTRONELLA OIL

M/s. Save Earth Plantations Limited
11A/33, WEA Karol Bagh
New Delhi - 110 005
Ph. : 57897495, 5766899
Fax : 5766899

M/s. Trade India Exports (Regd.)
209 E, Missionary Hill,
Post Box No. 13
Ootacamund - 643 002
Tamilnadu
Ph. : (O) 42553, 41413
Fax : 41413
C.P.: Mr. V.Narayanan
Mr. V.N. Ranjit

M/s. James Wright Ltd.,
Off. 909, Embassy Centre,
Mumbai - 400 021
Ph. : (O) 2047593
FAx : 2840645
C.P.: Mr. K.G. Jhajharia

JOJOBA OIL

M/s. Osom Extracts
Som Santi House, 152,
Patparganj Ind. Estate
Delhi - 110 092
Ph. : 91-11-2148207
2143195 ,2153077
Fax : 91-11-2143066,2154284
E-mail :som@ndb.vsnl.net.in

JOSS STICK/ GUTKHA FLAVOURS

M/s. Ultra International Limited
304/M-3, Connaught Circus
New Delhi - 110 001
Ph. : (011) 3324100, 3352200
Fax : (011) 3712563, 3317776

JUNIPER ROOT

M/s. Aum Aromas
V.P.O. Galma - 175021
Distt. : Mandi (H.P.)
Himachal Pradesh
Ph. : 01905 - 42281, 23204

LAVENDER

M/s. Osom Extracts
Som Santi House, 152,
Patparganj Ind. Estate
Delhi - 110 092
Ph. : 91-11-2148207
2143195 2153077
Fax : 91-11-2143066,2154284
E-mail :som@ndb.vsnl.net.in

LEMON GRASS OIL

M/s. D.V. Deo
V/1084, Pandit Road, Corner,
Cochin - 682 002 Kerala
Ph. : (O) 224196
226903, 373809
Fac : 422248, Fax : 373780
Telex : 885-7041
C.P. : Mr. Dhanajai D.Deo
Mr. Bobby Gulati

M/s. LA Aromatics
BG-6/25B, Paschim Vihar
New Delhi - 110 063
Contact Person :
Umesh Jha

M/s. Sandeep Chemicals
(Patiyali Sarai)
Near Nai Sarai Ki Chowki
Budaun - 243 601 (U.P.)
Ph. : 05832-24341

M/s. S.A.V. Aromatic
BG-6/25 B, Paschim Vihar,
New Delhi - 110 063
Ph. : 5672186, 5585022
Fax : 011-5672186

M/s. Save Earth Plantations Limited
11A/33, WEA Karol Bagh
New Delhi - 110 005
Ph. : 57897495, 5766899
Fax : 5766899

M/s. Swastik Eucalyptus Oil Co.
166, Main Bazar,
Ootacamund - 643 001
Bangalore - 560 010 Karnataka
Ph. : (O) 42527 Fac : 43489
C.P.: Mr. Shantilal B. Mehta

LIME JUICE

M/s. Manak Cirus Products Pvt. Ltd.,
At & Post. Utran, Tal. Erandol
Nagpur - 440 002 Maharashtra
Ph. : 40070
C.P.: Mr. Satish Sanghavi

LIME OIL

M/s. Manak Cirus Products Pvt. Ltd.,
At & Post. Utran,
Tal. Erandol
Nagpur - 440 002
Maharashtra
Ph. : 40070
C.P.: Mr. Satish Sanghavi

LINALOOL OIL

M/s. Arovision Industries
B-13, Industrial Estate,
Salarpur, Budaun - 243 601
(U.P.) Ph. : 05832-24250
(R) : 26126

M/s. Aroma Chemicals
Siddhi Sadan, Tiraha
Tubewell Colony
Moradabad - 244 001
Ph. : 414365, 418960 Fax : 424408

M/s. Dee Kay Exports
Shakuntla Bhawan
Malgodan Road
Budaun, (U.P.) - 243 601
Ph. : 05832-24331, 24922
(R) : 24883, 24507
Fax : 91-5832-25085

M/s. Evergreen Aromatics Pvt. Ltd.,
Fact. : 6-A, Industrial Estate,
Roshan Bagh,
Civil Lines,
Rampur - 244 901 (U.P.)
Fax : (0595) 350184, 350190
E-mail : evergreen@del5.vsnl.net.in

M/s. J.S. Traders
Dr. Ramswaroop Road
(Near State Bank of India)
Chandausi - 202 412 (U.P.)
Ph. : 05921-50777

M/s. K.K. Aromatics
Shree Ram Kunj (Behind Bankey Behari Mandir)
Indira Nagar, Bareilly (U.P.) 243122
Ph. : 91(0591) 448512, 448631
Fax : 91-(0581) 444188

M/s. Menthol & Allied Products
F-26/1, B.S. Road
Indl. Area, Site - 1
Ghaziabad - 201 009 (U.P.)
Ph. : 0120-4700257
4700442, 4701995
(R) : 4702693, 4750785
Fax : 0120-4700257
E-mail : menthol@satyam.net.in

M/s. Osom Extracts
Som Santi House, 152
Patparganj Ind. Estate
Delhi - 110 092
Ph. : 91-11-2148207
2143195 2153077
Fax : 91-11-2143066,2154284
E-mail :som@ndb.vsnl.net.in

M/s. Surya Aromatic & Essential Oils
D- 662, Saraswati Vihar
Pitampura, Delhi - 110 034
Ph. : 7019930
Fax : 011-7028516, 7022396

M/s. Singhal Export Corporation
Works : 6th km, Nainital Road,
Rampur- 244 901 (U.P.)
Admin.Office : 7, Kailash Colony
Civil Lines, Rampur - 244 901 (U.P.)
Ph. : (O) 91-595-350897, 352979
(W) : 91-595-325073, 325074
Fax : 91-595-350684
E-mail : sec@nde.vsnl.net.in

M/s. Virat Exports Pvt. Ltd.,
23/3, East Patel Nagar
Delhi - 110 008
Ph. : 0091-011-5767182
576183, 5730485
Fax : 0091-011-5755209
E-mail : viratexp@del2.vsnl.net.in

LINALOOL PURE

M/s. LA Aromatics
BG-6/25B, Paschim Vihar

New Delhi - 110 063
Contact Person :
Umesh Jha

M/s. S.A.V. Aromatic
BG-6/25 B, Paschim Vihar,
New Delhi - 110 063
Ph. : 5672186, 5585022
Fax : 011-5672186

LIQUID MENTHOL

M/s. Naini Essential Oils & Chemicals
Vill. & P.O. Khod Sharif
Tehsil : SUAR
Distt. : Rampur (U.P.) 244 924
Ph. : Maswasi (0595) 555527

LINALOOL (EXTRA)

M/s. Aroma Industries
DSIDC Shed No. 111, Okhla Industrial Area
SCHEME -1, Phase - II,
New Delhi - 110 020
Ph. : 6914573,6841353
Fax : (91)(11)6841353
Website:www:gogia.com
E-mail:gcipl@vsnl.com

M/s. Arihant Aromatics
Gali No. 1/3-A, C-36/2
Bhajanpura
(Behind Petrol Pump), Delhi - 53
Telefax : 2183876, 2265174

M/s. LA Aromatics
BG-6/25B, Paschim Vihar
New Delhi - 110 063
Contact Person :
Umesh Jha

M/s. S.A.V. Aromatic
BG-6/25 B, Paschim Vihar,
New Delhi - 110 063
Ph. : 5672186, 5585022
Fax : 011-5672186

LINALYL ACETATE

M/s. LA Aromatics
BG-6/25B, Paschim Vihar
New Delhi - 110 063
Contact Person :
Umesh Jha

M/s. S.A.V. Aromatic
BG-6/25 B, Paschim Vihar,
New Delhi - 110 063
Ph. : 5672186, 5585022
Fax : 011-5672186

LIQUID MENTHOL

M/s. Evergreen Aromatics Pvt. Ltd.,
Fact. : 6-A, Industrial Estate Roshan Bagh, Civil Lines
Rampur - 244 901 (U.P.)
Fax : (0595) 350184, 350190
E-mail : evergreen@del5.vsnl.net.in

M/s. Kali Agro Chemicals Limited
F-35, Okhla Indl.

Area Ph-1, New Delhi - 110 020
Ph. : 0091-11-6819362
Fax : 0091-11-6812492

L-LIMONENE OIL

M/s. Hindustan Mint & Agro Products Pvt. Ltd.,
Barehseni Street,
Chandausi - 202 412
Ph. : 91-5921-50540, 51900
Fax : 9105921-50074
Factory Deverkhera, Moradabad Road
Chandausi - 202 412
Ph. : 91-5921-51274, 51894
E-mail : hindustn@nde.vsnl.net.in

MARIGOLD

M/s. Cigma Essence & Aromatics Pvt. Ltd.,
910/1, Thimmampalayam
Karamadai, Coimbatore - 641 104
Tamilnadu
Ph. : (O) 72480, 72001
Fax : 04267-72690
C.P.: Mr. S.R.Varadharajan

MENTHYL ANTHRANILATE

M/s. Om Parkash Madan Lal (P) Ltd.
2190, Gali Hinga Beg
Tilak Bazar, Khari Baoli
Delhi - 110 006
Ph. : 3963657, 3967276
(R) : 7074650, 7082740
E-mail : opml62.hotmail

MENTHA CITRATA

M/s. LA Aromatics
BG-6/25B, Paschim Vihar
New Delhi - 110 063
Contact Person :
Umesh Jha

M/s. S.A.V. Aromatic
BG-6/25 B, Paschim Vihar,
New Delhi - 110 063
Ph. : 5672186, 5585022
Fax : 011-5672186

MENTHONE OIL

M/s. Arihant Aromatics
Gali No. 1/3-A, C-36/2
Bhajanpura (Behind Petrol Pump), Delhi - 110 053
Telefax : 2183876, 2265174

M/s. Dee Kay Exports
Shakuntla Bhawan
Malgodan Road,
Budaun, (U.P.) - 243 601
Ph. : 05832-24331, 24922
(R) : 24883, 24507
Fax : 91-5832-25085

M/s. Evergreen Aromatics Pvt. Ltd.,
Fact. : 6-A, Industrial Estate,
Roshan Bagh,
Civil Lines,
Rampur - 244 901 (U.P.)
Fax : (0595) 350184, 350190
E-mail : evergreen@del5.vsnl.net.in

M/s. Hindustan Mint & Agro Products Pvt. Ltd.,
Barehseni Street,
Chandausi - 202 412
Ph. : 91-5921-50540, 51900
Fax : 9105921-50074
Factory Deverkhera
Moradabad Road
Chandausi - 202 412
Ph. : 91-5921-51274, 51894
E-mail : hindustn@nde.vsnl.net.in

M/s. J.S. Traders
Dr. Ramswaroop Road, (Near State Bank of India)
Chandausi - 202 412 (U.P.)
Ph. : 05921-50777

M/s. K.K. Aromatics
Shree Ram Kunj (Behind Bankey Behari Mandir) Indira Nagar
Bareilly (U.P.) 243122
Ph. : 91(0591) 448512, 448631
Fax : 91-(0581) 444188

M/s. Kali Agro Chemicals Limited
F-35, Okhla Indl.
Area Ph-1, New Delhi - 110 020
Ph. : 0091-11-6819362
Fax : 0091-11-6812492

M/s. Menthol & Allied Products
F-26/1, B.S. Road, Indl. Area, Site - 1
Ghaziabad - 201 009 (U.P.)
Ph. : 0120-4700257
4700442, 4701995
(R) : 4702693, 4750785
Fax : 0120-4700257
E-mail : menthol@satyam.net.in

M/s. Naini Essential Oils & Chemicals
Vill. & P.O. Khod Sharif
Tehsil : SUAR
Distt. : Rampur (U.P.) 244 924
Ph. : Maswasi (0595) 555527

M/s. Osom Extracts
Som Santi House, 152,
Patparganj Ind. Estate
Delhi - 110 092
Ph. : 91-11-2148207,2143195
2153077
Fax : 91-11-2143066,2154284
E-mail :som@ndb.vsnl.net.in

M/s. Siddh Aromatic Chemicals
Dr. Ram Swaroop Road,
Chandausi - 202 412 (U.P.)
Ph. : (05921) 50792

M/s. Virat Exports Pvt. Ltd.,
23/3, East Patel Nagar,
Delhi - 110 008
Ph. : 0091-011-5767182,
576183, 5730485
Fax : 0091-011-5755209
E-mail : viratexp@del2.vsnl.net.in

MEN. ACETATE OIL

M/s. Osom Extracts
Som Santi House, 152

Patparganj Ind. Estate
Delhi - 110 092
Ph. : 91-11-2148207
2143195 2153077
Fax : 91-11-2143066,2154284
E-mail :som@ndb.vsnl.net.in

METHYL-CHEMICAL

M/s. Arihant Aromatics
Gali No. 1/3-A, C-36/2
Bhajanpura (Behind Petrol Pump), Delhi - 110 053
Telefax : 2183876, 2265174

MENTHA OIL

M/s. LA Aromatics
BG-6/25B, Paschim Vihar
New Delhi - 110 063
Contact Person :
Umesh Jha

M/s. Naini Essential Oils & Chemicals
Vill. & P.O. Khod Sharif
Tehsil : SUAR
Distt. : Rampur (U.P.) 244 924
Ph. : Maswasi (0595) 555527

M/s. S.A.V. Aromatic
BG-6/25 B, Paschim Vihar,
New Delhi - 110 063
Ph. : 5672186, 5585022
Fax : 011-5672186

M/s. Sandeep Chemicals
(Patiyali Sarai)
Near Nai Sarai Ki Chowki,
Budaun - 243 601 (U.P.)
Ph. : 05832-24341

M.P. ACETATE

M/s. LA Aromatics
BG-6/25B, Paschim Vihar
New Delhi - 110 063
Contact Person :
Umesh Jha

M/s. S.A.V. Aromatic
BG-6/25 B, Paschim Vihar,
New Delhi - 110 063
Ph. : 5672186, 5585022
Fax : 011-5672186

MENTHA OIL

M/s. Save Earth Plantations Limited
11A/33, WEA Karol Bagh
New Delhi - 110 005
Ph. : 57897495, 5766899
Fax : 5766899

M.PIPERITA OIL

M/s. Naini Essential Oils & Chemicals
Vill. & P.O. Khod Sharif
Tehsil : SUAR
Distt. : Rampur (U.P.) 244 924
Ph. : Maswasi (0595) 555527

MENTHA PIPRATA

M/s. LA Aromatics
BG-6/25B, Paschim Vihar

New Delhi - 110 063
Contact Person :
Umesh Jha

M/s. S.A.V. Aromatic
BG-6/25 B, Paschim Vihar,
New Delhi - 110 063
Ph. : 5672186, 5585022
Fax : 011-5672186

MENTHYLE ACETATE

M/s. Kali Agro Chemicals Limited
F-35, Okhla Indl. Area
Ph-1, New Delhi - 110 020
Ph. : 0091-11-6819362
Fax : 0091-11-6812492

MENTHYL CHAVICOL

M/s. Aroma Chemicals
Siddhi Sadan, Tiraha
Tubewell Colony
Moradabad - 244 001
Ph. : 414365, 418960
Fax : 424408

M/s. Evergreen Aromatics Pvt. Ltd.
Fact. : 6-A, Industrial Estate,
Roshan Bagh,
Civil Lines, Rampur - 244 901 (U.P.)
Fax : (0595) 350184, 350190
E-mail : evergreen@del5.vsnl.net.in

MITHYL CHEVICOL

M/s. LA Aromatics
BG-6/25B, Paschim Vihar
New Delhi - 110 063
Contact Person :
Umesh Jha

MIMOSA

M/s. Cigma Essence & Aromatics Pvt. Ltd.
910/1, Thimmampalayam,
Karamadai,
Coimbatore - 641 104
Tamilnadu
Ph. : (O) 72480, 72001
Fax : 04267-72690
C.P.: Mr. S.R.Varadharajan

MIMOSA CONCRETES

M/s. Jasmine Concrete Exports Pvt. Ltd.
19, Josier Street,
Nangumbakkam,
Chennai - 600 034
Tamilnadu Ph. : 8279451
Mr. A.K. Venkatasamy, Mr. S.Natarajan

MINT TERPENE

M/s. Evergreen Aromatics Pvt. Ltd.,
Fact. : 6-A, Industrial Estate,
Roshan Bagh,
Civil Lines, Rampur - 244 901 (U.P.)

Fax : (0595) 350184, 350190
E-mail : evergreen@del5.vsnl.net.in

M/s. K.K. Aromatics
Shree Ram Kunj (Behind Bankey Behari Mandir)Indira Nagar
Bareilly (U.P.) 243122
Ph. : 91(0591) 448512, 448631
Fax : 91-(0581) 444188

M/s. S.A.V. Aromatic
BG-6/25 B, Paschim Vihar,
New Delhi - 110 063
Ph. : 5672186, 5585022
Fax : 011-5672186

M/s. Siddh Aromatic Chemicals
Dr. Ram Swaroop Road
Chandausi - 202 412 (U.P.)
Ph. : (05921) 50792

MINT PRODUCTS

M/s. Kali Agro Chemicals Limited
F-35, Okhla Indl.
Area Ph-1, New Delhi - 110 020
Ph. : 0091-11-6819362
Fax : 0091-11-6812492

MENTHOL CRYSTALS

M/s. Indira Dinesh Chemicals
Factory : 131, HSIDC Industrial Estate,
Kundli (Sonepat) Haryana - 131 028
Ph. : (01264) 70123, 70131
Fax : 91-11-6830158
(R) : 91-11-7860411
E-mail : idchem@vsnl.com
Web: http://dinesh.vsnl.com/menthol

METHYL CHAVICOL

M/s. J.S. Traders
Dr. Ramswaroop Road, (Near State Bank of India)
Chandausi - 202 412 (U.P.)
Ph. : 05921-50777

METHYL SALICYLATE

M/s. Om Parkash Madan Lal (P) Ltd.
2190, Gali Hinga Beg,
Tilak Bazar, Khari Baoli
Delhi - 110 006
Ph. : 3963657, 3967276
(R) : 7074650, 7082740
E-mail : opml62.hotmail

6-METHYL COUMARIN

M/s. Aroma Aromatics & Flavours
67-68-69, Industrial Area,
Baddi, Distt. Solan - 173 220 (H.P.)
Ph. : 91-1795-44431
Fax : 91-1795-44430
New Delhi
Fax : 91-11-6840763
E-mail : gcipl@vsnl.com
Website : www.gogia.com

METHYL EUGENOL

M/s. Aroma Industries
DSIDC Shed No. 111, Okhla Industrial Area
SCHEME -1, Phase - II,
New Delhi - 110 020
Ph. : 6914573,6841353
Fax : (91)(11)6841353
Website:www:gogia.com
E-mail:gcipl@vsnl.com

METHYL ISO EUGENOL

M/s. Aroma Industries
DSIDC Shed No. 111
Okhla Industrial Area
SCHEME -1, Phase - II
New Delhi - 110 020
Ph. : 6914573,6841353
Fax : (91)(11)6841353
Website:www:gogia.com
E-mail:gcipl@vsnl.com

M.PIPERITA OIL

M/s. Evergreen Aromatics Pvt. Ltd.,
Fact. : 6-A, Industrial Estate,
Roshan Bagh,
Civil Lines,
Rampur - 244 901 (U.P.)
Fax : (0595) 350184, 350190
E-mail : evergreen@del5.vsnl.net.in

M.CITRATA OIL

M/s. Evergreen Aromatics Pvt. Ltd.,
Fact. : 6-A, Industrial Estate,
Roshan Bagh,
Civil Lines,
Rampur - 244 901 (U.P.)
Fax : (0595) 350184, 350190
E-mail : evergreen@del5.vsnl.net.in

MENTHOL OIL

M/s. Indira Dinesh Chemicals
Factory : 131, HSIDC
Industrial Estate,
Kundli (Sonepat)
Haryana - 131 028
Ph. : (01264) 70123, 70131
Fax : 91-11-6830158
(R) : 91-11-7860411
E-mail : idchem@vsnl.com
Web: http://dinesh.vsnl.com/menthol

M/s. Naini Essential Oils & Chemicals
Vill. & P.O. Khod Sharif
Tehsil : SUAR
Distt. : Rampur (U.P.) 244 924
Ph. : Maswasi (0595) 555527

MENTHOL FLAKES

M/s. Indira Dinesh Chemicals
Factory : 131, HSIDC Industrial Estate,
Kundli (Sonepat) Haryana - 131 028
Ph. : (01264) 70123, 70131

Fax : 91-11-6830158
(R) : 91-11-7860411
E-mail : idchem@vsnl.com
Web: http://dinesh.vsnl.com/menthol

MOUTH FRESHER FLAVOURS

M/s. Ultra International Limited
304/M-3, Connaught Circus
New Delhi - 110 001
Ph. : (011) 3324100, 3352200
Fax : (011) 3712563, 3317776

MUSK AMBRETTE

M/s. Aswathi Chemicals Pvt. Ltd.
56, Bommasandra Industrial Area, Hosur Road,
Bangalore - 560 020
Ph. : (O) 3363692
Fac : 8395799
Fax : 3697352
C.P. : Mr. K. Venkataramani

MUSK KETONE

M/s. Awasthi Chemicals Pvt. Ltd.
56, Bommasandra
Industrial Area,
Hosur Road,
Bangalore - 560 020
Karnataka
Ph. : (O) 3363692
Fac : 8395799
Fax : 3697352
C.P. : Mr. K. Venkataramani

M/s. Maschmeijer Aromatics (India) Ltd.,
P.B. NO. 3, G.S.T. Road,
Chromepet Chennai - 600 044
Tamilnadu Ph. : (O) 2368788, 2368789, 2368790
Fax : 2366808, 2341375
C.P.: Mr. S.A. Md. Shareef

MUSK XYLOL

M/s. Awasthi Chemicals Pvt. Ltd.
56, Bommasandra
Industrial Area, Hosur Road,
Bangalore - 560 020 Karnataka
Ph. : (O) 3363692
Fac : 8395799
Fax : 3697352
C.P. : Mr. K. Venkataramani

M/s. Maschmeijer Aromatics (India) Ltd.
P.B. NO. 3, G.S.T. Road,
Chromepet
Chennai - 600 044 Tamilnadu
Ph. : (O) 2368788,
2368789, 2368790
Fax : 2366808, 2341375
C.P.: Mr. S.A. Md. Shareef

NEEM OIL

M/s. Malve Chemicals
"Shabri" Building,
Kapar Road,
Ahead of Santoshi Mata Bldg.,
Dombivli (W) - 421 202
Maharashtra

Ph. : (O) 452336,
Fac : 590846 Fax : 452336
C.P.: Mr.Datta Malve
Mr. Suhas Malve

M/s. Osom Extracts
Som Santi House, 152,
Patparganj Ind. Estate
Delhi - 110 092
Ph. : 91-11- 214820
2143195 ,2153077
Fax : 91-11-2143066,2154284
E-mail :som@ndb.vsnl.net.in

NATURAL FLORAL EXTRACT

M/s. Indrag Pvt. Ltd.
S-913, Manipal Centre,
Dickenson Road,
Bangalore - 560 042
Ph. : (O) 5589521,
Fax : 5589521, 5560594
C.P.: Mr. Philip Samuel

NATURAL PRODUCTS

M/s. Nat-Con
No. 490 (L), Phase,
Peenya Indl. Area,
Bangalore - 560 058
Ph. : (O) 8396545
Fax : 8392956
C.P.: Mr. Sujit Mukund

NATURAL GERANIUM OIL

M/s. Trade India Exports (Regd.)
209 E, Missionary Hill
Post Box No. 13
Ootacamund - 643 002
Tamilnadu
Ph. : (O) 42553, 41413
Fax : 41413
C.P.: Mr. V.Narayanan, Mr. V.N. Ranjit

ORANGE OIL

M/s. Aroma Industries
DSIDC Shed No. 111, Okhla Industrial Area
SCHEME -1, Phase - II,
New Delhi - 110 020
Ph. : 6914573,6841353
Fax : (91)(11)6841353
Website:www:gogia.com
E-mail:gcipl@vsnl.com

M/s. Osom Extracts
Som Santi House, 152,
Patparganj Ind. Estate
Delhi - 110 092
Ph. : 91-11-214820
2143195 2153077
Fax : 91-11-2143066,2154284
E-mail :som@ndb.vsnl.net.in

OTHER ESSENTIAL OILS

M/s. Haritwal Essential Oils Exports
272/273, Hind Rajasthan,
Shopping Centre, Block No. 113,
1st Floor, SION (West) Mumbai - 400 022
Maharashtra Ph. : (O) 4075865
Fax : 022-4015998
C.P.: Mr. Haritwal

ORANGE OIL

M/s. Kushalchand Sons
Devkaran Mansion,
Room No. 07/3, Block No. 1,
2nd Floor, 79,
Princess Street
Mumbai - 400 002
Ph. : 2052190, 2080937
Fax : 2084265
C.P.: Mr. Lalit Hirani
Mr. Amit Hirani

OLIBANUM RESINOID

M/s. Parekh Perfumery Works
128, Bhuleshwar Road,
Kabutarkhana
Mumbai - 400 002
Ph. : (O) 3739711, 3739712
Fac : 3727052
C.P.: Mr. Harkrishan R. Parekh

PATCHOULI OIL

M/s. Osom Extracts
Som Santi House, 152,
Patparganj Ind. Estate
Delhi - 110 092
Ph. : 91-11-2148207,2143195
2153077
Fax : 91-11-2143066,2154284
E-mail :som@ndb.vsnl.net.in

PALMAROSA OIL

M/s. D.V. Deo
V/1084, Pandit Road, Corner
Cochin - 682 002 Kerala
Ph. : (O) 224196, 226903, 373809 (F) 422248
Fax : 373780 Telex : 885-7041

M/s. Hindustan Mint & Agro Products Pvt. Ltd.,
Barehseni Street,
Chandausi - 202 412
Ph. : 91-5921-50540, 51900
Fax : 9105921-50074
Factory Deverkhera, Moradabad Road, Chandausi - 202 412
Ph. : 91-5921-51274, 51894
E-mail : hindustn@nde.vsnl.net.in

M/s. Haritwal Essential Oils Exports
272/273, Hind Rajasthan,
Shopping Centre, Block No. 113, 1st Floor, SION (West)
Mumbai - 400 022
Ph. : (O) 4075865
Fax : 022-4015998
C.P.: Mr. Haritwal

M/s. Osom Extracts
Som Santi House, 152,
Patparganj Ind. Estate
Delhi - 110 092
Ph. : 91-11-2148207
2143195, 2153077
Fax : 91-11-2143066,2154284
E-mail :som@ndb.vsnl.net.in

M/s. Save Earth Plantations Limited
11A/33, WEA Karol Bagh
New Delhi - 110 005

Ph. : 57897495, 5766899
Fax : 5766899

M/s. Virat Exports Pvt. Ltd.,
23/3, East Patel Nagar,
Delhi - 110 008
Ph. : 0091-011-5767182, 576183, 5730485
Fax : 0091-011-5755209
E-mail : viratexp@del2.vsnl.net.in

PERFUME & FLAVOUR

M/s. Anthea Aromatics Pvt. Ltd.
Takshila, Mahakli Caves Road,
Andheri (E), Mumbai - 400 093
Maharasthra
Ph. : (O) 8300507
Fac : (F) 7691746
Fax : 8228949

M/s. Vina Fragrances
459, Ashoka Pillar Road,
Jayanagar,
Bangalore - 560 011 Karnataka
Ph. : (O) 663944
Fac : 642472
Fax : 6650338
C.P : Mr. K.L. Negendra

PERFUMERY COMPOUND

M/s. Maschmeijer Aromatics (India) Ltd.,
P.B. NO. 3, G.S.T. Road,
Chromepet
Chennai - 600 044 Tamilnadu
Ph. : (O) 2368788
2368789, 2368790
Fax : 2366808, 2341375
C.P.: Mr. S.A. Md. Shareef

PERFUMERY COMPOUNDS FOR SOAPS, TOBACCO AGARBATTI, COSMETICS TOILETRIES

M/s. W.Southern Aromatics Pvt. Ltd.
7, Venkatachala Mudali St., Park Town Chennai - 600 003
Tamilnadu Ph. : (O) 581841

PINE OIL

M/s. Hindustan Mint & Agro Products Pvt. Ltd.,
Barehseni Street,
Chandausi - 202 412
Ph. : 91-5921-50540, 51900
Fax : 9105921-50074
Factory Deverkhera, Moradabad Road Chandausi - 202 412
Ph. : 91-5921-51274, 51894
E-mail : hindustn@nde.vsnl.net.in

P.C.P.A.

M/s. LA Aromatics
BG-6/25B, Paschim Vihar
New Delhi - 110 063
Contact Person :
Umesh Jha

M/s. S.A.V. Aromatic
BG-6/25 B, Paschim Vihar,
New Delhi - 110 063

Ph. : 5672186, 5585022
Fax : 011-5672186

PECTIN

M/s. Manak Citrus Products Pvt. Ltd.
At & Post. Utran, Tal. Erandol,
Nagpur - 440 002
Maharashtra Ph. : 40070
C.P.: Mr. Satish Sanghavi

PETITGRAIN OIL

M/s. Osom Extracts
Som Santi House, 152,
Patparganj Ind. Estate
Delhi - 110 092
Ph. : 91-11-2148207,2143195
2153077
Fax : 91-11-2143066,2154284
E-mail :som@ndb.vsnl.net.in

P.E.M.E.

M/s. LA Aromatics
BG-6/25B, Paschim Vihar
New Delhi - 110 063
Contact Person :
Umesh Jha

M/s. S.A.V. Aromatic
BG-6/25 B, Paschim Vihar,
New Delhi - 110 063
Ph. : 5672186, 5585022
Fax : 011-5672186

P.E. ISO BUTYRATE

M/s. LA Aromatics
BG-6/25B, Paschim Vihar
New Delhi - 110 063
Contact Person :
Umesh Jha

M/s. S.A.V. Aromatic
BG-6/25 B, Paschim Vihar,
New Delhi - 110 063
Ph. : 5672186, 5585022
Fax : 011-5672186

P.E.P. ACETATE

M/s. LA Aromatics
BG-6/25B, Paschim Vihar
New Delhi - 110 063
Contact Person :
Umesh Jha

M/s. S.A.V. Aromatic
BG-6/25 B, Paschim Vihar,
New Delhi - 110 063
Ph. : 5672186, 5585022
Fax : 011-5672186

PEPPERMENT OIL

M/s. Aroma Industries
DSIDC Shed No. 111, Okhla Industrial Area
SCHEME -1, Phase - II,
New Delhi - 110 020
Ph. : 6914573,6841353
Fax : (91)(11)6841353
Website:www:gogia.com
E-mail:gcipl@vsnl.com

M/s. Naini Essential Oils & Chemicals
Vill. & P.O. Khod Sharif
Tehsil : SUAR
Distt. : Rampur (U.P.) 244 924
Ph. : Maswasi (0595) 555527

M/s. Aroma Chemicals
Siddhi Sadan, Tiraha
Tubewell Colony
Moradabad - 244 001
Ph. : 414365, 418960
Fax : 424408

M/s. Arihant Aromatics
Gali No. 1/3-A, C-36/2
Bhajanpura (Behind Petrol Pump)
Delhi - 110 053
Telefax : 2183876, 2265174

M/s. Evergreen Aromatics Pvt. Ltd.,
Fact. : 6-A, Industrial Estate, Roshan Bagh,
Civil Lines, Rampur - 244 901 (U.P.)
Fax : (0595) 350184, 350190
E-mail : evergreen@del5.vsnl.net.in

M/s. Kali Agro Chemicals Limited
F-35, Okhla Indl. Area
Ph-1, New Delhi - 110 020
Ph. : 0091-11-6819362
Fax : 0091-11-6812492

M/s. LA Aromatics
BG-6/25B, Paschim Vihar
New Delhi - 110 063
Contact Person :
Umesh Jha

M/s. S.A.V. Aromatic
BG-6/25 B, Paschim Vihar,
New Delhi - 110 063
Ph. : 5672186, 5585022
Fax : 011-5672186

M/s. Siddh Aromatic Chemicals
Dr. Ram Swaroop Road,
Chandausi - 202 412 (U.P.)
Ph. : (05921) 50792

PHENYL ACETIC ALDEHYDE

M/s. Surya Aromatic & Essential Oils
D- 662, Saraswati Vihar,
Pitampura, Delhi - 110 034
Ph. : 7019930
Fax : 011-7028516, 7022396

PHENYL ACETIC ACID ETC.

M/s. Arihant Aromatics
Gali No. 1/3-A, C-36/2, Bhajanpura
(Behind Petrol Pump), Delhi - 53
Telefax : 2183876, 2265174

M/s. Sabari Chemicals P. Ltd.
A/2/236 GIDC Estate, Nandesari
Baroda - 391340 Gujarat
Ph.(O) : 23081, 338334
Fac : 840429, 840143
Fax : 481265, 840890
C.P. : Mr. Ravi Nair Mr. Mohan Nair

PHENYL ETHYL ALCOHOL

M/s. Sanghi Organics & Phytochem Ltd.
144, Piplia Rao Agra - Mumbai Road, Indore - 452 001
Madhya Pradesh
Ph. : 62651, 65830, 67308
Fac : 07292, 47239, 47360
Fax : 474392
C.P.: Mr. Rajeev Sanghi
Mr. K.K. Jain

M/s. Surya Aromatic & Essential Oils
D- 662, Saraswati Vihar,
Pitampura, Delhi - 110 034
Ph. : 7019930
Fax : 011-7028516, 7022396

PHENYL ETHYL METHYL

M/s. Sanghi Organics & Phytochem Ltd.
144, Piplia Rao Agra - Mumbai Road Indore - 452 001
Madhya Pradesh
Ph. : 62651, 65830, 67308
Fac : 07292, 47239, 47360
Fax : 474392
C.P.: Mr. Rajeev Sanghi
Mr. K.K. Jain

PHENYL ETHYL FORMATE

M/s. Sanghi Organics & Phytochem Ltd.
144, Piplia Rao
Agra - Mumbai Road
Indore - 452 001
Madhya Pradesh
Ph. : 62651, 65830, 67308
Fac : 07292, 47239, 47360
Fax : 474392
C.P.: Mr. Rajeev Sanghi, Mr. K.K. Jain

PHENYL ETHYL ACETATE

M/s. Sanghi Organics & Phytochem Ltd.
144, Piplia Rao
Agra - Mumbai Road
Indore - 452 001
Madhya Pradesh
Ph. : 62651, 65830, 67308
Fac : 07292, 47239, 47360
Fax : 474392
C.P.: Mr. Rajeev Sanghi, Mr. K.K. Jain

PIPERATA OIL

M/s. Indira Dinesh Chemicals
Factory : 131, HSIDC Industrial Estate,
Kundli (Sonepat)
Haryana - 131 028
Ph. : (01264) 70123, 70131
Fax : 91-11-6830158
(R) : 91-11-7860411
E-mail : idchem@vsnl.com
Webpage: http://dinesh.vsnl.com/menthol

M/s. Sandeep Chemicals
(Patiyali Sarai)
Near Nai Sarai Ki Chowki,
Budaun - 243 601 (U.P.)
Ph. : 05832-24341

PARACRESYL ACETATE

M/s. R.C. Aromatic & Chemicals
69, Narayan Rao Koli Marg (Bhansari Street,) Koliwada Mandvi, Near Vadagadi
Mumbai - 400 003
Ph. : (O) 3432235,
Fac : 6247635, 6246809
C.P.: Mr. Anil R. Shah
Mr. Vikram R. Shah

PARA CRESYL METHYLETHER

M/s. Aroma Industries
DSIDC Shed No. 111
Okhla Industrial Area
SCHEME -1, Phase - II,
New Delhi - 110 020
Ph. : 6914573,6841353
Fax : (91)(11)6841353
Website:www:gogia.com
E-mail:gcipl@vsnl.com

PROPENYL GUAETHOL

M/s. Aroma Aromatics & Flavours
67-68-69, Industrial Area,
Baddi, Distt. Solan - 173 220
(H.P.) Ph. : 91-1795-44431
Fax : 91-1795-44430
New Delhi Fax : 91-11-6840763
E-mail : gcipl@vsnl.com
Website : www.gogia.com

M/s. Odochem Industries
C-71, II Stage,
Peenya Indl. Estate
Bangalore - 560 058
Karnataka Ph. : (F) 8392229
Fax : 839229
C.P.: Mr. P. Annapumaiah, Mr. M.S. Raikar

POTPOURRI OILS

M/s. Ultra International Limited
304/M-3, Connaught Circus, New Delhi - 110 001
Ph. : (011) 3324100, 3352200
Fax : (011) 3712563, 3317776

PAN MASALA/ GUTKHA FLAVOURS

M/s. Ultra International Limited
304/M-3, Connaught Circus,
New Delhi - 110 001
Ph. : (011) 3324100, 3352200
Fax : (011) 3712563, 3317776

PERFUME OILS

M/s. Ultra International Limited
304/M-3, Connaught Circus,
New Delhi - 110 001
Ph. : (011) 3324100, 3352200
Fax : (011) 3712563, 3317776

RAW MATERIALS OF AGARBATTI, PERFUMES,

M/s. Meenakshi Chemicals & Trading Co.,
113, Mangal House, 1st floor,
S.V. Road, Malad (West)
Mumbai - 400 064 Maharashtra

ROSE CRYSTAL

M/s. LA Aromatics
BG-6/25B, Paschim Vihar
New Delhi - 110 063
Contact Person : Umesh Jha

M/s. Malve Chemicals
"Shabri" Building, Kapar Road,
Ahead of Santoshi
Mata Bldg., Dombivli (W) - 421 202
Maharashtra
Ph. : (O) 452336,
Fac : 590846 Fax : 452336
C.P.: Mr.Datta Malve
Mr. Suhas Malve

M/s. S.A.V. Aromatic
BG-6/25 B, Paschim Vihar,
New Delhi - 110 063
Ph. : 5672186, 5585022
Fax : 011-5672186

ROSEMEARY OIL

M/s. Osom Extracts
Som Santi House, 152,
Patparganj Ind. Estate Delhi - 92
Ph. : 91-11-214820
2143195 2153077
Fax : 91-11-2143066,2154284
E-mail :som@ndb.vsnl.net.in

RESORCINOL DIMETHYL ETHER (SO CALLED DI-METHYL RESORCINOL)

M/s. Aroma Aromatics & Flavours
67-68-69, Industrial Area,
Baddi, Distt. Solan - 173 220 (H.P.)
Ph. : 91-1795-44431
Fax : 91-1795-44430
New Delhi Fax : 91-11-6840763
E-mail : gcipl@vsnl.com
Website : www.gogia.com

RESINOIDS

M/s. Bush Boake Allen India Ltd.,
102/103, T.V. Indl. Estate S.K.
Ahire Marg Worli
Mumbai - 400 025
Maharashtra
Ph. : (O) 4929906, 4947013
Fax : 4950577
C.P.: Mr. G.S. Rande

M/s. J.D. Savant & Co.
Goverdhandas Khimji Bldg.,1st
Floor, 35, Vithaldas Road,
S.G. Marg, Mumbai - 400 002
Ph. : (O) 2017456,
Fac : 6243558, 6207969
Fax : 6249780
C.P.: Mr. A.J.Savant
Mr. B.A. Savant

M/s. Siva Essential Oils & Chemicals
Shubh Aromatics 52, Patpar Ganj Industrial Estate
Delhi - 110 092
Ph. : 2204207, 2204195
Fax : 011-2154284
011-2456772
Telex : 031-62434 SIVA IN

M/s. Synthite Industrial Chemicals Ltd.
Ajay Vihar, M.G. Road,
Cochin - 682 016 Kerala
Ph. : (O) 355794, 360698
Fac : 04853-60316, 60285
Fax : 370405
C.P. : Mr. C.V. Jacob,
Mr. George Paul

M/s. S.H. Kelkar & Co. Ltd.
Devkaran Mansion,
36, Mangaldas Road,
Mumbai - 400 002
Ph. : (O) 2069609, 2019130
Fax : 2081204
C.P.: Mr. G.D.Kelkar, Mr. S.V. Vaze

M/s. Technagi Laboratories
53, 3rd Cross, MICO Layout
Bangalore - 560 076
Karnataka
Ph. : (O) 6636165
Fac : 646486 Fax : 6636165

M/s. Naresh Trading Co.
36, K.V. Temple Street
Bangalore - 560 053 Karnataka
Ph. : (O) 2871800
Fax : 8392986
C.P.: Mr. Naresh Khakhar, Mr. Manoj Khakhar

SAMBAC CONCRETE

M/s. Natural & Essential Oils Pvt. Ltd.
No. 224, 8th Cross, Gokulam III Stage, Mysore - 570 002
Karnataka
Ph. : (O) 512021,
Fac : 77738, 77587, Fax : 512021
C.P.: Mr. Tyagarajan, Mr. T.Gowrishankar

SAMBAC ABSOLUTE

M/s. Natural & Essential Oils Pvt. Ltd.
No. 224, 8th Cross
Gokulam III Stage
Mysore - 570 002, Karnataka
Ph. : (O) 512021,
Fac : 77738, 77587, Fax : 512021
C.P.: Mr. Tyagarajan
Mr. T.Gowrishankar

SANDALWOOD OIL

M/s. Liya Aromatics
40/396, Azad Road,
Kaloor Cochin - 682 017
Kerala
Ph. : (O) 348599, 348782,
Fax : 348782
Telex : 885-5023 LIYA IN

SPICE EXTRACTS

M/s. Universal Oleoresins
VIII/946, Navaratna House,
Jawahar Road,
Cochin - 682 002, Kerala
Ph. : (O) 223671,226673
225029, Fax : 226542
C.P. : Mr. Chetan Shah, Mr. Dipak Shah

SPEARMINT OIL

M/s. Aroma Industries
DSIDC Shed No. 111
Okhla Industrial Area
SCHEME -1, Phase - II
New Delhi - 110 020
Ph. : 6914573,6841353
Fax : (91)(11)6841353
Website:www:gogia.com
E-mail:gcipl@vsnl.com

M/s. Arihant Aromatics
Gali No. 1/3-A, C-36/2, Bhajanpura,(Behind Petrol Pump), Delhi -53
Telefax : 2183876, 2265174

M/s. Aroma Chemicals
Siddhi Sadan, Tiraha
Tubewell Colony
Moradabad - 244 001
Ph. : 414365, 418960
Fax : 424408

M/s. Dee Kay Exports
Shakuntla Bhawan, Malgodan Road,Budaun, (U.P.) - 243 601
Ph. : 05832-24331, 24922
(R) : 24883, 24507
Fax : 91-5832-25085

M/s. Evergreen Aromatics Pvt. Ltd.,
Fact. : 6-A, Industrial Estate, Roshan Bagh, Civil Lines,
Rampur - 244 901 (U.P.)
Fax : (0595) 350184, 350190
E-mail : evergreen@del5.vsnl.net.in

M/s. Indira Dinesh Chemicals
Factory : 131, HSIDC Industrial Estate, Kundli (Sonepat)
Haryana - 131 028
Ph. : (01264) 70123, 70131
Fax : 91-11-6830158
(R) : 91-11-7860411
E-mail : idchem@vsnl.com
Webpage: http://dinesh.vsnl.com/menthol

M/s. K.K. Aromatics
Shree Ram Kunj (Behind Bankey Behari Mandir)
Indira Nagar, Bareilly
(U.P.) 243122
Ph. : 91(0591) 448512, 448631
Fax : 91-(0581) 444188

M/s. LA Aromatics
BG-6/25B, Paschim Vihar
New Delhi - 110 063
Contact Person : Umesh Jha

M/s. Naini Essential Oils & Chemicals
Vill. & P.O. Khod Sharif
Tehsil : SUAR
Distt. : Rampur (U.P.) 244 924
Ph. : Maswasi (0595) 555527

M/s. Nova Menthochem
D-93, Phase VII,
Mohali Industrial Area,
Chandigarh, Haryana
Ph. : 670798

M/s. Osom Extracts
Som Santi House, 152,
Patparganj Ind. Estate
Delhi - 110 092
Ph. : 91-11-2148207,
2143195,2153077
Fax : 91-11-2143066,2154284
E-mail :som@ndb.vsnl.net.in

M/s. S.A.V. Aromatic
BG-6/25 B, Paschim Vihar
New Delhi - 110 063
Ph. : 5672186, 5585022
Fax : 011-5672186

M/s. Sandeep Chemicals
(Patiyali Sarai), Near Nai Sarai
Ki Chowki,
Budaun - 243 601 (U.P.)
Ph. : 05832-24341

SPECIALISE MENTHOL CRYSTALS

M/s. Kali Agro Chemicals Limited
F-35, Okhla Indl. Area Ph-1,
New Delhi - 110 020
Ph. : 0091-11-6819362
Fax : 0091-11-6812492

SALICYLIC ACID

M/s. Om Parkash Madan Lal (P) Ltd.
2190, Gali Hinga Beg,
Tilak Bazar, Khari Baoli
Delhi - 110 006
Ph. : 3963657, 3967276
(R) : 7074650, 7082740
E-mail : opml62.hotmail

SODIUM BENZOATE

M/s. Sabari Chemicals (P). Ltd.
A/2/236 GIDC Estate,
Nandesari, Baroda - 391340
Gujarat
Ph.(O) : 23081, 338334
Fac : 840429, 840143
Fax : 481265, 840890
C.P. : Mr. Ravi Nair
Mr. Mohan Nair

TERPENYL ACETATE

M/s. LA Aromatics
BG-6/25B, Paschim Vihar
New Delhi - 110 063
Contact Person : Umesh Jha

M/s. S.A.V. Aromatic
BG-6/25 B, Paschim Vihar
New Delhi - 110 063
Ph. : 5672186, 5585022
Fax : 011-5672186

TERPINEOL EXTRA PURE

M/s. Prabhat General Agencies
154/6, Mittal Tower, 'B' Wing,
Nariman Point, Mumbai - 400 021
Ph. : (O) 2823680
2825055, 2828182
Fax : 2842147
C.P.: Mr. V.T. Chudiwal
Mr. J.P. Singh

TERPINEOL BP.

M/s. Prabhat General Agencies
154/6, Mittal Tower, 'B' Wing,
Nariman Point, Mumbai - 400 021
Maharashtra
Ph. : (O) 2823680
2825055, 2828182
Fax : 2842147
C.P.: Mr. V.T. Chudiwal, Mr. J.P. Singh

TERPINYL ACETATE

M/s. Prabhat General Agencies
154/6, Mittal Tower, 'B' Wing,
Nariman Point, Mumbai - 400 021
Ph. : (O) 2823680
2825055, 2828182
Fax : 2842147
C.P.: Mr. V.T. Chudiwal
Mr. J.P. Singh

M/s. R.C. Aromatic & Chemicals
69, Narayan Rao Koli Marg,
(Bhansari Street,)
Koliwada, Mandvi, Near
Vadagadi, Mumbai - 400 003
Ph. : (O) 3432235,
Fac : 6247635, 6246809
C.P.: Mr. Anil R. Shah
Mr. Vikram R. Shah

TEA TREE OIL

M/s. Osom Extracts
Som Santi House, 152
Patparganj Ind. Estate
Delhi - 110 092
Ph. : 91-11-2148207
2143195,2153077
Fax : 91-11-2143066,2154284
E-mail :som@ndb.vsnl.net.in

TERPINENE OIL

M/s. Osom Extracts
Som Santi House, 152
Patparganj Ind. Estate
Delhi - 110 092
Ph. : 91-11-2148207
2143195,2153077
Fax : 91-11-2143066,2154284
E-mail :som@ndb.vsnl.net.in

TERPENES OIL

M/s. Dee Kay Exports
Shakuntla Bhawan

Malgodan Road
Budaun, (U.P.) - 243 601
Ph. : 05832-24331, 24922
(R) : 24883, 24507
Fax : 91-5832-25085

M/s. Hindustan Mint & Agro Products Pvt. Ltd.,
Barehseni Street,
Chandausi - 202 412
Ph. : 91-5921-50540, 51900
Fax : 9105921-50074
Factory Deverkhera
Moradabad Road
Chandausi - 202 412
Ph. : 91-5921-51274, 51894
E-mail : hindustn@nde.vsnl.net.in

M/s. J.S. Traders
Dr. Ramswaroop Road, (Near State Bank of India)
Chandausi - 202 412 (U.P.)
Ph. : 05921-50777

M/s. Singhal Export Corporation
Works : 6th km, Nainital Road,
Rampur- 244 901 (U.P.)
Admin.Office : 7, Kailash Colony,
Civil Lines,
Rampur - 244 901 (U.P.)
Ph. : (O) 91-595-350897, 352979
(W) : 91-595-325073, 325074
Fax : 91-595-350684
E-mail : sec@nde.vsnl.net.in

TOBACCO & GUTKHA PERFUME

M/s. LA Aromatics
BG-6/25B, Paschim Vihar
New Delhi - 110 063
Contact Person : Umesh Jha

M/s. S.A.V. Aromatic
BG-6/25 B, Paschim Vihar,
New Delhi - 110 063
Ph. : 5672186, 5585022
Fax : 011-5672186

TERPIONAL OIL

M/s. Hindustan Mint & Agro Products Pvt. Ltd.,
Barehseni Street,
Chandausi - 202 412
Ph. : 91-5921-50540, 51900
Fax : 9105921-50074
Factory Deverkhera
Moradabad Road
Chandausi - 202 412
Ph. : 91-5921-51274, 51894
E-mail : hindustn@nde.vsnl.net.in

TERPENE LESS MENTHOL

M/s. Naini Essential Oils & Chemicals
Vill. & P.O. Khod Sharif
Tehsil : SUAR
Distt. : Rampur (U.P.) 244 924
Ph. : Maswasi (0595) 555527

Chapter-7

MANUFACTURER/EXPORTERS/ SUPPLIERS OF PERFUMES

ANDHRA PRADESH

Amreli Industrial Aromatics
301, Royal Plaza, 3rd Floor
Kandaswamy Lane
4-14933/35, Sultan Bazar
Hyderabad - 500 195
Andhra Pradesh
Ph: 516880, 592323 F: 501080

Aromatic Chemical & Oil Pvt. Ltd.
D-7-8, Industrial Estate
Visakhapatnam - 530007 (A.P)
Ph: 559039 Fax: 556014

Bharat Bottle Stores
Afzal Gunj
Hyderabad - 500012 (A.P)
Ph.: 4619064, 636612

Chunial Dayaldas Batliwala
15-5-97, Afzal Gunj
Hyderabad - 500012
Ph.: 524998, 557001

Deccan Bottle Stores
Maharani Jhansi Road
Afzalgunj Hyderabad - 500012
Ph.: 500237

Deccan Chemical & Essences Mart
15-9-382/5, Maharani Jhansi Road, Afzalganj
Hyderabad - 500012 Ph.: 500970

Dubey Perfumers
19-2-422, Chandulal Baradari Colony Hyderabad - 500001
Ph.: 523350 Fax: 524083

Flora Cosmetics Pvt. Ltd.
509, Topaz Bldg. 5th Floor, Amruta Hills, Pajagutta
Hyderabad - 502482 Ph.: 314116

Hyderabad Zarda Works
22-6-183, Pathergatty
Hyderabad - 500002
Ph.: 523294, 522966

Mattupalli Sambaurthy
2/4, Brodipet Guntur - 522002 (A.P) Ph.: 235821

Mysore Y.G. Agarbathi Works
Metro Mansion Purani Haveli Road (A.P) Ph.: 522864, 521307

Purandas Ranchhoddas & Sons
No. 22-6-786, Gulzar Houz East Panjeshah, Guruvannagalli
Hyderabad - 500002
Ph.: 520343, 522203
Fax: 565009

Synat Aromatic Pvt. Ltd.
P.O. Box 793, 40-3-4
Krishna Nagar
Vijayawada - 520010 (A.P)
Ph.: 471184 Fax: 473433

BIHAR

N.H. Enterprises
82, Purani Godown Road
Gaya - 823001 Ph.: 21765

NEW DELHI

Mir Products
1436, Bazar Chitli Qabar
Jama Masjid , Delhi - 110006
Ph.: 3275061

Arihant Fragrances
17MM, Janpath
New Delhi - 110001 Ph.: 3353949

Attar House
633, Chitli Qabar Jama Masjid
Delhi - 110006 Ph.: 3286237

Bhaiji Attar Wale
853 Qutab Road , Delhi - 110006
Ph.: 3670722

Bush Perfumery Company
E-108, Shastri Nagar Delhi - 52
Ph.: 3645762

Chachaji Attar Wale
6510 Chowk Bara Hindu Rao
Delhi - 110006 Ph.: 3613470

Devi Lal Jee & Company
A-71, G.T. Karnal Road Indl. Area, Delhi - 110033
Ph.: 7233829

Dhupar Sales Organisation India Pvt. Ltd.
1202, Vikram Tower, Rajendra Place, New Delhi - 110008
Ph.: 5715710

Floral Insence India
10, Rishi App. 25/4 Sector - 9
Rohini Delhi - 110085
Ph.: 7871538

Gupta & Co. Ltd.
XIV/294-95, Gali Pan Mandi
Sadar Bazar, Delhi - 110006
Ph.: 3674742, 3528923
Fax: 3619215
E-Mail : aroma@del2.vsnl.net.in

Mumbai : 2089859
Kolkatta : 225933
Bangalore : 2877570

Mittal Aroma Essential Oils P. Ltd.
4435-36/3, First Floor
7, Ansari Road, Darya Ganj
New Delhi - 110002
Ph.: 3242341
E-Mail : rpmittal@del2.vsnl.net.in
Web : aromanoilf.com

Nishat Enterprises
8142, Chimni Mill,
Bara Hindu Rao Delhi - 110006
Ph.: 3677184

Oscar Perfumes
14/29, Shakti Nagar
Delhi - 110007
Ph.: 7214975, 7144404
E-Mail : karonac@hotmail.com

Schimmer Fragrances
2348, Tilak Bazar, Delhi - 110006
Ph.: 3978659, 5793961, 5795228 Fax: 5793961

Arcko Aromatics
1419 Raj House Ground Floor
Gali Telian, Tilak Bazar
Delhi - 110006 Ph.: 3960700

Ajit Traders
6629, Main Bazar, Khari Baoli
Delhi - 110006
Ph.: 235146, 3919242
Fax: 011-3919242

Bhaiji Attar Wale
853, Qutab Road , Delhi - 110006
Ph.: 7770722, 7519531

Dharam Pal Satyapal
7/22, Ansari Road, Darya Ganj
New Delhi - 110002
Ph.: 3271363, 3274101
Fax: 011-8522592, 3286335

Gupta & Company Ltd.
XIV/294-95, Gali Mandi Pan
Sadar Bazar, Delhi - 110006
Ph.: 7774742, 528923, 7518383
Fax: 91-11-7519215

Gogia Chemical Industries
A-127, Okhla Industrial Area
Phase - II, New Delhi - 110020
Ph.: 6836007, 6910329, 6915194
Fax: 91-11-6840763

Gulati & Company
1487, S.P. Mukherjee Marg
Delhi - 110006 Ph.: 2512986

H.B. Chemicals
100, Chowk Tilak Bazar
Khari Baoli, Delhi - 110006
Ph.: 3979071, 3913551

Harish C. Khosla & Co. Pvt. Ltd.
Zinat Mahal, Lal Kuan Bazar
Delhi - 110006
Ph.: 7524803, 733160
Fax: 011-7524403

Japan Bottle House
2124, Tilak Bazar
Khari Baoli, Delhi - 110006
Ph.: 3932100, 3935100

Jeju Chemicals
205, IInd Floor, 2280, Gali Hinga Beg, Tilak Bazar, Delhi - 110006
Ph.: 3918689, 3918591, 3919246

Kanta Chemical Company
133, Tilak Bazar, Delhi - 110006
Ph.: 3978650, 3928109, 3928110, 3928119
Fax: 91-11-3911267
E-Mail : spiceoil@del3.vsnl.net.in

M.P. Fragrances
A-13/A, Mayapuri Indl. Area
Phase-I, New Delhi - 110064

Red Club Flavours Pvt. Ltd.
Off. 70-A, Rama Road Delhi-15
Ph.:5451142, 5431556
Fax: 91-11-5104412

Rishabh & Company
G-22, Lawrence Road
New Delhi - 110035
Ph.: 7183922, 7180824
Fax: 011-545554, 5434849

R.N. Chemicals
A-30, Pocket-I, Sector-4, Rohini
Delhi - 110085
Ph.: 7275795, F: 011-8-314467

Reviera Overseas Corporation
116, Model Basti, New Delhi - 5
Ph.: 3542136, 7723013
Fax: 7534989

Seth Brothers
C-197, Naraina Area, Phase-I
Delhi - 110028
Ph.: 3918000, 3978659

Seth Bros. (Perfumers) P. Ltd.
Ph.: 5793961, 5795228
Fax: 5793961, 2940020

Ultra International Ltd.
304/M-3, Connaught Circus
New Delhi - 110001
Ph.: 3324100, 3352200
Fax: 3712563, 3317776
E-Mail : ultraintl@vsnl.com
Web : ultraintl.com

Anurag Enterprises
A/19, Gujarat Apts., Pitam Pura
Delhi - 110034 Ph.: 7016162
Fax: 7016162

S.K. Florescences
B-1711, Shastri Nagar
Delhi - 110052
Ph.: 7533560, 521337
Fax: 91-11-7522834
E-Mail : S-K-florescences@shammikapoor.com
Web: shammikapoor.com/cheetah

Ultra International Ltd.
304, AVG Bhawan
M-3, Connaught Circus
New Delhi - 110001
Ph.: 3324100, 3352200
Fax: 11-3317776, 3712563

GUJARAT

Anant Fragrances P. Ltd.
1-2, Everest Estate, Rakhial
Ahmedabad - 23
Ph.: 2741484, 6610808
Fax: 6611818

Chinu Bhai Moti Lal Saraiya
3101, Three Gate
Ahmedabad - 380001
Ph.: 5351022

Delhi Wala Hari Bhai & Co.
1st Floor, Opp. Jumma Masjid
Gandhi Road, Ahmedabad - 1
Ph.: 5356070

G. Aromas C.
M/37, New Madhupura Market
Shahi Baug Road
Ahmedabad - 4
Ph.: 5624877 Fax: 5623244

Hem Sales Corp.
Near Kavishwar's Pole
Gandhi Road
Ahmedabad - 380001
Ph.: 2110537

Natwar Lal Natha Lal & Co.
1st Floor, Hira Prabhu Complex
Bala Hanuman, Ahmedabad - 1
Ph.: 2140147

Alka Chemi-Cosmetics
1578, Lallu Raijis Vanda
Opp. Jansatta Bldg. Mirzapur
Ahmedabad - 380001
Ph.: 5505183, 5351150, 5351022

Ambica Agencies
26, Professor Colony
Opp. Memnagar
Fine Street,
Near Vijay Char Rasta
Navrangpura - 380009
Ph.: 491403

Bharti Perfumers
9, Pragati Industrial Estate
Gujarat Bottling Road
Rakhial, Ahmedabad - 380 023
Ph.: 2744691 Fax: 2744586

Chinubhai Motial Saraiya
3101, Three Gates
Ahmedabad - 380001
Ph.: 5351150, 5351022
Fax: 5505183

Dayalal Velji & Sons
Ranjit Road, Jamnagar - 361 001
Ph.: 551092, 78396

G. Aromas
2, Jyotika Park Society
Shahihbag Road
Ahmedabad - 380004
Ph.: 2112877 Fax: 2112878

Gujarat Aromatic
416, Sugandh Ghar
Jethbhai's Pole, Khadia
Ahmedabad - 380001
Ph.: 2148949 F: 7459754

J.B. Shah & Co.
Pankaj Society
Ahmedabad - 380007
Ph.: 6620072, 6620202

M.M. Khambhatwala
Akashethkuva's Pole
Ahmedabad - 380001
Ph.: 2146400, 2146500
F: 5324148, 5326918

M.L. Rathod & Co.
7/8, Galaxy Commercial Centre
1st Floor, Jawahaer Road
Post Box No. 224
Rajkot - 360001
Ph.: 55903 F: 43905

Nicon Traders
Chokshi Bazar, Mahatma Gandhi
Road, Vadodara - 390001
Ph.: 551844, 66205

Natwarlal Nathalal & Co.
9, Balahanuman-Gandhi Road
Ahmedabad - 380001
Ph.: 2140147 Fax: 2144807

P.M. Rathod & Co.
0/11, Empire Tower
Panchwati, C.G. Road
Ahmedabad - 380009
Ph.: 6420261, 466846
Fax: 6420261

P.C. Lalani & Co.
Chauta Bazar, Kelapith
Surat - 395001 Ph.: 423280

R.D. Agencies
, Raghuvir Park, Shriji Complex
Dhebar Road, Rajkot - 360001
Ph.: 22272

R.R. Gondal Wala & Co.
Tower Road
Surendranagar - 363001
Ph.: 20032, 23640

S.M. Associates
1, Bapudas Apts. Navrangpura
Ahmedabad - 380009
Ph.: 402708 Fax: 6420819

Sanjay Chemicals
3, Sanjay Society No. 2
Shahibag, Ahmedabad - 380004
Ph.: 386458, 2140147

Saraiya Brothers
3101/1, Three Gates
Ahmedabad - 380001
Ph.: 5351561

Saraiya Ramlal
Maganlal & Sons
3106, three Gates
Ahmedabad - 380001
Ph.: 5351640

Shah Agency
1574/1, Kalupur Road
Ahmedabad - 380001
Ph.: 337974, 334695

Varia Sunderji Virji & Co.
Natakshala Road
Jamnagar - 361001
Ph.: 77277, 551071
Fax: 553121

Varia Sunderji Virji
Main Road

Surenderanagar - 363001
Ph.: 21524, 31206
F: 23142, 25142

Wala & Company
13-B, Nanbha Wadi
Bhavnagar - 364001
Ph.: 0278-424628

KERALA

G.R. Associates
V/905, G.K. Avenue
Cochin - 682002 Ph.: 226081
Fax: 0484-226081

Syed Attars
Syedna Ground Floor
Masjid Lane, S.R.M. Road
Ernakulam Cochin - 682018
Ph.: 341783

T.M.V. Shenoi
Mahakavi Bharathiyar Road
Ernakulam , Kochi - 682035
Ph.: 361330, 373121
Fax: 373121

KARNATAKA

Aromatic Agencies
36, K.V. Temple Street
Bangalore - 560053
Ph.: 2870238 F: 605484

Aromatik (India)
28, (46)III Cross,
Kumarapark West
Bangalore - 560020
Ph.: 3363692, 8395799
Fax: 3697352

Benson Co.
167, Chamarajpet
Bangalore - 560018
Ph.: 605228, 6621402,
Fax: 6602697

Devson Organics
No. 38, 6th Cross
Pipeline, Chelurapalya
Vijaynagar, Magadi Road
Bangalore - 565086
Ph.: 3300076, 3350104
Fax: 3350562

Dinamit Enterprises
12, 11th A Cross II Stage
West of Chord Road
Bangalore - 565086
Ph.: 3323132, 3321799
Fax: 3326621

Florale (India) Pvt. Ltd.
1768, 15th Main 34th Cross
Banashankari II Stage
Bangalore - 560070
Ph.: 6610108, 642141
Fax: 6610474

High Tech
Flavours & Fragrances
C-133, Peenya Indl. Area
2nd Stage, Bangalore - 560058
Ph.: 8393689, 8394804
Fax: 3334802

Indian Aromatics (Bangalore)
2, KMK Building
Magadi Main Road
Bangalore - 560053

Kohinoor Aroma Enterprises
20-A, Block, Balaji Complex
125, Sultanpet
Bangalore - 560053
Ph.: 2877512, 622703

Nasir & Bros.
1101, Akbar Road
Mandi Mohalla
Mysore - 570021
Ph.: 31677, 23742 Fax: 37540

Naresh Trading Co.
36, K.V. Temple Street
Bangalore - 560053
Ph.: 2871800 Fax: 8392986

Perfumery Industries
FKCCI Building
K.G. Road, Bangalore - 560009
Ph.: 2268498

Saibaba Sugandh Bhandar
P.B. 7905, 53, Snathusapet
Bangalore - 560053
Ph.: 2879762, 2874802

Sona Rome Chemicals P. Ltd.
C-133/136, 2nd Stage
Peenya Indl. Area
Bangalore - 560058
Ph.: 080-8360595

Shilpa Aromatics
K.C. Rani Road
Post Box No. 30
Gadag - 582101 Ph.: 8658

Sathyanarayana & co.
61, Mamulpet
Bangalore - 560053
Ph.: 7870125, 2874326
Fax: 6601141

Sonarome Chemicals Pvt. Ltd.
C-136, Peenya Industrial Area
II Stage, Banagalore - 560058
Ph.: 8394804, 8395595
Fax: 3334802

Suresh Chemicals
298/2, N.S. Palya
Bannerghatta Road
Bangalore - 560076
Ph.: 6634118 Fax: 628912

Vina Fragrances
459, Ashoka Pillar Road
Jayanagar Bangalore - 560011
Ph.: 6639344, 642472
Fax: 6650338

Vinarom Ltd.
1101, Bartor Centre
M.G. Road, Bangalore - 560001
Ph.: 5091104, 5091105, 425343
Fax: 425344

MAHARASHTRA

Asian Chemicals Works (Bombay) P. Ltd.
Asian House 29 Ram Krishna Mandir Road, Andheri East
Mumbai - 400059 Ph.: 8341114

Attar Exports
3 Phd Chinoy Bldg.
45 A, Dock Yard Road
Mumbai - 10 Ph.: 3741923

Attar Mohd. Dawood & Bros.
14/17, Dev. Bank Building
Crawford Market, Palton Road
Mumbai - 1 Ph.: 2622604

Attari International
1-4, Kamal Mansion
Arthur Bandra Road, Colaba
Mumbai - 5 Ph.: 2841438

Attari Sales Corp.
3, Commercial Chambers
Yusuf Meherali Raod
Mumbai - 400003 Ph.: 3410110

Contemporary Perfumes India Ltd.
1/17, Prabha Devi Indl. Estate
Mumbai - 25 Ph.: 4314806

D.G. Gore Fragrances
31, Mangal Das Road
Mumbai - 2 Ph.: 2080909

Firmenich Aromatic India Ltd.
Sterling House, 5/7, Sohrab Ji Santok Lane, Off Kawasjee Marg, Dhobi Talao
Mumbai - 400002 Ph.: 2073300

Hemani Aromatics
Minerva Estate, Bunder Road
Sewri East, Mumbai - 400015
Ph.: 4124605

Khanna Aromatics
54, Mangal Das Building No. 1
3rd Floor, Pricess Street
Mumbai - 2 Ph.: 8211931

A.R. Attarwala
Jumma Masjid, 325, Sheikh Memon Street , Mumbai - 2
Ph.: 022-3429923

A.S. Attarwala & Sons
160 A, Rehman Street
Mumbai - 3 Ph.: 022-3423974

Aco Impex
82/84, Clare Road, Mumbai - 8
Ph.: 022-3085321

Annex
1-B/10, Sonal App.,
Jai Praksh Road No.2
Goregaon East, Mumbai - 63
Ph.: 022-8737444

Aromatic Products & Chemicals Pvt. Ltd.
42, Prospect Chambers Annexe
Dr. D.N. Road Fort
Mumbai - 400001
Ph.: 2047991, 2824773
Fax: 2873811

Bush Boake Allen India Ltd.
102/103, T.V. Indl. Estate
S.K. Ahire Marg, Worli
Mumbai - 400025
Ph.: 4929906, 4947013
Fax: 4950577

Cosmair Fragrances Pvt. Ltd.
101, Centre Point, Jijibhai Lane
Lalbaug, Mumbai - 400012
Ph.: 4114991, 4123214, 4124208
Fax: 4148226

D.D. Shah Fragrances Pvt. Ltd.
Cambata Building , 5th Floor, North/East Wing, 42M, Karve Marg, Mumbai - 400020
Ph.: 22288, 223019,2850577
Fax: 91-22-2850581

Hitesh Chemical Works
Shankar Niwas, Maskasath
Nagpur - 440002
Ph.: 43610, 43620 Fax: 43487

Himanshu Aromatics
Mahalami Indl. Estate
Unit No. 11, 2nd Floor
Gandhi Nagar, Lower Parel
Mumbai - 400013
Ph.: 4937877, 4927105

Hindustan Aromatics
166, Ebrahim Rehmatullah Road
Mumbai - 400003
Ph.: 3762194, 2018005
Fax: 3738075

Industrial Aromatics
2/32, Verma Nagar
Old Nagardas Road
Mumbai - 400069
Ph.: 8349352, 8720138

Industrial Perfumes Ltd.
Hay Bunder Road, Tank Road
P.O. Mumbai - 400033
Ph.: 3711001, 3711003, 3711004 Fax: 3739313

Interchemie
243/3-B, Mangaldas Bldg.
Mangaldas Road
Mumbai - 400002
Ph.: 2017409, 2053823, 2064673 Fax: 2064688

IVY Fragrances
Unit No. 108 Creatice Indl. Estate, N.M. Joshi Marg
Mumbai - 4000113 Ph.: 3088302

J.D. Savant & Co.
Goverdhandas Khimji Bldg.
1st Floor, 35, Vithaldas Road
S.G. Marg, Mumbai - 400002
Ph.: 2017456, 6243558, 6207969 Fax: 6249780

K.H. Dhamdhrer
45/47, Shamaldas Gandhi Marg
Mumbai - 400002 Ph.: 2081683

K.K. Enterprises
16-A, Mulchand Mansion
1st Floor, S.G. Marg
Mumbai - 400002
Ph.: 2058495, 4455466
Fax: 4226527

Kanta Flavouring Industries
A-15 & A-16, Royal Indl. Estate
5-B, Naigaum Cross Road
Wadala (West)
Mumbai - 400031
Ph.: 4123165, 4124347, 4126784, 4136154

Keva Fragrances Ltd.
Devkaran Mansion, 36
Mangaldas Road
Mumbai - 400002
Ph.: 2069609, 2019198, 5645274, 5645274
Fax: 5645271, 2081204

Khanna Aromatics
Sharaf Mansion, 2nd Floor
32, Princess Street
Mumbai - 400002
Ph.: 2012853, 8211961

Lana Floressens Pvt. Ltd.
13, Swastik Indl. Estate
178, C.S.T. Road, Kalina
Mumbai - 400098
Ph.: 6122928, 6127440

Laveesha Enterprises
216/217, Anjani Complex
2nd Floor, Pereira Hill Road
Andheri Kurla Road
Mumbai - 400099 Ph.: 8216159
Fax: 8216261

M. Rawji Brothers
Gulai House, 4th Floor
111/115, Kazi Syed Street
Mumbai - 400003
Ph.: 3429598, 3445455, 3448769
Fax: 3419694

Maneklal & Bros.
61/A, Devkaran Mansion, S.G. Marg, Princess Street
Mumbai - 400002 Ph.: 2011671

Mangal Perfumes
304, Prabhadevi
Unique Indl. Estate
Bombay Dying Compound
V.S. Marg, Prabhadevi
Mumbai - 400025, Ph.: 4303680

Megha Enterprises
197/1, Sion (West)
Post Box No. 6754
Mumbai - 400022
Ph.: 375950 Fax: 3737064

Mohan Aromatic Pvt. Ltd.
349/53, Samuel Street
Indu Chamber, 4th Floor
Mumbai - 400003
Ph.: 3441981, 3442875
Fax: 91-22-3441981

Mohini Perfumers Pvt. Ltd.
13, Krishnakunj, 144/145, M.G. Road, Ghatkopar
Mumbai - 400077
Ph.: 5133092, 7685454
Fax: 5160729

Mukesh Industries
7, Anjiwadi, 2nd Floor
Charnpsi Bhimji Road
Mazgaon, Mumbai - 400010
Ph.: 3750896, 3739557
Fax: 5160729

Multiflor
72, Mangaldas Road
Dwarkadas Building
Lohar Chawl, Mumbai - 400002
Ph.: 2080666 Fax: 6400128

Mysore & S. Agarbathi Works
6, Arab Lane, Mumbai - 400008
Ph.: 3082444

M.M. Nabikhan & Co.
135, Bhandara Road
Ganja Khet, Nagpur - 440002
Ph.: 44460

N. Chimanlal & Company
Post Box No. 2574
160, Princess Street
Chikhal House, Mumbai - 400002
Ph.: 2012010, 2019890
Fax: 2012010

Nagpur Chemicals
W-36, M.I.D.C. Indl. Area
Hingna Road, Nagpur - 440016
Ph.: 37627

New India Aromatics Co.
Mukund Madhav Udyog Nagar
Unit No. 2, Plot No. 142
Village Navghar Vasai (E)
Thane - 400601 Ph.: 326280

New Barouliya Aromatics Co.
14 Dhanlaxmi Chambers, II Floor
Thane - 400601
Ph.: 5332280, 5331208, 5429076
Fax: 5331208

National Essence Supply Co.
12, Shalimar, Gulmohar Cross
Lane, 10 Juhu Scheme, Juhu
Mumbai - 400049
Ph.: 6206831

Nemat Enterprises
Devkaran Mansion, 2nd Floor
43 Princess Street
Mumbai 400002
Ph.: 20119816, 2068917
Fax: 2085977

Odhawji Lawji & Co.
Gold Mohar Building
1st Floor, R.No. 4
174 Shamaldas Gandhi Marg
Mumbai - 400002 Ph.: 2050273

Oriental Aromatics Pvt. Ltd.
Sion Trombay Road , Govandi
Mumbai - 400088
Ph.: 5563613, 5559837
Fax: 5560708

P.M. Ratho & Co. Pvt. Ltd.
Chikhal House , 1st Floor
453 Kalbadevi Road
Mumbai - 400002
Ph.: 2010103
2089160, 5611688
Fax: 5670598

Perfume Centre
94-C, Mohamedial Road
Mumbai - 400003
Ph.: 7682323, 7681322
Fax: 7672537

Praful J. Parekh
45, Mangaldas Bldg. No. 1
Above Grindlays Bank
Mumbai - 400002
Ph.: 2088051, 2088057

Pranav Perfumes
61/A, Devkaran Mansion
Princess Street
Mumbai - 400002 Ph.: 2011671

Pravinkumar Hiralal
35, Kazi Sayed Street
Mumbai - 3450620, 3438431
Fax: 3737064

Quest International India
Plot No. 6, Saki Vihar Road
Sakinaka, Mumbai - 400067
Ph.: 5782305, 5782306, 5782308, 5782307
Fax: 5787787

R.D. Corporation
42/44, Bapu Genu Road
2nd Floor , Room No. 5, Princess Road
Mumbai - 400002
Ph.: 2061122, 2068961, 2068961 Fax: 2068961

R.K. Shapurji & Co.
Prospect Chambers
4th Floor, R.No. 8
319, Dr. D. Naoroji Road
Mumbai - 400001
Ph.: 2047408 Fax: 3865951

Radhakishan Rajaram & Co.
141, Shamaldas Gandhi Marg
Mumbai - 400002
Ph.: 2081094, 4936450
Fax: 2081094

Rajasthani Trading Co.
349, Samuel Street, Vadgadi
Mumbai - 400003
Ph.: 3441981, 3411807, 3442875
Fax: 3411806

Ram & Company
73, Princess Street,
Devakaran, Mansion
Mumbai - 400002 Ph.: 2069996

Rayon Industries
21, Navyug Mansion
N. Bharucha Marg
Near Grant Road, Station (W)
Mumbai - 400007, Ph.: 3878801

Remlin Laboratories
39, Nand Bhavan
59, Bapu Genu Road
Mumbai - 400002
Ph.: 2069885, 7670551
Fax: 2051593

Vaishali Aromatics India Pvt. Ltd.
30 M.I.D.C Chikal Thane
Aurangabad - 431001
Ph.: 484193, 484120
Fax: 0240-482078

MADHYA PRADESH

Arochem Industries
454, Ram Bagh Ratlam - 457001
Ph.: 31026

Opal Aromatics
35-A/4, Industrial Estate
Indore - 45006 Ph.: 410177

PUNJAB

Fab Flavours & Fragrances Pvt. Ltd.
B-16. Phase II, Indl. Area
S.A.S. Nagar , Mohali - 160055
Ph.: 5451142, 5431556
Fax: 3913599

RAJASTHAN

Parnami Perfumery Works
Adarsh Nagar , Jaipur - 302004
Ph.: 620131, 48633, 605751

Parasmani Products
1st B Road, Sardarpura
Jodhpur - 342001
Ph.: 34283, 37378
Fax: 0291-34896

TAMIL NADU

Bush Boake Allen (India) Ltd.
Seven Wells Street
St. Thomas Mount
Chennai - 600016
Ph.: 2341131, 2341132,2341133
Fax: 2346017, 2346158

Chemifuture
No. 2, 4th Cross, 6th Street
Surendranagar, Adambakkam
Chennai - 600088 Ph.: 2346099

Dragoco India Ltd.
144, 1st Street, Seevaram Village, Perungudi
Chennai - 600096
Ph.: 4926172, 4926539
Fax: 4925773

Gogia Chemicals Industries
133, Walltax Road
Chennai - 600003
Ph.: 5626253 Fax: 567735

Hawarden Traders
50 South Masi Street
Post Box No. 170
Madurai - 625001
Ph.: 24002, 25764

Madras Aromatic Co.
48, Ellis Road, Post Box No. 374
Mount Road, Chennai - 600002
Ph.: 840556 Fax: 833770

Maschmeijer Aromatics Ltd.
P.B. No. 3, G.S.T. Road
Chromepet, Chennai - 600044
Ph.: 2368788
2368789, 2368790
Fax: 2366808, 2341375
E-Mail : maschmeijer@pobox.com

Shri Rathod Trading Company
532, Mount Road
Chennai - 600018 Ph.: 4349757

Sunrise Chemical Industries
66, Bazullah Road, T. Nagar
Chennai - 600017
Ph.: 8252516, 8282219
Fax: 8286971

The National Trading Co.
57, Velachery Road
P.B. No. 2622
Chennai - 600032
Ph.: 2352317, 2350771
Fax: 2352317

W. Southern Aromatics Pvt. Ltd.
7, Venkatachala Mudali Street
Chennai - 600003 Ph.: 581841

UTTER PRADESH

Fakirchand & Sons
Lohar Gali, Agra - 282003
Ph.: 405186

Progressive Enterprises
Shastri Nagar
Dtt. Udham Singh Nagar
Bazpur - 262401
Ph.: 88359, 88465, 88135

AFF Aromatics Pvt. Ltd.
A-83, Sector-IV, Noida - 201301
Distt. Ghaziabad
Ph.: 543161, 543162, 543163
Fax: 91-11-91-543164

Sachee Fragrances & Chemicals
D-11 & 12, Sector-2
Noida, Ghaziabad
Ph.: 36111, 36222, 20134

Glorious Perfumes Centre
608, 609, 6th Floor "City Centre"
63/2, The Mall, Kanpur-208001
Ph.: 354528, 313483, 317343
Fax: 91-512-312977

Hafiz-Ji-Ki Mashoor Qadimi Dookan
33/220, Moolganj
Kanpur - 208001
Ph.: 261169, 248935

Kanpur Sandalwood Oil Distillery P. Ltd.
D/54/27, Naya Ganj
Kanpur - 208014
Ph.: 310362, 363483, 363585
Fax: 0512-363483, 368204

Moolchand Nanakchand
W/9, MIG, Juhu Gaushala, P.O.
Kanpur - 208014
Ph.: 271973, 277010

National Aromatics
98-Y-I Block, Kidwai Nagar
Kanpur - 208001 Ph.: 276829

Rakesh Sandal Industries
7/117-A, Swaroop Nagar
Kanpur - 208002
Ph.: 214071, 210236, 294793
Fax: 294675, 214993

Hargovind Dass & Sons
Deedarganj Kannauj - 209725
Ph.: 34317, 34614
Fax: 05694-34114, 34617

Indian Fragrances & Chemicals Works
G.T. Road, P.O. Makarand Nagar
Kannauj - 209725 Ph.: 34716
Fax: 05694-34286

Jagat Aroma Oils Distillery
Main Road, Kannauj - 209725
Ph.: 34401 Fax: 34335

Kumud Products
Bara Bazar, Kannauj - 209725
Ph.: 34294 Fax: 05694-34894

Lala Praggdutt & Co.
Perfumers, Makrandnagar
Kannauj - 209726
Ph.: 34209, 34459
Fax: 05694-34234

Munna Lal Sons & Co.
Hina Bidg. Kannauj - 209725
Ph.: 34242, 34542
Fax: 05694-34599

Pragati Aroma Oil Distillers Pvt. Ltd.
Deedarganj, Chhipatti
Kannauj - 209725
Ph.: 34317, 34614
Fax: 35694-34114

Prayag Dutt Sunder Lal
Perfumers, Kannauj - 209726
Ph.:34258

Pt. Chandrabali & Sons
Kannauj - 209725 Ph.: 34257
Fax: 05694-34157

R. Misra & Sons
(H.O.) : 1/62, Shiva Villa
Deedarganj, Kannauj - 209725
Ph.: 34536, 34652

Perfumers (India) Pvt. Ltd.
4, Nanpara House
P.O. Box No. 87, B.N. Road
Lucknow - 226001
Ph.: 224244, 248804
Fax: 218090

Perfumers & Essential Oils Co.
47-48, New Market
P.O. Box No. 165, Kesarbagh
Lucknow - 226001
Ph.: 272309, 242040, 371361
Fax: 234927

Satyanarain Sundarshan Lal & Co.
11, Khun Kuhnji Road, Chowk
Lucknow - 226003 Ph.: 269176

Shaivi Industries
Post Box No. 50 42/2, Saket
Palli, Lucknow - 226001
Ph.: 225694, 213847
Fax: 213847

Suman Industries
46, Diamond Dairy
Kabir Marg, Lucknow - 226001
Ph.: 34573, 34179

Fragrance Lab
Chowk Bazar, Mathura - 281001
Ph.: 405186

Mehrotra Brothers Perfumers
K-61/57, Bula Nala
Varanasi - 221001
Ph.: 333280, 335918, 335917,
358244

Mehrotra Brothers Perfumers
Semra, Ram Nagar
Varanasi - 221001 Ph.: 333163

WEST BENGAL

AFF Aromatics Pvt. Ltd.
17, Ezra Street
Kolkatta - 700001
Ph.: 2250234 Fax: 033-2259832

B. Kamar & Co.
1, Sun Yat Sen Street
Kolkatta - 700012 Ph.: 270643

Basha Perfumery House
8, Ezra Street Kokatta - 700001
Ph.: 2254347

Keshavlal Khanderia & Co.
167, Old China Bazar Street
Kolkatta - 700001 Ph.: 2422334

Lakshmi Bottle Stores
17, Ezra Street,
Post Box No. 450
Kolkatta - 700001
Ph.: 253703, 259903

Latin Flavour Synthesis Co.
161/1, Mahatma Gandhi Road
2nd Floor, Bangur Building
Kolkatta - 700007, Ph.: 2382243

Makhu Lal Ayodhya Prasad Grand Sons
4B, Madan Mohan, Burman Street, Kolkatta - 700007
Ph.: 2393340, 2390447

Mansukh Lal Brothers
1, Bonfield Lane, 1st, Floor
Kolkatta - 700001
Ph.: 2428091, 2426315, 255636, 256256
Fax: 2423617

Keshavlal Khanderia & Co.
167, Old Bazar Street
Kolkatta - 700001 Ph.: 2422334

Lakshmi Bottle Stores
17, Ezra Street
Post Box No. 450
Kolkatta - 700001
Ph.: 253703, 259903

Latin Flavour Synthesis Co.
161/1, Mahatma Gandhi Road
2nd Floor Bagur Building
Kolkatta - 700007 Ph.: 2382243

Makhu Lal Ayodhya Prasad Grand Sons
4B, Madan Mohan, Burman Street, Kolkatta - 700007
Ph.: 2393340, 2390447

Mansukh Lal & Brothers
1, Bonfield Lane, 1st Floor
Kolkatta - 700001
Ph.: 2428091, 2426315, 255636, 256256
Fax: 2423617

Mukti Agencies Pvt. Ltd.
23 A, Netaji Subhash Road
11th Floor , Kolkatta - 700001
Ph.: 2208595

National Perfumery House
44, Ezra Street
Post Box No. 328
Kolkatta - 700001
Ph.: 258144, 255547, 256426
Fax: 250617

Neshat Perfumery House
212, Parsee Church Street
Kolkatta - 254859, 277985

O.T. Kader Basha Sahib
17, Ezra Street
Kolkatta - 700001 Ph.: 257970
Fax: 2254402

Praj Enterprises
10, Ezra Street
Kolkatta - 700001
Ph.: 2479541, 2471759
Fax: 2479738, 2407173

Quality Perfumery Centre
5/5, Elive Row , 5th Floor
Kolkatta - 700001
Ph.: 2209057 Fax: 2429834

Raj Aromatics
14/2, Old China Bazar Street
3rd Floor. Room No. 193
Kolkatta - 700001
Ph.: 2423606, 2422564
Fax: 2421615

Reprocess
103 B, Dhan Devi Khanna Road
Kolkatta - 700054
Ph.: 346314, 347278

S.D. Bose
63, Radha Bazar Street
Kolkatta - 700001
Ph.: 2422110, 2422186
Fax: 742987

Seth Brothers (Perfumers) Pvt. Ltd.
11, Rabindra Sarani, 1st Floor
Kolkatta - 700073
Ph.: 2250792

Soni Aromatics
70, Canning Street
Kolkatta - 700001
Ph.: 258580, 258931

Swastik Industries
32, Ezra Street, 3rd Floor
Room No. 321
Kolkatta - 700001
Ph.: 250306, 250207
Fax: 250207

Tulsi Fragrances
17, Ezra Street G.P.O. Box 2491
Kolkatta - 700001
Ph.: 252939, 253098
Fax: 409899

Madanlal Burnwal
Munshi Bazar, P.O. Asansol
Burdwan - 700013
Ph.: 203455

Grovers & Co.
13 Roydstreet, 2nd Floor
Kolkatta - 700016 Ph.: 2291176

Chapter 8

PROJECT PROFILES

PLANT ECONOMICS OF NON-ALCOHOLIC FLAVOURS

Rated Plant Capacity = 100.00 Kgs./Day

LAND & BUILDING

Total Land Area Required 200 Sq.Mt. = 1,40,000.00

PLANT & MACHINERY

1. Mixing Machine with stirrer
2. Storage tanks
3. Various containers for handling chemicals
4. Weighing scale 1-small & 1-large
5. Pouch filling machines
6. Other accessories, motors, pumps etc.

FIXED CAPITAL

1.	Land & Building	Rs.	1,40,000.00
2.	Plant & Machinery	Rs.	5,30,000.00
3.	Other Fixed Assets	Rs.	1,70,000.00
	Total	Rs.	8,40,000.00

RAW MATERIALS

1. Various essence and concentrator
2. Modifers

3. Solvent Glycerine

TOTAL WORKING CAPITAL/MONTH

1.	Raw Material	Rs.	9,50,000.00
2.	Salary & Wages	Rs.	34,800.00
3.	Utilities & Overheads	Rs.	14,800.00
	Total	Rs.	9,99,600.00

TOTAL CAPITAL INVESTMENT

Total Fixed Capital	Rs.	8,40,000.00
Total Working Capital For 3 Months	Rs.	29,98,800.00
Total	Rs.	38,38,800.00

TURN OVER/ANNUM

By Sale of By sale of 100 x 300 kgs. of various flavour	Rs.	1,50,00,000.00

PROFIT SALES RATIO = Profit / Sales x 100 = 14.48%

RATE OF RETURN = Operating profit / T.C.I x 100 = 56.59%

BREAK EVEN POINT (B.E.P) = 33.01%

PLANT ECONOMICS OF SCENT AND PERFUMES

Rated Plant Capacity = 10.00 Kgs./Day

LAND & BUILDING

Total Land Area Required 1000 Sq.Mt.= 9,30,000.00

PLANT & MACHINERY

1. Feeding Hopper with Bucket elevator
2. Rotary Extractor to extract flower oil,
3. S.S. Jacketed evaporation tank with vacuum system
4. Condenser
5. Vacuum still (SS) for final Concentration
6. Solvent Storage tank (SS)
7. Baby Boiler
8. Pipes, fittings, vacuum pumps, valves, motor and other miscellaneous
9. Solvent Recycling Unit.
10. Laboratory testing Equipments & Instruments

FIXED CAPITAL

1.	Land & Building	Rs.	9,30,000.00
2.	Plant & Machinery	Rs.	6,50,000.00
3.	Other Fixed Assets	Rs.	1,35,000.00
	Total	Rs.	17,15,000.00

RAW MATERIALS

1. Flower Fresh (Jasmine, Lily)
2. Solvent Petroleum ether
3. Glass bottles & Lables.
4. Carton made of Cardboard

TOTAL WORKING CAPITAL/MONTH

1.	Raw Material	Rs.	13,03,250.00
2.	Salary & Wages	Rs.	63,780.00
3.	Utilities & Overheads	Rs.	48,700.00
	Total	Rs.	14,15,730.00

TOTAL CAPITAL INVESTMENT

Total Fixed Capital	Rs.	17,15,000.00
Total Working Capital For 3 Months	Rs.	42,47,190.00
Total	Rs.	59,62,190.00

TURN OVER/ANNUM

By Sale of 3000 Kg. Flower Oil Rs. 2,40,00,000.00

PROFIT SALES RATIO = Profit / Sales x 100 = 24.21%

RATE OF RETURN = Operating Profit / T.C.I x 100 = 97.47%

BREAK EVEN POINT (B.E.P) = 23.04%

PLANT ECONOMICS OF AGARBATTI SYNTHETIC PERUMERY COMPOUND

Rated Plant Capacity = 100.00 Kgs./Day

LAND & BUILDING

Total Land Area Required 500 Sq.Mt. = 5,20,000.00

PLANT & MACHINERY

1. Grinder electrically operated, medium size 100-200 kg.capacity/hr.
2. Mixer fitted with agitator (S.S)
3. Weighing Machines with varying capacities
4. Storage Vessels for liquid ingradients
5. Storage Vessels for solid ingredients
6. Packing Unit Semi Automatic
7. Miscellaneous equipments includes pipe and fittings

FIXED CAPITAL

1.	Land & Building	Rs.	5,20,000.00
2.	Plant & Machinery	Rs.	2,48,000.00
3.	Other Fixed Assets	Rs.	1,70,000.00
	Total	Rs.	9,38,000.00

RAW MATERIALS

1. All the raw materials as per the formulations (4 & 5) including citonellol, phenol ethyl alcohol,
2. Miscellaneous Chemicals
3. Packing Materials includes Bottle of various capacity

TOTAL WORKING CAPITAL/MONTH

1.	Raw Material	Rs.	4,25,000.00
2.	Salary & Wages	Rs.	29,520.00
3.	Utilities & Overheads	Rs.	40,400.00
	Total	Rs.	4,94,920.00

TOTAL CAPITAL INVESTMENT

Total Fixed Capital	Rs.	9,38,000.00
Total Working Capital For 3 Months	Rs.	14,84,760.00
Total	Rs.	24,22,760.00

TURN OVER/ANNUM

By Sale of 5000 kg of synthetic otto rose perfume 15000 kg of synthetic red rose perfume	Rs. 79,50,000.00

PROFIT SALES RATIO = Profit / Sales x 100 = 19.07%

RATE OF RETURN = Operating profit / T.C.I x 100 = 62.57%

BREAK EVEN POINT (B.E.P) = 35.40%

PLANT ECONOMICS OF FRUIT FLAVOURS (WHISKEY,VODKA,GRAPE,BUTTER,SCOTCH & RUM)

Rated Plant Capacity = 500.00 Kgs./Day

LAND & BUILDING

Total Land Area Required 600 Sq.Mt. = 9,70,000.00

PLANT & MACHINERY

1. Stainless steel mixer with 1/2 HP motor and stainless steel stirrer
2. Stainless steel vessel with stirrer 1/2 HP motor
3. Packing M/C (Filling & Sealing Machine)
4. Lab. Testing Equipments Viz.Beakers Flasks.

FIXED CAPITAL

1.	Land & Building	Rs.	9,70,000.00
2.	Plant & Machinery	Rs.	4,10,000.00
3.	Other Fixed Assets	Rs.	1,45,000.00
	Total	Rs.	15,25,000.00

RAW MATERIALS

1. **FOR RUM FLAVOUR :** Oil of Birch tar (rectified)
2. Amyl butyrate
3. Amyl Acetate
4. Amyl Vanillin
5. Oil of Cloves
6. Balsam of pern
7. Ethyl butyrate
8. Styrax
9. Amyl formate

10. Ethyl Oenanthate
11. Ethyl Acetate
12. Ethyl formate
13. Ethyl propionate
14. **FOR WHISKEY FLAVOUR :** Ethyl Acetate
15. Ethyl Nitrate
16. Caraway oil
17. Anise oil
18. Juniper oil
19. Worm wood oil
20. Ginger oil
21. Conander oil
22. Calamus oil
23. Bitter Almond oil
24. Ethyl Alcohol
25. **FOR GRAPE FLAVOUR :** Green Cognac oil
26. Methyl Anthranilate
27. Ethyl Cinnamate
28. Propyl Cinnamate
29. Ethyl butyrate
30. Ethyl Alcohol
31. **FOR BUTTER SCOTCH FLAVOUR :** Ethyl oenanthate
32. Ethyl pelarganate
33. Butyl butyrate
34. Amyl acetate
35. Ethyl butyrate
36. Butyric acid
37. Orange Oil
38. Ethyl Alcohol

TOTAL WORKING CAPITAL/MONTH

1.	Raw Material	Rs.	17,79,901.38
2.	Salary & Wages	Rs.	56,625.00
3.	Utilities & Overheads	Rs.	41,500.00
	Total	Rs.	18,78,026.38

TOTAL CAPITAL INVESTMENT

Total Fixed Capital	Rs.	15,25,000.00
Total Working Capital For 3 Months	Rs.	56,34,079.14
Total	Rs.	71,59,079.14

TURN OVER/ANNUM

By Sale of Rum Flavour 30,000 kgs.
By Sale of Whiskey Flavour 30,000 Kgs.
By sale of Vodka Flavour 30,000 kgs.
By sale of Grape Flavour 30,000 kgs.
By sale of Butter Scotch
Flavour 30,000 kgs. Rs. 2,91,00,000.00

PROFIT SALES RATIO = Profit / Sales x 100 = 17.56%

RATE OF RETURN = Operating profit / T.C.I x 100 = 71.37%

BREAK EVEN POINT (B.E.P) = 27.37%

PLANT ECONOMICS OF ESSENCES FOR BISCUIT CONFECTIONERY

Rated Plant Capacity = 80.00 Kgs./Day

LAND & BUILDING

Total Land Area Required 400 sq.mt. = 8,07,500.00

PLANT & MACHINERY

1. Mixer with stirrer
2. Storage tanks
3. Various containers for handling chemicals
4. Weighing scale 1-small & 1-large
5. Bottle filling machines
6. Lab. Equipments
7. Instrumentation and process control equipments.
8. Miscellaneous accessories, motors, pumps, valves etc.

FIXED CAPITAL

1.	Land & Building	Rs.	8,07,500.00
2.	Plant & Machinery	Rs.	8,80,000.00
3.	Other Fixed Assets	Rs.	2,45,000.00
	Total	Rs.	19,32,500.00

RAW MATERIALS

1. **PINE APPLE ESSENCE :** Amyl Butyrate
2. Ethyl Butyrate
3. Acetaldehyde
4. Chloroform
5. Vanillin

6. Diethyl Glycerine
7. **ORANGE ESSENCES :** Orange Oil
8. Acetaldehyde
9. Ethyl Formate
10. Ethyl Acetate
11. Ethyl Butyrate
12. Ethyl Benzoate
13. Methyl Salicylate
14. Amyl Acetate
15. Tartaric acid
16. Diethyl Glycerine
17. **VANILLA FLAVOUR :** Vanilla/Vanillin
18. Coumarin
19. Monoethyl Glycerol
20. Carmel
21. **CHOCOLATE FLAVOUR :** Vanillin
22. Aldehyde C-18,
23. Amyl Phenyl Acetal
24. Vevatraldehyde
25. n-Butyl Phenyl Ethyl Acetal
26. Propylene Glycol
27. Cocoa Flavouring extruct
28. Cardamom oil
29. Paraffin oil (Food Grade)
30. Glycerine
31. Propylene Glycol
32. **COCONUT ESSENCE :** Gamma Nonyl acetone
33. Monoethyl Ether
34. **RASBERRY FLAVOUR :** Monoethyl Ether
35. Orris Concrete
36. Benzyl Acetate
37. Vanillin
38. Rhodinol
39. Ionone
40. Amyl Butyrate
41. Ethyl Palargonate

42. Ethyl Benzoate
43. Amyl Acetate
44. Rasberry Juice
45. **CHERRY FLAVOUR :** Engenol
46. Cognac oil
47. Cinnamic Aldehyde
48. Benzoic Aldehyde
49. Coumarin
50. Ethyl Caprylate
51. Amyl Acetae
52. Ethyl Acetate
53. Bourbonol
54. Caramel Colour
55. Black Current Ester
56. Rose Essence
57. Sweet Orange Essence
58. Lemon Essence
59. Iris Essence
60. Packing material Glass bottles for packing of 2000 kgs of all essences in 40,000 Nos. Bottles (50 gm each)

TOTAL WORKING CAPITAL/MONTH

1.	Raw Material	Rs.	7,57,232.33
2.	Salary & Wages	Rs.	1,09,375.00
3.	Utilities & Overheads	Rs.	60,000.00
	Total	Rs.	9,26,607.33

TOTAL CAPITAL INVESTMENT

Total Fixed Capital	Rs.	19,32,500.00
Total Working Capital For 3 Months	Rs.	27,79,821.99
Total	Rs.	47,12,321.99

TURN OVER/ANNUM

By sale of 4,80,000 Nos. Bottles
(50 gm each), Rs. 1,44,00,000.00

PROFIT SALES RATIO = Profit / Sales x 100 = 14.98%

RATE OF RETURN = Operating profit / T.C.I x 100 = 45.79%

BREAK EVEN POINT (B.E.P) = 47.29%

PLANT ECONOMICS OF SPRAY SCENT (PERFUME)

Rated Plant Capacity = 2400.00 BTL/day

LAND & BUILDING

Total Land Area Required 250 Sq.Mt. = 3,52,500.00

PLANT & MACHINERY

1. Different Storage tank made by mild steel of capacity 100 litres each with eight glass and close
2. Mixing vessel arrangments with storrer, Jacketed vessel, bottom become conical, vessel volume 1000
3. Refrigeration unit
4. Distillation Unit
5. Liquid filling M/c
6. Labelling M/c
7. Heater Unit
8. Miscellaneous

FIXED CAPITAL

1.	Land & Building	Rs.	3,52,500.00
2.	Plant & Machinery	Rs.	2,50,000.00
3.	Other Fixed Assets	Rs.	1,70,000.00
	Total	Rs.	7,72,500.00

RAW MATERIALS

1. Essence compounds
2. Ethyl Alcohol

TOTAL WORKING CAPITAL/MONTH

1.	Raw Material	Rs.	5,70,000.00
2.	Salary & Wages	Rs.	15,600.00
3.	Utilities & Overheads	Rs.	76,300.00
	Total	Rs.	6,61,900.00

TOTAL CAPITAL INVESTMENT

Total Fixed Capital	Rs.	7,72,500.00
Total Working Capital For 3 Months	Rs.	19,85,700.00
Total	Rs.	27,58,200.00

TURN OVER/ANNUM

By Sale of 25 ml capacity bottles 360000 Nos.
By Sale of 50ml capacity bottles 240000 Nos.
By Sale of 100 ml capacity bottles 120000 Nos. Rs. 1,04,40,000.00

PROFIT SALES RATIO = Profit / Sales x 100 = 17.32%

RATE OF RETURN = Operating profit / T.C.I x 100 = 65.55%

BREAK EVEN POINT (B.E.P) = 38.46%

ALL FOLLOWING PROJECT REPORTS ARE READILY AVAILABLE

PAINT, ENAMEL, SOLVENTS, THINNERS, INKS & VARNISH
PAINT, ENAMEL, SOLVENTS, THINNERS, INKS & VARNISH

- Acrylic Emulsion Paints
- Acrylic Cement Paint (Dry Powder)
- Aluminium Paint
- Automobile Paints
- Ball Point Pen Refill Ink
- Bituminious Road Emulsion
- Bitumen
- Bituminious Felts For Water & Damp Proofing
- Bituminious Road Emulsion Rapid Medium & Slow Setting
- Buffing & Polishing
- Cement Paint For White & Grey Cement
- Dispersant
- Dry Distemper
- Dry Distemper & Cement Paint
- Duplicating Ink Black For Gestner Duplicator
- Emulsion Paints (Water Based)
- Hammertone Paint
- Insulating Varnish & Wire Enamel
- Iron Oxide Pigments
- Insulating Varnish (Poly Vinyl Butyral Based, Ffc Grade)
- Lime Colour (Cement Colour)
- Synthetic Red Oxide For Floorings
- Solvent & Thinners
- Marking Inks (Water Proof)
- Metal Naphthanate (As Drier For Paints)
- N.C.Putty
- Offset Printing Ink
- Oil Bound Distemper Paint
- Paint Brushes
- Paint Manufacture For Rolling Coating Of Aluminium And Steel Coil
- Paint Removers
- Paint Industry
- Paint & Varnish
- Picture Varnish
- Powder Coating Paint
- Printing Inks (Offset,Flexo & Roto Gravure)

- Primer Paint & Enamel Paint
- Putty & Water Proofing Paint
- Printing Inks (Flexo-Graphic Ink)
- Putty (Metal Casement)
- Red Oxide Primer (Anti Corrosive)
- Refractory Paint (Graphite Based)
- Screen Printing Inks
- Silk Screen Printing Ink Formulation For Plastic, Paper, Cloth
- Stamp & Pad Ink
- Stoving Paint
- Spirit Soluble Maleic Resin
- Texture Paint
- Thinners And Its Allied Products
- Toner Ink
- Varnish Thinner (Solvent)
- Vacuum Metallizing Lacquers
- Wood Primer

PHARMACEUTICAL, DRUGS, AYURVEDIC/HERBAL COSMETICS & MEDICINES, HOMOEOPATHIC MEDICINES, HOMOEOPATHIC MEDICINES, DISPOSABLE SYRINGE, DENTAL COLLEGE & FINE CHEMICALS ETC. MEDICINES, HOMOEOPATHIC MEDICINES, DISPOSABLE SYRINGE, DENTAL COLLEGE & FINE CHEMICALS ETC.

- Aromatic Pills
- Alumina From Bauxite
- Aspirin
- Ayurvedic Pain Balm Ointments
- Ayurvedic Churan And Tablets
- Ayurvedic Tablets (Hajmola Type)
- Ayurvedic/Herbalpharmacy
- Ayurvedic Sherbats
- Ayurvedic Products
- Bulk Drugs (E.O.U)
- Blood Bags
- Calcium Gluconate
- Capsule, Tablet & Injection With Modern Instruments
- Cashew Feni
- Chloroquinone Phosphate (Bulk Drugs)
- Clinical Thermometer
- Dental Clinic
- Dental College
- Dental Grade Eugenol
- Dextrose Monohydrate, Liquid Glucose
- Dehydrated Onion & Onion Powder
- Dextrose Powder (Anhydrous From Starch)
- Dextrose Saline Solution
- Distillery (I.M.F.L)
- Disposable Needles For Syringes
- Disprin
- Distilled Water
- Empty Hard Gelatine Capsules
- Fairness Cream
- Filling & Packing Of Capsules
- Glucose - D - Powder
- Glycerine
- Hair Colour Mate (Formulations And Process Only)
- Herbal Cosmetics
- Herbal Shampoo
- Herbal Shampoo And Cream
- Herbal Hair Oils (Ayurvedic)
- Homoe & Bio-Medicines With Mother Tincture
- Homoepathic Medicines
- Hypodermic Needles
- I.V. Fluids
- Ibuprofen
- Infusion & Transfusion Sets (I.V. Set)
- Injectable For Pharmaceuticals
- Injection Ampoules Packaging Box
- Integerated Surgical Cotton
- Ice Making Plant
- Ice & Cold Storage
- Lactose & By Products Processing From Milk
- Lichen (Jatamansi Charila)
- Liquid Glucose And Its By-Products
- L-Lysine Monohydro Chloride
- Liquid Glucose From Potatoes
- Medical College
- Methanol (Hpcl Grade)
- Nicotine From Tobacco Waste
- Ointment-Ayurvedic (Yellow & White)
- Pharmaceutical And Food Grade Gelatine
- Pharmaceutical Industry (Tablets, Capsules, Liquid, Gel, Ointment Powder Injectable)
- Pharmaceutical Unit (Eou) With Formulations, Injectables, Etc.
- Pyridine & Derivatives
- Salt (Iodized Salt)
- Saline & Injection Water
- Saline Water & Dextrose Solution (I.V.Fluid In Plastic Bottles)
- Sorbitol
- Starch (Maize)
- Surgical Adhesive Plaster
- Surgical Bandages
- Surgical Gloves
- Surgical Cotton
- Surgical Cotton And Bandage
- Synthetic Camphor Powder
- Tablets & Capsules
- Tissue Culture
- Tincture From Rectified Spirit
- Trimethopime
- Veterinary College With Hospital
- Veterenary Medicines (Only Formulations)
- Vitamin 'C', Sorbitol' Anhydrous Dextrose, Starch

Market Survey Cum Detailed Techno Economic Feasibility Report on all Projects are available Contact.
"ENGINEERS INDIA RESEARCH INSTITUTE", 4449, Nai Sarak (D), Main Road, Delhi-110006 (India)
Ph.: 09811437895, 91-11-23918117, 23916431, 45120361, 64727385 Fax : 91-11-23916431
E-mail : eiriprojects@gmail.com, eiribooks@yahoo.com • website: www.eiri.in, www.eiriindia.org

ALL FOLLOWING PROJECT REPORTS ARE READILY AVAILABLE

- Pulp From Tarmarind
- Readymate Processed Food
- Rice & Corn Flakes
- Rice Basmati (Trading)
- Rice Polishing & Packaging In Pouch
- Roasted/Salted/Masala/Cashew Nuts Almonds & Pea Nut
- Roller Flour Mill
- Vanaspati Unit

INFOTECH / IT PROJECT

- Medical Transcription
- Business Process Outsource (Bpo)
- E-Commerce
- Cybercafe
- Computer Software
- Internet Service Provider (Isp)
- I.T. Park
- Computer Education Centre
- Portal (Website Design)
- Call Centre (Domestic)
- Call Centre (International)

PROFITABLE PLANTATION, CULTIVATION & FARMING PROJECTS

- Amla Plantation
- Amla Plantation, Processing & Preservation
- Bio Fertilisers
- Coffee Plantation
- Coconut Plantation
- Dairy Farming
- Eucalyptus Tree Plantation
- Floriculture - Gladiolus
- Goat Farming
- Green House
- Hybrid Seeds
- Herbs Cultivation
- Jatropha (Bio Diesel) Cultivation & Extraction
- Mushrooms
- Mushroom Growing And Processing With Air Condition
- Medicinal Plantations (Neem)
- Nursery Farms
- Organic Manure
- Papaya & Tomato Cultivation
- Papaya Cultivation
- Poplar Plantation
- Rubber Plantation
- Strawberry Cultivation & Processing
- Safed Musli Cultivation & Processing (Extract & Powder)
- Stevia Cultivation & Extraction
- Sunflower Plantation
- Sugar Cane Plantation
- Teak Plantation

- Turmeric Plantation
- Tea Plantation
- Vermi-Composting

PROFITABLE GUMS, ADHESIVES & RESINS PROJECTS

- Adhesive For Stickers
- Adhesive For Corrugation Dry Powder & Paste
- Adhesive Based On Polyure Thane
- Adhesive Industries (Laminated, Favicol,Sticker, Dda & Other Types Of Adhesives)
- Adhesive For Corrugation (Dry Powder)
- Alkyd Resins
- Adhesive Manufacturing For Joining Hdpe Pipes & Joints
- Adhesive Based On Vinyl Acetate (Fevicol Type)
- B.O.P.P Self Adhesive Tapes
- Cnsl Based Resin In Liquid & Powder Form
- D.O.P And Other Plasticizers
- Ester Gums (Food Grade)
- Epoxy Resin
- Guar Gum
- Glue Stick
- Latex Rubber Based Adhesive
- Leather Based Adhesive
- Liquid Adhesive For Corrugated Board & Boxes
- Leather To Leather Adhesive (Latex Based Adhesives)
- Melamine Formaldehyde Powder
- Office Paste
- Paper Label For Beer Bottles
- Polyester Resins
- Phenol Formaldehyde Resin
- Potato Starch
- Poly Amide Resin
- Printing Gums (Guar Gum Based)

- Rubber Adhesive
- Synthetic Adhesive For Decorative Laminates Bonding
- Starch & Dextrin Based Adhesive
- Thermosetting Adhesive
- Urea Formaldehyde Resin
- Urea Formaldehyde Moulding Powder
- Unsaturated Polyester Resins
- Water Based Latex Adhesives

TEA PLANTATION & PROCESSING BASED INDUSTRIES

- Caffeine From Tea Waste
- Decaffineated Tea
- Instant Tea And Coffee (Premixed With Sugar And Milk)
- Instant Tea From Black Tea
- Tea Bags (Dip - Dip Types)
- Tea Botique
- Tea Packaging Industry
- Tea Bags
- Tea Packaging & Distribution
- Tea Industry

ALUMINIUM AND ALUMINIUM BASED INDUSTRIES

- Aluminium Powder
- Aac & Acsr Aluminium Conductors
- Aluminium Silicate
- Aluminium Utensil
- Aluminium Wire Drawing
- Aluminium Paint
- Aluminium Ingots From Scrap
- Aluminium Alloy & Ingots
- Anodizing Of Aluminium
- Aluminium Chloride
- Aluminium Channels
- Aluminium Rolling Mill
- Aluminium Bottles
- Alumnium Foil Cutting & Roll Making
- Aluminium End Caps
- Aluminium Door And Windows
- Aluminium Collapsible Tubes
- Aluminium Phosphide
- Aluminium Ingots From Bauxite
- Aluminium Caps
- Aluminium Furniture & Hardware
- Aluminium Beverage Cans
- Aluminium Cans For Capacitors
- Aluminium & Aluminium Alloys From Aluminium Scraps To Make Utensils (Induction Furnace Melted)
- Aluminium Hot & Cold Rolling Mill (Aluminium Sheets & Circles)
- Anodic Aluminium Labels
- Aluminium Slugs & Circles

Market Survey Cum Detailed Techno Economic Feasibility Report on all Projects are available Contact.
"ENGINEERS INDIA RESEARCH INSTITUTE". 4449, Nai Sarak (D), Main Road, Delhi-110006 (India)
Ph. : 09811437895, 91-11-23918117, 23916431, 45120361, 64727385 Fax : 91-11-23916431
E-mail : eiriprojects@gmail.com, eiribooks@yahoo.com • website: www.eiri.in, www.eiriindia.org

EIRI PROCESS TECHNOLOGY BOOKS

EIRI PROCESS TECHNOLOGY BOOKS

03 Paint, Pigment, Solvent, Coating Emulsion, Paint Additives & Formulations
04 Technology Of Coating, Resins, Pigments & Inks Industries
05 Manufacturing Technology & Formulations Hand Book On Thinners, Putty, Wall & Industrial Finishes And Synthetic Resins
06 Technology of Synthetic Resins and Emulsion Polymers
07 Technology of Paints and Coatings with Formulations
08 Powder Coating Technology Hand Book

PLASTIC/POLYMER PROCESS, COMPOUNDING, INJECTION MOULDING, ROTATIONAL MOULDING, PLASTIC FILM, FIBRE GLASS, PLASTIC WASTE RECYCLING, MOULDS, PET & RESINS INDUSTRIES

01 Moulds Design & Processing Hand Book
02 Hand Book Of Plastic Materials & Processing Technology
03 Injection Moulding Of Plastics
04 Plastic Processing and Packaging Industries
05 Plastic Waste Recycling Technology
06 Technology Of Plastic Films
07 Rotational Moulding Technology Hand Book
08 Plastic Compounding, Master Batches, Pet & Other Plastics
09 Synthetic Resins Technology With Formulations
10 Technology Of PVC Compounding And Its Applications
11 Hand Book of Polymer And Plastic Technology
12 Hand Book of Fibre Glass Moulding
13 Technology of Reinforced Plastics
14 Plastic Additives Technology Hand Book
15 Technology of Pet Bottles, Preform and Pet Recycling
16 Modern Technology of Extrusion & Extruded Products
17 Technology of Synthetic Resins & Emulsion Polymers
18 Technology of Plastic Additives with Processes and Packaging
19 Technology of Disposable Medical Products

BAKERY, CONFECTIONERY & BREAKFAST, PASTA & CEREALS

01 Hand Book Of Bakery Industries
02 Hand Book Of Confectionery With Formulations
03 Breakfast, Dietary Food, Pasta & Cereal Products Technology
04 Hand Book Of Modern Bakery Products
05 Modern Bakery Technology & Fermented Cereal Products With Formulae
06 Technology of Confectionery, Chocolates, Toffee, Candy, Chewing & Bubble Gums, Lollipop and Jelly Products with Formulations

AGRO CULTIVATION, ANIMAL FARMING, AGRO PLANTATION & AGRO CHEMICAL/ PESTICIDES/ FLORICULTURE & BEE KEEPING

01 Poultry Farming & Feed Formulations
02 Hand Book of Pig Farming
03 Agro Based Hand Book of Plantation, Cultivation & Farming
04 Agro Based Plantation Cultivation & Farming
05 Agro Chemical Industries (Insecticide & Pesticides)
06 Modern Bee Keeping & Honey Processing

EIRI PROCESS TECHNOLOGY BOOKS

Complete Hand Book Of Ayurvedic & Herbal Medicines)

STEEL, S.S., NON FERROUS METALS, ROLLING MILL

01 Modern Technology of Non Ferrous Metals and Metal Extraction

02 Processing Technology of Steels and Stainless Steels

03 Modern Technology of Rolling Mill, Billets, Steel Wire, Galvanized Sheet, Forging & Castings

04 Manufacturing Technology of Non-Ferrous Metal Products

WOOD, VENEER, PLYWOOD, PARTICLE, BOARD, FIBREBOARD, BAMBOO & FOREST PRODUCTS

01 Modern Technology Of Wood, Veneer, Plywood, Particle Board, Fibreboard, Bamboo & Forest Products

BIO GAS PRODUCTION

01 Modern Technology of BIOGAS Production

WASTE BASED PRODUCTS INCLUDING INDUSTRIAL, AGRICULTURE, MEDICAL, MUNICIPALITY, ORGANIC & BIOLOGICAL

01 Technology Of Products From Wastes Industrial, Agriculture, Medical, Municipality, Organic & Biological

02 Products from Waste Technology Handbook

FOOD CHEMICALS, FOOD ADDITIVES, PIGMENTS, AROMA, SWEETENERS AND FOOD EMULSIFIERS

01 Technology of Food Chemicals, Pigments and Food Aroma Compounds

02 Modern Technology of Food Additives, Sweeteners and Food Emulsifiers

SOYBEAN

01 Technology of SOYBEAN Products with Formulae

02 Technology of Soya Milk, Tofu, Hydrlyzate and allied Soyabean Products with Project Profiles

EIRI Multiple Project Reports in CD ROM

01 92 New Lucrative Project Reports In Cd

02. 45 Infotech/It, Hospitality, Hospital, College, School & Club

03. 23 Profitable Construction Projects

04. 56 Agro Based & Food Processing Projects

05. 52 Food, Dairy, Bakery, Confectionery & Snacks Foods

06. 45 New Chemicals & Allied Project Reports

07. 100 Profitable Plastic, Polymers & Allied Projects

08. 44 Textile, Garments, Hosiery & Allied Products In Cd

09. 23 Dairy Farming (Buffalo & Jersey Cow, Dairy Products & Other Milk Processing Ind.

10. 42 Paper, Pulp & Paper Converting Products Reports

EIRI PROCESS TECHNOLOGY BOOKS

07 Technology Of Modern Rice Milling And Basmati Rice
08 Hand Book Of Goat Farming
09 Floriculture Hand Book (Flowers Growing Technology)
10 Aloe Vera Cultivation, Processings, Formulations And Manufacturing Technology
11 Poultry Farming, Hatchery and Broiler Production

DAIRY FARM, MILK PROCESSING AND ICE CREAM

01 Hand Book of Dairy Formulations, Processes & Milk Processing Industries
02 Milk Processing And Dairy Products Industries
03 Hand Book Of Dairy Farming to Produce Milk with Packaging
04 Hand Book Of Ice Cream Technology And Formulae
05 Hand Book Of Milk Processing Dairy Products And Packaging Technology
06 Dairy Farming for Milk Production Technology
07 Commercial Dairy Farming with Project Profiles

HERBS & MEDICINAL CULTIVATION

01 Herbs, Medicinal & Aromatic Plants Cultivation
02 Aushidhi And Sungndhit Paudho Ka Vaysayik (Hindi)
03 Hand Book Of Aromatic & Medicinal Plants And Biodiesel (Jatropha)
04 Hand Book Of Medicinal & Aromatic Plants (Cultivation, Utilisation & Extraction Processed)

FOOD & AGRO PROCESSING, PRESERVATION, SNACK FOOD, DEHYDRATION, FRUIT BEVERAGE, POTATO, MAIZE, MEAT PROCESS

01 Fruits & Vegetables Processing Hand Book
02 Fruit Beverage & Processing With Mango
03 Food Processing & Agro Based Industries
04 Manufacturing Technology of Snacks Food, Namkeen, Pappad & Potato Products
05 Preservation & Canning Of Fruits and Vegetables
06 Hand Book of Food Dehydration & Drying
07 Meat Processing & Meat Products Hand Book
08 Technology of Food Preservation & Processing
09 Hand Book of Food Packaging Technology
10 Agro Based & Processed Food Products
11 Potato & Potato Processing Technology
12 Technology of Maize & Allied Com. Products
13 Technology of Food Processing Industries
14 Technology of Sweets (Mithai) with Formulae
15 Modern Technology of Frozen Food Products
16 Technology of Water and Packaged Drinking water
17 Complete Hand Book on Frozen Food Processing and Freeze Drying Technology
18 Technology of Sweets (Mithai), Namkeen and Snacks food with Formulae
19 Complete Book on Banana Cultivation, Dehydration, Ripening, Processing, Products and Packaging Technology

EIRI Multiple Project Reports in CD ROM

11. 31 Essential Oils, Perfumes, Flavours & Aromatic Compounds
12. 28 Surgical And Disposable Medical Projects
13. 36 Profitable Printing & Allied Projects Reports
14. 63 Profitable Packaging & Allied Project Reports
15. 99 Profitable Printing & Packaging
16. 42 Electroplating, Anodizing & Allied Projects
17. 31 Profitable Plantation & Cultivation Projects
18. 55 Profitable Products From Agro And Other Industrial Wastes
19. 35 Profitable Gums, Adhesives, Sealants And Resins Projects
20. 54 Paint, Varnish, Solvents, Lacquers, Resins, Enamel, Pigments, Thinners & Powder (54 Project Reports In Cd)
21. 43 Iron, Steel, Casting, Fabrication, Wire Drawing & Rolling Mills Projects
22. 26 New Educational Projects (Schools, Colleges, Training/ Management Institute, Hostels Etc.)
23. 12 Mosquitoes Preventive Projects (Coils, Mats, Liquids, Agarbatti, Nets, Spray Etc.)
24. 21 Bakery And Allied Products
25. 67 Rubber And Rubber Goods Industries
26. 37 Aluminium And Aluminium Based Industries
27. 14 Potato And Potato Based Industries
28. 50 Electrical, Electronics And Computer Based Industries
29. 52 Cosmetics (Herbal & Synthetics) Technology Projects (52 Project Reports)
30. 10 Molasses Based Lucrative Projects
31. 24 Fruits/Veg. & Allied Food Dehydration Projects
32. 7 Power Plant Projects (Thermal, Hydro, Solar, Wind Energy And Lignite Coal Based)
33. 35 New Profitable Industries
34. 160 New Export Oriented And Profitable Projects (160 Project Reports In Cd)
35. 5 Ginger & Ginger Processing Industries
36. 13 Fish Farming And Fishery Products
37. 6 Agarbatti And Allied Projects
38. 28 Fruit Juices, Food Dehydration And Allied Products
39. 9 Tea Plantation And Processing Based Industries
40. 14 Roasted/Salted Cashew Nuts, Almonds, Namkeens, Spices Projects
41. 23 Injection Moulded Plastic Products (23 Project Reports)
42. 38 Biofertilizer, Biofuel, Enzyme, Organic Farming & Manure, Protein And Allied Lucrative Projects
43. 10 Maize & Corn Processing Projects
44. 11 Profitable Solar & Solar Based Products
45. 11 Infotech/It Projects
46. 42 Hospitality, Building Material, Power Steels, Alcohol & Other Food Products
47. 24 Soap & Detergents (Scouring Powder, Toilet Cleaner, Laundry Soap, Detergent Cake & Powder, Toilet Soap, Enzyme Based Detergents, Phenyl & Soap Coated Paper)
48. 10 Coconut And Coconut By Products
49. 22 Alcohol, Beer, Imfl, Country Liquor, Wine & Other Related Projects

EIRI PROCESS TECHNOLOGY BOOKS

20 Technology of Chicken Meat and Poultry Products
21 Agro Food Processing and Packaging Technology
22 Modern Technology of Tomato Processing and Dehydration (Ketchup, Juice, Paste, Puree, Soup and Drying)
23 Modern Technology of Agro Processing and Food Packaging Products with Project Profiles
24 Start Your Own Coffee and Coffee Processing

SOAPS & DETERGENTS

01 Household Soap. Toilet Soap & Other Soap
02 Profitable Small Scale Manufacture Of Soaps & Detergents
03 Synthetic Detergents With Formulations
04 Modern Technology of Acid Slurry, Surfactants, Soap and Detergents with Formulae

ORGANIC FARMING AND FOOD

01 Hand Book Of Organic Farming And Organic Foods With Vermi-Composting And Neem Products

FISH FARMING & FISHERY PRODUCTS

01 Hand Book Of Fish Farming And Fishery Products

COSMETIC (SYNTHETIC & HERBAL)

01 Cosmetics Processes & Formulations
02 Herbal Cosmetics & Beauty Products With Formulations
03 Profitable Small Scale Manufacture Of Cosmetics (Synthetic & Herbal)
04 Hand Book Of Synthetic & Herbal Cosmetics (How to Make Beauty Products)
05 Technology Of Herbal Cosmetics & Toiletries Products With Formulae

OIL AND FATS

01 Hand Book of Oils, Fats And Derivatives With Refining & Packaging Technology
02 Technology of Oilseeds Processing, Oils & Fats and Refining

ESSENTIAL OILS & AROMATIC

01 Essential Oils Manufacturing & Aromatic Plants
02 Modern Technology Of Essential Oils
03 Technology Of Perfumes, Flavours & Essential Oils
04 Essential Oils Processes & Formulations

PERFUMES AND FLAVOURS

01 Hand Book Of Flavours & Food Colourants Technology
02 Hand Book Of Perfumes & Flavours
03 Hand Book of Perfumes With Formulations
04 Technology Of Perfumes, Flavours & Essential Oils
05 Hand Book Of Flavours Technology

BUILDING MATERIALS & CHEMICALS

01 Technology Of Building Materials & Chemicals With Processes

EIRI PROCESS TECHNOLOGY BOOKS

TEXTILE, GARMENTS, DYEING

01 Modern Technology Of Bleaching, Dyeing, Printing & Finishing Of Textiles
02 Technology Of Textiles (Spinning & Weaving, Dyeing, Scouring, Drying, Printing And Bleaching)
03 Garments Manufacturing Technology

SPICES & COLD STORAGE

01 Spices & Packaging With Formulaes
02 Start Your Own Cold Storage Unit

PULP & PAPER TECHNOLOGY

01 Hand Book Of Pulp & Paper, Paper Board & Paper Based Technology

NON WOVEN TECHNOLOGY

01 Complete Technology of Nonwovens Fabrics, Carry Bags, Composite, Geotextiles, Medical Textiles, Fibres, Felts, Apparels, Spunlace and Absorbent Nonwoven

TEXTILE AUXILIARIES & CHEMICALS

01 Textile Auxiliaries And Chemicals With Processes And Formulations

PHARMACEUTICALS & DRUGS

01 Pharmaceuticals And Drugs Technology With Formulations

LEATHER & LEATHER PRODUCTS

01 Hand Book Of Leather & Leather Products Technology

BIOTECHNOLOGY

01 Hand Book Of Biotechnology

CERAMICS

01 Hand Book of Ceramics and Ceramics Processing Technology

TREE FARMING

01 Hand Book Of Tree Farming

MUSHROOM CULTIVATION/ PROCESS

01 Hand Book Of Mushroom Cultivation, Processing and Packaging

BIOFERTILIZERS & VERMICULTURE

01 Hand Book Of Biofertilizers & Vermiculture

MINERAL AND MINERALS

01 Hand Book Of Minerals And Minerals Based Industries

RUBBER CHEMICALS, COMPOUND & RUBBER INDUSTRIES

01 Rubber Chemicals & Processing Industries
02 Modern Rubber Chemicals, Compounds & Rubber Goods Technology
03 Technology Of Rubber & Rubber Goods Industries

AYURVEDIC MEDICINES

01 Ayurvedic & Herbal Medicines With Formulaes
02 Hand Book Of Ayurvedic Medicines With Formulations (A